THE
DICTIONARY
OF
ESPIONAGE

THE DICTIONARY OF ESPIONAGE

Christopher Dobson
and
Ronald Payne

Harrap · London

First Published in Great Britain 1984
by HARRAP LIMITED
19–23 Ludgate Hill, London EC4M 7PD

© *Christopher Dobson and Ronald Payne* 1984

ISBN 0 245–54201–9

Designed by Robert Wheeler
Printed and bound in Great Britain by
R. J. Acford, Chichester

CONTENTS

INTRODUCTION

The Enigma code machine developed by the German Third Reich to ensure the secure transmission of its most secret military commands finally fell into British hands in the summer of 1939 through the joint endeavours of French, Polish and British espionage.

General Bertrand, a senior French military cryptologist, described delivering the actual Enigma device to the head of the British SIS, the Secret Intelligence Service. Major-General Sir Stewart Menzies — 'C', none other — went down in person to Victoria Station, London, wearing evening dress and the Legion of Honour. The French general exclaimed, *'Quel acceuil!'*

There could be no more striking picture of the two worlds of espionage coming together at a crucial moment in the history of Europe than in this ceremonial handing over of the first fruit of the new technology of espionage to a clubman hero of the old-style intelligence service from the age of Bulldog Drummond. It is a suitable starting-point for *The Dictionary of Espionage* to begin its roll-call of the most famous, the most important, and the most significant spies and spymasters of the period between the Second World War and 1984.

It is less than half a century since new technology intruded into the cosier old world of secret intelligence. The Enigma machine was the core of the espionage revolution. With it the Germans could encode signals automatically. It consisted of two joined-up electric typewriters linked to mechanical wheels bearing symbols, to render secret signals transmitted by radio.

In breaking the Enigma codes with the help of the Poles and the French, British mathematicians and experts eventually used the Turing machine, invented by Alan Turing, which was the basis for the first electronic computer. Machines were used to break machine codes in order to supply what was called Ultra information about enemy plans and orders. When correctly used and interpreted, Ultra gave a tremendous advantage to Allied commanders in the field.

For the first time since the invention of codes, and of invisible ink, scientists were providing new tools for spies. The arrival of miniature cameras and microdots for sending intelligence inconspicuously also helped the agents in place.

Further technical developments came swiftly, and by 1984 the new espionage was moving into the age of *Star Wars*. Satellites spy upon satellites, and whirling orbs in space record military small-talk a hundred miles below. It is only a question of time before one listening and photographic device in the service of either the Soviet Union or of the United States blasts out of the sky a similar enemy device. Already it is reported that the Americans keep reserve satellites in deep space where they are safer, ready to be moved into another orbit to replace casualties.

Since the 1950s intelligence services have been using specially designed spy aircraft. In the aftermath of the shooting down of a Korean civil airliner which had strayed into hostile airspace over the Soviet Far East island of Sakhalin in 1983 indications became public which showed the extent of aerial and electronic espionage being practised by both sides.

The United States puts more money and effort into the National Security Agency — which controls electronic spying — than into the more traditional activities of the better-known Central Intelligence Agency. In Britain, where the government is more secretive about secret service matters, it is highly likely that the comparable institution at Cheltenham, the Government Communications Headquarters, which co-operates with NSA, has a budget more than rivalling that of the Secret Intelligence Service.

Yet it would be wrong to assume that signals intelligence — 'Sigint' in the cant — has replaced 'Humint', human intelligence. For as Alexander Haig aptly said when he was US Secretary of State, somebody has to tell the satellites and the spy aircraft where to look, and what to look for. Those controllers are among the people who make up the assorted community of present-day intelligence-gatherers.

A book detailing the lives and personalities of more than three hundred people involved in espionage (directly or peripherally) — some included, it must be admitted, because of the fascination of their stories, rather than because of the effect of their activities — makes it possible to see just how greatly the art of espionage and its agents have changed in less than half a century.

In 1939 Sir Stewart Menzies controlled British Intelligence, while the United States had no real foreign intelligence service at all. J. Edgar Hoover, the opinionated gang-buster in a fedora hat, presided over the Federal Bureau of Investigation, only just turning its attention from tommy-gun shoot-outs with bootleggers to the finer crafts of spycatching, and establishing its first intelligence agents in Latin America.

Lavrenti Beria, the archetypal secret policeman, a revolutionary returned to the traditions of the Tsarists, was in the Kremlin as head of the KGB conglomerate, then in business under different initials. While he purged the Red Army of traitors suspected by Stalin, and spied upon Soviet citizens, he spread his espionage networks in a Western world too sympathetic to Russia as a victim of the Hitler invasion even to notice.

A study of the entries on individual spies demonstrates how different are the spymasters of 1984, while the intelligence officers and the spies have also greatly changed in the comparatively short period of history covered. Although the objectives of spying remain the same, to discover what is happening on the other side of the hill, the increasing complexity of the kind of information which is useful has made it necessary to recruit more intelligent and better-trained agents. For spying is not simply a question of stealing secret plans; an agent must be able to judge the quality of the material by understanding it. He must also be capable of assessing the significance of hostile intentions. When a wartime Soviet agent in North America asked a scientist what was new in radar

development the Canadian replied that people were much more interested in research into nuclear physics. Because the Russian understood the significance of the remark he and his comrades were able to concentrate on the still highly secret research behind the making of the first atomic bombs.

Intelligence-gathering has become a profession. Men and women join with an eye on the career structure, promotion and pensions. They have replaced the gifted amateurs, the clubmen and the adventurers. At the top in each country, whether East or West, capitalist or communist, there is an élite of intellectuals, clever, university-trained people who frequently have more in common with their rivals and enemies than with the rest of the population.

Alexander Solzhenitsyn has shown in the *Gulag Archipelago* how tempting it is for a talented young Russian to take service with the KGB as a step into the privileged world of secret-service power and influence. The rewards are by no means as high in the British Secret Intelligence Service and the MI5 Security Service, and the powers are far more limited; but there is no shortage of capable volunteers from the universities and from the armed forces, no lack of dons to recommend such a career. Certainly in the United States many able young men and women came forward when the Central Intelligence Agency after the years of its decline in scandal began expanding again in 1983 to a strength of around 1,000. The same is true of the FBI.

American advertisements planned to attract new recruits to the CIA make it clear what kind of people they are looking for by stressing that intelligence 'has less to do with cloaks and daggers than with painstaking, generally tedious collection of facts, analysis of facts, exercise of judgement and quick clear evaluation'. The same advertisements carry a picture of Sir Francis Walsingham, the Elizabethan royal spy, and not the kind of person who would attract the rougher elements of the world of espionage.

It is fascinating to observe that methods of recruitment are very similar in both the Western intelligence communities and in those of the Soviet

Union. Suitable people are spotted at university or in the armed forces, or in the government service, and they are brought into their new careers in exactly the same way that they would be attracted into any other form of work for the government. These remarks apply, of course, only to those in the permanent and respectable structure of intelligence; the recruitment of agents who do the dirty work of supplying information is part of a different social world.

Those who rise to the top of the ladder are men of unusually high talent. William J. Casey, head of the CIA, is at the age of seventy a man of many success stories. He is a millionaire lawyer, a tax and investment specialist, a politician, and an amateur historian as well as being an intelligence man with long experience. In Britain the rule of discretion is still observed that it is not 'suitable' to mention in print the names of heads of MI5 and 6. In fact the very names of these organizations are camouflaged from the public at large which still calls them by those titles, although in fact the departments are correctly known as DI5 and 6, *defence* having replaced *military* intelligence in official quarters. Throughout this book we stick to the old and better-known designations.

Despite the convention of anonymity it may reasonably be assumed that the present heads of the departments are experienced and skilful officers. When Sir Maurice Oldfield retired from the SIS in 1978 with a knighthood it was known that he had spent a lifetime in military intelligence, and that he was a cheerful man opposed to violence, and whose hobby was farming. Perhaps spymasters have a taste for quiet philosophic pursuits, for James Angleton, a former CIA director of counter-espionage, favoured fishing.

Yuri Andropov of the Soviet Union was said to enjoy listening to nostalgic popular music, but whether or not that is so he was clearly a man of outstanding ability, and far subtler and more sophisticated than Beria, his predecessor. He became the supreme Soviet leader through a long and successful political career in the communist party, which then took him to the top in the KGB, before he left it to become President.

Soviet agents in the field long ago abandoned their baggy suits and wide trousers. On the surface they now appear to be very similar to their counterparts in the West, smartly dressed, intelligent and persuasive, like Captain Anatoli Zotov, the naval attaché expelled from London in 1983, who professed not to be able to see what all the fuss was about.

In the 1980s intelligence services are still under the control of officers and gentlemen, but as in the Duke of Wellington's army, they command other ranks who are the scum of the earth. At the seedy end of the trade, those who help to provide the product are ready to betray, destroy, and sometimes to kill in return for money, sexual favours, or to save themselves from blackmail, disgrace or death. In their ranks are to be found psychopaths, ego-boosters, and knaves and fools of all kinds.

Grudge-bearers abound. A dim and boozy American NCO, Sergeant Robert Lee Johnson, took service with the Russians because he had been passed over for promotion, and stayed on for the money. Lance-Corporal Aldridge of the Intelligence Corps in the British Army offered to sell secrets so that he could buy a car. Servicemen of every rank from private to general have sold out their country for a variety of squalid reasons.

Maureen Bingham, wife of a Royal Navy officer promoted for his skills from the lower deck, went to the Soviet Embassy in London to market her husband's information, so that she could keep up socially in the officers' wardroom. And Harry Houghton, an old petty officer in the Portland spy ring, got involved, as he put it, through 'chasing a bit of skirt behind the Iron Curtain'.

By no means all spies are prompted by unworthy motives. There are those who seek out information and provide it to a foreign Power, convinced that by so doing they are helping to save the world from war. Such a man was Georges Paques, a French government servant, by no means a Marxist, who supplied Russia with Nato secrets, and calling himself a 'negotiator', refused to accept that by so doing he had become a secret agent.

Ideological doubts also affect high-placed officials and officers who come to believe that only one side or the other in the cold war represents the best hope for the future. Colonel Oleg Penkovsky, a stylish Soviet officer, convinced himself that Nikita Khruschev was a monster and a danger to the world, and offered important secret information to the British and Americans in order to foil his plots. He provided assessments of the power behind Russian threats, as well as details of missile resources. Such men bring the spy trade into good, rather than ill, repute.

The Colonel's counterpart in the West, it has to be recognized, was 'Kim' Philby, traitor to the British, a hero to the Russians, and a born secret agent recruited while still at Cambridge, and named after the Kipling spy hero. He is still convinced, as he first was at university before the War in a totally different atmosphere, that communism is right.

Mention of Philby raises the question of the defectors and moles who play such a part in present-day espionage. So far as the West is concerned, a Soviet mole represents the highest danger; a Soviet defector is the greatest asset. The best source of information about the Soviet Union is the evidence of government officials and KGB officers who for a whole variety of reasons, including joy, doubt, fear and sorrow, decide that they want to live in the non-communist world, and are prepared to pay the price by bringing secrets with them. They have been able to reach parts of the Soviet apparatus where foreign agents would be incapable of penetrating within the tightly regulated society of the Eastern Bloc.

One thing that all these categories of spies do share in common is the ability to dissemble. For the most important feature of their activity is that they should be able to conceal what they are doing from friends, relations and spouses, and be capable of leading at least two lives at once. That is perhaps why so many people in espionage already have practice in leading secret lives, because they are homosexuals or people used to conducting clandestine love-affairs.

Even when they are most successful, constant dissembling puts them under stress and strain. Only to his case officer, his immediate controller, can a spy unwind through being able to talk freely about what is forbidden, and boast of his achievements.

It is this deep and sometimes urgent need to tell which often accounts for the full confessions which secret agents make once they have been caught. For them it is a positive relief to be able to speak out frankly about what they have been doing in secret, to share the experience. The interrogator if he is skilled and understanding can easily slip into the role formerly occupied by the case officer.

A remarkable example of this was provided in the lengthy statement made by Klaus Fuchs, the atomic spy, after Jim Skardon, the MI5 interrogator, had won his confidence in lengthy and sympathetic sessions of questioning. The statement revealed some of the tortuous processes of his brilliant mind induced by the pressures of leading the double life of a spy. Fuchs explained that he had used his Marxist philosophy to establish two separate compartments of his mind in 'a controlled schizophrenia'. A less intellectual spy might have said that under the stress and strain he had found it difficult to live out a continual lie.

A spy is always most effective when he is operating in his own country. The high old days of secret agents who were masters of disguise and capable of speaking the lingo impeccably through the burnt cork and false moustache are gone for ever. The modern world is too well documented for such people to last for long enough in an alien atmosphere. Even the Israeli secret service, which enjoys the advantage of being able to use agents born in many countries, and accustomed to their ways and languages, no longer registers great successes in this field. Their people in the Soviet Union are under great pressure. In the Middle East a number of their best men — Eli Cohen, to name one, who lived in Damascus and mingled with top government people — were in the end detected and executed.

For the same practical reason that foreigners are more noticeable than natives when probing secrets, the Russians make use of native 'moles', who over the years work their way into positions of authority and responsibility. An obvious example is the Cambridge-recruited Britons

Burgess and Maclean, Philby and Anthony Blunt. They also place 'sleepers', persons who go about a normal life until the occasion arises for spymasters to make use of their services. The most dangerous enemies of moles and sleepers are defectors who know about them and can denounce them. Defectors themselves can be, and have been, undermined by a KGB tactic which consists of deliberately sending to the West false defectors, whose task is to throw doubt on the testimony of the genuine ones and generally to discredit their information.

All the world loves spy stories, and a taste has been created through fiction for the most devious and complicated espionage activities. But in no country does a spy scandal — and there have been plenty — arouse more interest, indignation, and indeed self-pity, than in Britain. Even when some quite minor affair comes to light, Members of Parliament rush in, ill informed though they frequently are, to demand explanations, and stricter control over the hard-pressed intelligence services. On such occasions the impression is given that Britain is the only country in the world where spies operate; and the only one with an incompetent government, lax security and unsuitable security chiefs.

A survey of spies and spymasters from other parts of the world detailed in *The Dictionary of Espionage* should at least serve to show that Britain is not unique in her suffering by espionage. To point this out is by no means to minimize the damage done in Britain through the penetration of its services by such traitors as Philby, Burgess and Maclean, Blunt and Blake. Because the intelligence services had failed to take precautions in recruitment they ended up with a multitude of betrayers from within. The final blow came when suspicion fell upon Sir Roger Hollis, head of MI5, the counter-intelligence organization itself.

However, it is in the nature of spying organizations to be in danger of penetration by spies. The American CIA boasts that it has never had a traitor in its ranks, but one of its grandees, Dick Helms, thoughtfully spoke of the nightmare of every intelligence director, 'that one day he will be told that somebody inside his immediate

organization has been spying for a foreign power'.

When Congress began to investigate the undoubted excesses of the CIA its then director, William Colby, not only told them the truth but revealed operational secrets to such an extent that senior colleagues believed he was doing irreparable harm to the whole organization, because those secrets leaked from Congress and became known to the KGB.

Indeed, James Angleton, head of counter-intelligence, who was manoeuvred into bitter resignation by William Colby in 1974 when his obsession with Russian infiltration became very marked, actually wondered out loud if Colby was not a KGB agent, out to wreck the CIA.

Dick Helms declared that he did not believe that this was so, nor did he believe that there was any KGB agent at all in the Agency. So far as William Colby himself was concerned, he declared that Congress had a constitutional right to know, and that he was simply doing his duty, and doing his best to protect the CIA. Nevertheless, suspicions there were.

Commendable though the record of the Central Intelligence Agency may be in fending off Russian attempts to infiltrate the service itself, it must not be forgotten that it was in the United States and Canada in the 1940s that the Soviets scored their greatest spy triumphs. Several networks succeeded in discovering the processes and secret research which produced the first atomic weapons. In face of such activities the United States was forced to reactivate its foreign intelligence service, which had been over-hastily demobilized at the end of the Second World War, and to establish the CIA.

Senator McCarthy gave his name to a new term of abuse in denouncing communist agents everywhere, and launched a national spy scare comparable only to similar obsessions in the USSR. Then in the wake of Cuba and Vietnam scandals came Watergate, which reduced the effectiveness and reliability of the nation's intelligence agency to such an extent that even its loyal British ally, the Secret Intelligence Service, felt compelled to withhold from it some sensitive intelligence information.

American traitors were just as willing to provide

the Russians with secret intelligence as were European and British ones. Christopher Boyce and his friend Daulton Lee revealed at least as much about electronic espionage and the National Security Agency to the Russians as the KGB obtained from the British spy at GCHQ Cheltenham, Geoffrey Prime. Indeed, it was hypocritical to pretend in 1982 that the CIA and the Pentagon were deeply shocked by lack of security at Cheltenham, when they knew perfectly well that their own installations in Fort Meade, Maryland, were every bit as porous.

We shall never know what recriminations go on in the Kremlin about Russian security leaks to the West, or ever discover the terrible denunciations for laxity and treachery. Even electronic ears have not yet successfully penetrated those ancient walls.

It is nevertheless well known that the principal European countries have had their troubles in the espionage wars. France emerged from the Second World War with a battered intelligence service composed of Gaullist exiles from London mingled with members of the old service which had remained loyal to the Vichy regime of surrender to the Germans. Communist networks had established themselves in and through the Resistance movement, and as General de Gaulle tried to unify the nation by taking communists into the government loyal party members infiltrated the administration. For several years after his first departure from office France was in danger of a Moscow-ordered coup d'état, like the one which converted Czechoslovakia into an Eastern Bloc state.

It was not until 1957 that General Paul Grossin took command of the SDECE intelligence service, and a start was made to clean out that organization. Even after that France had to withstand one espionage offensive after another, first from the Eastern Bloc services and then from the KGB itself. Naturally, there were scandals, and when Charles de Gaulle himself returned in triumph as President in 1958 a Soviet defector claimed that the KGB had a 'mole' in the entourage of the President. 'Absurd', declared de Gaulle, who took a lofty view of espionage (which he described as an affair *vulgaire et subalterne*).

Germany, while still divided into occupation zones controlled respectively by the Western allies and by the Russian ex-ally in the East, became the battleground of the espionage cold war. General Gehlen, formerly one of Hitler's intelligence chiefs, set up his freelance organization with American help and encouragement.

Ernst Wollweber, an experienced revolutionary in charge of East German intelligence, fought a bitter series of battles with Gehlen across the battered streets of Berlin. Each side had its successes and failures, for both enjoyed the advantage of employing Germans on each side of the Iron Curtain. Heinz Felfe, as a double agent for the East Germans, succeeded in becoming head of counter-espionage in the West German BND intelligence service, from which advantageous position he also betrayed that organization to the Soviet KGB, his principal employer. Defectors betrayed former colleagues, and there were arrests and suicides of generals, and senior officials in West Germany. General Gehlen had his men and women in Wollweber's entourage.

When the younger men started taking over Lieutenant-General Markus Wolf, the most successful new-generation Eastern Bloc spymaster, managed to place Gunther Guillaume as a mole who became a confidential adviser to Chancellor Willy Brandt.

General Wolf is also notable as the officer who brought women into espionage on the grand scale, exploiting not only their sexual attraction (as in the old days) but their professional capabilities. He realized that nobody in a government office has easier access to secret papers than the women secretaries who type them, or the female personal assistants to ministers. It was also obvious that many such women employed after the War at a certain age were likely to be unmarried, and unlikely to find husbands among the depleted male population. He used this cynical calculation by sending specially instructed men to recruit through the bedroom, and even if necessary up the aisle, to persuade secretaries to make extra copies of secret documents to please their agent lovers and husbands.

'Can there really be any need for all this spying?'

is the question most frequently put — and expecting the answer 'No' — when espionage is talked about by those not involved in it. Nikita Khruschev, at the height of his rampaging as the Soviet leader, once professed to express the same view in a bantering exchange.

He suggested to Allen Dulles that the Americans and Russians should exchange spy lists because it would not make much difference. Anyway, he thought, a good many of them would turn out to be the same people. Nevertheless, he did not expect to be taken seriously, for he knew that spying is not an end in itself but a symptom of the political quarrels which divide the world. Every country has a right to defend itself, and in order to do that effectively it must know in advance about the weapons which are being developed by its opponents. Even more important, a nation must try to discover what are the intentions of its enemies, and when they plan to carry out those intentions.

To take for a moment the Kremlin-eye view of recent espionage activities, it is clear that all the effort put into the training of thousands of agents and arranging networks of spies in Britain and North America, in particular towards the end of the 1939-1945 war, was worthwhile. The Russians were able to learn through it, and through information from scientists like Klaus Fuchs and Dr Nunn May, how the first atom bombs were made. It gave them an undoubted advantage in producing their own nuclear armoury, enabling them to catch up with the West.

Even now they are saving years of effort and millions in money, which otherwise would need to be spent on research and development, by spying out technological developments in the West. That is another justification for the size and cost of the KGB.

The United States, Britain and the Nato countries remain confident enough of their capability to conceive and produce industrial as well as military innovations. However, to preserve their way of doing things from Soviet attempts to spread revolution they certainly need to know what are the plans and dispositions of the Soviet leaders. Had it not been for advance intelligence

provided by Colonel Penkovsky, and by the flights of spy planes over Cuba in 1961, President Kennedy would have been taken by surprise at the installation there of Soviet missiles. Without that intelligence he most certainly would have found it impossible to handle the crisis as he did, and to force their withdrawal.

Even when it comes to peacemaking and attempts to control the quantity of missiles and nuclear weapons, both super-Powers need to practise espionage. Without control over treaties announced in this field international agreements for arms-reduction would not be worth the paper they were written on. That indeed is why electronic spying from aircraft and satellites over hostile territory is now customary, and even tolerated. That is why embassies on both sides have staffs of military, naval and air attachés to act as 'legal' spies.

The need for vigilant espionage services is further proved by the record of what happens when intelligence services, or the governments they serve, have failed in their duty to forecast events. When Mossad, the Israeli intelligence service, failed to provide evidence to convince the government that a joint Egyptian and Syrian attack was imminent in 1973 Israel was taken by surprise and very nearly defeated.

When the CIA reported that Iran was not in even a pre-revolutionary situation shortly before the Ayatollah Khomeini overthrew their friend the Shah the consequences were dire and humiliating for the United States. The failure of Britain's Secret Intelligence Service to provide enough information to convince Mrs Thatcher's government that the Argentines really did mean to invade the Falkland Islands involved Britain in a costly war which need never have been fought, had an advance warning been followed by suitable precautions.

For all these reasons espionage really is necessary. It will remain with us as it has always been, technical and fascinating in its direction; sordid (though equally fascinating for that reason) in its execution.

As for the scale of spying in the present decade, the statistics speak for themselves. In January

1984 the US State Department announced that during the year 1983 no less than 147 Soviet spies in the guise of diplomats and trade delegates had been unmasked and expelled from a range of non-communist countries around the world. Apart from Britain and the US, countries included in the list were Bangladesh, Belgium, Denmark, Holland, Iran, Italy, West Germany, Norway, Ireland, Japan and Switzerland.

The comparative figures for 1982 were 49 expulsions, and for 1981, only 27. The huge increase in Soviet-spy detection-rates in 1983 came about partly because Nato countries were pooling their intelligence resources more tellingly. The American CIA had come back into action after its years in the wilderness, although it should also not be forgotten that the KGB and the GRU had stepped up *their* activity, in an attempt to trawl in scientific and technological intelligence for both civil and military use. Their top priority was to supply information to enable the USSR to catch up with the West in such fields.

So intent were they upon this work that they were willing to accept losses of agents by expulsion *en masse*. They even abandoned the traditional policy of reciprocal expulsions, contenting themselves with sharp counter-attack by means of protesting statements.

In Moscow Viktor Chebrikov (who had taken Yuri Andropov's former job as head of the KGB) claimed successes in spy-catching of Western agents early in 1984. He said that the KGB had trapped and neutralized 'scores' of Western spies. Though he did not go into detail — beyond saying that CIA men had been caught red-handed — he declared that 'the state security organs frustrate the criminal designs of the special services of the imperialist states and take drastic measures against those who encroach upon our state and social system.'

Clearly both sides in the cold war are still highly active in their spy campaigns.

It is not the aim of this book to justify such campaigns, or argue the need for espionage. It is our aim, by providing short lives of the most notable spies and spymasters of the last half-century, to provide material by which readers may become their own analysts, and decide for themselves about the motivations and justifications of the people concerned.

Inevitably, the formula chosen of listing them by alphabetical order has given rise to some difficulties. For example, the Portland spy story has a cast of at least half a dozen main characters — the Krogers, a KGB couple; the English ex-naval man Houghton; his mistress (later wife) Ethel or 'Bunty' Gee; 'Gordon Lonsdale', a Soviet agent; not to mention Jim Skardon of MI5. In telling the story by way of a series of brief lives there is a certain amount of repetition but in such cases we have tried to keep overlap to a minimum by attempting to recount events from individual viewpoints.

Finally, a disclaimer. Out in the field it is sometimes difficult to know whether there are more spies pretending to be journalists or more journalists giving the impression that they are spies. We fall into neither category. Like all good newspapermen, we have met spies and have written on spy stories. We wrote the book, as somebody once said to justify climbing Everest, because espionage is there.

THE SPIES

A

ABDOOLCADER, Siroj Husain

'The dirty rotten Russian swine blackmailed me into it.' declared Siroj Husain, the son of an influential Malaysian lawyer, reverting to the language of an earlier age of espionage at his trial at the Old Bailey. The 33-year-old failed law student was sent to prison for three years in 1972.

After meeting a Soviet trade-delegation man in a North London pub he was put in touch with Oleg Lyalin, a Russian agent who eventually defected to the West. He was used as a messenger, and was also asked to provide registration numbers of cars used by British security officers from files in the London local government office where he worked.

The defence of this rather agreeable, low-level operator was that he had in fact provided false and misleading information which, in the words of his lawyer, 'must have bemused rather than assisted the Russians'. He only took service with them because he was put out that as a Malaysian he found it difficult to get lodgings in the London of the early 1970s. In return for his services the Soviets gave him an electric razor, a watch and a toilet set.

Although he might not have realized it, the information he provided detailing the registration numbers of MI5 vehicles gave KGB men in London under surveillance an enormous advantage. A later defector reported that a senior officer at headquarters in Moscow had boasted, 'We have the numbers of all British security cars in London.'

ABEL, Colonel Rudolph

The odd thing about this experienced professional Russian spy was that nobody was ever able to discover, far less to prove, precisely what he had done. Under his 'illegal' buried-away name of Emil R. Goldfus, photographer and artist, he was arrested in New York and later sentenced to thirty years for espionage in March 1960.

For nine years he had remained undetected until he was betrayed by a corrupt and drunken assistant named Reino Hayhanen, who, sent back to Moscow for disciplining, paused in Paris, defected to the US Embassy, and denounced Abel. When they searched the Brooklyn studio of this dapper and well-liked little man they discovered there all the paraphernalia of espionage — transmitter, microdots *et al.* — but no evidence about agents operating to Abel or signs of any secret material actually dispatched to Moscow Centre.

One interesting find was a pair of photographs of the Cohens — who later turned out to be the Krogers, caught in London in the Portland Spy Ring exposure. But even that clue could not be followed up in time.

The conclusion of American security investigators was that Abel must have been planted in New York for use later when a sufficiently high-quality American supplier of secrets had been recruited. The alternative explanation must be that Abel was of such high technical proficiency that he had totally concealed a network from the FBI and CIA, which is unlikely.

It was the Russians themselves who drew attention to the high importance they attached to Abel by making such a fuss about securing his return in exchange for the shot-down American U2 pilot, Gary Powers. The impression was later reinforced by Abel's own disinformation book on his activities, which in fact gave away very little.

Although even his original name still remains a mystery, it is known that Abel was the son of Russian émigrés and that he lived in England from 1903 to 1921. He worked in Europe for the Soviets during the Second World War, and when that ended Moscow Centre began preparing him at once for his North American mission.

He was placed in a camp for displaced persons under the name Goldfus and then emigrated to Canada, making his way from there to New York after spending several years establishing his new identity. He arrived in North America shortly after the defection of Gouzenko in Canada, and this may account for the care taken by his masters to make him lie low and to perfect his cover at a time when many agents were blown.

As a quiet and modest self-employed businessman he was able to travel without attracting suspicion among his circle of friends and acquaintances in New York. After his return to Moscow in 1962 Soviet honours were poured upon him, and there were constant stories that he had begun operating again in the West. What is more likely is that the KGB used his talents by making him a lecturer and instructor in the skills of espionage for the new generation.

He died at the age of sixty-eight on 16 November 1971.

ADNONI, Nahum

Appointed head of Mossad, the Israeli intelligence service, in June 1982 after serving as number two in the organization, he replaced General Yekotiel, who had been appointed head, but who was ambushed and killed by Palestinian guerrillas in Lebanon before he could take up the post.

Nahum Adnoni, unlike most of his predecessors (who were either generals or flamboyant war heroes), was unknown outside the service. His appointment was a stopgap measure by Menachem Begin, the then Prime Minister. The appointment of a functionary as head of Mossad did, however, serve the useful purpose of putting the service under tighter control, and reducing its influence on policy-making.

It was a difficult time for Adnoni. The Israeli army was still at the gates of Beirut, and Mossad was fully occupied with events in the city. It was Adnoni's misfortune that he had barely taken over when after the assassination of Bashir Gemayel, the President-elect, the Lebanese Phalangist militia moved into Palestinian refugee camps under the eyes of the Israelis and brutally murdered hundreds of men, women and children.

Adnoni was exonerated from blame by the official Israeli inquiry into the massacre on the grounds that he had taken up his duties just before it took place.

AGCA, Mehmet Ali

The man who shot and wounded Pope John Paul in St Peter's Square in May 1981. He was a crop-headed and bearded 25-year-old Turkish fanatic, who although he was groomed in terrorism by a right-wing group in his own country called the 'Grey Wolves', claimed after his conviction that he had carried out the assassination attempt in co-operation with the Bulgarian secret service.

Questioned by an Italian magistrate, Ilario Martella, he made ever wilder allegations about the origins of the plot, claiming that the Soviet KGB also was involved. Indeed, if it can ever be proved that the Bulgarian secret service really did inspire his actions, then it follows automatically that the KGB (with whom they work hand in glove) must also have been involved. Both the Russians and the Bulgarians stoutly denied any connection, saying that, 'There are no facts to bear out directly or indirectly the socialist countries' complicity in this dastardly plot.'

Agca himself has also claimed that he went first to Rome with the aim of killing Lech Walesa, the Polish Solidarist leader. That mission had to be aborted, declared Agca, who admitted that he was a fully trained international terrorist.

The case for him being an agent of Eastern Bloc intelligence services stands or falls on the circumstantial evidence he has provided about three Bulgarians in Rome. According to his version, Sergei Antonov, a Bulgarian state airline manager in Rome, was actually present with him during the murder attempt. He was later arrested to face complicity charges. Agca also alleged that he had planning sessions with two Bulgarian diplomats who had later left Rome.

There is little doubt that Agca was in touch with international terror groups. In brief, the Agca dossier has all the elements of a classic mystery, and it seems most unlikely that the whole truth will ever emerge from the partisan accounts.

He was visited in prison by Pope John Paul in December 1983. Two months later the Turkish newspaper *Hurriyet* claimed to have a copy of a film made during the interview, during which the Pope questioned Agca about who had sent him to St Peter's Square.

AGEE, Philip Burnett Franklin

The CIA has always boasted that it has never had a traitor within its ranks. No Philby, no Burgess, no Maclean. But it did have Philip Agee, who was a CIA case officer in Latin America for most of his twelve years with the Agency. He resigned in Mexico in January 1969, giving 'personal reasons' for leaving, but later claimed that he had turned against 'my work in the CIA as a reaction against the corruption, ineffectiveness and greed I found among the traditional political forces that we were supporting'.

He enrolled at the National Autonomous University of Mexico in a graduate programme of Latin American Studies, but soon began to think of writing a book about his career in the CIA to 'show the hypocritical, corrupt and self-defeating nature of the CIA's clandestine intervention to subvert institutions of friend and potential adversary alike'.

But he did more than that. He spent six months in Cuba 'researching' his book. He was given a house to work in, and two university students to help him. He swears that 'the Cuban government did not exert pressure for any relationship having an intelligence content', but the CIA view is that he was recruited by the DGI, the Cuban secret service, itself a surrogate of the KGB. While working in Paris he maintained close contact with the Cubans, and in 1974 again visited Cuba — the CIA insist he made a number of visits to Havana — and in 1975 he published *Inside the Company: CIA Diary*.

It did a great deal of damage, not because of what it revealed about the workings of the CIA — it had been overtaken by events in Washington — but because it printed the names of several hundred CIA employees, local agents and organizations. It caused the withdrawal of a number of agents who were put in danger by these revelations, and cost the CIA a great deal of money. But Agee did not stop there; he mounted a continuing campaign of identifying agents.

Many of the agents identified were named in a publication called *Counterspy*. One of the men named in *Counterspy* as a Chief of Station was Richard Welch. In December 1975 an Athens newspaper picked up this story, and checking through the American Embassy list discovered that Welch was working in Athens under diplomatic cover.

It published this story, identified Welch as Athens Chief of Station and published his home address. On 23 December, he was gunned down on his own doorstep. Agee was immediately blamed. He protested that he had not given Welch's name as a CIA agent to anybody, and was not responsible for the *Counterspy* article.

However, in his protestations he ignored the fact that the edition of *Counterspy* which fingered Welch also contained this advice from Agee:

The most effective and important systematic efforts to combat the CIA that can be undertaken right now are, I think, the identification, exposure, and neutralization of its people working abroad, the CIA people can be identified and exposed through periodic bulletins disseminated to our subscribers, particularly individuals and organisations in the foreign country in question. Photographs and home addresses in the foreign capital or Consular cities should be included. Having this information, the peoples victimized by the CIA and the economic exploitation that CIA enforces can bring pressure on their so-often compromised governments to expel the CIA people. And, in the absence of such expulsion, which will not be uncommon, the people themselves will have to decide what they must do to rid themselves of CIA.

This, especially the final sentence, was taken by the CIA as a clear exhortation for their agents to be murdered. Agee was also accused by Congressman Larry McDonald in the House of Representatives of betraying Colonel Jerzy

Pawlowski, the Polish Olympic fencer, to the Russians as a Western agent. Pawlowski was sentenced to twenty-five years in 1976 for spying for the CIA.

Later that year Agee was ordered to be deported from Britain — where he had lived since 1969 — on the grounds that he 'has maintained regular contacts harmful to the security of the United Kingdom with foreign intelligence agents'. He appealed against the order, along with Mark Hosenball, another American ordered to be deported on security grounds.

It was an appeal which caused considerable excitement among left-wingers in London. An Agee-Hosenball Defence Committee was set up, and all the fashionable names of the protest industry joined in. Agee, dapperly suited, with modish long hair softly contrasting a harsh mouth, loved it. He gave press conferences after each hearing at the Institute of Contemporary Arts. But he lost, and had to leave Britain.

Agee remains a blot on the CIA's record, but although he does his best to cause trouble, and stays close to the Cubans, he has been thoroughly sanitized and is no longer capable of doing overmuch damage. The Agency has, though, no intention of forgiving and forgetting. In January 1981, after a long legal battle, the Supreme Court ruled that Agee no longer had the right to hold an American passport.

ALDRIDGE, Philip Leslie

An official enquiry after the sentencing to four years' imprisonment of this 19-year-old Intelligence Corps lance-corporal revealed alarming laxity in British security procedures in 1983. MI5 was ordered to overhaul arrangements within the defence intelligence staff at the Ministry of Defence as a result of its revelations.

While working at the Ministry Aldridge telephoned the Soviet Embassy and told them that if they were interested in buying secret information they should place an item in the *Daily Telegraph* personal column. It duly appeared as: 'I love you, Spider, Love: Mum', and a meeting was arranged.

Aldridge had never been positively vetted. Yet, despite that and his junior position, he had been left without supervision with orders to destroy seventeen pages of a Joint Intelligence Committee digest and to file the rest of it. It was this intelligence assessment for eyes at Prime Minister level which he purloined and offered to sell to the Russians so that he could buy a car.

Swift counter-intelligence action prevented him from handing over the papers. However, he was able to destroy them, and it was not until after his trial in January 1983 that he revealed under questioning in prison which important papers had been in his possession.

ALLEN, Staff-Sergeant Percy

Intent on making money quickly to solve his domestic financial problems, Allen went to a telephone box near the War Office where he worked, in the Land/Air War Directorate. It was March 1965, and he simply offered Western estimates on the Egyptian armed forces to the Iraqi Embassy. He also got in touch with the Egyptian military attaché, and some of the documents he sold there were eventually published in the Cairo press. He removed documents on seven different occasions before restoring them to their files.

He was easily spotted by the intelligence watchers, and Special Branch arrested him in the act of handing over some papers to Major Abdul Al-Abbasi, the Iraqi military attaché. All he had made from his espionage activity was £75. He was sentenced to ten years in prison.

ALMEBERG, Captain Alvar

He was the captain of a Swedish air force DC3 which disappeared while on a signals intelligence mission along the Baltic Sea borders of Sweden and the Soviet Union in June 1952. The weather was good, and no distress call was recorded from the aircraft with a crew of seven, which was packed with radio listening devices.

Three days later a Catalina flying-boat, one of the aircraft searching for the DC3, was itself shot down by Soviet MiG fighters, though the crew were rescued. No protest was ever made, but the general conclusion was that Captain Almeberg's aircraft also had been shot down near the Soviet border.

When thirty years later his son Roger Almeberg wrote a book on the subject, *The Flyer who Disappeared*, an Estonian exile informed him that in the 1950s he had met captured Swedish airmen in a Soviet prison camp. The affair remains an unsolved puzzle of aerial espionage.

AMIT, General Meir

A kibbutz-educated Israeli, born in Tiberias, he became head of Mossad, the Israeli secret service, in 1962, having already been head of the military intelligence organization. He controlled the service in the great days of Mossad, when it was operating high-powered agents in both Damascus and Cairo, the capitals of his country's two principal enemies.

Meir Amit had long military experience which he put to good use in effectively fighting the first assaults of international terrorists. After joining Haganah, the Jewish guerrilla group in Palestine, and then rising to command a brigade in the 1948 war with the Arabs, he moved into intelligence work.

While serving with military intelligence he travelled widely, and during a visit to the United States he met many influential people who were to prove useful later. Among them was Dick Helms, director of the CIA, whom he first encountered at the University of Columbia. Co-operation between the American Agency and Mossad became so close later that intelligence men used to speak of the 'Mossad desk' at the Langley, Virginia, headquarters.

It was General Amit who succeeded in persuading the Americans that the Russians were encouraging the Arabs to make war in the Middle East in 1967. He successfully canvassed for US support of Israel when its pre-emptive war of that year was being planned.

Because he had experience as head of both the Israeli intelligence services he was able to put an end to the fierce and harmful rivalry between them. During his time in office he doubled the size of the service and modernized its equipment, especially in the way of modern technology. He was one of the most successful of Israeli spymasters.

AMORY, Robert

Amory was the amiable, eloquent professor of law from Harvard, the archetypal upper-crust New Englander, or 'educated Easterner', who became Deputy Director of Intelligence at the CIA. He was one of Allen Dulles's most trusted lieutenants, played a good game of tennis, and was convivial company at the spymaster's parties. Related to the Heathcoat Amory family, he could call on the British Establishment for help. Above all, he brought a keen intellect to a department filled with brains. His job was to collate information and present assessments, and he did it with panache until 1961 when, shortly after John McCone succeeded Dulles as Director, Amory found that he was being cut off from the kind of direct relationship he had enjoyed with the latter. He resigned to become general counsel for the National Gallery of Art in Washington.

ANDROPOV, Yuri Vladimirovich

Although he had controlled the KGB, the world's most active, repressive and conspiratorial security and espionage service, for fifteen years before achieving supreme power as President of the USSR, Yuri Andropov was not a professional secret policeman. He clawed and conspired his way up the ladder as a party man.

The inscrutable man behind the thick glasses which give him a slightly academic air began life near the Volga in Southern Russia as the son of a 'railway official', not quite proletarian enough.

While doing odd jobs he joined Komsomol, the Young Communist League, and so took the path to fame and fortune.

After graduating from a technical college Yuri in his twenties found himself a youth leader in Karelia, on the northern border, at the time of the Soviet-Finnish war. In the Leningrad region he survived the great war against fascism as a party official without ever being involved with the army, and it is significant that he had no military decorations.

Andropov seized his big chance, first as counsellor, then as ambassador, in Budapest at the time of the Hungarian uprising in 1956. It was an odd appointment, for he had no previous diplomatic experience.

Nevertheless, he played a key role preparing the way for the Soviet tanks which crushed the uprising. According to some accounts, it was he who lured the leaders to their arrest and doom by promising them safe conduct. By such means did he attract the attention of the Kremlin, and in 1967 Khruschev appointed him chairman of the Committee of State Security.

Abroad the KGB promptly stepped up its spying campaigns in the US, Britain and Europe — it was during his reign at secret police headquarters that the British government detected and expelled 105 Soviet agents at the London embassy. At home Andropov made war upon the dissidents who, encouraged by Khruschev's denunciation of Stalinist methods, believed that a new era was dawning.

Andropov demonstrated that they were wrong, for during his time as KGB master he broke the dissident movement. He did so not by the old-fashioned Beria methods of purge and extermination, but by subtler tactics. Indeed, his claim to fame was as an innovator, a KGB boss who improved and modernized tactics without changing the aims.

Prominent dissidents were silenced either by being deported to the West or by being encouraged to leave, so that they could do less damage at home. It was during Andropov's time that increasing use was made of psychiatric treatment for opponents of the regime, used on the grounds that anyone who questioned communism must be mad anyway. While he was at Dzerzhinsky Square headquarters the number of 'psychiatric prisons' increased from one to eleven, and later there were thirty such establishments.

He also gave a new look to KGB people operating in the West, encouraging the new-model spies to abandon the old raincoat, baggy suit and broad-brimmed hat in favour of Western-cut suits. They were urged towards a smoother approach in their dealings with the West, to appear as sophisticated and reasonable persons — though their aims remained the same as before.

Naturally, the hard men were still there in case of party need, but on the surface everything seemed more reasonable. It was remarkable that such tactics should have been worked out by a man who had no experience of the non-communist world, for there is no record of Andropov ever having visited a Western country.

He made great efforts to learn English, no doubt as a preparation for his international role, and he is said to have known German and perhaps other languages too. Andropov was also a firm believer in the use of disinformation. One of his first acts as KGB chairman was to upgrade the department responsible and rename it Directorate A. He was quoted as remarking, 'The political role of the USSR must be supported abroad by the dissemination of false news and provocative information.'

A Soviet diplomat defector, Vladimir Sakharov, who was a friend of Andropov's son, claimed that the KGB chief had consulted Kim Philby, the British renegade, in this matter. 'Andropov', he wrote, 'knocked the rough edges off the KGB', to give it a new and more attractive image.

He used Soviet novels, films and television to feature spy stories in which KGB heroes, clean-cut and decent, battled against seedy and crafty imperialist forces. Unlike the heroes of many films in the West, they were ideologically sound and highly intelligent.

After he became President there were signs that Andropov — who had already partially succeeded in spreading the word in the West that he was

sophisticated, cultured and quite different from
the brutal old heads of the USSR — was making
use of similar techniques to encourage the anti-
defence lobby in the West. Moscow continually
made helpful noises to spread the belief that
Russia was the centre of peace, always willing to
talk about nuclear-free areas and ending the arms
race.

But behind the façade Andropov remained head
of Russian imperialism, promoted his henchmen
from the KGB to high office, took a tough line at
home, and an aggressive stance abroad. He also
had to fight against ill health, which manifested
itself soon after he became President, and which
led finally, in February 1984, to his death at the
age of sixty-nine.

ANGLETON, James Jesus

A tall, lean introvert who served alongside his
father in the OSS in Italy, Angleton was one of the
few kept on after President Truman disbanded the
organization in 1945. He remained in Italy, and
played a part in preventing that country from
going communist. At the same time he kept up his
friendship with left-wingers he had first met as
partisans during the war. He maintained one
particularly fruitful relationship with Palmiro
Togliatti, the communist leader.

It was during this period that he made his first
connections with the Jewish underground, which
later blossomed into a close collaboration between
Mossad and CIA's Israeli desk, which Angleton
took under his wing.

However, although he was good in the field, his
true vocation was counter-espionage, and it was in
this area that he carried out his best work for the
Agency. He approached it like a medieval
inquisitor, examining every aspect of an affair
before pronouncing judgment. His inquiries about
a single defector were quite likely to go on for
years. He believed absolutely in the great world-
wide KGB plot; wrongly suspected that Tito's
quarrel with Stalin was merely play-acting, and
that the split between China and Russia was a plot
to lure the West into dropping its guard.

It was Angleton who first suspected Philby,
more by instinct than anything else. Philby, in his
apologia *My Silent War*, says that they used to
lunch once a week in Harvey's, a Washington
restaurant, and that 'Our close association was, I
am sure, inspired by genuine friendliness on both
sides.... But the real nature of my interest he did
not know.' It seems likely that Philby was also
unaware of the real nature of Angleton's interest
in him.

As the years passed, so Angleton grew more
cadaverous — though he ate hugely — and more
zealous about counter-espionage. He became
something of a joke to the younger men in the
Agency, but still retained a great deal of power. He
had a large budget, and virtually ran his world-
wide network of counter-espionage operations
without reference to anyone else. He could walk
into Allen Dulles's office without knocking, and
Richard Helms let him get on with his arcane
business.

There had never been any love lost between him
and another OSS veteran, William Colby, and
when Colby became Director of the Agency he set
about forcing Angleton out. In December 1974 he
relieved Angleton of his responsibility for counter-
intelligence and for liaison with Israel, which
effectively left him with nothing to do. Colby said
he could stay on as a consultant, expecting him to
resign, but when that did not work he leaked the
story that Angleton had been responsible for the
CIA opening domestic mail. Angleton, certain
that there was a plot against him, resigned, telling
friends that Colby, by giving up the CIA's secrets
to the Church Commission and by destroying the
counter-espionage branch, could not have done
more damage if he had been working for the
KGB.

When Angleton disappeared from the Agency
to enjoy his singularly apt pursuit of fly fishing it
was as if the last of the CIA old guard had
vanished. The Agency was never the same again,
though as David Phillips wrote in *The Night
Watch*, 'CIA has the best record of any intelligence
service in history in defending itself against
penetration by hostile services. Perhaps that will
be Angleton's monument.'

ARTAMONOV, Lieutenant-Commander Nicolai Fedorovich

From a Western intelligence officer's viewpoint it seemed too good to be true when in June 1959 a brilliant 35-year-old Soviet naval officer simply turned up on the beach of Oland Island off the Swedish coast. He had with him a beautiful Polish girl doctor named Ilja, and a Russian seaman whom he claimed to have tricked into helping him sail a launch across the Baltic from Gdynia.

The Commander's story was that he was in love with the Polish girl, and fearing that an imminent posting would separate them for ever, and not being too keen on the regime, he had decided to change sides.

Naturally, this caused a stir. The Swedes were interested, but the CIA and the British MI6 were even more enthusiastic at the idea of debriefing a talented naval officer, who said he was captain of one of the latest Russian destroyers. His name was, moreover, on the record, for he had taken his ship on goodwill visits to European ports.

Artamonov accepted an American offer of asylum, and was flown off to West Germany. After a stay there he went on to the United States to the defector-processing centre. By September 1960 he was considered a star discovery, and was able to testify, partly in English, before the Un-American Activities Committee, to utter warnings that the Soviets had instructed senior officers to be ready to launch surprise nuclear attacks.

Tall, dark-haired and wearing horn-rimmed glasses and a full moustache, he made quite an impression. He said that he had been brought up as a hundred per cent Soviet citizen of the new generation, and had been trained in the best naval schools, including the Frunze Naval Academy.

He said he had been described as one of the most brilliant Soviet naval officers. The Commander had never had connections with foreign intelligence until he sailed across the Baltic, and he was reluctant to give away detailed naval information, though happy to expose the errors of the communist leadership.

With such credentials American intelligence did not hesitate to employ him, though not at a very

high level. They had, however, checked out his credentials by allowing him to take over for a while on the bridge of an American destroyer, where he proved his seamanship skills.

But heavy doubts began to emerge about the activities of Commander Artamonov, who had seemed at first such a splendid catch, and who indeed had provided a good deal of useful information about the Soviet Navy. Major Anatoli Golytsin, who defected west from the KGB in 1961, had seen a good deal of the Commander in America, but in 1965 he refused to see him again, and denounced the naval officer as a 'plant' sent over as part of a Soviet deception operation.

From this point onward he was treated with suspicion, and it seems more than likely that the CIA struck back by attempting to use him as a double agent. He seems to have been in touch with both the KGB and the CIA.

The Commander was last seen in Vienna just before Christmas 1975, where he was supposed to have a rendezvous with the Russians. It is still far from clear whether he returned home to the Soviet Union at the end of his mission, or whether he was forced back. But it was the end of the Commander's story.

ASSAD, Rifaat

Head of Syria's security services, he is the brother of President Hafez el Assad, and protector of the regime. He has four wives, eleven children and is enormously rich. He is also completely ruthless, and is considered to be the most hated man in Syria. He commands detachments of Defence Companies of divisional strength, which are equipped with heavy weapons and tanks and are recruited from the ruling Alawite minority to which the Assads belong. These detachments guard the Presidential Palace, and have been used to put down uprising by the Moslem Brotherhood and other religious sects with great cruelty, especially in the city of Homs.

Apart from these uniformed forces, Rifaat Assad and his colleague Ali Duba also run Syria's espionage organization, which in fact carries out little orthodox spying but concentrates on sending hit teams abroad to murder opponents of the Assad regime. It was one of these teams which murdered Benan El-Attar, wife of Essam El-Attar, the leader of the Moslem Brotherhood, who was working against the Assads from exile in West Germany. The hit-team planned to kill him, but when they rang the doorbell of his Aachen home his wife opened the door and was gunned down.

In 1982 Rifaat Assad paid more than a million dollars in cash for a house near Washington. Perhaps he intends to retire there.

AUGUSTENBORG, Lon David

An American vice-consul in Leningrad seized with his wife and daughter by a roadside near the city, and according to the Russians caught red-handed collecting highly secret documents to do with the Soviet navy. In September 1983, announcing his expulsion, the Russians said that he had taken his wife Denise and his young daughter on a Sunday afternoon drive so as to use them as cover.

Mrs Augustenborg retrieved a tin containing documents from a dead drop, and when Soviet security men arrived she threw it into the back seat of the car while her husband (who kept the engine running) tried to drive away. From this the KGB assumed that she too was experienced in espionage. No name was announced of a Soviet citizen said to have been recruited by the Americans to provide information, but later the Russians published pictures of code sheets, documents and money used in this spying enterprise.

One curious feature of the Augustenborg story was that four months before the Russians announced his expulsion *Pravda* had published a story that a US vice-consul in Leningrad had been caught spying as he collected material from a drop. They named him as D. Shorer, and the US Embassy said they had no such person on their staff in Leningrad.

It may well be that the newspaper story was intended as a warning that they intended to take

action against Mr Augustenborg and were testing for any reaction.

BACHMANN, Colonel Albert

Attention was first drawn to the activities of this officer, the director of Swiss intelligence services, by a rather old-fashioned spying episode of comic-opera dimensions. He was suspended from duty in 1979 after the Austrian police, to their intense embarrassment and that of the Swiss authorities, arrested one of his officers spying on Austrian military manœuvres.

The officer in question, Lieutenant Karl Schilling, was so inexperienced in such activities that he succeeded in drawing attention to himself while trying to discover 'secrets' which were freely revealed to foreign official observers of the war games. Both Austria and Switzerland are neutral countries, having excellent relations the one with the other, and the whole thing seemed absurd.

The Lieutenant was given a five-month suspended sentence by the Austrians, and was promptly sent back home.

Colonel Bachmann was later discharged from his position as a civil servant in the National Defence Department after a parliamentary inquiry into his activities. It criticized him for running a private intelligence organization as well as government intelligence services.

BARBIE, Klaus

The now notorious 'Butcher of Lyons', alleged to be responsible for the murder of 4,000 French Jews and the deportation of 7,500 others when he acted as the local Gestapo chief in occupied France, was recruited after the war as an informer by American intelligence. In 1947 the US Army Counter Intelligence Corps hired Barbie after he had offered his services to British intelligence in post-war Germany.

Barbie made the approach, offering to provide information about his former Nazi friends, and also no doubt placing at the disposal of Western intelligence his dossiers on communists, both German and Russian. He had additionally a good deal of secret information about the communist party in France of value to the Americans, alarmed at the possibility of a Red takeover in France after the coup which made Czechoslovakia a People's Republic.

It was probably fear that this might become known which decided American intelligence to help smuggle out Barbie via the so-called Rat Line to Latin America, when in 1950 the French tracked him down and wanted to bring him to justice for wartime crimes. It was for this action that the United States offered a frank and formal apology to President Mitterrand in August 1983.

By that time Barbie (aged eighty-two) had been extradited from Bolivia and was in prison in Lyons, being interrogated by magistrates preparing the case against him.

BARGHOORN, Professor Frederick C.

An amiable political scientist from Yale University who had been a temporary diplomat in Moscow during the war, he fell victim to the machinations of the KGB, and was briefly branded by them as a spy in 1963. The fantastic story of his distressing experience did not emerge in detail until after the later defection of Yuri Nosenko, who at the time ran the department documenting American visitors to the USSR.

It all came about because the FBI in New York arrested three KGB officers in October 1963. Two were covered by United Nations diplomatic immunity and had to be released, but the third, Igor Ivanov, posing as a chauffeur, had no such protective cover, and there was strong evidence against him.

The KGB reflex was at once to grab an American in Moscow and hold him as a potential swop to recover their man in New York. Nosenko was at once summoned by his general, who asked him for any likely visitors. He had to admit that, it being the end of the season, there was nothing much about at the time, except the unhappy Professor Barghoorn.

Unfortunately for them, the KGB had nothing to even suggest that he was a spy. A diligent agent in Tbilisi only a few days before had made the Professor poorly by drugging his coffee in order to have a chance of going through his belongings — without result.

As the matter was pressing and Khruschev, the Soviet leader at the time, was demanding urgent action, they simply decided to *make* Barghoorn a spy. It was arranged that as he returned to the Hotel Metropole after lunch at the US Embassy a young KGB apprentice should approach him and thrust into his hand a packet of defence documents. Hardly was this done before a security team pounced to arrest them and convey the Professor to the Lubyianka.

Luckily for the Professor, prompt action was taken by President Kennedy, who having assured himself that there was no possibility of Barghoorn being employed on secret work, denounced the Soviet action at a press conference and demanded his immediate release. Khruschev in a rage ordered that he be freed and reprimanded his security officers — not for framing an American, but for choosing one who was a friend of the American President.

BARTSCHATIS, Ella

The private secretary of the East German political boss Otto Grotewohl, a lady with excellent shorthand which enabled her to furnish West German intelligence with verbatim reports on his important conferences in 1953. She also provided secret papers at Cabinet level.

A 42-year-old spinster, she had been recruited through her infatuation for a former legal adviser, Dr Laurenz, who had himself been approached by the West Germans. After several months she was detected and executed following a secret trial. Frau 'Red Hilde' Benjamin — the hanging judge, as she was known — had recently been appointed Minister of Justice, and restored the death penalty for treason.

Another West German woman agent caught at about the same time was Fräulein Halm, who worked in the State Security Ministry itself. Although two of her colleagues were executed, she only received a life sentence.

BEER, Israel

A friend and confidant of Israel's first Prime Minister, David Ben Gurion, a colonel of the reserve and an official defence adviser to the government of Israel, he was also a Soviet agent carefully implanted. Beer even had his own room at the Ministry of Defence, where he was writing an official history of the war of independence.

Counter-intelligence caught up with him only because of his heavy spending, which attracted attention in Tel Aviv. They took him red-handed with a brief-case full of documents, including Ben Gurion's official diary, which had just been photographed by a Russian agent.

When Ben Gurion was told that his friend was about to be arrested he remarked sadly, 'Do your duty.' For several years Beer had been handing over highly secret documents about installations, nuclear research and foreign arms-suppliers.

At his trial in 1961 he did not deny the facts but justified his actions by saying that he felt it his duty to save Israel from falling into the hands of the Western Powers when it ought to ally itself to Russia. In prison during his ten-year sentence — raised on appeal to fifteen years — he wrote a book of self-justification. He died there in 1968 of a heart-attack.

The account which Beer gave of his life was full of fantasy, and Mossad had little difficulty in proving it so. But they never managed to discover his true origins, though it was proved that the real Austrian named Israel Beer had disappeared in 1938, the year that the spy emigrated to Israel. This supported the belief that he had been placed in deep cover during the immigrations from Europe, ready to be exploited later after he had embedded himself in the Israeli establishment.

BERIA, Lavrenti Pavlovich

The Grandfather of the KGB. This archetypal secret policeman with the steel-framed glasses and the sharp face, like his master Joseph Stalin, came from Georgia. An early Bolshevik, he was given his first intelligence job by Lenin himself. From 1921 until the end of his days his entire working career was taken up with the business of conspiracy, espionage both internal and external, murder and execution.

Among his first tasks when Stalin appointed him head of the KGB — it was then called the NKVD (People's Commissariat for Internal Affairs) — was to arrange the execution of his predecessor, Nicolai Yezhof, a 'liquidation' expert himself, and known as the 'Bloody Dwarf'.

Under Beria's control the KGB became a state within a state, with its own uniformed army and police force, spies, executioners and death squads. It was in charge of industries, labour camps, and publishing enterprises. To join the KGB became a sought-after privilege for the brightest and most ambitious young men, for though membership carried obvious risks of denunciation and death at the slightest suspicion of treachery, it also offered promise of social advantage, wealth and prestige.

Beria's men carried out the great pre-war purges of the Red Army which almost destroyed it through the blood-letting of professional officers not considered sufficiently communist. They had killed thousands in bringing the peasants to heel. His squads had assassinated 'enemies' of the regime at home and émigrés abroad.

After the German invasion in 1941 Stalin entrusted Lavrenti Beria, as deputy Prime Minister, with the job of keeping security behind the war-front. This energetic little man behaved with the utmost brutality towards those who failed to carry out orders or showed signs of defeatism. Beria worked on the principle that soldiers should be more afraid of the secret police than of the enemy. As a reward he became a Marshal of the Soviet Union.

This greatly feared man had also made many enemies, and although he was certainly among the most powerful men in the Soviet Union he failed to move quickly enough. Since they were terrified at what might happen, once Stalin died in 1953, Khruschev, Malenkov and a few colleagues of the so-called collective leadership banded together.

In a swift and daring pre-emptive move they managed to do what Beria himself had done many times, to arrest their enemy as he arrived for a meeting with them. He was shot, after, they said being tried for anti-party and anti-State activities. Among the more fanciful of charges publicly made against him was that Beria was a British secret agent.

The NKVD died with the appalling Beria, for the following year it was decided that the organization should be renamed KGB.

BETTANEY, Michael

Who on earth was responsible for allowing this strange and silly fellow into MI5, the counter-espionage service, and for keeping him on as a middle-ranking officer after obvious indiscretions? That was the question most commonly asked after the spy scandal which ended with his conviction in April 1984 on ten spying charges under the Official Secrets Act. To make matters worse, he had hardly begun serving a 23-year term in prison before he wrote to the *Observer* newspaper about low morale in MI5.

The trial was held *in camera*, but the case against him was that he had made blundering attempts to get in touch with Arkady Gouk, whom he believed to be a KGB man at the Soviet Embassy in London offering secret papers. When the embarrassed Mr Gouk — no doubt scenting a heavy-handed attempt to compromise him — ignored the attempts, Bettaney decided to fly to Vienna and and offer his ideological wares to the Russians there.

It was clear that he had proved himself a thoroughly unsuitable officer. After Oxford and a

teaching spell in Germany, the podgy-faced man who once wanted to be a Catholic priest took an interest in Nazism before switching to Marxism. His personal behaviour was absurd. Bettaney was taken to court for fare-dodging on the railway, and when approached by the police for being drunk and disorderly in a London street he shouted, 'You can't arrest me, I'm a spy'.

Even that did not attract disciplinary attention from his superiors. He was in fact promoted to the Russian desk, and was able to filch files without attracting attention.

Bettaney attempted to justify his actions by issuing through his lawyers a long and naïve statement in the language of nineteenth-century Marxism which must have embarrassed even the Russians. In passing sentence Lord Lane, Lord Chief Justice, accurately described him as 'puerile, self opinionated and dangerous'.

Yet another inquiry into the security and methods of the British security service was ordered by the government.

BINGHAM, Sub-Lieutenant David James

This clever and ambitious young naval officer, promoted from the lower deck, was not recruited by Soviet intelligence. He was just one of the many cases in Western Europe of a man who volunteered secret material to the Russians in return for cash payment. Or rather his wife did so on his behalf by the simple process of calling at the Soviet Embassy in London.

Maureen Bingham was a waitress when she married her young sailor husband in Portsmouth. She did her best to look after their young family of four, but she had an insatiable appetite for bingo, and felt unable to cope with the new life of her husband when he won the sword of honour on a promotion course and became a sub-lieutenant.

By 1969 the Binghams were crippled with debts. They owed money everywhere, and had sold their car without telling the hire-purchase company. So Maureen Bingham took herself to London and coolly announced that her naval officer husband would like to sell secrets for cash.

As the prosecution put it at the subsequent trial (in March 1972), 'He treacherously converted his knowledge of defence secrets into money to pay his household expenses and hire purchase debts on his car.' The Soviets got a bargain, for Bingham was an electronics expert serving as a torpedo officer aboard the frigate HMS *Rothesay*. He was able to photograph and supply to the Russians Fleet Operations Tactical Instructions which gave details of combined naval operations against hostile submarines, wavelengths and call signs.

In addition he supplied details of the American nuclear depth-charge being used by the Royal Navy. All that the Russians had to do was to arrange a series of meetings with him and to pay over £2,800 in all, a bargain basement of espionage.

Although Lieutenant Bingham was an anxious and incompetent spy who on at least one occasion had to get his wife's help in finding the spot where he was to make a 'drop', he was never detected by naval security. His fellow-officers were surprised when finally (and by now worried out of his mind) he asked to speak to the ship's First Lieutenant and made a full confession of his activities.

Incredibly enough, Bingham's first meeting with the Russians was at the West London apartment of the assistant naval attaché, Lory Turifmovich Kuzmin. After warning him in writing not to speak, and turning up the radio as a primitive anti-bug precaution, the Russian offered vodka and cash payment for certain information, in that order. When the Bingham affair came to light Kuzmin disappeared back to Moscow. He was never allowed to return to his post in Britain.

Bingham's trial was short and sharp, for he had pleaded guilty and made full confession. Sentencing him to twenty-one years, Mr Justice Bridge declared, 'The damage you may have done is incalculable.'

The extraordinary Mrs Bingham later had the effrontery to organize a campaign against the 'savage' sentence upon her husband, and to try to recruit the support of the Soviet Embassy. She even asked them for more money. Wisely, a Soviet diplomat refused her request for an official statement from the Embassy that Bingham's

information had been 'worthless'. He did not think that anybody would believe such a statement.

As a result of his activities NATO naval forces had to revise their procedures and change tactics in the all-important matter of anti-submarine defences against the threat of the huge Soviet submarine fleet.

David Bingham was released on parole after serving seven years in prison. He had divorced Maureen and remarried. In 1982 he got a job with the probation service supervising offenders doing community work.

BISSELL, Richard

A studious and engaging economist who had worked as a Marshall Plan administrator in Germany and for the Ford Foundation in Washington before being brought into the Central Intelligence Agency, despite his lack of experience in that field. He was regarded at first as the protégé of Allen Dulles, the director, but soon adapted to his new role as a 'dirty tricks man'.

His most solid achievement came when he was put in charge of the programme announced by President Eisenhower in 1954 to begin building specially designed U2 spy planes at an initial cost of $22 million. By the following year the first aircraft were operational. Richard Bissell also foresaw that eventually they would be replaced by spy satellites, and began preparations by ordering the development of special camera equipment.

Unfortunately for his career, the CIA recruit also became deeply involved in the more squalid covert operations being mounted at the time. His first experience of such things was as a joint organizer of the agency-backed coup d'état which overthrew the government of Jacobo Arbenz after he had nationalized the United Fruit Company owning America's banana plantations in Guatemala. It was a textbook operation.

But the next enterprise of the director in charge of covert operations led to disaster. After Jack Kennedy had been elected President in 1960 he was ordered to begin counter-revolutionary operations in Cuba, with the eventual aim of destroying the Fidel Castro regime. Although Richard Bissell had doubts about the affair, he was soon busy plotting with his eccentric scientific adviser, Dr Sidney Gottlieb, who put forward bizarre plans to murder Castro. Other third-world statesmen on their death list were Patrice Lumumba of the Congo, Rafael Trujillo of the Dominican Republic, and General Kassem of Iraq. Although these all came to a violent end, there is little evidence that the CIA was responsible.

Full information on Richard Bissell's part in these bloodthirsty schemes came to light years later in the report of the Church Committee on alleged assassination plots involving foreign leaders.

His downfall as an Agency man came about through the total failure of the most ambitious of the operations against Fidel Castro. President Kennedy enthusiastically supported plans to land a Cuban rebel army on the beaches of the Bay of Pigs, convinced that they could eventually march on Havana, the capital. But although he had ordered CIA backing, and B-26 bombers had been provided for the assault, he hesitated about giving the full air support which Bissell had recommended. When grudging air support was given at the CIA man's insistence it was too late, and the Cuban army of Fidel Castro had little trouble in mopping up the invasion force.

The President blamed the CIA, and threatened to break it up. Seeking a scapegoat, he picked upon Allen Dulles, and dismissed him in November 1961. Three months after his patron, Richard Bissell also had to resign. He went back to his career as an economist in practice as a business consultant, and his only further connection with intelligence was as a witness before the committees investigating CIA misbehaviour.

BLAKE, George

Long before he took the unlikely path which led him to become an officer in Britain's Secret Intelligence Service while acting on behalf of the KGB, George Blake had passed through a complicated cosmopolitan childhood. His father was Albert Behar from Cairo, whose Sephardic Jewish family cut him off because of his marriage to a Dutch Christian lady named Catherine Beijdervellen.

Behar senior became a British citizen after serving in the French Foreign Legion and in the British Army. When he died in 1936 he left his widow and the young George (who later changed his name to Blake) in reduced circumstances. One of the Behar sisters had married a wealthy banker in Cairo named Henri Curiel, and he offered to look after the boy provided that he went to live with the family in Egypt.

After much heart-searching George (then aged thirteen) was packed off from Rotterdam aboard a freighter. It was only during his stay in Cairo that he learned English at the English school there, and became closely involved with Middle Eastern life. While the authors were researching their book *The Carlos Complex* they discovered another fascinating link in George Blake's past.

He fell very much under the influence of his cousin Henri Curiel, in whose father's house he lived. Curiel is a most enigmatic figure, who was a founder of the Egyptian communist party, and who much later in life went to live in Paris, where he was involved with not only the KGB but also with a number of terrorist and liberation movements. He was murdered by unknown assassins in 1978.

So it is obvious that quite early in his life Blake was, to say the least, on close terms with communist activity while living in the home of a Jewish banker. When the war broke out in 1939 George Blake was on a visit to his mother in the Netherlands, and was trapped there. After escaping from German internment and making contact with the Resistance he finally escaped to Britain.

He joined the Royal Navy, and no doubt because of his linguistic skills, found a job with naval intelligence in Hamburg after the Allies occupied Germany. From there this withdrawn yet ambitious young man did not have too much difficulty in joining the Foreign Office after eading modern languages, including Russian, at Downing College, Cambridge.

At the Foreign Office his first posting was to the Far Eastern department, where he was befriended by Guy Burgess. Appointed consul-general in Seoul, he arrived there just before the Korean War, and during it fell into the hands of the North Koreans. He was held for three years, part of that time by the Chinese communists.

On his return to England he went into the field as a Secret Intelligence Service officer, but from 1953 until he was unmasked by a German double agent in 1961 he faithfully served the KGB, and in this capacity betrayed at least forty Allied agents to the Russians.

Blake held a highly sensitive MI6 post in Berlin at the height of the cold war, bringing him into contact with General Reinhard Gehlen, which gave him the chance of spying on West German intelligence. Among the most damaging of his acts was to inform the Russians about Operation Gold.

This was a joint Anglo-American exercise to construct a tunnel 350 feet long under the Iron Curtain to tap Red Army communications. After it was finished the Russians struck, and moved into its eastern end, winning a great propaganda victory as well as ruining its usefulness.

Blake also revealed to his KGB bosses the 'order of battle' of the SIS, and betrayed dozens of individual agents. Furthermore, he helped East Germany to get back some of their people who had fled to the West.

In 1959 Blake was alarmed to discover that one of his agents was not only working for the Russians as well but was also in the pay of the Gehlen Organization. Blake was able to get himself posted back to London, and then for a spell to the Arabic language school at Shemlan in Lebanon out of harm's way.

The double agent was eventually discovered and arrested, and he did indeed inform on Blake's true activities. SIS summoned Blake back to London on a routine matter and arrested him, and during a long interrogation he admitted that he had spied for the Russians for years.

Both the British Government and the SIS, embarrassed by the seemingly endless procession of spy scandals involving highly placed Britons working for the KGB, was happy to have the confession. For it meant that there was no need for a long public trial. Evidence was heard briefly in camera, and the Lord Chief Justice sentenced George Blake to no less than forty-two years' imprisonment.

In fact he managed to escape from Wormwood Scrubs prison after serving only six years, and it was generally assumed at the time that the KGB were looking after their own. However, Sean Bourke, an Irish criminal who got to know Blake in prison, insisted that the escape plan was a private one worked out by the two of them, and came as a surprise to the KGB.

There is no doubt that the British authorities regretted that such a long sentence had been imposed, for they believed that it discouraged other traitors from confessing, and it may even have had a bearing on the Philby affair, because it deterred Philby from making a confession.

BLUNT, (Sir) Anthony Frederick

It was the publication in 1979 of an exceptionally well-researched book, *The Climate of Treason* by Andrew Boyle, which led to the public disgrace of this very 'English' spy and traitor. Because no formal charge had ever been made against an outwardly distinguished art historian who had been knighted by the Queen, and the laws of libel being what they are in Britain, he was referred to in the book simply as 'Maurice'.

'Maurice', it emerged, had on several occasions played a key part in the espionage activities on behalf of the Soviet Union of the Cambridge trio, Philby, Burgess and Maclean. In November 1979 Mr Ted Leadbitter, MP asked in Parliament whether the Prime Minister would make a statement on the actions 'of an individual... in relation to the security of the United Kingdom'.

Several Prime Ministers in reply to similar questions about similar people had been content to fudge the issue in their replies. It therefore came as a great surprise when Mrs Thatcher replied, 'The name ... is that of Sir Anthony Blunt.'

At last Blunt's disgraceful past as an agent of the KGB had come to light. Within a short time he was stripped of the honours with which he had been loaded. The Queen removed the knighthood awarded to him as Keeper of the Royal Pictures. Trinity College, Cambridge, where it had all started, revoked his Fellowship.

The beginning of the end of his spying career came in 1964, when Arthur Martin of MI5 called at his apartment in Portman Square with direct evidence that he had worked for the Soviets. That evidence had been provided shortly before by Michael Whitney Straight, a well-to-do American who had been his friend at Cambridge in the early 1930s.

Whitney Straight was being considered for an appointment which involved security clearance, and thought it better to tell the FBI about his communist past. In the process he revealed that he had been recruited by Blunt to work for the Russians, even though he claimed that he had never provided them with hard material. This information was passed on to the British security service, which had long suspected Blunt's heavy involvement with the Cambridge trio of spies, but in the course of eleven interrogations had failed to get him to admit his guilt.

The officer who questioned him in 1964 had the benefit of the tardy Straight revelations and was authorized to do a deal with Blunt, promising him immunity from prosecution in return for confession and information about his activities and contacts. Like a common criminal, the artistic knight 'turned Queen's evidence' in order to save himself.

His upbringing as the son of a Church of England parson had been conventional — public school at Marlborough, followed by university. At Trinity College the clever and talented young aesthete fell in with the smart left-wing set, who considered that the Soviet Union was the world's only hope.

Blunt as a young don was himself recruited and appointed as the talent-spotter who helped to enmesh both Burgess, his fellow-homosexual, and Maclean. What the Soviets were doing was to get supporters who as they built successful careers in the British establishment would eventually be in a position to supply high-class intelligence material.

At the outbreak of war in 1939 Blunt displayed all the outward signs of patriotism by taking a commission in the British Army, despite the fact that Stalin had just signed a pact with Nazi Germany. After a brief period of service in an Army field intelligence unit with the BEF in France he casually passed into the security service.

Serving there throughout the war in a section which dealt with security among the many European exile groups in England, he was well placed to provide his Soviet control with information about them. Serving in counter-intelligence, he was also able to oblige by furnishing lists of British operators in this field, at home and abroad, which no doubt were of use to the KGB in the post-war period of cold war with the Soviet Union.

Whether or not he may be held responsible for the killing of agents by Soviet death squads is open to debate. George Young, a former British security service officer, believes that such charges could be levelled against him.

Ostensibly his espionage career ended in 1945, when he left MI5 to resume his academic and artistic career. However, there was still waiting for him a star role in the continuing saga of the Cambridge three, Burgess, Maclean and Philby.

As the intelligence net finally tightened around Burgess and Maclean, he learned some of the details. According to Andrew Boyle in *The Climate of Treason*, he knew from his old MI5 friends that Maclean was about to be interrogated, and he supplied the date to Burgess and Maclean, who two days before slipped into the escape plan prepared for them by the KGB, and defected to Russia.

In the words of Mrs Thatcher, 'There is no doubt that British interests were severely damaged by his activities.' A further question still unanswered is how far Blunt continued aiding the Soviets even after his retirement. After the flight of Burgess and Maclean he was a terrified man, in fear that the past might catch up with him still, and therefore remained open to Russian pressure.

Although he had no access to official papers, it must be remembered that there is more to espionage than microdots and military plans. The Soviets are always seeking among persons of influence for titbits about reactions to situations and personalities in power; and as a distinguished man moving in high society Blunt was in a position to provide such material.

After his exposure Blunt, his long, cultured face crumpled in an attempt at sincerity, told TV viewers, 'I did not betray my conscience.'

When pressed with questions at a Press conference, full of self-justification, the old man had the impertinence to shelter behind the Official Secrets Act — to which he had paid remarkably little attention while he was furnishing intelligence to a hostile state. There was little sympathy for him.

Four years later he died at the age of seventy-six.

BOGDANOV, Radomir Georgiyevich

KGB agent who served for ten years in the Russian Embassy in New Delhi, where he is believed to have been the 'Resident'. He was appointed Deputy Director of the Institute of the USA and Canada of the USSR Academy of Sciences in 1975.

This Institute is the Soviet Union's only research organization devoted exclusively to American and Canadian affairs. Bogdanov openly supervised the Institute's study of US social, ideological and arms matters, but his covert duties included espionage and disinformation aimed at the US.

BONNET, Yves

A 47-year-old senior civil servant appointed in 1982 as part of the reorganization of French intelligence services head of the DST (Direction de la Surveillance du Territoire), the internal counter-intelligence branch. He replaced a police officer in this branch, which consists almost entirely of policemen.

Apart from acting in a role comparable to that of the Special Branch in Britain against foreign spies, the DST is heavily committed to action against terrorists. M. Bonnet has at his disposal computer files on some 30,000 terrorist suspects which are readily available to provide instant information at frontier posts, ports and airports.

His service also receives copious information from the RG police service (Renseignements Généraux) which keeps millions of files on private citizens, even those who have no criminal records. Among those carefully logged in these files are foreigners, trade unionists, journalists and civil servants.

'BORIS'

The name given to a Soviet defector described as a desk man from Moscow Centre who on one of his rare ventures into the field to Western Europe seized the opportunity to defect. His arrival was exclusively reported in *The Daily Telegraph* in London in April 1983.

No public announcement about the defection was made in 1983 — debriefing is a long process. However, American press reports hinted that 'Boris' was regarded as a big catch by the CIA.

The story was that he contacted British intelligence while in London, and was later passed on to the Americans. The first fruits of his information about KGB activities world-wide were passed on to the French Government. In April 1983 there was great activity in a number of Western countries as Soviet KGB officers were expelled.

Within a short period five were ordered to leave Britain. The French made an unprecedented move and expelled no less than forty-seven Russians for espionage, including forty diplomats. In Washington the FBI picked up Lieutenant-Colonel Yevgeny Barmyantsev, a Soviet military attaché, caught red-handed collecting film of defence documents. Two other Russians were expelled with him.

Expulsion of spies from a number of countries almost simultaneously is usually a sure sign that a Soviet defector with wide knowledge of field activities has begun talking.

BOSSARD, Frank Clifton

A resentful man who had no doubt had a hard start in life but who managed to do well in the RAF during the War and to become a flight lieutenant specializing in radar, despite the fact that he had a pre-war record for passing dud cheques. After leaving the Service he got a job with the rank of Second Secretary at the British Embassy in Bonn, interviewing refugees.

Back home in London, he began drinking heavily, and appropriately enough it was in a pub that he was first approached by the KGB. By that time in 1961 he was working in the Air Ministry department involved in guided-missile research.

Bossard needed money; the KGB needed information about research. The operation was commercial, and he delivered film of documents on at least nine dead, and live, drops in and around London in return for large sums of money, before being arrested in March 1965 at the Ivanhoe Hotel in Bloomsbury, London. It was his custom to collect his espionage outfit from the left luggage at Waterloo station and then go to the hotel to photograph secret material during the lunch-hour.

He was instructed when to make drops by Moscow Radio in a code based on the playing of five numbers, such as *Volga Boat Song* and *Moscow Nights*.

In May 1965 he was sentenced to twenty-one years in prison. Although his case aroused little public interest at the time, there is no doubt that the Russians valued his services highly, and that he had provided them with high-grade material in quantity.

BOURKE, Sean

He was described at the time as the man who master-minded the 1966 escape from Wormwood Scrubs Prison, London, of George Blake, the Soviet agent, for it was generally assumed that the Russians had carefully organized the springing of the man who had worked so hard on their behalf.

Things were not quite like that: Sean Bourke was very far removed from being a master-mind of

any kind. An ex-RAF clerk convicted of petty crime in Ireland, he went to London with a chip on his shoulder and worked as a labourer, and in this capacity sent a letter bomb to a police officer. For the offence he was sent to the Scrubs for seven years, and there he met George Blake.

The springing of George Blake was not a great KGB operation but a simple do-it-yourself affair contrived with some difficulty by the amiable Irishman. For one thing, he could not drive, and therefore had bother about the getaway car. Blake was to come over the prison wall at a place marked by a flower-pot, but on the exceptionally wet day chosen it was difficult to locate.

While Bourke waited nervously outside the prison a warder came up surrounded by dogs and started whistling frantically. Bourke stood transfixed, waiting to be arrested, but was amazed to see the warder run away from him still whistling, apparently in search of one of his dogs which had gone missing.

Blake eventually got over the wall and found his rescuer, but then he could not start the car, and it was some time before they managed to get clear of the prison. George Blake was eventually smuggled across the Channel in a caravan and after he arrived in Moscow he kindly invited Bourke to go and stay in a smart apartment as a guest of the KGB.

In September 1967 Bourke turned up at the British Embassy in Moscow saying that he now wanted to go back home. He had been alarmed to overhear a conversation in the flat about what was to be done with him. Apparently there was a debate about whether to let him go later, or simply to liquidate him.

In London the Foreign Office, grateful to have hard news at last that Blake was in Moscow, made an official announcement that Bourke was in the USSR, thus making it more difficult for the Russians to take action against him. From a KGB point of view the fact that Bourke had helped to organize the freelance springing of Blake was highly suspicious. Although they helped to get both men to Moscow by way of a flight with false passports to West Berlin via Frankfurt, they must have assumed at first that Blake had been turned y British intelligence as a double agent, and then llowed to escape from prison. Blake's debriefing annot have been a very pleasant experience for .im.

Bourke was eventually allowed to return home o Dublin a year later after the Russians had inished their investigations. He died of a heart-attack in 1982.

3OXHALL, Lieutenant-Colonel Edward

When he died at the age of eighty-six in January .984 he was described by the newspapers as 3ritain's oldest spy. He served in intelligence luring the First World War, and in the twenties ınd thirties he represented British firms in Romania where his father had served as consul.

It seems that he was still in service almost until :he time of his death. A long memory and his ınrivalled knowledge of the Special Operations Executive during the Second World War ensured :hat the security service considered him indis-pensable for vetting books written by ex-officers subject to the Official Secrets Act.

In 1979 when a British magazine published a photograph taken in the twenties of British intelligence officers, including himself in uniform and Sydney Reilly, the ace spy from earlier days, there was an official complaint from him that by so doing the publication had 'blown' his cover.

BOYCE, Christopher John

The more interesting member of the Boyce-Daulton Lee spy team which sold to the Russians the most closely guarded secrets of the Special Projects Office of TRW at Redondo Beach, California. He was twenty-two when the two of them hatched their plot, a college dropout but by no means stupid. His father, a former FBI agent, helped him to get his job.

Boyce well understood the significance of the work being done at the establishment where he worked, even though he was employed in a modest job as clerk at 140 dollars a week. In order to do his job — which involved changing cypher key settings daily — he needed top security clearance to get access to two important satellite projects for Sigint, signals intelligence, which were code-named Rhyolite and Argus.

Rhyolite was a permanent spy satellite designed to hang over the Soviet Union and China to monitor the sounds of missile engines and even whispered telephone conversations 18,000 miles below.

The first prototype was placed in orbit in 1972. Signals from its continual eavesdropping were passed to ground stations in Britain and in Australia. When it began operating a special security clearance was demanded from anyone who needed to see the targeting or the messages received from it.

Rhyolite was described by an expert on space espionage, Dr Desmond Ball, as 'perhaps the most successful development in technical intelligence since the "Ultra" operation of the Second World War'. Christopher Boyce was among the chosen few who had the right passes to know details of this operation, and he was the man who through his friend Daulton Lee offered his services to the Soviets, simply by knocking on the door of their Embassy in Mexico City.

Although Boyce was not himself in touch with the Russians directly until October 1976, he had provided the material for his courier, Daulton Lee, to pass on to them. By 1976 he was convinced that Daulton Lee was swindling him by failing to pass on his full share of the large sums being paid by the Russians, so he went to Mexico City to see for himself.

For the first time he met the Soviet controller of the operation, Boris Alexei Grishin, over dinner (caviar included) in the Embassy basement. He was surprised to find that Boris was not the fictional Russian agent in a baggy suit but one of Andropov's new-model KGB men, stylishly dressed and long-haired in the Western manner.

They got along very well, and Boris was obviously pleased to be in touch for a change with a serious and intelligent young American rather than with the drug addict Daulton Lee. Indeed, he suggested that his organization would be happy to finance some kind of scholarship for Boyce to take a degree in a suitable subject so that he could eventually join the State Department or the CIA.

The Soviets are always alert to the possibility of recruiting young men — as they did in the 1930s — who will eventually mature in office and rise high enough to make the espionage investment worth-while. Here was a potential American Kim Philby, to be trained and allowed to mole his way into the hierarchy for future Soviet use. Boyce was tempted by the idea, and accepted Boris's offer, having also agreed, in return for a payment of $75,000, to make one last bulk delivery from TRW.

Before resigning from the office, Boyce worked hard to photograph a thick report on the development of a covert satellite network being developed on behalf of the CIA under the code name 'Pyramider'. It was to be operated through miniature receiver/transmitters in areas of the world denied to the CIA.

It was at this point, when all seemed to be going well for the American duo, that Daulton Lee — unreliable at the best of times — made a fatal blunder by drawing attention to himself at the Soviet Embassy in Mexico City. He was desperate for money to buy a fix from his drug-dealer. While trying to contact Boris he slipped into the Embassy a book cover on which he had written the initials KGB, and was arrested by Mexican police, who believed he was a terrorist.

At the subsequent trial in April 1977 Daulton Lee received a life sentence and Christopher Boyce was sent to prison for forty years. Boyce escaped from jail three years later, apparently on his own initiative.

The conjunction of the Boyce-Daulton Lee case with that of the British electronics spy at Government Communications Headquarters, Geoffrey Prime, caused bitter Anglo-American recrimination. The American sensitivity about their failure to detect the Californian spies increased their indignation at the disclosures about Prime, because the GCHQ works closely with the American National Security Agency, which controls satellite and electronic espionage.

BRITTEN, Douglas

'Golf Three Kilo Foxtrot Lima,' said the Russian called Yuri when he introduced himself to Douglas Britten, a chief technician in the RAF, as he wandered around the Science Museum in Kensington. It was a surprising though shrewd move, for Britten was a radio ham and that was his call sign.

The KGB had done its homework before making this approach in 1962 by seeking out radio enthusiasts who were also Servicemen. At that time Britten was stationed in Lincolnshire at RAF Digby, working at a secret signals unit.

Yuri's first request was low-level. He simply wanted a radio transmitter which both parties knew was obsolete. This seemed harmless enough, and the RAF man supplied it and collected the money.

But that was just a beginning. When Britten was posted to Cyprus a new case officer had him photographed accepting money, and then began blackmailing him in traditional fashion.

Back in London he went on providing sensitive signals and code information to a Soviet agent named Borisenko, who was ostensibly a First Secretary at the Soviet Embassy. This continued until February 1968, when British watchers photographed Britten delivering material by hand to the Soviet Consulate, after, it turned out, his case officer had missed a rendezvous.

At the trial in 1968 Britten pleaded guilty. He was sentenced to twenty-one years in prison, after which he co-operated fully with security investigators in assessing the real extent of the damage he had done.

BROOKE, Gerald

A young British university lecturer who smuggled pamphlets into the Soviet Union while on a tourist visit in 1965. The pamphlets, attacking the communist regime, had been produced by NTS, the Russian émigré organization based in West Germany, but this had been penetrated by KGB agents and the Russians knew that Brooke was carrying what they regarded as 'subversive' literature.

He was certainly not a spy, but it was convenient for the Soviets to pretend that he was and to sentence him to four years in the camps, where they made sure he suffered great privations — and that the West knew about it.

The Russians simply wanted to hold him ready for one of their lopsided exchanges against their professional agents captured in the West. They already had someone in mind, two people in fact, the Krogers who had been sentenced to twenty years in 1962 for their role in the Portland Spy case. They planted stories that Brooke was being ill-treated, that his health was suffering and that he was likely to die if he was not released. The British Government came under pressure to secure his release.

The deal was made in 1969. Brooke for the Krogers. One man who had done nothing wrong by British standards in exchange for two highly professional spies. It was a deal which outraged the British security services. It meant that no Briton travelling behind the Iron Curtain would be safe if Britain held a Russian the Soviets wanted back. And it gave encouragement to the KGB professionals, who had once again been shown that Moscow Centre would always get them back.

BROOMAN-WHITE, Dick

A diffident and usually disinterested former SIS officer who was head of the wartime Iberian section in which Kim Philby served. Indeed, it was Brooman-White who originally smoothed his passage into the service.

He felt almost hero-worship for Philby. Believing that the suspicions about him raised in the United States were false and unfair, he was extremely sympathetic towards his old friend in trouble, especially at the time of Philby's forced resignation from the service.

By this time Brooman-White had become Conservative member of parliament for Rutherglen, and was determined to raise political support for Philby. He made approaches to the then head of MI6, in Philby's interest.

He was totally convinced that Kim was in the clear, and gave his personal assurance to Malcolm Muggeridge, the journalist and author — and himself an ex-military intelligence man — of his innocence. On the strength of that Muggeridge tried to get Philby taken on as a foreign correspondent for the *Daily Telegraph*, of which he was then deputy editor. He failed, but did recommend him to the *Observer*, which assigned him to Beirut.

Brooman-White was totally shaken by the triumphal announcement from Moscow that Philby had escaped there, and his health was affected. He died a year later, a betrayed friend.

BURGESS, Guy Francis de Moncy

Frivolous, brawling drunk, flauntingly homosexual, totally disreputable, witty and amusing — that was Guy Burgess, not at all the *beau idéal* of a Soviet agent, or come to that of a Foreign Office spokesman. Yet in his comparatively short life he simultaneously filled both posts.

The conventional picture is that at Cambridge, after Eton and a spell at Dartmouth naval college — shortened because he had bad eyes — the young Burgess fell in with the communists. The reasons put forward are that he believed only Stalin could stop Hitler; and that he worried about the plight of the English working class.

Neither emotion seems very likely in the bosom of such a person as Burgess. Certainly so far as the working class was concerned it is unlikely that he came in touch with members of it, other than those young men he took delight in seducing.

Nevertheless, he did frequent the posh left-wing circles at the university, and the most probable explanation for his enlistment in the KGB is that he joined for the hell of it. His recruiter no doubt brought him in on the totally justified assumption that no one would really believe that Guy was a communist.

Never did he display any of the communist virtues. There is not the slightest indication that he liked the Russians, and it is almost impossible to imagine him reading Marx. When finally he fled to Moscow — apparently by mistake rather than intent — he hated it, thought only of things English, became ever drunker and sadder in his search of the bars for people who could remind him of the old days at home, and died at fifty-two.

Burgess had visited Moscow once before on a sort of university outing from Cambridge. Even then he was discovered hopelessly drunk in the Park of Rest and Culture, though that is by no means a great offence in the Soviet Union.

In early wartime London Guy Burgess was well known and knew many influential people, so it was not surprising that he easily drifted by way of friends from the BBC to one of the mushrooming intelligence services. Gifted amateurs from the nation's gilded youth, especially those who were amusing and good company, were welcome in such military intelligence sub-cultures of the time.

Before that, and no doubt because the communist party approved, he associated with a fashionably pro-German faction in London, helped by the homosexual connection. This rather fooled his friends, but seemed to be no bar to his future career.

Since he had been a sort of freelance intelligence man he was offered a temporary job in the Foreign Office in 1944, which despite his continued appalling behaviour then became permanent. From being a spokesman he was taken on as personal assistant to Hector McNeil, Labour Minister of State at the Foreign Office, who we are told was dazzled by his brilliance. He was dismissed from a different department by another Labour minister who rightly described him as 'dirty, drunk and idle'.

Despite this small setback, and while he was still happily circulating confidential papers to his Soviet masters, the British appointed him to the Washington embassy to look after Far Eastern affairs, which were particularly sensitive at the time of the Korean War in 1950.

Before he set off Hector McNeil gave him some good advice about how to behave in the United States — to avoid homosexual incidents, race-relations talk and left-wing aggression. Guy gaily summed up, 'In other words, Hector, you mean I mustn't make a pass at Paul Robeson.'

So Guy Burgess left behind the wild parties of his London apartment (painted incidentally in red, white and blue) and plunged into the chic diplomatic salons of Washington, to provide more material for the boys in Dzerzhinsky Square.

He went to stay in the house on Nebraska Avenue of his old Cambridge friend and fellow Soviet agent at the British Embassy Kim Philby — to the chagrin of the then Mrs Philby. Philby was becoming increasingly worried by secret reports to which he had access showing that it would not be long before counter-intelligence got to grips with Donald Maclean, by now back in London after his spying stint in the Washington embassy.

It was decided after consultation with their Russian control that Maclean must be warned, and the chosen instrument was Burgess. Burgess, long experienced in outrage, had no difficulty in getting himself sent back to London in disgrace. He simply drove around like a maniac, made trouble with American police officers who stopped him, and threatened to invoke diplomatic immunity from speeding tickets.

Back in London, in May 1951, he popped into the Foreign Office, looked in on his old friend Donald Maclean, and to avoid any risk of detection handed over a slip of paper with the warning on it. With the further help of Anthony Blunt, another of the traitorous clique, and a message from Kim coded in a reference to the car he had left behind in America, Burgess activated the escape arrangement.

His task was to visit Maclean at home in suburban Surrey, which he did under an assumed name, and then drive him in a hired car down to Southampton en route for the Soviet Union via France. Either because he was in a panic, or simply by accident, Burgess decided at the last minute to sail with Maclean, and then there was no going back.

It is comforting to be reminded that Soviet as well as Western agents make mistakes. This might have been a fatal one for Philby, still *en poste* in Washington, because he was directly linked with Burgess, who had been living in his house.

In fact it did result in the recall of Philby, though not for some years in putting him out of action. As the boat sailed from Southampton a dockhand shouted to ask about the car which Burgess had clumsily left on the dockside because of his last-minute decision. 'Back on Monday,' cried Guy — but he never did come back, though he may have wanted to. The Channel was his Rubicon.

BURT, Commander Leonard

From 1946 until his retirement in 1958 he commanded the Special Branch of the Metropolitan Police, responsible for the police end of spycatching. In this capacity he arrested a number of notable spies, including Klaus Fuchs and Allan Nunn May.

He began his career on the beat and rose to serve during the Second World War as a colonel in military intelligence. He died in 1983 at the age of ninety-one.

BUSH, Vice-President George

During the few months that he served as interim director of the CIA from January 1976 to March of the following year, he earned the respect of people within the Agency and of the politicians. It was his delicate task to restore morale within the CIA after the scandals and revelations of the years 1974–76.

President Ford chose him because of his wide experience in many fields of activity, even though he had never been engaged in intelligence work. George Bush had been a Congressman, the US Ambassador to the United Nations, and had also served in China as representative of the US government.

With such a background he had the weight and respectability to help the new President to reform the intelligence community and get it working

again. During his time as director, President Ford took a number of steps to set it in order. He made director Bush responsible for all intelligence-gathering, and appointed him chairman of a three-man committee on foreign intelligence.

One of the restrictions on CIA activity imposed at the time by Presidential order announced, 'No employee of the United States government shall engage in, or conspire to engage in, political assassination.' It was a very necessary touch of discipline to agencies which had plotted murders in a number of countries.

After President Carter was elected in 1976 he decided to put his own candidate in to direct the CIA, and George Bush's brief period of control came to an end. Mr Bush himself went back to politics, fought a vigorous campaign for the Republican nomination, and in 1980 became Vice-President to President Reagan.

His views on the future of the Agency he had directed were crisply put in his nomination speeches. On one occasion he declared, 'We are up against a tough adversary (Russia) and we have to have the best intelligence service money can buy.'

C

CAHAN, Samuel Borisovich

The task set this pre-war resident director of the Soviet secret service in London was to spot and recruit likely lads in the British intelligentsia who might be expected to act as moles later. The theory was that if the Comintern, as it was then called, could get the right people who were recommended by communist academic sympathizers they would be of great use when they had succeeded in their regular careers.

His greatest success was to enlist Kim Philby, the British spy. He was also in touch with the Cambridge trio Burgess, Maclean and Blunt. The method of spotting and persuading was very much the same as that used to provide new entrants to the British intelligence service, which also relied upon bright young men from the old universities.

Operating from the Soviet Embassy, Cahan had two assistants. One was Leonid Tolokonsky, an ex-commissar posing as a Second Secretary, and Georgi Askalov. They gave elementary espionage instruction to the new boys, and received their first reports.

CAIRNCROSS, John

It was not until after the public exposure of Anthony Blunt that the name of John Cairncross was mentioned publicly. In 1981 Mrs Thatcher, in answering parliamentary questions, referred to the case of a man who had been persuaded to confess by 'an indication that he was unlikely to be prosecuted'.

Cairncross, a former civil servant, worked for MI6 during the war, and later for the Foreign Office and the Treasury. Interrogated in 1967 by MI5, he confessed to having been a Soviet agent from the 1930s until 1952. He was allowed to resign without further action being taken, and went to work in the UN Food and Agriculture Organisation in Rome, where he still lives.

During the War he had been on the staff of the Bletchley code and cypher centre where German codes were cracked. He later confessed that at that time he used to drive to London at weekends in a car provided by the Russians to pass on decoded German messages.

Later, while working in the London HQ of MI6, he handed over Allied plans about the future of Yugoslavia. The case is interesting for the light it sheds on how far British security was prepared to go in offering deals not to prosecute known agents so long as they provided information leading to the detection of others. In Cairncross's case it was presumably considered an extenuating circumstance that at the time he was most active as a Soviet agent, Russia was a wartime ally of Britain and America.

'CARLOS', Ilich Ramirez Sanchez

The notorious international terrorist responsible for the kidnapping in 1975 of eleven Oil Ministers gathered for an OPEC conference in Vienna. He was heavily involved with both Palestinian extremists and violent groups of European terrorists, among whom he led a clandestine life for nearly twenty years.

The son of a wealthy Venezuelan communist lawyer who became a property-developer, Carlos, like his brothers, was given one of the names of Lenin. His first move into the underground life was in Venezuela at the age of fourteen. Then he went into a training-camp in Castro's Cuba, and took what amounted to a course in subversion.

It was at that period that the rather podgy young man known to his acquaintances as 'Fatty' began serious training, and for the first time came into contact with the Cuban DGI, the Dirección General de Inteligencia. The Russians were watching over that organization, and had installed a KGB officer, General Simenov, as a kind of intelligence overlord.

Whether 'Carlos' was a volunteer or whether he had been talent-spotted by the Russians is not known for certain, but in 1968 he enrolled at the Patrice Lumumba University in Moscow, an educational establishment devoted to training third-world intakes either as KGB agents or simply as future leaders who are expected to favour Soviet policies.

He was in fact given the benefit of the best schools for espionage and subversion before going off to make his bloodthirsty career in the world of international terrorism.

After he had been driven out of Beirut in 1982's forced retreat from that city of Palestinian guerrillas under attack by the Israelis he again went underground. The following year he was variously reported to be in South Yemen and in Libya.

CASEY, William J.

President Reagan insisted in 1981 on appointing his old friend and campaign manager William

Casey to be director of the Central Intelligence Agency, with the task of restoring its morale, building up the service and providing 'desperately needed' intelligence capability. Congress was less than enthusiastic about his choice, expressing a preference for Admiral Bobby Ray Inman from the National Security Agency, who for a brief and unhappy period did serve as number two in the CIA. For this reason they raised difficulties over the declaration of financial interests required of the new director, a seventy-year-old multi-millionaire who seemed to them forgetful about some of his assets, and reluctant to place them into a blind trust.

Within the Agency itself the principal worry was that although William Casey had built a great reputation with his wartime intelligence career he had had no direct experience in the business for thirty-five years, which is a long time in espionage. It was as a young and successful lawyer whose bad eyesight kept him out of operations in the field that Mr Casey made his way into the wartime precursor organization of American intelligence known as OSS. He did so by way of a friend in the law office of William Donovan, its founder-member, who tended to recruit through the New York cocktail circuit.

For William Casey that began his long and fascinated connection with the world of spies and clandestine operations. He became station chief in London for OSS, built extremely friendly relations with British intelligence officers, and was kind enough to tell Mrs Thatcher years later that America had learned all that it knew about foreign intelligence work from the British. In fact he served a proper apprenticeship, organized the penetration of Europe with OSS agents, and mastered the art of intelligence analysis, at which he was specially gifted.

Back in the United States, it was as a lawyer and entrepreneur with a knack for producing publications which concisely explained complicated legal and financial dealings that he made his fortune. He is a voracious reader, and has himself written a book on the history of the American Revolution. He has also prepared his own account of the OSS, ready for publication when he

considers that the secrets can properly be revealed, and after his own retirement from the CIA.

A rather quizzical man with jowls and thinning white hair, he had the advantage of being exceptionally close to President Reagan, who made him the first director of the CIA ever to hold Cabinet rank. There is no doubt that he is a hard-boiled and aggressive intelligence chief, who favours covert operations. Once he began making his weight felt there were signs that he intended to expand the staff of the Agency, which had been cut down in the lean years of unpopularity. He also increased funding and took steps to make CIA activities more secret once again, perhaps as a result of his experience with the British service.

William Casey emphasized the importance of assessing intelligence material. An advertisement placed by the agency to attract new recruits made it clear that intelligence 'has less to do with cloaks and daggers than with the painstaking, generally tedious collection of facts, analysis of facts, exercise of judgement and quick, clear evaluation'.

Despite that, the US Congress suspected him as a forceful risk-taker, and the intelligence watch-dog committees kept a careful eye over his activities. When the director appointed Max Hugel as his chief of clandestine operations in August 1981 Congress forced Hugel to resign on the grounds that his qualifications for the post were not good enough. The Senate Intelligence Committee had grudgingly admitted that William Casey himself was not 'unfit to serve'.

Another attempt was made to associate the CIA director with the purloining of briefing papers from the Democrats during the 1980 presidential campaign. Hopeful journalists by calling the affair Debategate no doubt saw a chance of stirring memories of Watergate. Casey denied that he had in fact received the papers.

In April 1984 he came under further attack when the CIA admitted laying mines in Nicaraguan ports.

CHAMBERS, Whittaker

A shiftless 1930s American journalist who found himself at the centre of the famous Alger Hiss affair. He joined the communist party in New York, and became editor there of the *Daily Worker*. Then under the influence of his wife, Esther, he joined a communist group.

In Baltimore he acted as a courier for passing secret US government documents to a Soviet agent known as 'Karl'. It was during this period that he claimed to have been in close contact with Hiss.

Just before the War he left the communist party, shocked by the Nazi-Soviet Pact, and turned informer on his earlier comrades. In his own book on the subject Chambers further claimed that he had tried to persuade his friend Hiss to leave the party at that time.

He died in 1961, still loathed by American liberals, but in March 1984 President Reagan awarded him posthumously America's highest civilian honour, the Medal of Freedom.

CHEBOTAREV, Anatoli Kuzmich

Mystery still surrounds this major in the GRU — Soviet military intelligence — described as an engineer attached to the trade mission in Brussels, who in 1971 walked into the US Embassy in Brussels and asked to go to America. He made this move only a few days after the mass expulsion of 105 Soviet officials from London.

In Washington he was debriefed by US officials, who said that he had given them a good deal of valuable information. Yet only two months later, after a meeting with Soviet diplomats at their request, Chebotarev left his apartment to go for a walk and did not return, and nothing more was heard until the Soviet chargé d'affaires announced that he had asked to be allowed to return to Russia to his wife and children.

American security men questioned him at the airport and were convinced that he was going home of his own free will and without duress. This inevitably aroused the suspicion that Chebotarev had been a plant to pass on false information, and his debriefing by CIA men had to be checked out in detail.

The possibility remains that he had simply become homesick and fed up with his American

life and decided to return, knowing that if he had been marked down as a defector, even a temporary one, he would be severely punished by Moscow.

There were nevertheless repercussions in Brussels, where the Belgians cautiously expelled four people named as Soviet agents by Chebotarev.

CHEBOTOK, Stanislav

A KGB officer specializing in providing support, and in some cases money, for organizers of movements advocating causes favoured by Moscow. While serving at the Soviet Embassy in Denmark in 1981 he made contact with left-wing groups and advocates of nuclear disarmament.

To avoid expulsion by the Danes — who had discovered that KGB money had been given to a prominent Danish author to pay for a publicity campaign for a nuclear-free zone — he returned to Moscow. There he handed over his Danish contact list to a colleague named Vladimir Merkulov, who replaced him in Copenhagen. Chebotok was then posted to Oslo as First Secretary.

Merkulov continued the same pattern of activity, cultivating political figures on social occasions and making 'gifts'. He co-ordinated the Peace March from Scandinavia to Paris. Such activities are a growing part of the work of KGB officers working in the West under diplomatic cover.

CHEBRIKOV, Viktor

When this energetic sixty-year-old with fair hair and glasses was appointed head of the KGB in December 1983 it caused some surprise. For General Fedorchuk, who was known to be a close friend and colleague of Yuri Andropov, had held that position in charge of state security for only five months. The explanation for General Fedorchuk's brief tenure of office was that President Andropov needed his services elsewhere to clean up the Soviet police and try to stamp out corruption.

Viktor Chebrikov owed his own rapid promotion in the state security organization to the fact that he was a member of the so-called Dnepropetrovsk clique of party members who worked under Brezhnev when he ran the city and district of South Ukraine. Like Brezhnev before him, he had attended the Metallurgical Institute there, and was active in party organization.

In 1967 he was suddenly switched to Moscow as head of the KGB personnel department. For a man who hitherto had no experience of work in that department of state, this was considered a challenging and difficult appointment, and it is still not known precisely why he was chosen.

His first appearance in public was on May Day 1983 when he was seen near the Lenin Mausoleum in Red Square awaiting the arrival of President Andropov and the rest of the Politburo. Before becoming head of the KGB, according to some sources, he had been transferred from personnel to a new task as overlord of KGB electronic operations — not just the old-fashioned bugging, but the new technology of espionage.

CHERNOV, Vladimir Alexandrovich

When Vladimir Chernov, a translator employed by the International Wheat Council, was given seven days to leave London because of his Russian spying activities, his wife Valentina spoke out. 'It is ridiculous to call my husband a spy. He doesn't even look like a spy.'

And there she hit the nail upon the head, for indeed her portly, chubby-faced Russian of a husband dressed in conservative English sports clothes, and even ready to risk English-style jokes, did not look in the least like the conventional picture of a *fictional* Red plotter. But the whole point of being a successful *factual* agent is not to arouse suspicion by looking like one.

Chernov was the second Soviet agent to be sent home from London within six weeks early in 1983, the first being the more obvious naval attaché Captain Zotov. The truth of the matter is that the Soviet Union is always ready to use extra citizens working in the West to play their part in

intelligence-gathering. It is often easier for a man like Chernov, modestly employed — as a translator in his case, with an international body organizing the import and export of wheat — to operate than it is for the more obvious type of Service attaché at an embassy.

Chernov was no doubt controlled by Department Twelve of the KGB in Moscow, which is responsible for intelligence men in the field with the cover of working as international civil servants and journalists.

Since Andropov first took over the KGB it has become more subtle in handling expulsions of its agents from foreign capitals. In the old days those ordered to leave used to go to ground and say nothing. Both Chernov and Zotov were happy to talk to reporters and appear on TV as ordinary officials, claiming that they had been wrongly identified and punished by the cruel capitalist government in London.

The Soviets are learning how to manipulate a free Press in order to try to convince the man in the street of their innocence. However, Chernov in his pleadings went a little too far playing his mock-English role and crying 'Not Guilty,' for he claimed the British government had picked on him for political reasons — in order to distract attention from the nuclear arms negotiations. That may well be the way they do things in Moscow, but in London government control is not quite like that.

CHETVERIKOV, Nicholas

As First Counsellor of the Soviet Embassy in Paris he enjoyed the distinction of being the senior — in diplomatic rank, that is — of the forty diplomats and seven others expelled from Paris in April 1983 for spying. The diplomats all expressed surprise, and naturally, all said that they had nothing to do with such unpleasant activities.

It is extremely rare for the French to go in for such public and large-scale weeding-out operations, and it has to be assumed that they had good reason for taking the measures they did. At about the same time the DST counter-espionage group arrested five French citizens for passing confidential material.

Notable among them were Patrick Guerrier, a young archivist with an engineering firm, and Monsieur Juge, a 57-year-old engineer and inventor, accused of betraying secrets to a Soviet trade-mission official.

Curiously, the Russians made no attempt to hit back by expelling French citizens from their country. President Andropov himself went on the record as saying, 'I do not want blame for the grossly provocative action against the Soviet people to fall on French socialists, or even the communists.'

There were four communist Ministers in the French government, but Mr Andropov was also no doubt aware that in Paris there are no less than 2,400 Soviet citizens, an astonishing 700 of them being on diplomatic passports. The number had trebled within the preceding ten years.

Because the French expulsions coincided with action taken in Britain, the United States and several other Western countries, it seemed likely that a recent Russian defector had been providing lists of names of KGB agents active in the West. Numerous expulsions usually provide evidence of the arrival in the West of a well-informed KGB man. There were two known new defectors in early 1983 but the most fascinating speculation was that a Moscow Centre desk man simply referred to as 'Boris' was at the time being debriefed by the Central Intelligence Agency.

CHISHOLM, Ruari

The British SIS agent working under diplomatic cover in Moscow in 1961 who did a fine job of running Oleg Penkovsky, the Russian intelligence colonel who gave many of the Soviet Union's most sensitive secrets to the West. According to *The Penkovsky Papers*, one of the methods by which Penkovsky passed on his microfilmed information was in a box of sweets which he gave to one of the Chisholm children, as they played under the eyes of their mother, who sat on a near-by bench in Moscow's Tsvetnoy Boulevard.

Chisholm was the perfect example of the post-Philby SIS. Tough, intelligent and skilful, he had a wicked sense of humour. At one period he lived in Sussex close to the weekend house used by members of the Soviet Embassy and Trade Delegation. The Russians would often use the local pub — always in groups. One night Chisholm got behind the bar, and when the Russians ordered their drinks he answered them in perfect Russian. They fled.

After he had been blown by the trial of Penkovsky, he resumed his diplomatic career and spent a long posting in South Africa, where he wrote a book on the siege of Ladysmith. Encouraged by its success, he took early retirement to start a new career as an author, and he made his way home via Dar-es-Salaam in order to research a book on General von Lettow-Vorbeck, the German commander in East Africa in the First World War. There Chisholm contracted cerebral malaria, but not knowing he was ill, came home, stopped taking his anti-malaria pills, went on holiday to Scotland and died.

CLINE, Ray S.

A Harvard historian who was recruited into the Research and Analysis Branch of the OSS in the Second World War, Cline became a professional intelligence operative and eventually rose to become Deputy Director for Intelligence for the CIA. He was at one stage talked of as a possible Director of the Agency.

He was an accomplished field agent, serving in London from 1951 to 1953 and as station chief on Taiwan, where he ran US flights over China, Tibet and Manchuria. He also parachuted Chinese agents into China using CAT, a CIA-financed supposedly commercial airline.

It was CAT's B26 bombers which were used in the CIA's disastrous attempt to overthrow President Sukarno of Indonesia. One of them was shot down and its pilot, Allen Pope, captured, much to the embarrassment of the United States.

Cline was also largely responsible for the

publication of Khruschev's 'secret' speech attacking Stalin at the 20th Party Congress in Moscow in 1956. Having acquired the speech — probably through the Gehlen organization — James Jesus Angleton, that most secretive of men, wanted to keep it under wraps and use it as disinformation material. But Cline argued that its publication in full would have more impact. He won — but Angleton still managed to slip some paragraphs of disinformation into Khruschev's text.

Cline's star began to fade when Admiral William F. Raborn became Director of the CIA in April 1965. Cline thought Raborn ineffectual as Director, and allowed Raborn to feel his contempt. Early in 1966 Cline decided he had to get away from Washington, so he asked for and was given an overseas posting. He became station chief in Frankfurt, and finally left the CIA in 1969 to become Director of State Department Intelligence.

COHEN, Eli

Super-Power spying has become rather a cosy game. Many agents are covered by diplomatic privilege: they are licensed to spy, and when detected they are simply declared *persona non grata*. Although non-diplomats arrested in the field may be given long sentences, they are often exchanged after a while for someone caught by the other side.

For spies engaged in the cruel wars of the Middle East, be they Israeli or Arab, the stakes are much higher — death is still the penalty for being caught. In May 1965 Eli Cohen, the most effective of all Israeli spies, was hanged in the full view of thousands and of the TV cameras in Martyr's Square, Damascus.

After prayers with the Rabbi of Syria the hangman threw a rough white shroud over him. They pinned upon the garment a sheet of paper recording his offences, and details of sentence passed. What that paper failed to register was the fact that the high-quality military intelligence about Syrian military dispositions which he had discovered and relayed to Tel Aviv was vital to the success of the Israeli assault upon the Golan Heights during the Six Day War.

Eli Cohen, son of a Jewish family in Alexandria, Egypt, spoke perfect Arabic. In his teens he worked undercover with Jewish organizations in Egypt before going to Israel and volunteering for service in Mossad, the Israeli intelligence organization.

After careful preparation which involved perfecting his Syrian dialect — for Arabs are sensitive to nuances of speech — he went into deep cover in Damascus. To prepare the ground he spent some time in Buenos Aires, Argentina, for his cover was to enter Damascus as Kamil Amin Taabes, a Syrian expatriate from Latin America returning home. During his stay in Buenos Aires he became friendly with Major Amin Al-Hafez, the Syrian military attaché.

Al-Hafez too returned home, became a general and then President of Syria. This meant that Cohen-Taabes had excellent credentials and an entrée to the highest circles in Damascus. By the mid 1960s he was so well known and respected that there was talk of him joining the Syrian government as Minister of Propaganda, and they also began grooming him as deputy Minister of Defence.

With such advantages he was able to inspect defence positions, and he even managed to send to Israel detailed pictures and plans of the whole military installation at Kuneitra on the Golan Heights. He communicated with Mossad headquarters through a radio in his apartment. More detailed plans and information were hidden in the legs of chairs and tables, which he sent out under cover of his antique import-export business.

Cohen photographed the Soviet MiG 21 fighter for the first time, reported the arrival of 200 T54 tanks from the Soviet Union, and delivered to Tel Aviv the detailed plan worked out by Soviet military advisers for the Syrian forces to cut off Northern Israel in a surprise attack. He also had full details of the Jordan water-diversion scheme organized by the Syrians.

His downfall was due not to the vigilance of Syrian counter-intelligence, which claimed credit for his unmasking, but to a complaint made by the

Indian Embassy. The Embassy was near to his apartment, and its radio operators complained of frequent interference with their wireless transmissions.

The Syrians, lacking equipment, were unable to trace the source of interference, so they called in Soviet advisers who had special radio tracking material. With their aid the Syrians narrowed down the field, and eventually burst into Cohen's apartment while he was transmitting.

Cohen was forced to use the radio to transmit a message dictated by the Syrians: 'To the Prime Minister of Israel and the chief of the Secret Service in Tel Aviv. Kamil and his friends are our guests in Damascus. You will hear of their fate soon. Signed: the counter-espionage service of Syria.'

They tortured Cohen to get information from him. For a long time President Al-Hafez hesitated whether or not to execute the man he thought he knew so well. Despite a campaign for clemency launched in the outside world by the Israelis, the President finally decided that mercy might compromise his own political position, and signed the execution order.

COLBY, William

Short, lean, inscrutable, Bill Colby was one of the original OSS action men. In his early twenties he was involved in secret operations, code-named Jedburgh, behind the German lines in France, and commanded an operational group parachuted into Norway to sabotage German communications in 1945. He returned to Princeton to finish his law studies after the war, but quickly resumed his intelligence career with the CIA. He spent some time as a field agent before being appointed station chief in Saigon from 1959 to 1962. He succeeded Desmond Fitzgerald as head of the Far Eastern Division in 1963, and was destined to become head of the Soviet Division of the CIA, but in a move which he later had cause to regret he was sent back to Vietnam to run the controversial Phoenix programme of 'resettlement and pacification'.

Thousands of Vietnamese suspected of being Viet Cong sympathizers were killed or imprisoned under this programme, and its unsavoury reputation clouded Colby's. Later he was to acknowledge that it was the greatest cross he had to bear when he was trying to set the CIA to rights after Watergate.

Colby returned from Vietnam to become Deputy Director for Operations in February 1973. A few months later he was appointed first Executive Director-Comptroller, and then promoted to be Director from September 1973 until January 1976. It was this last period of Colby's intelligence career which remains the most controversial within the CIA. It was he who handed the 'Family Jewels' — the CIA's 'bad secrets' — over to the Church Committee, and gave the Committee the internal report which led to Richard Helms being charged with perjury. This caused such consternation within the CIA that he was accused of deliberately setting out to wreck the Agency. He fired James Angleton from his post as head of counter-intelligence, and Angleton fumed that he could not have done more damage if he had been working for the Russians. However, it can now be seen that Colby was changing the CIA so that it could survive as an organization in the post-Watergate era. A strict Roman Catholic, he was known to his colleagues in the Far East as 'the soldier-priest'.

COPLON, Judith

A tiny, intelligent, aggressive woman from a middle-class New York Jewish background who became an enthusiast for the Soviet Union while still at school. She signed editorials in her school newspaper calling for a Second Front against the Germans, and she was active in war relief and exchange programmes between Russian and American youths.

Despite this background she passed a security check and went to work at the Department of Justice, where her job in the foreign agents' registration department made it possible for her to read FBI reports on Soviet espionage in the United

States. Soon, according to a 1952 report by the Un-American Activities Committee, 'highly confidential investigative reports being conducted by the FBI concerning Soviet and Russian satellite diplomats were finding their way back to these individuals.'

These reports were judged so important by the Russians that they sent a special agent, Valentin Gubitchev, to America specifically to handle the material she provided. Her method of operation was simple. She took home quantities of documents and typed out copies before handing them over to Gubitchev, who was posing as a Russian functionary at the United Nations.

The precise methods by which she was exposed as a spy have never been revealed. Certainly she had a taste for requesting secret papers which had nothing to do with her department, and just as certainly a wire-tap was involved. It is most likely that she was discovered when the FBI ran checks to discover the source of the leak.

By the first week in 1949 both Coplon and Gubitchev were under surveillance, and when she told her boss she was going to New York on 4 March they fed her two spurious 'secret' documents. She was followed to New York, where she met Gubitchev, and when they were both arrested the documents were found in her handbag along with thirty-four data slips from the Justice Department.

When her flat was searched FBI agents found a hoard of incriminating material. It seemed to be an open-and-shut case, and at their trial the following year Gubitchev — whose plea of diplomatic immunity was turned down because he was a United Nations employee and not a Soviet diplomat — was sentenced to fifteen years. However, the sentence was suspended at the request of the State Department and he was shipped back to Russia — along with $2,000 in severance pay from the United Nations.

Judy Coplon was sentenced to twenty years, with the judge reading her the usual lecture on the evil of her ways: '... You have brought dishonour on the name you bear ...'

But her conviction did not stick. It was overthrown in December 1950, on the grounds that the prosecution had failed to show its case was not based on illegal wire-taps and that the judge had not shown the defence certain documents. Judge Learned Hand ruled that: 'The conviction must be reversed, but we will not dismiss the indictment because the guilt was plain.'

Not long after the trial Judith Coplon married Albert Socolov, a 41-year-old lawyer from the firm which had handled her defence — as a headline at the time put it, 'she married her mouthpiece'. Once the publicity had died down she lived quietly as a housewife, bringing up four children.

COURTNEY, Commander Anthony

A tough and opinionated former naval officer and Member of Parliament who denounced the government of the day and the Foreign Office for softness in permitting Soviet and Iron Curtain diplomats to abuse their privileges for espionage purposes. He pointed out the folly of allowing them 'chauffeurs' enjoying diplomatic immunity while British diplomats in their countries had to be driven by secret-police informers.

So irritated was the KGB by his constant and reasoned attacks that they trapped him in a scandal, and with the unseemly help of electors in his East Harrow Conservative constituency, were responsible for depriving him of his seat in Parliament.

The Commander, a fluent Russian-speaker, on a visit to Moscow in 1961 had gone to bed with his Intourist guide, Zinaida Grigorievna Volkova, who was a regular KGB seduction agent. He was at the time a widower, and there was no reason why he should not have done so, except that the act took place in Moscow and the KGB secret photographers were on hand.

They attempted to blackmail Courtney into stopping his parliamentary attacks. When he refused they circulated the rather sad, compromising pictures, to Members of Parliament and business associates. *Private Eye*, the London satirical journal, lent a helping hand by publishing them, and despite the relative innocence of the

Commander's heterosexual brief encounter his business suffered. At the next elections he lost his seat by 378 votes.

Despite that, Commander Courtney continued to speak his mind and campaign against Soviet mischief in London.

It has been suggested that the Soviet action was also intended as a warning to others in prominent positions who had been similarly compromised. In particular this might have applied to Tom Driberg, the Labour MP, who had been photographed in homosexual encounters in Moscow.

CRABB, Commander Lionel Phillip Kenneth, GM, OBE, RNVR

At the end of an adventurous career, first in the Merchant Navy and then as a commissioned frogman in the Royal Navy, Buster Crabb (as they called him) died in mysterious circumstances near the Soviet cruiser *Ordzhonikidze*, berthed by King's Stairs in Portsmouth Harbour in 1956.

The cruiser had brought Nikita Khruschev and Nikolai Bulganin, then the joint masters of the Soviet Union, on a State visit to Britain. She was escorted by two destroyers. Rear-Admiral Kotov of the cruiser asked Commander-in-Chief Portsmouth for an explanation of the fact that on 19 April his watch had reported the appearance of a frogman wearing black diving-suit and flippers near the destroyer *Smotryashchi*. The British government made an embarrassed apology which raised a parliamentary storm.

Later the Admiralty announced that Commander Crabb was presumed dead as a result of trials with underwater apparatus in Stokes Bay. Another suspicious circumstance was then revealed — a police officer had visited the Sallyport Hotel, Portsmouth, where Crabb had stayed with a man named Smith and had taken four pages from the hotel register.

It was not until a year later that a headless and handless body dressed in frogman outfit was recovered by fishermen from Chichester Creek. This was presumed to be the body of Commander Crabb, though in the circumstances identification was not easy.

What really happened has never entirely come to light, though it is generally assumed that the retired Commander had been sent on a covert mission to get up-to-date information about Soviet warships. Many other theories were put forward, including an improbable one that the Russians had captured Crabb and had taken him back to the Soviet Union.

Harry Houghton, a naval petty officer later convicted on charges of selling secret information to the Russians, claimed after being released from prison that he had been told what happened by his Soviet contacts, including 'Gordon Lonsdale', an experienced Russian agent.

According to this account Commander Crabb had been sent down to attach a limpet device to the Soviet warship which was capable of registering signals from underwater detection equipment on board. The device would have enabled the Royal Navy to discover how modern this equipment was, before explosively detaching itself from the hull and disappearing.

However, the Russians were on the alert, because according to Houghton, his contact had overheard a conversation in a country pub about special operations during the Russian visit. Underwater sentries were on duty, and they overpowered the Commander and took him on board, where he died of a heart-attack.

To dispose of the body they attached it by a light line under water so that as they departed it would break free. If this version (from an unlikely source) is correct, then the body must have fouled underwater obstructions which mutilated it.

Neither the British government nor the Royal Navy ever made further comment on the affair.

CUMMING, Captain Sir Mansfield, RN

The naval officer who after years of service in foreign parts was summoned to London in 1911 and requested to organize a spy system to match those already in being in continental Europe. The Secret Intelligence Service came into being under his direction as the organization responsible for carrying out intelligence operations abroad.

Cumming left a permanent mark upon MI6, which he controlled until his retirement in 1929. In style it was Edwardian: its officers were mostly gentlemen, though there was a sprinkling of more exotic persons who were certainly not.

A striking example of the latter category was Sydney Reilly, a cosmopolitan adventurer dispatched to the Soviet Russia of the early Bolsheviks, at a time when there was a shortage of agents capable of operating there with success. Compton Mackenzie the novelist worked for the service in Athens, and in the best traditions of British intelligence was fined £100 for writing about his experience afterwards in a prosecution under the Official Secrets Act.

Curiously, the communist Russians greatly respected Cumming's British service, and in some respects took it as a model for their own. Certainly the élitist style was passed on to the Russians, and when they recruited British agents they carefully selected, not workers, but impressionable young bourgeois from Oxford and Cambridge.

Ever since Cumming's time, it has been customary for the head of the SIS to be referred to as 'C'. To this day boring arguments may be heard in the better London clubs about whether 'C' originated as his initial, or whether it means Chief, or something else altogether.

CURIEL, Henri

This mysterious person frequently involved on the fringes of espionage once boasted, 'My dossier is one of the biggest that the DST [French counter-espionage service] has. But they can do nothing against me.'

Not only the DST but many of the world's secret services kept files on Henri Curiel, the son of a Cairo banker of Jewish descent, who helped to found the Egyptian communist party before being expelled by President Nasser. He went off into exile, and as a convinced Stalinist is thought to have begun working for the KGB in Eastern Europe and later in France.

George Blake, the British spy for the Russians who was sentenced to forty-two years' imprisonment, was a cousin of Henri Curiel. Blake was the son of Albert Behar, a member of a Sephardic Jewish family living in Cairo. Behar became a British subject, but on his death left the widow and her son (who changed his name to Blake) in straitened circumstances.

One of the Behar sisters was married to a wealthy banker named Curiel in Cairo. He undertook to educate the nephew, provided that he went to Egypt. At the age of thirteen Blake went there, and grew up with his older cousin Henri Curiel.

Curiel eventually went to live in Paris, where he was involved with a number of support groups for terrorist and liberation organizations in Europe and in Latin America and South Africa. French security men believe that he then supplied information about such organizations to the Russians.

During the Algerian war Curiel was active in many left-wing groups supporting the Algerian National Liberation Front. On one occasion when he feared that arrest was imminent he began throwing papers from the window of his apartment. Among those recovered were confidential French and German government papers. French security, although they suspected that he was a spy, were unable to prove it conclusively.

Henri was well into his seventies when unidentified gunmen murdered him in Paris in 1978.

DANSEY, Colonel Sir Claude

One of the grandees of the old wartime British intelligence service so devastatingly penetrated by the team of British traitors on behalf of the Soviet

Union. A rugged bear of a man who graduated to intelligence work in the First World War by way of the Territorial Army, and became vice-chief of the SIS. The title had been carefully chosen for him shortly before his retirement in order not to offend his rival Colonel Vivian, who had been deputy chief.

Between the wars he involved himself in a series of unsuccessful business affairs. For a while he ran a curious English-style country club in the United States, staffed by servants wearing country-house kit.

Dansey returned to the SIS in London, and worked hard to establish networks of agents in Italy and Switzerland. At the beginning of the war his networks were rolled up by the Germans, and Himmler publicly named all the chief officers of the British service from 'C' downwards.

Professor Hugh Trevor-Roper, the historian who worked during the war in intelligence, commented on the old-style service controlled by Stewart Menzies, and Colonels Vivian and Dansey: 'When I looked coolly at the world in which I found myself, I sometimes thought that, if this was our intelligence system, we were doomed to defeat...'

Colonel Dansey too was sharply critical, usually of Colonel Vivian. He had developed a taste for the comfortable life, was a bit of a snob and a clubman, with a marked distaste for university recruits to the service. He once described Vivian's staff as 'a lot of old women in red flannel knickers'.

He was a man of intrigue and some mystery. He was acid in his comments and capable, according to his friends, of thinking nine ways at once.

One reason for his dislike was that Vivian was director of security, and Dansey thoroughly disapproved of counter-espionage. He always favoured expansion of overseas networks in the more aggressive role.

Yet one of his blunders shortly before retirement was over an affair in Switzerland. In the closing stages of the war a well-placed German liaison officer presented himself at the British Embassy in Berne offering secret information. His offer was spurned, for British diplomats and agents were reluctant to engage in anything which

might look like an attempt at peace-making by anti-Nazi plotters against Hitler, when government policy insisted on unconditional surrender.

The German rejected by the British got in touch with Allen Dulles — then running the American OSS operation in Switzerland — and provided valuable information. Indeed, Dulles declared he was 'one of the best secret agents'.

When copies of his documents reached Colonel Dansey he promptly — and without even checking — rejected them as having been planted on the Americans. This marked the end of his career in the secret service, and he died shortly after D-Day in 1944.

DEJEAN, Maurice

'*Eh bien, Dejean, on couche*', which might be roughly translated as 'So you sleep around, Dejean' was what President de Gaulle said to his old friend, until then the distinguished ambassador of France to the Soviet Union. The French diplomat had been caught by the KGB in what is called, in the cant language of espionage, 'a honey trap'.

To make matters worse, the intelligence report with its damning and detailed evidence came from the British intelligence service. The defector who knew all about the operation was Yuri Krotkov and he had given himself up to the British. Although in fact the ambassador, a well-preserved 56-year-old, had done absolutely nothing disloyal to France, and was guilty of no offence save a fondness for women, he had allowed himself to be placed in a position where he was susceptible to blackmail.

It had been a devious trap carefully prepared by whole teams of KGB men in Moscow to lure M. Dejean into bed with one of their part-time attractive lady assistants. It was all done on orders from Nikita Khruschev, who had been persuaded that because Dejean was a friend of de Gaulle he would one day be promoted to high government office in France, where he might be useful to them.

Over a period of months the KGB people posing

as cultural persons or senior functionaries wheedled themselves into the ambassadorial social set. His Excellency was introduced to stunning actresses, themselves lured by the KGB with promises of better accommodation in Moscow, and opportunities were presented for intimate meetings.

The flattered ambassador fell first into the arms of Lydia Khovanskaya, a sensual French-speaking divorced woman, and then of Larissa Kronberg-Sobolevskaya, a beautiful long-legged actress. The dénouement of the ambassador's *affaire* with this lady was worthy of Feydeau himself.

For suddenly there burst into the apartment the 'husband' of Larissa, who affecting to be freshly back from a Siberian geological expedition, was kitted out with boots and clothes to prove it. 'It's my husband!' screamed Larissa in a stagey voice.

The indignant geologist proceeded to beat the ambassador, no doubt to the pleasure of the KGB technical recording and filming crew in the next room. Larissa pleaded on his behalf, and he was allowed to leave.

It was at this stage that M. Dejean made a worse mistake still. In his distress he asked for help in hushing up the affair from a Soviet friend who unbeknown to him was a KGB man. No news was allowed to leak, but this meant that the Russians had a firm hold over the diplomat — a goodwill loan which one day they planned to redeem.

So determined were the state security men to get a hold over the French that they also attempted, though without success, to entrap the ambassador's wife, Marie-Claire.

Similar seduction techniques were also tried on an air force attaché, Colonel Louis Guibaud, who did have an affair with a Russian woman. In his case the KGB were less subtle, and when they confronted him with compromising photographs they offered a straight choice between collaboration or exposure. The unhappy officer went straight back to the embassy and shot himself dead.

It was this act which stirred the conscience of Yuri Krotkov (who had been heavily involved in Operation Seduction) and helped to persuade him

to defect. He did so on an official visit to London in 1963, and revealed for the first time exactly what had happened.

DERIABIN, Peter

A large part of the activity of the KGB is concerned with home duties in the repression of the Soviet population. It came as a great shock, therefore, to Russian agents serving in the outside world to realize that immediately to the west of them lived people whose governments do not feel it necessary to spy on their own people. Such realizations are quick to produce doubts about the perfection of communism. That is what happened to Peter Deriabin when he was posted to Vienna in 1954.

It was the duty of this lifelong communist — who had fought bravely at Moscow and at Stalingrad against Hitler's Germans before being rewarded with promotion into the state security service — to spy upon the Russian community in the Austrian capital, then under four-Power control. Only a part of his job was to spy on the Austrians, a relatively 'clean' task.

Within a few months he went over to the Americans and was given refuge in the United States. Because he was among the first of the high-ranking defectors, the CIA kept him under cover for five years. During that time he made valuable contributions to American knowledge of the workings of the KGB and its agents.

Deriabin wrote his autobiography entitled *The Secret World* exposing the activities of the KGB. He worked for the CIA, and like all good converts was ever ready to give the benefit of his experiences on the other side of the hill by drawing attention to Soviet agents at work in the West. One example of his work was the exposure of a senior KGB officer, Vladimir Pavlichenko, who was working in the United Nations Public Information Office in New York.

Naturally, the Russians denied this with proper indignation, but Deriabin refreshed their memories in a letter which was placed in the

Congressional records. In it he said that he knew Pavlichenko was a veteran agent because they had worked together at Moscow Centre's First Chief Directorate of the KGB, and for good measure he named their immediate superiors. He then went on to make the point which has become generally accepted, that the United Nations is a nest of Soviet spies.

DIAKANOV, Dmitri Alikseevich

The Soviet Embassy in Mexico in 1971 over which this rather unkempt senior KGB officer presided, thinly disguised as the chargé d'affaires, was much more like an outpost of Soviet state security in Latin America than a diplomatic mission. Of the inordinately large staff of fifty-seven, only eight were in fact diplomats.

This was not surprising, for the aim of this strict, old-fashioned puritan of a communist agent and his staff was really to organize a revolution in Mexico. It was a tempting target, for the successful overthrow of the government of Mexico on the doorstep of the US and at the crossroads to Latin America would indeed have been a coup.

With the help of his colleagues — and especially that of Oleg Nechiporenko, a specialist in Latin American work — Diakanov had recruited a band of fifty-seven Mexicans and arranged for their guerrilla training in North Korea. They called themselves the Revolutionary Action Movement, and their leader was Gomez Souza, specially trained for the task back in Moscow.

Unfortunately for the plotters, a village policeman stumbled by accident on a naïve cell of the Movement at a training session before a blackboard. He bravely arrested all four, and promptly informed Mexico City. As a result of all this Mexican security in turn arrested Gomez when he went to check on the cell, and broke the movement. They also discovered the Soviet connection.

On 17 March 1971 the Foreign Minister, Emilio Rabasa, summoned Diakonov and ordered him and four KGB colleagues to leave Mexico at once.

When asked the reason he simply replied, 'You, I, and the State Security Committee of the Soviet Union all know.' So blatant was the plotting that the Soviet Union, anxious not to lose its embassy altogether, did not even bother to protest.

Although Diakanov was not in the strict sense of the word a spy, he was a specialist in arranging strikes, riots and violence, and already had a record for fermenting such troubles in both Argentina and Brazil. He deserves inclusion in this spy collection, for there is no doubt that he will go down in Soviet records as the man who could not even organize a revolution in Mexico.

DONOVAN, James

A name which should be venerated among field workers in the world's espionage services, for this American lawyer pioneered the theory that convicted spies should be saved up ready for exchange rather than executed. James Donovan was a New York trial lawyer before joining the wartime US Navy and then the Office of Strategic Services. At the end of the war he was among those who prosecuted Nazi war criminals at Nuremberg.

He defended Colonel Rudolf Abel, the Soviet spymaster in the United States. After Abel's conviction Donovan successfully appealed against the death penalty on the then novel grounds that the time might come when Abel could be swapped for an American similarly convicted in the USSR.

Three years later the Russians shot down Francis Gary Powers at the controls of the famous U2 on an espionage mission over their territory. Powers was sent to prison and labour camp.

Mr Donovan successfully negotiated an exchange with the blessings of both governments, and through Wolfgang Vogel, an East German lawyer. In 1962 the exchange took place in Berlin, ushering in a new age in the spy wars when any captured agent might hope to avoid execution or imprisonment and qualify for exchange.

In the same year Donovan looked after arrangements to pay Fidel Castro for the release of invaders taken prisoner during the forlorn landings in the Bay of Pigs, Cuba.

DONOVAN, General William J.

A Wall Street lawyer and hero of the First World War, in which he won the Congressional Medal of Honor and the nickname 'Wild Bill'. In 1941, in the Second World War, he organized the Office of Strategic Services, the forerunner of the CIA, the first ever American comprehensive intelligence service. Donovan was greatly influenced by William Stephenson, the Canadian who ran British Security Co-ordination in wartime New York.

After a visit to Special Operations Executive in London he also received help from that organization, and a great deal of advice from the Secret Intelligence Service. Like the British service, OSS recruited its people from the upper crust of the old universities. Donovan also poached from Wall Street, and brought in old friends. It was a pattern which prevailed later in the CIA.

After an exciting war, including field work, William Donovan, worried by Soviet expansionism, wrote a memorandum to President Roosevelt, with whom he had been in close contact. It suggested the establishment of a permanent 'general intelligence organization' modelled on the OSS. But in post-war America there was strong opposition.

J. Edgar Hoover, ever diligent to protect the FBI, leaked the memorandum, and Roosevelt's intentions, to the *Chicago Tribune*. This provoked a great row about what was described as an 'American Gestapo', and the project was killed.

In October 1945 President Truman dismissed Donovan and disbanded the organization. Donovan returned to private life, but when two years later the obvious exigencies of the cold war made it necessary to establish the Central Intelligence Agency, he again offered his advice.

Before his death in 1959 at the age of seventy-six, William Donovan served for a while as American ambassador to Thailand. President Eisenhower described him as 'the last hero'.

DOUGLAS-HOME, Sir Alec (Lord Home)

By no stretch of the imagination a spy, but he made a considerable impression on the twilight world of espionage by taking the decision in 1971 to order the immediate expulsion from London of no less than 105 Soviet diplomats. At the time he was Foreign Secretary, and had urged this course of action upon the then Prime Minister, Edward Heath, after detailed examination by the Foreign Office of the proof of Soviet espionage activity collected by MI5, the British counter-intelligence service, who had received a good deal of help in spy-spotting from the well-informed Soviet defector Oleg Lyalin.

The Soviet Union riposted by ordering five Britons to leave Moscow within fourteen days, and issued orders to prevent thirteen others from re-entering the country. There is no doubt that the action of the British government served warning on the Russians that they had gone too far in the matter of espionage in Britain. It also set an example to other NATO countries.

Sir Alec's bold decision also helped to restore the morale of officers in the intelligence service, who were resentful about what they believed was the reluctance of the previous Labour government headed by Harold Wilson to take action, for fear of offending the Russians at a time when he was trying to promote détente.

A political row broke out in London when Mr Wilson, displaying his undoubted talent for phrase-making, and stung by allegations that he had been soft on spies (which he angrily denied), spoke of the defector being 'a semi-drunken playboy attracted by the lights of Mayfair and the fair hair of some lady'. He said the expulsion affair was 'a bit of a phoney'.

That was not the impression abroad, and certainly the Russians took it all most seriously.

DOWNEY, John T.

John Downey must be one of the unluckiest members of the Central Intelligence Agency.

Recruited directly from Yale, he was captured by the Chinese on his first mission and spent the next twenty years in Tsao Lan-Tze (Grass Basket) prison, Peking. And he need not have gone on the mission.

His job was to train Taiwanese agents for dropping into China during the Korean War. It was no part of his mission to fly with them, but he decided to go on one run for the experience. He set out from Seoul on 29 November 1952 with nine Taiwanese agents and another CIA man, Richard Fecteau. Their destination was Manchuria, where they were to drop their agents and pick up other men who had been operating in another district. They never made it. Possibly betrayed, they were captured and put on trial.

The Taiwanese were executed. Downey, 'the arch-criminal of all the American prisoners', got a life sentence. Fecteau got twenty years. Later Downey admitted that he had confessed everything to his captors, and that once he had done so his gaolers removed his leg-irons.

The trial did not take place until 1954, and both men were suffering from the effects of two years of harsh solitary confinement. However, after their show trial they were treated reasonably well. They received family visits, and on one occasion were taken on a tour of several cities to see the progress China was making.

Their capture was, of course, an embarrassment for the CIA. The US authorities first announced that the two men had been lost at sea, and even when it became known they had been captured, they were still listed as civilian employees of the Army Department. The US government refused to admit that Downey and Fecteau were engaged in subversion.

They were used by the Chinese as pawns in their campaign to secure diplomatic recognition by the United States, and admission to the United Nations, but the Americans would not budge, even though they knew very well how hard it was for Fecteau and Downey. It was not until they were released in 1973 that the CIA admitted that they were its agents. Undoubtedly, the Agency was generous to them. But what could recompense them for twenty years in the Grass Basket?

DRIBERG, Tom

It came as no great surprise in London when this talented and charming journalist and politician revealed in his autobiography *Ruling Passions* that he was a compulsive homosexual, and then retailed a variety of outrageous stories to prove it. What was less well known was the fact that Driberg — by then ennobled as a life peer, Lord Bradwell — had for years been a double agent working on behalf of both MI5 and the KGB.

There is also evidence from a defector that as a sideline he had peddled information to the Czech secret service. According to Chapman Pincher, the London journalist who specializes in security matters, he was recruited into the British service while still at school, with instructions to join the communist party in Brighton.

He did so and after continuing his education at Christ Church, Oxford, made friends with British communist leaders and reported on their activities. He was brusquely expelled from the party when they discovered his MI5 connection during the war.

Before that Tom, as he was generally known, had become a successful columnist on Lord Beaverbrook's *Daily Express*. But he became more valuable in espionage after his election to Parliament, first as an Independent and then as Labour. Late in life indeed he became Chairman of the Labour Party and was ennobled on the recommendation of Michael Foot, who became leader of the party.

In 1956 Driberg visited Moscow to see his friend Guy Burgess, the British defector who had fled there. The purpose of the trip was to discuss the writing of a book about Burgess, but while he was there the KGB asked him to provide them with information about happenings in the Labour Party, which he was well placed to do. All this he reported back to MI5.

He delivered regular reports on what he learned as a member of the Labour party executive to both the British service and the KGB, who paid him thousands of pounds, most of which he dutifully handed over to MI5. Through him the British officers learned a good deal about the activities of crypto-communists within the party.

When he wrote the Guy Burgess book (which was in fact a work of KGB disinformation intended to discredit the British intelligence service) Driberg handed the English proofs over to his British spymasters. This gave them the opportunity to arrange a little disinformation of their own.

By this time Driberg was mockingly known to British intelligence officers as the 'Lord of the Spies', but he was playing a dangerous game, for the KGB always had it in reserve to produce pictures of his homosexual affairs — some even conducted ostentatiously in Moscow — and threaten to shatter his public career if he failed to do their bidding.

Despite that, Driberg continued until his death in 1976 to serve two masters, and still maintain his public life as a successful politician. A friend at his funeral found himself making a bad-taste joke when he paid tribute to Lord Bradwell — 'At least, I suppose we should call him that though he was only a "life" peer.'

DRUMMOND, Yeoman Nelson B.

An American sailor who during his service in London was bought as a going-concern spy by the Soviet Union for a down-payment of 250 dollars — for which the Russian recruiter made him sign a receipt. Once a signed receipt is in KGB hands, they know that it can be used at any time as blackmail to assert control over their spy.

Between 1962 and his trial two years later Yeoman Drummond had supplied the Russians with quantities of operating manuals and defence dossiers from the Newport Naval Base. In return he received a total of 20,000 dollars.

He was sentenced to life imprisonment because of the extent and range of the effects of his treachery. It was estimated that it cost the US Navy a thousand times as many dollars to repair the damage as Drummond had received.

DUFF, Sir Anthony

Mrs Thatcher, the Prime Minister, in 1983 appointed this 63-year-old government servant as chairman of the Joint Intelligence Committee (JIC), the most authoritative intelligence body in Britain, in response to recommendations in the report on the Falkland Islands conflict that in future the JIC should serve under a chairman who was not provided by the Foreign Office.

Sir Anthony could reasonably fit such a description, for as co-ordinator of the security and intelligence secretariat of the Cabinet Office he was strictly speaking not a member of the Foreign Office, despite the fact that he had been a diplomat for thirty-four years.

The new appointment placed him in a position of great power and influence in intelligence. He kept his old job (thus retaining supervision over the accounts of the intelligence service) and gained control over the Joint Intelligence Organization which channels information to the JIC. The new combination of jobs gave Sir Anthony overlordship of the intelligence-gathering and analysis, as well as supervision over the budgets of all the British secret services.

Sir Anthony, a member of an old naval family, was educated at the Royal Naval College, Dartmouth, served in the Navy during the war, and was awarded the DSO and the DSC. In 1946 he entered the Foreign Service. After a number of postings abroad he became deputy Under-Secretary of State in 1975. In 1979 Sir Anthony was appointed deputy governor of the African country then known as Rhodesia, in order to prepare for its independence under the name Zimbabwe.

He joined the Cabinet Office in 1980.

DULLES, Allen Welsh

America's first completely professional spy, he neither looked like one nor acted like one. A big, wide-shouldered man with rumpled white hair and a moustache, charming, talkative and a determined party-goer.

When he first became head of the Central Intelligence Agency in 1952, after being a prominent member of the committee which had recommended restructuring the infant body four years earlier, he was already an experienced veteran of field work in two world wars.

The Dulles family had always been deeply involved in government. Allen Dulles's grandfather and uncle had both served as Secretary of State, and in his own lifetime his brother John Foster Dulles held that same office under President Eisenhower.

Allen Dulles had reinforced his reputation for espionage as top man in the Office of Strategic Services in wartime Berne, into which he was introduced by Bill Donovan. There he built networks covering practically the whole of Europe, and was particularly successful in running German anti-Nazi agents hoping for a peace arrangement to avoid unconditional surrender.

Dulles's men provided useful information about the construction of the first German V2 rockets deployed against Britain towards the end of the war. His agents helped to unmask Cicero, the German spy in the British Embassy in Ankara. He secretly negotiated for the surrender of German troops in Italy.

Skilled though he undoubtedly was in the trade of espionage, Allen Dulles was really a leftover man from an earlier age who found it difficult to adapt to the new one. In the cold war with the Russians he stuck to wartime techniques, was responsible for the famous Berlin tunnel to tap Soviet communications which ended in disaster. He was in charge of CIA operations of U2 high-altitude spy planes, and got into trouble when Gary Powers was shot down in one on the eve of the 1960 East-West summit.

Cuba brought the downfall of the ageing spymaster. In 1961 he urged upon the enthusiastic ears of President Kennedy the plan for a landing by Cuban exiles in the Bay of Pigs, designed to bring about the end of Fidel Castro and his pro-communist regime. The invasion collapsed, and although Dulles blamed its failure on the Presidential decision to deprive the operation of air cover, he was forced to resign as director of the CIA.

Shortly before he left he had the satisfaction of opening the grandiose new headquarters of the CIA at Langley, Virginia, though he was never able to use the splendid office suite which had been specially designed for him. He wrote industriously in his declining years to defend the organization he had done so much to establish, and Langley, bigger and better than KGB headquarters in Dzerzhinsky Square, remains as a memorial to this giant of old-style espionage.

DUMOV, Alexei

The expulsion from Berne of this local head of the Soviet news agency *Novosti* in April 1983 again drew attention to the new-style KGB operations conducted by its officers in the guise of journalists. For the Swiss government, always cautious though vigilant in such matters, had discovered that Novosti's extra-journalistic activities presented a threat to the country's security.

It was not that Dumov was in search of defence secrets, but that with the aid of the Swiss citizens he employed he had been infiltrating the peace movement and youth activists in order to bend them to the Soviet interest. This type of KGB disinformation and interference in the affairs of other countries has become quite common in recent years, and their agents are now active in almost every European country.

The Swiss closed down the bureau and gave the bespectacled, intellectual-looking Dumov ten days to leave the country in face of Russian protestations of innocence. Within eighteen months the Swiss government had been compelled to get rid of the local manager of Aeroflot, as well as a brace of military attachés, and two Soviet diplomats.

The peace movement is a favourite objective of Soviet agents. By misleading innocent peace-lovers about Soviet intentions, and in some cases by providing money for their organizations, the Russians hope to lull European countries into a false sense of security and to weaken their defences.

DUNLAP, Jack Edward

Like its British outpost, the Government Communications Headquarters at Cheltenham,

America's National Security Agency has Soviet spies as old houses have mice. One such agent at Fort Meade, headquarters of the NSA, remained undetected for nearly three years.

To the security men checking new arrivals at the establishment Sergeant Jack Dunlap of the US army looked a pretty safe bet. He had three good-conduct badges, and had collected a Purple Heart and a Bronze Star for coolness under fire in the Korean War. They found no sign of sexual deviation (which was the fashionable fault to look for at the time); he displayed no significant political views.

Jack drank a fair amount of beer, had a wife and five children, and was a sound family man. Yet when he was taken on by the Agency as a chauffeur to drive around Major-General Garrison Cloverdale and was then promoted to be a messenger, a Soviet agent who knew the system and the rates of pay rightly assumed that Dunlap was short of money.

And it says in the KGB instruction manual that Americans will do anything for money. That proved true in this case, and Jack Dunlap was the man to whom highly secret messages were given to carry to some more important person before being carefully coded (for security reasons) for transmission to yet more important persons.

By June of 1960 the impoverished sergeant was able to put down $3400 for a smart cabin cruiser. He traded in an old station wagon and bought a couple of Cadillacs and a Jaguar. He set up a blonde mistress for relief from family life, and in general displayed all the external signs of wealth. The estimate is that during the first year in return for services rendered in merchanting top secrets Jack Dunlap pocketed the best part of $40,000. That was a lot of money in the 1960s, and a good indication of the keenness of the Russians to find out about NSA.

The neighbours noticed, but were told that he had inherited a plantation. The security people were busy with other things, and failed to spot this amazing change of fortune.

Jack Dunlap's increasing greed finally drew him to their attention, for in order to avoid transfer to another post and continue his profitable stay at NSA he decided to leave the army and take a civilian job there. Unlike soldiers, civilians were forced to take a lie-detector test and twice the polygraph caught out Dunlap on minor points. That was enough to start an investigation.

He was promptly deprived of security clearance and sent elsewhere to an orderly room job. Within a month he made two unsuccessful attempts at suicide, first with drugs, then with a revolver. Finally, in the summer of 1963 he drove down a country road, ran a pipe to the engine exhaust and gassed himself to death.

Despite that, he was buried with military honours at Arlington National Cemetery, Washington. Not until his wife, Diane, reported the discovery at their home of quantities of high-classification documents did the story of his traitorous activities emerge.

By then it was too late even to make a full assessment of the damage he had done, for only the KGB knew for certain which documents, and how many of them, they had received. But it is certain Dunlap's spying had been of enormous assistance to the Russians.

DZHIRKVELOV, Ilya Grigorevich

One of the most articulate of the defectors to Britain who had spent his whole working career of more than thirty years in the service of the KGB, this Georgian-born officer was able to reveal not only the workings of Soviet agents, but also a good deal about their social life as members of the Soviet élite.

He joined the uniformed branch of the service at the age of seventeen, passed through the rigours of the training school in Moscow, and spent ten years at headquarters, which was in Dzerzhinsky Square. By then he was considered ready for work in the field. A full-time officer until 1956, he then worked with the Union of Journalists before going off to Zanzibar thinly disguised as a correspondent of TASS, the Soviet news agency.

By the 1970s he found himself in the Sudan, using his journalistic cover to ask questions which were more pressing than those a regular KGB man would have considered suitable. According to him, all Soviet journalists are at the disposal of the espionage service, though some are more journalistic than others. The hard men file through their own channels. One of his criticisms was that some such operators are over-anxious to present the kind of reports they know their masters would like to read. For this reason they misinform Moscow, and this sometimes results in wrong policy decisions.

In Khartum he had a regular morning meeting with the 'Resident' agent to report on his conversations and to be briefed for intelligence-gathering tasks. He was worried to discover that Moscow took far too rosy a view of the Sudan's ripeness for a communist coup.

His own judgment was more accurate, for when the coup was attempted in July 1970 the government quickly reacted. Ringleaders were rounded up and shot, the Soviet ambassador was asked to leave and Dzhirkvelov himself exited discreetly soon afterwards. By this time he had been identified as a KGB man, and African states were unwilling to accredit him. For this reason he was seconded in 1977 to the World Health Organisation in Geneva as an information officer.

His own career shows clearly how a state security officer can be used in a variety of roles during his period of service. Nevertheless, despite the incentives of a comfortable, well-paid life which provides privileges and special comforts for its own men, he became disillusioned with his job. One reason he mentioned was that so sycophantic had field reporting become that in Moscow the leadership and the élite frequently checked the reports they received against those broadcast by the BBC and the Voice of America. They also measured the accuracy of their party-line dispatches against those provided by Reuter's news agency.

Since arriving in the West in 1980 Dzhirkvelov has settled down to live a quiet suburban life in Britain.

EICHMANN, Adolf

The transport manager of the Holocaust, tracked down by Mossad and kidnapped in the streets of Buenos Aires in 1960. He was clandestinely flown to Israel, and after a show trial was found guilty of crimes against humanity and hanged in 1962. His body was cremated and the ashes scattered at sea so that his burial-place could never become a place of pilgrimage for any future Nazis.

An early recruit to the Nazi party, he specialized in Jewish affairs, learning the rudiments of Hebrew and Yiddish in order to get promoted as head of the police and security force sections persecuting the Jews.

He took part in the meeting which decided to implement the 'Final Solution', and was in charge of sending Jews to the death camps. After the war he escaped to Latin America and assumed a new identity, knowing that he was one of the most wanted war criminals. He was eventually discovered partly through the researches of Simon Wiesenthal, the man who has made it his life's work to seek out the Nazis who exterminated so many Jews.

ELLIOTT, Nicholas

An experienced SIS officer who had once thought of Kim Philby as a friend deserving of professional admiration. Indeed, even after Philby had ostensibly been forced to resign from the service following the flight of Burgess and Maclean, he still believed that Kim had been unfairly treated.

When Nicholas Elliott arrived in Lebanon in 1959 to take over as SIS station director in Beirut, and took his wife for lunch in a restaurant, the first people they met there by chance were Kim Philby and *his* then wife, Eleanor. At that period Philby was working as a newspaper correspondent and only freelancing as a spy.

Elliott met Kim often during his time in Beirut, and indeed benefited from his Middle East experience. So friendly were the two men that their meetings must have caused misgivings to the Soviet agents, who may even have feared that Philby was working more for British intelligence than for them.

By 1963, and after he had left the Beirut station, Nicholas Elliott had completely changed his view of Philby. Evidence of his treachery had become conclusive, and Elliott was the more angry and indignant because he felt that he had been taken in.

In this state of mind he volunteered to fly back to Lebanon to force a confession, and Dick White, the head of SIS, accepted his offer. The brief was to get a confession, try to assess the damage caused by Philby, and attempt to persuade him to return to London.

Elliott already had experience of a similar delicate and unpleasant task, for in 1960 while still stationed in Beirut he had persuaded George Blake (freshly detected as a Soviet agent) to return to London. He had done so, moreover, by pretending that they wanted Blake in London simply to talk about a new and interesting job and about promotion.

On this occasion, in January 1963, Elliott was in a different mood and his technique was quite different. He went straight to the Philby apartment and confronted his former friend, saying roundly, 'You took me in for years. Now I'll get the truth out of you even if I have to drag it out.'

He made it quite plain that he despised Philby as a traitor; and Philby, shocked by this direct attack, did indeed make a general confession of his guilt. As for returning to London, Philby asked for time to think about it, and unlikely as it may seem, Elliott then dined with the Philbys.

That was the last time that the two men met, for shortly afterwards Philby made a run for it and took refuge with his KGB friends in Moscow. Some time later he did write to Elliott suggesting a meeting on neutral territory in Helsinki.

It was a tempting offer, for many questions remained unanswered. But the head of SIS, Dick White, ordered Elliott not to go, and not even to reply to the letter.

ESTRADA, Armando Ulises

One of the original 'band of brothers' of Fidel Castro when he was fighting in the mountains before his takeover in Cuba. The *Commandante* led a guerrilla force and was known as the 'Black Panther', but once Castro was installed in government he moved into the DGI, the Cuban intelligence service, formed with the help of the KGB.

He soon became head of the section dealing with subversion in Africa, and made many clandestine visits to that continent. In 1968 he went off to Moscow to attend a KGB course for senior Cuban intelligence men.

The next move took him to the Middle East, where he was busily involved with the most extreme sections of the Palestine liberation movements. With so much active service behind him, Armando Estrada was then appointed deputy to his friend Manuel Losada, who was put in charge of the Americas department of the DGI in 1971. It specialized in subversion and encouraging armed revolution.

In July 1979 the spymaster emerged from the shadows to become ambassador to Jamaica. Despite his diplomatic title, he was known to be highly active in stirring troubles in that country by importing ammunition and encouraging a number of plots. One of the first acts of the new regime in Jamaica, after Edward Seaga became the country's more moderate leader, was to declare Armando Estrada *persona non grata*.

After a spell back at base in Cuba he was appointed to another diplomatic post in a strategic area, and became ambassador to the People's Republic of South Yemen in 1982. Its capital, Aden, is an ideal base for such an operator, on the edge of Arabia and close to Africa.

F

'FEDORA'

This was the Federal Bureau of Investigation's code name for a KGB double agent reporting also to the FBI in the decade 1960 to 1970. Although his identity has never been officially revealed, it is widely believed that Fedora was in fact Viktor Mechislavovich Lessiovski, who worked from the cover of his post at the United Nations from 1970 to 1973.

During earlier service at the Soviet Embassy in Burma he met U Thant, at that time Minister of Information, who later became Secretary-General of the United Nations. For three years in New York Lessiovski served as his personal assistant.

There is evidence that 'Fedora' supplied to Moscow an advance copy of *The Pentagon Papers*, a lengthy and secret account of American actions and policy-making, extracts from which were later published in the *New York Times*. They contained many sensitive passages, in particular details about American recordings made in Moscow of telephone conversations between Soviet leaders such as Brezhnev and Podgorny.

Although 'Fedora' supplied some useful information to the FBI and the CIA, it was mixed with what those organizations considered to be deliberate disinformation. The conclusion was that the good bits were placed deliberately by the KGB in order to make the lies more credible.

One useful tip from him was of help to the British, for he reported that the spy in the Admiralty in the 1960s sought by MI5 was a homosexual trapped while he worked in Moscow. This helped to identify Vassall.

However, 'Fedora' made a less helpful intervention in the Profumo scandal. He reported having a long conversation in Moscow with Ivanov, the Soviet naval attaché involved, during which he claimed to have installed a listening device in Christine Keeler's bedroom through which he learned atomic secrets. When the Americans passed this on MI5 made a search and concluded that no bugs had been placed. This fact helped to reinforce the impression that the Russians were busy trying to exploit the Profumo affair and stir up more mud. Fedora also hinted that the French intelligence service had been actively involved in a sinister way.

British intelligence concluded it was likely that the Vassall clues had been offered as bait. This was either in order to discard an agent no longer of much use to the Soviets or to take attention away from another Admiralty spy they valued more highly.

'Fedora' has no significance as a name. It just happened that the FBI was using hat names at the time, and the next agent was labelled 'Top Hat'. The CIA at the time used drink names, and to them 'Fedora' bore the title 'Bourbon'.

FEDORCHUK, Colonel-General Vitaly Vasilievich

In May 1982 Tass announced the appointment of a new chairman of the Committee of State Security (KGB) to replace Yuri Andropov, who was preparing himself for higher office still. For the first time since General Ivan Serov headed the committee thirty years ago a career officer of the KGB had risen to the top of the heap.

General Fedorchuk, born in 1918, began his career as a youthful journalist in the Ukraine before going into the army. Although he was recruited in 1939 as a state security officer in what was then known as the NKVD (forerunner of the present-day giant service), he did not become a member of the communist party until the following year. The more conventional path of Andropov was to be a stout party man first and then a KGB man.

By the early 1960s Fedorchuk was working with the Soviet Forces Group in Germany, involved in military counter-intelligence work. After this foreign adventure he was appointed head of the

Third Directorate, which is responsible for security within the Ministry of Defence and in the armed forces.

In July 1970 he became Chairman of the Ukrainian KGB. The Ukraine, second largest in population of the Soviet Republics, has 50 million people, plus a long tradition of nationalism and dislike of Russian control. Indeed, Piotr Shelest, first secretary of the Ukrainian party at the time, was accused of nationalist tendencies after his fall from power.

There was plenty to keep General Fedorchuk busy in Kiev as nationalists and human rights activists were brought to trial. The Academy of Sciences was also purged. The State continued its harassment and persecution of Christians, dissidents and Jews, and also acted sternly against Crimean Tartars trying to resettle in their ancient homeland, which is now an administrative part of the Ukraine.

Something of General Fedorchuk's philosophy can be gathered from the articles which he continued to write in party organs. For example, in 1980 he wrote of the need for increased vigilance in fighting against alien influences. Ominously, in another journal he emphasized the dangers of allowing harmful ideas to go unchecked, and cited Poland as an example.

At the age of sixty-four, and after taking up his new appointment in Moscow, the Colonel-General made his first publicized appearance at a Kremlin ceremony in the autumn of 1982. His picture appeared in the Soviet papers, revealing a podgy face with greying hair smoothed hard back, alert eyes and the snapped-shut mouth of a carp.

It appeared that he was settling in for a long stay as head of the KGB. But in December 1982, after only eight months in that job, President Andropov suddenly made him Minister of the Interior with the task of purging the Ministry of corruption and inefficiency. The police controlled by it were blatantly corrupt, and the dismissed Minister, Nikolai Shcholokov (accused of misappropriating police cars) was lucky to escape arrest himself. General Fedorchuk took with him two other senior KGB officers, Boris Zabotin and Kyril Vostrikov.

He was replaced as head of the KGB by General Viktor Chebrikov.

FELFE, Heinz Paul Johann

The KGB went to extraordinary lengths to build the career of this German double agent in General Gehlen's West German intelligence service, the BND. It was their help in providing him with genuine high-grade information on East Germany — thus betraying their Eastern Bloc ally — and in authorizing him to denounce other Soviet agents in the West which enabled Felfe to rise within twelve years from being a modest clerk to the rank of Higher Government Counsellor.

He had become head of the BND counter-espionage department dealing with communist affairs, and this gave him access to material immensely useful to the Russians. Before his detection and arrest in 1961 he had betrayed to the Russians no fewer than ninety-five BND agents; he had supplied tapes and 15,000 microfilm frames, and had played a part in the communist disinformation campaign to discredit General Gehlen.

His trial in July 1963 launched a national scandal in West Germany. It was a factor in the downfall of Dr Adenauer's government, and almost resulted in the dismissal of Gehlen as head of the BND. Small wonder that General Gehlen described the Felfe affair as the most damaging in the history of his intelligence service.

Heinz Felfe, son of a Dresden police officer, became an SS Gruppenführer, and served in the Nazi secret service under Himmler. After the war he was recruited by British intelligence before joining the Gehlen Bureau, and then being tempted by an ex-SS colleague to work for the KGB because he hated the Americans, as he later claimed.

But there is little doubt that this pasty-faced, slightly built man, balding at forty-two, with few friends was in it for the money, and eventually he boasted of how much he had been paid. He bought for himself without arousing suspicion a ten-room manor-house, where he lived in style with his secret radios and espionage equipment.

According to the BND version, his colleagues began having doubts because the information which Felfe was providing them was too good to be true, and they started to feel that there must be something wrong. But the first indications that he was a Soviet agent really came from defectors in 1960.

General Gehlen himself then organized a methodical internal security investigation, similar to those later conducted by the British MI5, with only five senior BND officers in the know. As the field narrowed down to Felfe they began keeping him away from sensitive material, using as an excuse a carefully organized quarrel between him and one of his colleagues.

Felfe, who was something of a fantasist, not only confessed but also boasted, and exaggerated his importance as a Nazi spy in the past. Two other West Germans who had worked with him, named Clemens and Tiebel, were also arrested.

In 1963 at a much-publicized trial he was sentenced to fourteen years in prison. The prosecution had described Felfe as the most dangerous and unscrupulous traitor who had ever stood in a German dock, and who had almost destroyed the entire system of German intelligence. He was indeed responsible for the liquidation of many agents.

However, he did not stay long in prison. The West Germans were persuaded six years later to make a one-sided exchange of Felfe, a very important agent, in return for the release by the East Germans and Russians of six persons of less consequence.

FELL, Barbara

There is no shortage of professional women who have ruined their careers through infatuation with foreign spies. Barbara Fell, who was Controller of Overseas Services at the Central Office of Information, had an affair with Smiljan Pecjak, press counsellor at the Yugoslav Embassy in London.

She was foolish enough to show her lover confidential documents. Although when questioned she admitted her fault, and although the prosecution admitted that she had betrayed no secrets prejudicial to British security, she was sentenced to two years. When her appeal was rejected Lord Justice Parker even went so far as to add to it a further six weeks.

FIELD, Noel Havilland

An American Quaker who was one of the idealistic young men who joined the communist party in order to work against fascism. After service with the US State Department and then the United Nations, he was employed by the Unitarian Service Committee, a relief organization operating in Europe. Because this had brought him in contact with German communists he was later used in a minor way by the Office of Strategic Services, the wartime American intelligence agency run in Switzerland by Allen Dulles.

After the war he drifted back to Europe from the United States on his way to take up a teaching appointment in Prague in May 1949. There he disappeared while staying at the Prague Palace Hotel, and the mystery deepened when his brother Hermann, and then his wife, Herta, also disappeared when they went in search of him.

Four months later, and to the mystification of all concerned, he was cited as the chief prosecution witness at the show trial of Laszlo Rajk, the Hungarian Foreign Minister, who was charged with sedition and the attempted overthrow of the State. He had indeed met Rajk years before in the Spanish civil war. But what caused a sensation at the time was that Rajk in his forced confession of guilt described Field as 'head of the American intelligence agency for central and eastern Europe'.

Noel Field himself made no appearance at the trial, but he emerged from it, and after the execution of Laszlo Rajk, with the reputation of being an American spymaster. In subsequent political trials in Eastern Europe — including that of Rudolf Slansky, the Czech communist leader sentenced to death in 1952 — Field's name kept cropping up. It seemed that anyone who had ever been in contact with him was in danger, yet the Americans considered that he had always been working for the communists.

In 1954, five years after Field's disappearance, he reappeared, together with the others who had gone to look for him. However, he and his wife refused to return to the United States and settled down comfortably in a State-owned villa on Sashegy Hill, overlooking Budapest. He apparently remained a keen communist, supporting the Soviet-installed Hungarian regime after the Hungarian revolt had been crushed. He died in 1968.

The mystery remained unsolved as to why the Russians should have picked upon him for use as a scapegoat in the purge trials in Eastern Europe. His connection with the American intelligence organization was known, as was his wide-ranging connection with many European communists through his relief organization work. But he was also known as a communist sympathizer. It may well be that he simply arrived in Prague at a convenient time to be exploited.

An even more devious theory has been put forward that Allen Dulles wanted to punish him for infiltrating his intelligence organization as a communist, and to do so carefully leaked information to the Soviets that Field was really an important CIA agent. If that theory is correct, then the Soviets seized upon the plant and used him as a tool in the great East European purges of the time.

FLOUD, Bernard

A Member of Parliament, and son of Sir Bernard Floud, a former Minister and a pre-war High Commissioner in Canada. His name emerged from Anthony Blunt's confession in 1964, and British security officers had reason to believe that he had been recruited by the Soviets while he was at Wadham College, Oxford, before the war.

Roger Hollis, Director-General of MI5, went to the Prime Minister, Harold Wilson, to ask permission to interview Floud, for he had been instructed that no Member of Parliament was to be investigated without the Prime Minister's authorization. Floud was then interviewed and denied ever having been a Soviet agent. MI5 remained suspicious.

Then in 1967 they had a second chance to question Mr Floud. It came about because Harold Wilson wanted to make him a junior Minister, and the rule is that all Ministers must be security-cleared before appointment. Bernard Floud was therefore questioned at length about his links with communists such as James Klugman while he was at Oxford. In the face of MI5 scepticism he persisted in his denials of having any connection with the Russian espionage apparatus.

It was at this stage that in October 1967 he killed himself by wrapping his head in a blanket beneath which he placed a gas poker. His son Professor Roderick Floud later declared that the suicide was not connected with security matters and that his father had personal problems. He has since demanded an official inquiry to establish the truth.

FOCCART, Jacques

A tubby, balding and rather benign-looking French businessman who through his early loyalty to General de Gaulle in exile in London became involved with the establishment of the Gaullist secret service BCRA, the ancestor of the present-day intelligence service. Before General de Gaulle's return to power in 1958 he was a faithful counsellor in the small group of the General's friends who helped to engineer public demand for him to take over.

Foccart helped to co-ordinate intelligence and police operations against the many right-wing and army plotters trying to overthrow the new regime. In France the Left openly accused him of involvement with the so-called *barbouzes*, squads of under-cover men operating against the French rebels, and with strong-arm groups in France. He firmly rejected claims that he was involved with what the French called 'parallel police'. He successfully sued newspapers, including the communist *Humanité* and the *Canard Enchaîné*.

He also cleared his name by legal action against right-wing papers which tried to build up his sinister reputation in another direction by claiming that he was the Russian spy in the presidential entourage denounced by a Soviet defector to the United States named Anatoli Golytsin in 1962.

The French presidential office dismissed such claims as absurd. M. Foccart served as a Minister concerned with African affairs under de Gaulle and his successor Georges Pompidou.

FOOTE, Alexander

For a boy born into a very ordinary family in Liverpool he had an outstandingly eventful career in the world of international espionage. As a good left-winger he went off to join the International Brigade in the Spanish civil war, and he was hardly back in England in 1939 before a Soviet agent recruited him for service in Switzerland in a network operating against Nazi Germany.

He became the radio operator (code-named 'Jim') for transmitting material from Sandor Rado, the communist Hungarian in command in Switzerland. It was high-class material largely supplied by the British, distilled from their code-breaking at Bletchley for onward transmission to Moscow so that the Russians could be kept in ignorance of the source.

From 1942 onward this material was passed on through the 'Lucy' network by Rudolph Roessler, who pretended that it came direct from Germany. Under German pressure the Swiss counter-espionage arrested three agents, forcing Rado underground. In a piece of fiction become reality Foote found himself burning papers and destroying his radio as Swiss officers battered down the door of his apartment.

After release from prison in Switzerland in 1944 he made his way to liberated Paris to rejoin Rado. There they received orders to fly to Moscow, but Rado skipped from the aircraft when it landed in Cairo. As a result Foote had a pretty rough time from the interrogators when he reached Moscow.

After the war he was posted to Berlin, and promptly moved over to the British in West Berlin. No charges were made against him, and he returned home for a more peaceful life, until his death in 1958.

The story was put about that his treatment at Moscow Centre had jaundiced his view of Soviet life and persuaded him to abandon the Russian cause. But it is possible that he had in fact been fed into the Rado network by the British secret service.

FRANK, Paul

This was just one name — on the British passport — of a secretive Israeli intelligence officer who on other occasions became Hans Hoffman or Avni Weisenfeld. His real name was Avraham Seidenberg, and he became a double agent in Cairo acting for the Israelis and the Egyptians.

He had gone to Egypt in the early 1950s claiming to be a German former SS officer, which made it possible for him to mix with the many Nazi fugitives then living there. He also made it his business to become friendly with Egyptian ministers and senior officers.

In 1953 he was the number-two man in the clandestine Israeli operation in Egypt to plant terrorist bombs in British and American offices, in the forlorn hope that by claiming the outrages were Egyptian they could influence those countries against President Nasser. Frank, however, had already been 'turned' by the capable head of Egyptian counter-intelligence, Colonel Osman Nouri. It emerged later that he had received 40,000 Deutschmarks from the Colonel.

When the Egyptian security men swooped on the eleven-strong Israeli network they held Frank briefly to establish his alibi, before allowing his escape to Vienna, where surprisingly the Israeli service promoted him.

However, suspicion began to gather round him, especially as he was still using the cover-name of

Paul Frank, under which he had been sentenced to death in absentia by the Egyptians, and was in contact with Egyptians he had met in Cairo.

He was put under pressure to return to Tel Aviv, and eventually did so, threatening to blow the lid off the Lavon Affair. Indeed, the evidence introduced at his secret trial in Jerusalem in August 1959 reopened the whole affair. He was charged with betraying Operation Suzanna; he was not found guilty of this but of photographing and possessing secret military intelligence documents, and with making unauthorized approaches to Egyptian officers in Europe.

For these comparatively minor crimes he was sentenced to prison for no less than twelve years — a sentence which indicated that while it could not be proved he had betrayed the Cairo plotters, the court was in no doubt about his guilt.

He served his sentence and went to live in the United States.

FRANKS, Sir Arthur

Unlike comparable services in other countries, the British Secret Intelligence Service, SIS, never announces the name of its director. Furthermore, it has always been the custom, at the insistence of the SIS and of the government, that newspapers should not publish the name. Even among SIS officers the initial 'C' is still in use to describe the boss.

However, in recent years London newspapers have begun to break with this tradition, to the distress of British intelligence officers. In July 1981 Chapman Pincher writing in the *Daily Mail* announced that a new chief had been appointed by Mrs Thatcher, the Prime Minister.

Although he did not mention the name of the new man, he did mention that of the man he was replacing — the 61-year-old Sir Arthur 'Dickie' Franks.

The following year the *Sunday Times* went one stage further by naming Colin Frederick Figures, an officer from inside the service, as its new head.

Recommendations for chiefs of SIS and its counterpart in counter-espionage, MI5, are made by a five-man committee which sifts through the short-list before making recommendations to the Prime Minister.

FRAUENKNECHT, Alfred

A very businesslike Swiss spy who briskly delivered to the Israelis no less than two tons of blueprints and plans of Switzerland's version of the French-designed Mirage III jet fighter at a rate of 110 pounds a week. His industrial espionage on the grand scale in 1968–69 enabled the Israelis eventually to develop the Kfir aircraft (sarcastically known as 'son of Mirage').

A chief engineer in the fighter division of the Winterthur company Sulzer Brothers, he himself suggested passing the plans to Israeli agents who had approached him to get spare parts for their Mirage squadrons. They had been trying to get round the ban on military sales to them imposed by General de Gaulle for failing to heed his advice not to go to war with Egypt in 1967.

The curious feature of the Frauenknecht story is that while he launched himself into espionage out of sympathy for Israel, and the guilt he felt about Nazi persecution of Jews, he was not a Jew.

His clever plan for appropriating the blueprints began with his suggestion to his own company that they could save money and storage space by burning plans no longer in current use after they had been photocopied. He worked out the arrangements for destroying them in the municipal incinerator under the supervision of Swiss security officers.

However, between the factory and the incinerator he and his cousin (who acted as driver) stopped for five minutes at a private garage he had hired and stocked with waste blueprints purchased from the Swiss patents office. The Mirage plans were stacked in the garage and the old patents papers were burned under the vigilant eyes of Swiss security, who never bothered to read them.

The second stage of the operation involved a mysterious man known as Hans Strecker, transport manager of a company with warehouses at Kaiseraugst on the West German frontier.

Strecker was originally introduced as a 'friend' of Colonel Nehemiah Kain, a Mossad agent working in Europe.

His task was to collect the cartons of papers in the boot of his Mercedes and take them into West Germany to a small airfield, from whence they were flown to Israel by way of Italy. The operation continued undetected for a year, until people living near the warehouse mentioned to its owners, the Rotzinger brothers, that a strange man appeared there every Saturday.

When the brothers went to investigate and hailed their employee, Strecker, he sped off at once, leaving one carton behind, and was never seen again. They saw that papers in the carton were stamped 'Top Secret. Property of the Swiss Military Department.'

Swiss security investigated, and arrested Frauenknecht. The engineer, shrewdly aware that revelation of the Mirage affair would cause trouble between France and Switzerland, boldly offered a deal, saying that in return for his release he would guarantee to keep silent about the whole business and thus prevent a political crisis.

It was eighteen months before he came to trial. He made no attempt to deny handing over the blueprints, nor did he express any regret, declaring indeed that he had good reasons for his actions. The court convicted him in April 1971 of industrial espionage and violation of Swiss military security, and sentenced him to four and a half years imprisonment.

After his release in 1975 Frauenknecht visited Israel for the first time, but received no kind of official welcome, for had they put out the flags the Israelis would have been forced to admit publicly that they carried out espionage operations in the territory of neutral Switzerland. Although Israel would willingly have paid vastly more at the time for fighter plans, Frauenknecht asked only for $200,000 (£85,000 then) as a kind of insurance to look after his wife if he was discovered.

FRENZEL, Alfred

A communist who had been expelled from the party for pocketing the funds, this Sudeten German born in Czechoslovakia fled to Britain to escape the Nazis in 1938, and served in the RAF as a cook before settling in post-war Germany. He prospered, and was elected to the Bundestag as a member of the Social Democrat party. He became an assiduous committeeman and it was as a member of a committee that he went on a parliamentary visit to Vienna in 1956. There the Czech secret service was waiting for him. They threatened him with blackmail over the missing party funds, and pointed out that he had a daughter living in Prague who might have an uncomfortable life if he did not co-operate.

He accepted a payment of 3,000 marks and was hooked. Soon he was handing over documents and plans filched from his committees to a Czech contact man known as Altmann, with whom he had twenty-two meetings in one year. He was eventually caught, like most spies, when a defector gave the game away. He was arrested in 1961, and in a four-day trial held behind locked doors he was sentenced to fifteen years, although he served only a short time before being exchanged for a prisoner held by the Czechs.

General Gehlen always had doubts about Frenzel's account of his recruitment. The head of West German intelligence believed that Frenzel had been recruited much earlier than 1956 by the Czechs, and that they had encouraged him to stand for parliament and to join committees, especially that dealing with defence, as a long-term mole.

FRIEDMAN, William

The most inspired of the cryptologists. This former head of the inter-war American Signal Intelligence Service succeeded in 1940 in breaking the main Japanese code known to the Americans as Purple.

This was an achievement matched only by that of the British cryptologists at Bletchley who broke the German code of the Enigma machine. Both the Japanese and the German machines consisted of twin typewriters, enabling an operator to type in plain language on one so that the result came out in code upon the other, having gone through rotors arranging random cryptographic signs.

It was thanks to Friedman's work in cracking the code that his department was able to intercept and translate the crucial Japanese orders to break off talks with the US at a precise time on 7 December 1941. Intelligence officers correctly interpreted this as the signal for an act of war, but the message was not passed quickly enough to warn the command at Pearl Harbor.

In 1941 Friedman visited Bletchley, and thereafter the British and Americans exchanged their code-breaking knowledge. This combination provided war-winning information on detailed German and Japanese military and naval operations. It also paved the way to later co-operation in signals intelligence.

Despite persistent depression and ill health made worse by high-pressure work in code-breaking, Friedman became the first cryptologist to join the newly established National Security Agency. He died in 1969.

FROLIK, Joseph

'Stop all activity. Frolik has defected.' That was the message which went out from Prague in July 1969 to Czech intelligence service stations world-wide, for at headquarters they knew that Joseph Frolik had gone to the CIA bearing gifts, and was in a position to name names and betray their men in the field.

For seventeen years this senior officer had worked both at headquarters and in London, Europe and the Middle East. After the Prague Spring, when colleagues were busily betraying their own country by arranging provocative anti-Soviet incidents which gave the Russians an excuse to invade the land, he decided he had had enough.

Frolik contacted a CIA man in Prague and was promised that if he could get to Bulgaria the Agency would get him out of the country. His plan involved a disagreeable stay at a special holiday camp in Byala on the Black Sea coast for state security officers.

In a smooth operation the CIA lifted him

together with his wife and son in a fast motor-boat which took them to Turkey. From there they were flown to Washington and met by Richard Helms, head of the CIA.

One of the few known spies who became a professional by way of accountancy, Frolik was posted to London for two years after serving on the British desk in Prague. Apart from uncovering KGB men (whom he hated), after his defection, he was able to provide useful information about British spies.

He told the SIS about at least two British members of parliament who had provided information for Czech intelligence. They were Will Owen, who admitted taking money, though he said he had never given military information; and Tom Driberg, the Labour party chairman, who was already known to be a freelance for the KGB, because he was also a double agent informing the British SIS. But until then it had not been known that on the side he was also supplying the Czechs. When questioned he simply said that he had written some stuff for them, but that it was all harmless. Joseph Frolik considered that the Czechs had succeeded in penetrating not only Parliament but also British trade unions and the Czech émigré movement.

It was thanks to his information that Nicholas Praeger, a Czech-born spy in the RAF who had sold details of radar-jamming devices, was arrested and convicted. Frolik also revealed the harm done earlier by Charles Zbytek, codenamed Light, who while working for an intelligence-gathering organization had revealed to Czech security the names of CIA, British and West German agents working in central Europe.

FUCHS, Emil Julius Klaus

The son of a German Lutheran pastor, he became embroiled as a young man in the confusing battles of the totalitarian Nazis and communists united only by their desire to overthrow democracy in pre-war Germany. At about the time that Hitler came to power he joined the communist party.

As a result he was later to become the scientist

who inflicted most damage upon the West by revealing to the Soviet Union details of construction of atomic bombs and plutonium bombs which were once a Western monopoly. It is estimated that he saved eighteen months for Russian scientists in their frantic efforts to catch up.

Klaus Fuchs was from the beginning a man of several loyalties warring within his own split personality. To escape from Hitler he was sent to Britain, where a Quaker family looked after him and his education, which set him upon the road to becoming a brilliant physicist. Although even in his early days in Bristol he had been denounced as a communist by the German consul nobody bothered when it became necessary to recruit scientists for the war effort, the more so as the denunciation came from the Nazis.

At the outbreak of war he was detained as an enemy alien, and eventually shipped off to a camp in Canada. Indeed, it is quite likely that it was during this stay that he first came into contact with Soviet intelligence.

After a while he returned to England and began working as a statistician for Professor Rudolph Peierls of Birmingham University engaged on the Tube Alloys project — a cover name for the co-ordination of atomic research. For this purpose he got security clearance and became a British subject.

When he took on this job he had already been in touch for some time with Simon Kremer in the military attaché's department of the Soviet embassy in London and began making reports. When as a member of the British team selected to co-operate with the Americans at work on a similar project he went to New York arrangements were made by the Soviet for him to contact an agent there. He was to go to the Lower East Side, carrying a tennis ball in his hand, and there to meet a man wearing gloves and holding an extra pair, as well as a book with green binding.

That man was Harry Gold, who remained his contact through the two and half years that he served two masters in the United States, the British and the Russians. Neither man knew the real name of the other.

Throughout that time Fuchs not only worked diligently on the Allied atomic bomb, the Manhattan Project, but he also provided constant and detailed reports in his own precise hand-writing which he handed over to Gold for onward transmission to Moscow. Pages and pages of neatly written notes provided test results, methods of manufacture and guidance on theory.

The last meeting between Fuchs and Gold took place after the successful firing of the first atomic bomb near Los Alamos, of which Fuchs had been a spectator. Before the British scientists left the Manhattan Project site following the A-bomb raids on Japan they had a party, and Fuchs volunteered to drive into Santa Fe to buy the drinks.

There he met Harry Gold and gave him full details about the test explosion, and a good deal about the bombs actually dropped on Nagasaki and Hiroshima. It was their final rendezvous, for with the war against Japan now at an end the British scientists were all leaving the United States.

Back home Klaus Fuchs was appointed head of the theoretical physics division of the Atomic Energy Establishment at Harwell. He threw himself into the work with accustomed zeal and even failed to make contact with his Soviet case officer as instructed, which was just as well, for he was found clean in a routine security check. But in 1947, the next year, he contacted Ursula Kuczynski — now known as Ursula Beurton — a Soviet agent codenamed Sonia by the British. She passed him on to another Soviet officer.

Indeed, it was not until two years later in 1949 that the backwash of American investigation into the atom-secrets ring revealed the presence of a British traitor. For the first time Fuchs became a suspect, though there was practically no hard evidence against him.

British security wanted to question him, but did not want to make their interest obvious in case this deprived them of other leads. Fortunately, Fuchs himself came to the rescue. It is a curious feature of his complicated personality that on one level he was a stickler for the nuts and bolts of security.

His old father, who had suffered at the hands of the Nazis, had been appointed as a teacher at the

University of Leipzig in East Germany, and Fuchs went to ask the Harwell security officer (a friend of his) whether that would compromise his position. MI5 seized the opportunity to send down William Skardon, their experienced specialist interrogator.

Using the relaxed and sympathetic approach for which he was already famous, Skardon set Fuchs talking. Eventually after many quiet sessions he confessed in great detail to his double life of espionage. He gave the impression that not only was it a relief to confess, but also that he believed that once he had made a clean breast of things his life could go on as before.

Curiously enough in the long confession which he signed in January 1950 Fuchs added a note of contrition. 'I know that all I can do now is to try to repair the damage I have done. The first thing is to make sure that Harwell will suffer as little as possible and that I have to save for my friends as much as possible of that part that was good in my relations with them.'

He had by this time become fiercely loyal to the Harwell establishment, rather as a boy is to his school. Since his return to Britain, moreover, this refugee from Germany had shown many signs of his respect and liking for his adopted country. He was bitterly disappointed when it was explained to him that his conviction meant that he would automatically be deprived of British citizenship.

His obsession with security was again revealed before the trial. He refused to give technical details of his atomic knowledge to William Skardon, on the grounds that this officer did not have clearance to receive such information. He insisted on reserving these details for the ear of a member of the scientific establishment.

In his own statement Fuchs revealed part of his own complicated persona when he described using his Marxist philosophy to establish in his mind two separate compartments in 'a controlled schizophrenia'. In less grand terms he had in fact mastered the spies' trick of lying to lead a successful double life.

Lord Chief Justice Goddard, a judge of the old school, was clearly impatient with such psychological talk, and sentenced Fuchs to fourteen years in prison, the maximum penalty. 'His state of mind merely goes to show that he is one of the most dangerous men that this country could have within its shores,' declared the judge.

In fact Klaus Fuchs spent only nine years in prison, as the librarian. On his release he chose to go to East Germany, where as a reward for his efforts on behalf of world communism he was appointed director of a nuclear research institute at Dresden working (or so it was claimed) only on peaceful uses of atomic energy. He married Greta Keilson, a German girl he had known since childhood.

He was without doubt the most important of the atom spies. Klaus Fuchs was also the model of the new-type technical-ideological spy, not a professional of espionage, nor yet a man in it for the money.

FURNIVAL JONES, Sir (Edward) Martin

Succeeded Sir Roger Hollis as head of MI5 in 1965 after two years as Sir Roger's deputy. He worked hard to pull the organization together after the dark period when 'Five' seemed to be riddled with treachery and rumours of treachery. Known to his colleagues as 'FJ', he began his career as a solicitor after leaving Cambridge, and some of his colleagues thought he always looked like one.

He joined the Security Service during the great expansion of 1940 to cope with the war — the same expansion which brought in Blunt and his gang. He served in security at Eisenhower's headquarters in Europe after the invasion, where he was mentioned in despatches and awarded the Bronze Star by the Americans, and he stayed with MI5 after the war.

One of the difficult tasks he had to carry out involved the detailed internal investigation of his service in search of moles. He was convinced of the loyalty of Sir Roger Hollis, although a number of other members of the service had serious doubts.

Indeed, in 1981 he and his former deputy Anthony Simkins took the unorthodox step of writing a joint letter to *The Times*, stating their belief in Hollis's innocence. Both men had by then retired, Sir Martin in 1972.

Before that he had expressed his views on the question of secrecy involving the service when giving evidence to the Franks Committee reviewing the Official Secrets Act. He pointed out that, although he had no relations with the press, there had been an erosion in the old, extremely rigid attitudes.

Both he and his predecessor had been publicly named, and he wondered where that process would stop. Sir Martin doubted whether other countries which had a less restrictive attitude to confidentiality concerning the security services derived any benefit from it.

Fittingly for a Director of MI5, his hobby is birdwatching.

GADDAFI, Colonel *see* QADDAFI

GARCIA, Luis

When in December 1981 suspicious immigration officers at Gatwick Airport searched the luggage of Luis Garcia and Antonio Sanchez, two Mexicans who said they had come to Britain on holiday, they discovered a complete spy's outfit including a radio transmitter, code pads and instructions. Apart from that they had 18,000 dollars and a number of false passports including two made out in the names of girls. Though well financed and in charge of the very latest in spying kit, both denied that they intended to spy and refused to offer any explanation.

The only comment from Garcia was, 'I have big trouble now', and so it turned out, for the two men were awarded seven years apiece.

British secret service men were not slow to use the radio with its high-speed morse code attachment, following the instructions on photographic paper for making contact. They received incoming messages, and then with the aid of a British warship on the West Indies station got bearings and cross-references which proved conclusively that the transmitted instructions under the call sign 'RMA' were coming from Havana, Cuba. What the message which came in ninety five-letter groups said has never been revealed.

The evidence was strong enough to convince British security that Garcia and Sanchez were operating on behalf of Fidel Castro's DGI, Dirección General de Inteligencia, the Cuban secret service, which marches hand in hand with the Soviet KGB. The DGI has often been used to do dirty work for the Russians.

It also has sinister links with international terrorist groups. For example, DGI officers in London and Paris gave support to Carlos, the Venezuelan-born international terrorist, who had earlier attended their training establishments at home.

It is perhaps unfortunate that the Mexican pair were arrested so promptly upon their arrival, for had they been allowed to get to London and begin operations they might well have led MI5 towards even bigger fish. However, prevention is sometimes better than possible later exposure.

It is impossible to know precisely what kind of operation the Cubans intended to mount with the equipment being smuggled in, or to know for certain whether it was for espionage or for terrorism. Obviously the two men, although professional smugglers, were not high-calibre intelligence operators. The fact that they brought in two passports for women, including one attractive lady named Maria Rodriguez, gives the impression that they were couriers.

They had with them instructions on how to get to rendezvous points in London where they were to make contact with other group members. But here again the trail went cold.

Suggestions were made in January 1984 that in fact Garcia and his colleague Sanchez had been acting in Spain as couriers for left-wing groups from El Salvador. Convinced that they were being pursued by a hit squad, they left in a hurry and fled to England.

GEE, Ethel Elizabeth

This portly daughter of a Hampshire blacksmith, looking after her octogenarian father, aunt and uncle and working in local shops, seemed the person least likely ever to be involved in the world of espionage. She was a good-hearted woman who enjoyed going to pubs in the evening, and after she landed an office job at the Underwater Weapons Establishment at Portland she soon fell in with a retired naval petty officer, Harry Houghton, who shared her tastes.

Although she did not know it at the time, he had already been hooked by the Soviets and was providing them with intelligence material. He was also quarrelling with his wife, Peggy, and it was not long before he bought a caravan with money lent by Miss Gee (who was generally known as Bunty). The couple spent a good deal of time there.

After Harry Houghton was posted to another naval establishment he relied upon Ethel Gee to provide him with secret reports from Portland. They made frequent trips to London to hand over the material. At first he pretended that the man they met was in fact an officer in the United States navy, though he was in fact a Russian spy.

Finally Ethel Gee, her shopping basket filled with four Admiralty files and film with details of naval equipment, was arrested near the Old Vic theatre in London early in 1962 with Houghton and the Russian agent, Gordon Lonsdale. 'I've done nothing wrong,' declared Ethel Gee.

The judge and jury at the Old Bailey thought otherwise and she was sentenced to fifteen years in prison. Released ten years later, she finally married Harry Houghton, which she had declined to do earlier when she felt it her duty to look after aged relatives.

GEHLEN, General Reinhard

A real spymaster's spymaster, this small, sharp-faced, thin-voiced, lonely, German army intel-ligence officer, totally immersed in the great game, dominated the world of espionage in the post-war years between 1953 and 1957 when divided Berlin was the world centre of intrigue. Founder and controller of the Gehlen Organization, a freelance espionage and counter-espionage body sponsored and financed by the United States, he fought out bitter campaigns against communism over the battered body of post-war Germany.

By no means all Americans favoured his operations. The outspoken General Arthur Trudeau denounced him in Washington as the man who ran 'that spooky Nazi outfit at Pullach'. That was the name of an estate built originally for Hitler's SS officers in a village outside Munich, where Gehlen set up the ultra-secret headquarters of his organization.

But his services were much appreciated by the Central Intelligence Agency, and by Chancellor Adenauer of West Germany, who always described Gehlen as 'my beloved General'. Gehlen had shown himself a born intelligence officer from the start of his career. He remained loyal to Hitler to the bunker end, even though the Führer refused to believe his accurate and depressing reports on the final disastrous situation on the Eastern Front.

Gehlen as military intelligence head of Foreign Armies East, the German forces in Russia, knew precisely how bad things were for them in 1944 and 1945. He had built up in the occupied areas of the Soviet Union powerful networks of informers. He had at his disposal a filing system with detailed information about the Soviet military and the political leaders.

This store of invaluable material was moved back westward under his orders, so that when the War ended and he himself was a prisoner, he possessed the most comprehensive documentation on the USSR available in the West. In the dawn of the cold war he shrewdly used his records as a powerful bargaining counter to secure his own rehabilitation despite his Nazi record, and so persuaded the Americans to pay for his semi-independent Gehlen Organization established in July 1946.

After moving the microfilmed intelligence hoard hidden in the Bavarian mountains to his new headquarters at Pullach, he began recruiting from among his old friends and colleagues in the German army. With remarkable enthusiasm and skill, he not only reactivated old networks among 'sleepers' still alive in Russia, and equipped with their army transmitters, but infiltrated fresh spies into the satellite countries and into Russia.

Germany was still administered by the wartime Allies, Britain, the US, France and the Soviet Union. As the Federal Republic developed in what had been the occupation zones of the Western Allies, and while the Russians established a German communist state in their zone, conflict raged around Berlin, which remained divided. It was in this period that the Gehlen Organization operated most effectively, providing high-level information by way of spies implanted high in the East German administration and in its espionage service.

Gehlen's 'trusties' fought out a bitter spy war with the East German MfSS, the Ministry for State Security, and the SSD, its political police, controlled by the notorious old revolutionary Ernst Wollweber. At one stage Wollweber put a price of one million Deutschmarks on the head of his hated rival in the West, General Gehlen, 'dead or alive'.

Wollweber did not survive in office as long as did Gehlen.

The 'Org', as Gehlen's volunteers called their service, had a number of coups to its credit. It provided the first information about the operations of SMERSH, the killer organization operated by the KGB; it discovered how to tunnel into East Berlin to splice lines into East German communications. General Gehlen claimed that he provided the West with the first full text of the famous secret speech of Khruschev at the 20th Soviet Congress denouncing Stalin in 1956.

It was in April of that year that the organization was formally transferred to the West German government and it became the Federal Intelligence Service, the BND. Gehlen was promoted to the rank of lieutenant-general of the reserve, and became President of the BND.

Thus at the age of fifty-four he began his third career as a spymaster. After serving first Hitler

and then the United States, he now controlled espionage on behalf of the Federal Republic. Although Gehlen continued to be successful, he was beginning to be under stricter political control. The time of intelligence freebooting in the cold war was coming to an end, and he had political enemies at home to contend with.

Although his prediction of the Hungarian uprising and the Soviet invasion which was their reaction to it was timely, he was suspected of encouraging anti-Russian Hungarians. Gehlen also got it right about the Soviet invasion of Czechoslovakia after the Prague Spring.

But he was less successful in forecasting the East German action in building the Berlin wall to separate the two halves of the city. In his defence, he wrote in his memoirs that he had predicted that they would act to prevent the mass movement of citizens westward, and that they were assembling stocks of building material.

Growing more ambitious, General Gehlen began spying on the Western Allies as well as on the communist states. He set up networks in the United States, Britain, and in France, where he had connections with the rebellious French generals who attempted to overthrow General de Gaulle for his liberal policy on Algeria.

One constant reproach against Gehlen was that he used so many former Nazi officers, especially from the old SS. He admitted himself that such officers were very popular with the Arab countries as he expanded his intelligence web into the Middle East, because they too hated Israelis and Jews.

In the 1950s when Colonel Nasser ruled in Egypt Gehlen was helping, as he put it, to 'inject expertise into the Egyptian secret service'. However, this did not prevent him being in touch also with Mossad, the Israeli secret service, for in his mind the fight against communism was the main consideration, and he believed that Israel was a strong outpost against Russia in the Middle East.

In 1961 Heinz Felfe, chief of his counter-espionage department, was uncovered as a double agent who had been spying for the Soviet for over ten years with the Gehlen service. When this spy scandal was exposed it hastened the fall of Chancellor Adenauer in 1963, and although General Gehlen remained in office for another five years, his influence and power were diminished.

He was by this time a man from another age. He had been a spymaster for over a quarter of a century, and had run the 'Organization', and then the BND, for twenty-two years.

He died in 1979.

GERHARDT, Commodore Dieter

When the Commodore and his wife Ruth were found guilty of high treason by the South African Supreme Court in December 1983 he was described by Western security men as the most important Russian spy since Kim Philby. Well-connected in Pretoria, known by the Prime Minister, and one of the most senior officers in the South African navy, he was commander of the Simonstown dockyard at the most important naval base on the southern continent, which guards the sea routes round the Cape of Good Hope. For more than two decades he had systematically betrayed to the Soviets an alarmingly wide range of Western defence and political secrets.

He had spied for the GRU, Soviet military intelligence, for almost twenty-three years after offering his services to the Russian Embassy in London while serving as a young officer on secondment to the Royal Navy. The Russians promptly signed him up and paid him, and the quality of intelligence material he was able to provide increased as he prospered and was promoted in the service.

At first he produced reports on British weapons and warship development. Ultimately he was able to furnish the GRU with detailed material about Simonstown and its possible use by the Western alliance to keep oil routes open in an emergency. He gave them the first specifications of the French Exocet missile. He also had access to Silvermines, the great electronic listening station and computer centre in South Africa, comparable to the National Security Agency establishment in the US

and GCHQ, Cheltenham in England. It plots maritime and air movements in the South Atlantic. It is feared also that Dieter Gerhardt furnished the Russians with information on movements of the British task force heading for the Falklands which they fed to the Argentines.

In addition he betrayed secret information about government policies and decisions in South Africa. It seems probable that his original motive for spying was to damage his own country, when, as a 25-year-old lieutenant, he took a day off from the weapons-training course he was attending in England to pay his first visit to the Soviet Embassy in London. He told them that he wanted to join the armed struggle for the liberation of South Africa, but the GRU considered that the new catch would be more use to them in espionage.

Dieter Gerhardt already bore a grudge against his adoptive country as the unhappy son of a German architect who had settled there and who was interned as an extreme right-winger during the war. An introverted young man, ungainly and of abnormal height — nicknamed 'Jumbo' — he became a hard disciplinarian in the navy, and was determined to get to the top. It was reported that spying made him rich, for he was also in search of money. After his arrest the Swiss froze one of his bank accounts containing £85,000.

After divorcing his English wife, Janet, he married a Swiss woman, Ruth Johr. She was already a Soviet agent, and it seems likely that this was a match arranged by the GRU, which often favours husband and wife teams. She acted as his courier, making frequent journeys to Geneva, ostensibly to visit her mother. It was one of Gerhardt's difficulties that as neither the Soviet Union nor any other Eastern Bloc country has diplomatic representation in South Africa, he could not use the services of their wirelesses or diplomatic bags. For that reason he had to deliver his material through his own courier or by radio. Several times both Dieter and Ruth visited Moscow, travelling undetected by way of Vienna. On these visits he received instruction on espionage techniques and communications.

The Commodore's second career — in espionage — came to an end because of information provided by a Soviet desk man known only as 'Boris', who on one of his few outings into the field sought refuge in western Europe. South African security services were astonished when American CIA and British MI officers revealed that the successful and top-ranking officer in their navy was in fact a spy.

In January 1983 a mixed team of American and British counter-intelligence officers burst into Gerhardt's room at a Ninth Avenue hotel in New York where he was drinking with a fellow-student from the advanced mathematics course he was attending at Syracuse University. The student was in fact an FBI agent.

Under questioning Gerhardt broke and made a full confession. One of his revelations which particularly alarmed British security was his statement that while serving as South African naval attaché in London he had advertised for Royal Navy and other technicians to join the South African navy, which at the time was commissioning its first modern submarines. That was all above-board, but Gerhardt further confessed that he had interviewed hundreds of candidates, and had then given his Soviet case officer a hundred names of sailors, some of them serving with the British nuclear fleet of Polaris submarines, who were either discontented in the service or who seemed to be short of money. 'It was like supplying the Russians with a list of potential spies,' commented a British intelligence authority.

After arresting Gerhardt, the CIA interrogated him at a safe house for eleven days before flying him back under British and American escort to be handed over to the South Africans. They also managed to prevent news of his arrest from leaking to the Russians.

The proof of their success was that on 25 January 1983 the Gerhardts' contact arrived in Geneva for a routine meeting. This GRU man, named Mikhail Nikolayev, had in his brief-case a list of secret radio co-ordinates and broadcasting times, together with banknotes in various currencies worth £50,000. The Swiss police followed him to Zurich and arrested him at the rendezvous point, which was in the museum of modern art, by a Rodin sculpture called *Hell's Gate*.

At the end of the Supreme Court trial held *in camera*, which lasted for three months, Dieter Gerhardt and his wife Ruth were found guilty of high treason and sentenced to life imprisonment. South Africa still enforces the death penalty for this crime, and the fact that it was not imposed in this grave case led to speculation that one day the Gerhardts may hope to be exchanged, and to go to Russia. Leave for them to appeal against conviction was later refused by a judge in February 1984.

GEYER, Hans Joachim

Possibly the only recorded example of a spy-thriller author turning into a spy and a double agent, out of vanity. Under the pen name Henry Troll, a paperback writer in Berlin, he was doing very nicely until he volunteered in 1951 to work for the Gehlen intelligence organization, and was sent to East Berlin to find prospective agents.

Once there Geyer was approached by security men from the East German SSD security service who turned him through cash offers and blackmail. He then proceeded to supply them with as many names of West German agents as he had access to.

But he was a girl-chaser, and trying to impress a prospective conquest, he boasted about his amazing deeds in dangerous activities. The girl thought that he must have something to do with the white-slave traffic and told her cousin, who was a detective. He called at Geyer's house announcing his rank to the servant, and this terrified Hans Geyer, who swiftly fled to East Berlin.

At a Press conference there in November 1953 he exaggerated his own importance and launched a bitter attack on his old boss, Gehlen, whom he described as 'the fascist lackey of dollar imperialism'. Finally he could not resist using the occasion to make publicity for his forthcoming book, *At the Beginning Was the End*.

GOLD, Harry

'That is my American contact', said the British traitor Klaus Fuchs, when after his arrest in January 1950 he was shown pictures of the chubby-faced man with generous lips and a broad-brimmed gangster hat. That face belonged to Harry Gold, who was an old hand in the espionage business on behalf of the Russians and had appeared before a committee of investigation.

He was proud that he had graduated to being the link-man in a chain of atom-bomb spies by way of industrial espionage. Indeed, he was boastful about it, for this was his most important assignment since he began working for the Soviets in 1935.

Anatoli Yakovlev was a GRU case officer under cover of being Soviet Consul in New York. He chose Gold to make contact with Fuchs when he arrived in New York to work on the Anglo-Soviet project which produced the first atomic bombs. Clutching a green bound book which was his identity sign, Gold recognized Fuchs, who had been ordered, incongruously enough, to carry a tennis ball; and they had lunch together. It was the first of seven or eight meetings in the course of which the British scientist handed over the secrets which enabled the Soviet Union to catch up in its efforts to produce nuclear weapons.

But Yakovlev in an access of zeal, or perhaps under orders to get speedy and widespread results, was also the master of other American atomic spies. After Gold had successfully renewed contact with Fuchs — who had slipped away from the scientists' headquarters at Los Alamos to meet him by the Castillo Bridge in Santa Fe to take delivery of an important package — Yakovlev ordered him by way of an encore to go on to Albuquerque.

There in New Mexico he was to contact David Greenglass, then serving in the US army, who had sketches and drawings of the bomb. Although Gold was a simple man, he was devoted to espionage, and he protested that this was a dangerous move because Fuchs might have been under surveillance. He was wrong on that score, but his instinct was right.

When the Soviet spymaster insisted he made the error of linking separate spy rings under his control. When Fuchs was detected for other reasons, his contact with Harry Gold led the American investigators to David Greenglass, and that in turn alerted them to the part played by the Rosenbergs. Finally both Gold and Greenglass talked, and the interconnection of espionage rings was exposed.

Although Yakovlev broke the rule of compartmentalization of spies' cells, he did maintain secrecy on his own identity, being known to Gold only as 'John'. It was not until the FBI showed Gold photographs that he realized his control was in fact the Soviet consul-general.

Harry Gold was the son of an immigrant family named Golodnotsky from Russia by way of Switzerland. He himself was born in Berne, and was probably never a party member. Educated in Philadelphia, he became a competent scientist specializing in chemistry. After his arrest, when he admitted that he had made a terrible mistake in spying against the United States, he was more than anxious to help. Before he was sentenced he was able to provide a good deal of evidence against Greenglass, and thereby against the Rosenbergs.

He was nevertheless sentenced to thirty years' imprisonment. After he was paroled in 1965 he returned to Philadelphia, where he died seven years later, at the age of sixty. The Russians rewarded him with the Order of the Red Star. This entitled him among other things to free rides on the buses in Moscow, a privilege which as J. Edgar Hoover tartly remarked he was never destined to enjoy.

GOLENIEWSKI, Michal

The piece of information which came into the hands of the British intelligence people in 1959 sounded like a crossword clue — 'there is a spy in the Admiralty and his name begins with the letter "H".' The same source then improved on the initial statement by adding, 'And he once served in the British Embassy in Warsaw'.

That helped a great deal, and the choice of suspects lighted upon Harry Houghton, who had indeed served in Warsaw before taking up espionage after his return to Britain. In such mysterious ways do spy-hunters their wonders perform.

The clue had come from a mystery informant signing himself 'Sniper', who began writing a series of fourteen letters to CIA stations in Europe in 1959. From the internal evidence of his letters they guessed that he was East European rather than Russian.

Finally 'Sniper' presented himself in December 1960 in West Berlin in the form of Michal Goleniewski, an officer of Polish intelligence. He arrived together with his mistress, and was promptly whisked off to Ashford Farm, Maryland, in the United States, the defectors' collection centre.

He brought no documents, for he had furnished a great deal of pre-defection material by post in order to ensure a proper welcome when he did come. However, as a bonus he had left behind a hoard of hidden photographs for later retrieval by American agents. He was also able to offer verbal details which pointed British spycatchers in the direction of George Blake, the British traitor based in Berlin.

It is ironic to record that 'Sniper', though only of middle rank, was so well informed by virtue of the fact that he had been planted as a KGB mole in Polish intelligence. The Russians could not resist boasting to him of their successes, and it was their overbearing manner that persuaded him to make contact with the West.

GOLYTSIN, Anatoli

No Russian defector from state security brought with him more fascinating information, or caused more argument, enthusiasm and doubt, in Western intelligence services than did Anatoli Golytsin. From the moment that he presented himself to the CIA after leaving his post in Finland in December 1961 it was obvious that he was no run-of-the-mill informant.

He declared that he was a major in the First Chief Directorate of the KGB, working against targets in the NATO alliance. His knowledge of Russian agents in the West seemed encyclopaedic. He provided over a hundred leads to spies, and evidence that NATO secrets were leaking everywhere.

When he first appeared — to the stupefaction of the CIA — at the door of their station chief in Helsinki asking for asylum in the US with his wife and daughter he produced as a sign of goodwill a complete list of KGB men in Helsinki, and a promise to name Soviet agents around the world.

Back in America CIA interrogators found him a difficult man to deal with, temperamental, grandiose and quarrelsome, with an ambition to set up a world-wide intelligence research organization to do battle with the KGB. Controversy raged at Langley headquarters as to whether he might have been specially sent by the KGB themselves as an *agent provocateur*. One of his notable supporters was James Angleton, director of counter-intelligence, who took him over.

Angleton was particularly impressed by his prediction that the KGB would be so alarmed at his defection that they would spare no efforts with their speciality, disinformation, in order to discredit him and repair the damage. In due course a pair of suspected disinformers codenamed Bourbon and Scotch did appear in New York, and a third one, codenamed Foxtrot, arrived later.

The British MI5 and MI6 each sent one of their officers to interrogate Golytsin. They were astounded by his information, which put another nail in the coffin of Kim Philby, but also led to the exposure of at least three other Russian agents in Britain. It was as a result of their mission that the Fluency Committee (a codename) was set up to examine all his detailed information in full. They began by testing it against the considerable body of known evidence against Philby.

In July 1963 Golytsin and his family moved to England. Their visit was cut short when the *Daily Telegraph* proposed to write a story about the arrival of a top-secret defector of great importance. British intelligence was horrified and demanded a D-Notice forbidding publication, which of course ruined the *Telegraph* scoop, and forced revelation of the defector's name to the whole of Fleet Street. An MI5 officer blundered by spelling the name, Dolnytsin. The *Telegraph* went ahead and published the story by John Bulloch, but without mentioning the name.

MI5 warned Golytsin, who convinced that this was a KGB plot against him, hastily returned to America. It has been suggested by Nigel West in his history of MI5, *A Matter of Trust*, that the newspaper leak was American in source, planned to secure the return of Golytsin.

The controversial ex-KGB man later undertook a world tour to expose more agents, and particularly impressed Sir Charles Spry, head of Australian intelligence. Opinions about his activity still divide cliques in Western intelligence.

GORDON, Betty

'Applications are invited from girls of good education for posts in London with good prospects and possibility of service abroad for periods; age 18–30; must be able to type; shorthand also required for some vacancies; minimum initial salary £5 p.w.'

That was the situations vacant ad. in *The Times* which recruited a lively, 22-year-old bored secretary at a publisher's into MI5 in June 1949. She was excited at the prospect of working in a patriotic way. Thirty-three years later and for no very good reason she blew her own cover to announce to one of the people she used to spy upon what her true role had been. Like many other spies, she was finally facing the need to confess.

From the beginning to the end of her career for a whole decade Betty Gordon had the task of infiltrating the British communist party at the top. In 1949 Clement Attlee, the Labour Prime Minister, worried by Russian espionage and communist party infiltration and support, ordered the security service to keep local communists under stricter surveillance.

That is where Betty Gordon, the young graduate, came in. It was easy for her to go to party meetings, sell the old *Daily Worker* on street corners, and impress members with her keenness.

She got a job on the English-language publication *Soviet Weekly*; she taught English to diplomats at the Chinese Embassy. She had a baby, and after the child was born she gratefully accepted the offer from Betty Reid and her husband John Lewis, both prominent communists, of accommodation in their house in return for help with their children. MI5 were delighted, and said, 'The baby is good cover.'

Harry Pollitt, the then British communist leader, took a keen interest in her career. All the time Betty Gordon was reporting back to counter-intelligence the titbits she heard and read.

Eventually she did get an opportunity, as promised in the original advertisement, of service abroad. In 1958 her communist friends arranged a job for Betty Gordon working in East Berlin on an English-language magazine published by the German Democratic Republic. She followed to the letter her instructions for visits to West Berlin to pass on information to British intelligence. It was, she reported, a lonely task. Finally she decided to resign so as to devote herself to her child, and reluctantly MI5 agreed, making her a modest payment of £200. Later she suffered a nervous breakdown which she attributed to the schizophrenia of espionage.

GOTTLIEB, Dr Sidney

By name, personality, and speciality — poisons — Dr Gottlieb could well have served as a model for the eccentric scientist in a spy novel. Bearing the title of special assistant for scientific matters at the headquarters of the Central Intelligence Agency, he lived on a 15-acre estate near Washington in what had once been a slave cabin. There he grew Christmas trees for sale, and kept goats — in fact, goat's milk was the only drink permitted to himself, his wife and four children. Despite the fact that he had a club foot, his hobby was folk-dancing.

This was the man who was chosen to prepare and deliver special poisons to kill foreign political leaders considered to be trouble-makers by the

United States in the 1950s and 1960s. His qualification was that he held a Ph.D. degree in bio-organic chemistry.

In September 1960 a direction came through from 'the highest authority' for Richard Bissell, of the Agency's dirty tricks department, to arrange the preparation of poisons to kill an African leader, who turned out to be Patrice Lumumba, then Prime Minister of the Congo (now Zaïre). Dr Gottlieb was called in, and had soon packaged for delivery to Africa by diplomatic pouch a number of likely poisons. The US Army Chemical Corps helped with the concoctions. He carefully assembled his assassination gear consisting of hypodermic needles, rubber gloves and gauze masks, before setting out for Leopoldville, capital of the Congo, to contact the CIA station chief, a man called Devlin.

The difficulty facing them was how to get close enough to Lumumba, and how to administer the fatal potion. One plan was that it should be administered by way of toothpaste or a toothbrush, but nobody was certain about the African leader's dental hygiene habits. While ways and means of approach were still being discussed the poisons began deteriorating. In October 1960 Dr Gottlieb decided they were becoming unsafe, and disposed of them by throwing them into the Congo river, before returning to the United States.

When questioned on his attitude to the assassination plan by a later Congressional inquiry Dr Gottlieb replied that he realized that he might have chosen to be a conscientious objector in the 'silent war' then being waged. But he added, 'I felt that a decision had been made at the highest level that this be done, and that as unpleasant a responsibility as it was, it was my responsibility to carry out my part of that.'

That was by no means the end of attempts made by the team under Dr Gottlieb, with the sinister name 'Health Alteration Committee', to kill foreign leaders. A poisoned handkerchief was sent to General Kassem, the Iraqi leader. Among the more extraordinary devices prepared for attempts to kill Fidel Castro were poisoned Havana cigars, a poisoned wet-suit, and an exploding conch shell placed to attract his attention while swimming

under water. Mercifully, none of them succeeded.

Nevertheless, the drug experimenters were held responsible for the death of one man, Dr Frank Olsen, who threw himself from a tenth-floor window at the Statler Hotel in New York under the influence of drugs. He had been taking part in experiments into the effects of mood-altering chemicals, during which the drug LSD had been administered. After that Richard Helms, head of the CIA, ordered Dr Gottlieb to destroy all records of these experiments when the Agency came under investigation as a result of the Watergate scandal.

GOUZENKO, Igor

In 1945 the disclosures of Igor Gouzenko when he fled from the Soviet Legation in Ottawa put an end to the era of innocence which had marked the attitude of the Anglo-Saxon alliance towards its *de facto* wartime ally, the Soviet Union. So powerful was the contemporary myth of 'Uncle Joe Stalin' and the gallant Russians that early signs of communist imperialism had gone unremarked.

The Gouzenko defection marked not the beginning of the cold war, but the beginning of the realization that a cold war had been, and was being, conducted by the Kremlin during as well as after the world war.

It was typical of the spirit of the times that this small Russian, a lieutenant in GRU military intelligence posing as a civilian cypher clerk at the legation, had great difficulty in making contact with Canadian officials who were loth to betray the Soviet 'ally'. An Ottawa newspaper refused to look at the papers he had brought with him; the Ministry of Justice was reluctant to give him sanctuary.

It was only when a helpful Canadian neighbour, an NCO in the air force, lent a hand, and when his clumsy Soviet ex-colleagues raided the apartment he had left, that the terrified Gouzenko managed to get through to the authorities. Even then there was talk of handing him back to the Soviets.

Yet he had amassed a stack of secret papers from Room 12 in the legation, cables to and from

Moscow, agent index cards with cover-names and comments — 'takes money', 'is afraid' — and pages from the casebook of the military attaché, Colonel Nicolai Zabotin. When he saw the weight of evidence the Canadian Prime Minister flew off at once to inform President Truman, and Clement Attlee in London.

For what the papers revealed were the workings of the atomic spy ring which enabled the Soviet Union to catch up on the West's monopoly of nuclear weapons. They led to the arrest of Dr Alan Nunn May, the British communist scientist who had passed on details of the first bomb tests and had supplied a sample of uranium to the Soviets in Ottawa. They helped to expose Klaus Fuchs, another British spy, and the trail ultimately led to the American network Alger Hiss, David Greenglass and Harry Gold.

Furthermore, the Gouzenko papers provided undisputed evidence on how the Soviets had taken over the Canadian communist party, which they used as an instrument of Soviet policy. They exposed over a score of highly placed Canadians working for the Kremlin.

The USSR had been using communist parties all over the world as an auxiliary branch of military intelligence. So horrified by the results of the Gouzenko defection was the Kremlin that steps were immediately taken to divorce foreign communist parties from intelligence duties, and much stricter precautions were enforced in Soviet embassies.

Unfortunately, the Western powers, though shocked by the revelations, and at last convinced that the Russians were plotting world-wide, did not take immediate and decisive steps to tighten their own security. Igor Gouzenko, who settled quietly in Canada with his wife and children under police protection, spoke out many times about security laxness in the West. He could not understand why it had taken the British five years to catch Professor Klaus Fuchs after he had been named in the Gouzenko papers.

In 1983 one mystery arising from the defection of Gouzenko remained unsolved. The ex-GRU lieutenant several times drew attention to evidence he had given during his debriefing to the effect that a Russian agent was working in the British counter-espionage MI5 under the codename 'Elli'.

He remembered an incident in military intelligence headquarters in Moscow in 1942, when his friend and colleague Lieutenant Lev Lubimov passed him a London telegram newly decoded. He did so because it contained the unusual and interesting information that the Russians had an agent in MI5.

It has been suspected that the man in question was Roger Hollis, later Sir Roger Hollis, who from 1956 to 1965 was director-general of MI5. Mrs Thatcher, the Prime Minister, in reply to a question stated that although it was impossible to prove a negative she was informed that Hollis had not spied for Russia.

Igor Gouzenko still complained that this part of his information about British counter-intelligence had not been properly followed through.

Even after more than thirty-five years as a peaceful Canadian citizen he himself still fears KGB retribution and takes many precautions. He has never allowed photographs of his face.

GRAHAM, Bill

When a man he met casually in a pub in North London in 1979 turned out to be a Russian, this 45-year-old Londoner was mildly surprised. He was even more surprised, and delighted, when as a result the Soviet Trade Mission in Highgate offered his company a £45,000 contract to do double-glazing work in their complex.

Graham told his story to a friend in the Special Branch of the Metropolitan Police, and before long he was being introduced to a man from MI6 who asked him to keep his eyes open while he was on the job and to report back. When this part-time spy boasted to the *Standard* newspaper about his successes in 1983 he said that he agreed eagerly to help, 'Because I'm loyal to my country.'

He had been warned that his task was very tricky because he would be working on what was diplomatically speaking Russian territory. The double glazing started in January 1980 and lasted some time, so that Graham and his men got to know their Russian guards pretty well.

Bill Graham managed to identify quite a number of mysterious Russians when MI6 showed him mug shots at their debriefing sessions which put them on the track of one who had gone underground. His final success was to plant a small bug in the Soviet lecture hall just before an important conference there.

This provided solid evidence about the activities of Viktor Lazine, an Embassy second secretary, who was expelled in August 1981 for trying to recruit a spy-ring in London. Proud of his achievements, Graham, unlike his more professional colleagues in the game, could not resist telling the papers about it.

GRAMSCH, Walter

A Gehlen Organization volunteer spy, shrewdly placed in the office of Ernst Wollweber, head of East German intelligence. After being a British prisoner of war he returned to his home in the East in 1946, still believing that East Germany would develop into a democratic state.

Thanks to his acquaintanceship with Wollweber, this capable transport expert won promotion to be director-general of shipping, and also acted as right-hand man for his boss. This gave him many opportunities to pass westward top-class information about infrastructure and military movements. It gave General Gehlen great satisfaction to know that he had planted his own man so close to his hated enemy Wollweber. Gramsch's reports led to the unmasking of numerous agents in the West and the break-up of spy-rings.

However, in 1953 when the espionage war between the two Germanys was hotting up, and after the defection to the communists of a double agent, Gramsch had to be pulled out hurriedly. He took to a quiet life in the West.

GREENGLASS, David

Public interest in the career of David Greenglass centred around the value of his evidence against his fellow-conspirators, the Rosenbergs, which led to their conviction, execution and the subsequent uproar about that affair.

Like his sister Ethel, who married Julius Rosenberg, he was a New Yorker educated (up to a point) in Brooklyn before going into the US army in 1943. In uniform he received some technical training and was eventually posted to Los Alamos in New Mexico, to a modest job with the atomic bomb project.

Both he and the girl he married, Ruth, were early converts to communism and members of the Young Communist League. For that reason it was easy for Julius Rosenberg to recruit him into his circle of atom bomb spies.

Rosenberg sent his sister-in-law, Ruth, down to Los Alamos to ask Greenglass to provide classified information for the Russians. The argument put forward to convince him was that if the Russians had atomic weapons as well as the Americans, that would help the cause of peace.

It was arranged that an agent — who would identify himself by producing one-half of a Jelly-O box, raspberry flavour, to match the one given to Greenglass — was to be given the package for delivery in New York. Anatoli Yakovlev, the KGB case officer at the Soviet consulate, made a bad mistake when he ordered Harry Gold to undertake collection immediately after he had collected a package from the British traitor Klaus Fuchs. After Fuchs's arrest the link could then be traced between two sensitive operations, to the Rosenberg ring.

By the time that the FBI questioned Greenglass and searched his apartment he had already handed over plans of the secret establishment to the Soviet agent, together with a rough sketch of the plutonium bomb dropped at Nagasaki and details about its detonator.

After his arrest Greenglass gave evidence against Rosenberg and against his own sister, Ethel, and revealed their major role in the espionage ring. He also claimed that when they jointly saw news of Harry Gold's arrest in the papers his brother-in-law urged him and his wife to make a run for it to Mexico, and gave him $1,000 for the purpose, saying, 'You will be next.'

Because Greenglass was so heavily involved himself, and because he had been willing to give information to the FBI before receiving his sentence, critics of the Rosenbergs' trial doubted his evidence. When only ten days before the trial began he produced fresh evidence incriminating Ethel Rosenberg more strongly, suspicions deepened that he had done a deal with the prosecution to protect his own wife.

Ruth Greenglass was indeed not charged. Interviewed on his release after serving two-thirds of his prison sentence of fifteen years, David said that it would be reasonable to protect a wife rather than a sister. He was, however, emotionally attacked by defence lawyers as a man willing to testify against his own flesh and blood. To preserve his privacy he later changed his name.

GRESKO, Alexander Alexeyevich

The man chosen by the Soviet Union as secretary-general of the preparatory committee for the 1980 Olympic Games was by no means a sporting fellow. He was better known as a rather incompetent member of the scientific and technical branch of the state security service.

Caught red-handed trying to bribe science writers in London to get secret technical information, he took his place among the 105 Soviet agents expelled from Britain at a blow in 1971. It was only after that setback that he moved into the physical culture section of the service, though his interest concentrated upon the more congenial side of the business, how best to control foreign athletes and visitors to sporting events in the Soviet Union.

Gresko took upon himself the task of minding Olga Korbut, the gold-medal winner from Russia. He kept strict control over her, and made sure that everything she said in public sounded like a propaganda handout.

He visited a number of foreign countries with Soviet police delegations, but he was indignant when his picture appeared in Canadian newspapers making a presentation to Mr Trudeau, with a caption drawing attention to his sinister past. As a result of that the Canadians turned down his application to attend the 1976 Games in Montreal as 'Olympic attaché'.

GRIBANOV, Lieutenant-General Oleg Mikhailovich

This stockily built and balding comrade, head of the second directorate of the KGB in the late 1950s after being decorated for his services to socialism in Budapest in 1956, was known as a shrewd plotter. Despite his exalted rank in the branch of the service responsible for overseeing all foreigners living in or visiting the Soviet Union, the General was not too grand to play an active role in the schemes he had prepared.

He was 'on stage' in the almost successful plan to compromise Maurice Dejean, the French ambassador, through a classic entrapment ploy which began in 1955. The ambassador was a ladies' man, and specially selected attractive women were placed in his path.

To help along the process by introducing the ambassador to influential people in the Soviet regime, Gribanov played the role of a senior functionary, and took the name Gorbunov. For the exercise he fixed himself up with a trade 'wife', Major Vera Andreyeva, a plump lady who had served in Paris and spoke decent French.

She met the Dejeans as though by chance on social occasions and spoke about her 'husband', who was a very important man, and who would very much like to meet the French diplomat. On a number of occasions the KGB husband-wife team, known as the Gorbunovs, entertained the French pair. Once they borrowed the impressive dacha of General Serov, then head of the KGB, to create the right impression.

The astuteness of Gribanov's preparations was revealed later when the entrapment was sprung. Eventually, after the French ambassador had been seduced by 'Lora', a professional at such operations, another agent posing as her husband surprised them in a compromising situation and threatened public court action against the ambassador.

Gribanov, who had arranged this denouement, had also invited M. Dejean to dinner that night, and in the course of it the ambassador told his now well-established Soviet friend about his misfortune. The General sympathized, promised to find out what could be done, and then said that he had used his influence to have the affair hushed up. In this fashion he brought both halves of the play-acting plot together, and placed the Frenchman under an obligation to the man he did not know was a very senior KGB officer.

In 1963 General Gribanov was the person responsible for the arrest of Professor Barghoorn, a Yale political scientist falsely accused in Moscow of being a spy. The General wanted to grab an American quickly for use as an exchange to get the release of a KGB agent arrested in New York.

When told that the only possible person around in Moscow at that time was the Professor, who was not a spy, Gribanov briskly ordered, 'Make him a spy.' In fact the Professor had to be released promptly on the orders of Khruschev, after a sharp and public protest from President Kennedy.

GUILLAUME, Gunther

'Dear Mr President, I accept political responsibility for negligence in connection with the Guillaume espionage affair and declare my resignation from the office of Federal Chancellor.'

The letter was signed Willy Brandt, and dated May 1974, and it marked the end of the political career of that German statesman who had tried through his *Ostpolitik* to end the great rift between East and West Germany. It was quite right that he should have accepted responsibility for a grotesque security failure which had allowed the East German state security ministry to implant an agent high in his personal staff and to run him undetected for four years.

Gunther Guillaume seemed harmless enough. Double-chinned, podgy-faced, and owlish behind his steel-rimmed glasses, he looked and acted like the ideal functionary. His diligence was the only characteristic that people noticed as he graduated from service with the Social Democrats to become one of the three personal assistants of the Federal Chancellor.

In this capacity all he needed to do was to read and copy the important papers placed upon his desk and pass them on. Such documents included a letter from President Nixon outlining the replanning of NATO, communications from heads of state, and details of Herr Brandt's plans for negotiation with the East Germans, revealing what concessions he was prepared to make.

Guillaume had none of the impedimenta of spying; not for him the vulgar stealing of secret plans and hasty photography. His high-powered sabotage was quietly conducted year after year from the top.

Yet he might well have been spotted right at the start of his operation, for German security knew that he came from East Berlin and that he had worked for a publishing company there, which was frequently used as a cover for spies. He put all that right by posing as a refugee from communism, a keen social democrat affecting slightly right-of-centre politics, anxious to oblige.

The East Germans had made a shrewd choice when they picked Guillaume, who at the time of his arrest in 1974 was aged forty-seven. He was trained for his mission by the KGB, who took over his operation when he became successful. He had served in the army as a captain.

Guillaume attracted attention only by his extreme hard-working reliability as an official at SDP party headquarters in Bonn. For eighteen years he kept up a steady output of espionage material of increasing importance by way of both dead and live drops, personal meetings with his case officer, and through the courier activities of his wife Christel.

West German security only began to suspect him on the evidence of a Soviet defector to the French, probably Vadim Belotzerkovsky, who recognized him on TV film at the elbow of Willy Brandt, as he always was. He declared that he had been on a course with Guillaume at the Kiev military academy.

Even when investigations began, Gunther Guillaume still remained for almost a year on Herr Brandt's staff while security men tried to discover his contacts. Despite the fact that Brandt had been informed, he continued to allow Guillaume sight of important papers, and he accompanied the Brandts on holiday to Norway in the summer of 1973.

Finally, Guillaume was arrested at Cologne airport on his arrival back from a French vacation in April 1974. A Federal court sentenced him to thirteen years' imprisonment, but as is frequently the case with spies, he served only half that sentence before being repatriated in 1982 to East Germany in return for the release of a number of political prisoners and alleged West German agents.

HAASE, Werner

On a dark and wet night in November 1953 this former German army signals major dressed as a telephone workman found himself launching a radio-controlled model boat with a thin line attached to it on the waters of the Jungfern Lake border between West and East Berlin near Potsdam.

As he did so a car screeched to a halt among the war-damage rubble near by and East German security men who had crossed over to the West seized him and took him back to their sector. It was the untimely end of a clever operation planned by the Gehlen Organization to splice a telephone cable into the communist communications system on the eastern side so as to eavesdrop.

Major Haase had been betrayed by a double agent who had recently fled to the East. At a show trial not long afterwards the communist regime sentenced him to life imprisonment, but in 1958 he was exchanged for an East German agent.

HAAVIK, Fru Gunvor Galtung

A woman clerk in the Norwegian Ministry of Foreign Affairs arrested at a secret meeting with a Third Secretary from the Soviet Embassy in January 1977. She was accused of having been recruited to the KGB during her long tour of duty at the Norwegian Embassy in Moscow from 1947 to 1958, where she often acted as an interpreter.

After her arrest this 64-year-old woman confessed that it was because she had been a lonely woman in Moscow that the Russians had succeeded in suborning her. Later she had been paid by them for handing over secret defence papers. A few months later she died after a heart-attack.

As a consequence of her arrest the Norwegians expelled the diplomat she was meeting, A.K. Printsipalov, together with G.T. Titov, who they named as head of the KGB at the Soviet embassy. Among others sent packing as a result of this affair were the Tass correspondent, Evgeny Zotin, and Alexander Dementiev, the man who was also handling the Norwegian double agent code-named 'Jan Hansen'.

HALM, Hilde

As a German army secretary in Berlin in 1945 she won the Iron Cross for bravery when saving important documents from an office being shelled. A good Nazi, she soon became a communist after the war, and went to work in the East German state security offices.

On a visit to West Berlin in 1950 to look up old friends she was recruited by West German intelligence and provided much information, especially during the Berlin uprising in 1953. For eighteen months, while she was employed as a secretary at the Ministry of State Security itself after 1954, she managed to report continually. Before her arrest in April 1956 she was able to recruit two other agents in the Ministry. She was sentenced to life imprisonment for treason and espionage.

HAMBLETON, Professor Hugh

One of the oddest fish to be trawled up in recent years by the spycatchers' net, a dashing, hail-fellow-well-met academic surfeited with the good life in Canada and Europe, a man of dual British-Canadian nationality who became over-confident of his immunity to punishment for spying on behalf of the Soviet Union.

Despite confessions to the Royal Canadian Mounted Police after he had been publicly and privately denounced by a double agent named Rudi Hermann, he was not prosecuted by the Canadians, who are notably lax in pressing espionage charges. So confident was the Professor that he brazenly flew into Britain in the summer of 1982 and appeared mildly surprised that he should be arrested and charged.

In fact he had been passing highly sensitive NATO and other classified material to his KGB minders for thirty years. Apparently he thoroughly enjoyed the romantic drama of it all. For this good-looking sixty-year-old it fitted well with his travelling life, keeping a mistress in Yugoslavia and a villa in Spain where he could peacefully write historical biography.

Hambleton boasted about being flown to Moscow in clandestine fashion to have dinner with Yuri Andropov, then head of the KGB, for a chat about the US defence budget and the future of the Common Market. He found time for a crash course in up-to-date electronic spying equipment, and brought back for use in the West a smart Soviet-made decoder device. He said that he identified not so much with the KGB as 'with the officer class' — a bit of an international élitist, a gossip columnist of a spy.

That was certainly the way he presented himself when he came to trial at the Old Bailey in London. Yet for all that he was a well-trained KGB agent, given the rank of colonel by that organization, a professional agent who had inflicted grave damage on the Western alliance. During his time at NATO he procured for the Soviets thousands of documents invaluable for Moscow in assessing Western defence preparedness. So well did the spymasters know NATO that they actually ordered documents by their correct reference numbers.

Hambleton's career demonstrates the care and attention which the Russians devote to grooming their agents and operating them. The Professor was recruited, symbolically enough, at an Ottawa cocktail party in 1947 by Vladimir Bourdine, the Soviet cultural attaché.

In his twenties, and having served in Canadian army intelligence, he was a suitable candidate for the treatment. At first there were suggestions that he might go in for Canadian politics — on behalf of the KGB, naturally — a suggestion which was renewed later with offers to finance his election campaign.

But ten years after he had been recruited — meanwhile he had taken a degree at the Sorbonne, and was taking a doctorate at the London School of Economics — Bourdine suggested that the time had come for him to take a job with NATO as an economist. Conveniently, with his 'cosmic' security clearance there he had the run of the secret files.

The Professor no doubt enjoyed playing spy games in the back streets of Paris, though he must have stuck out like a sore thumb in some of the working-class areas where he met his spy-minders with curious conversation about 'Have you the etchings?'

Nevertheless, he survived. After all that he returned happily to live in Canada, travelling widely, passing on useful bits of information to the Russians about, for example, Western oil reserves in an emergency and the state of affairs in Israel. Even when he was denounced by the double agent and kindly informed the Canadian Mounties about his past activities, nothing very much happened.

It was only when he decided to make his summer trip to Spain by way of London that retribution came. Hard questioning from Sir Michael Havers, the Attorney-General, did succeed in breaking down the debonair defences of the smooth professor and compel him to admit his guilt. For until then the jury must have half believed the casual assertion that he was really a double agent and a dilettante.

Sometimes it must seem to the KGB master-minds that spying in the West is really just too easy for them. Perhaps they should take to heart the words of Mr Justice Croom-Johnson, sending Hambleton to prison for ten years: 'The gravity of this offence has to be recognized. Although it is a long time ago you committed those acts, they caught up with you in the end.'

A final verdict came from a security officer: 'Hambleton was very big indeed. After all, Andropov would not have dined with any old agent.'

As for the Russians, they loftily denied that Hambleton had anything to do with them. They denied that he had met Andropov, for even to mention such a social occasion shocked their sense of the protocol of espionage.

HAREL, Isser

When David Ben Gurion, Prime Minister of Israel, was reorganizing the intelligence services of the new state in 1953 he chose as head of Mossad this diminutive sandals-and-open-shirt veteran of a kibbutz and of Haganah, the Israeli guerrilla organization. The nickname 'Little Isser' seemed inappropriately harmless, for Harel was a hard man with cold eyes, ruthless ambition as well as Zionist fervour, and totally without humour.

Through the next decade he built Mossad in his own image. He had a positive passion for secrecy, keeping his own files walled into a special building. He never hesitated to launch violent and questionable operations whenever he considered them necessary. He gathered into his own hands supreme intelligence power in one of the most devoted intelligence communities in the world.

Isser Harel's most notable coup was to plan the snatch of Otto Adolf Eichmann, the Nazi persecutor of the Jews, from his refuge in Argentina, and to lead the team of five which captured him and took him back to Israel for trial. Eichmann was sentenced to death in December 1961 and hanged.

After the Suez operation in 1956 Isser Harel, who was the son of an immigrant family from Russia, became obsessed with the danger to Israel implicit in the development of new weapons in Egypt. A number of German scientists and military technicians, some of them with Nazi connections, had been lured to Cairo by offers of high salaries from President Gamal Abdul Nasser.

Nasser wanted to equip his forces with ground-to-ground missiles for use in a war of revenge upon the Israelis, and hoped that the Germans would provide them. In 1962 it was announced that such a weapon called Al Kahir was ready for action, though that turned out to be an overstatement.

At the orders of Harel, Mossad began a terrorist campaign to frighten the German scientists into leaving Egypt. Letter bombs were sent, among them one to Dr Wolfgang Pilz, and his secretary was wounded. Other terrorist devices went to German offices and workshops, and attempts were made in Europe to threaten violence and kidnapping against those in the service of Egypt.

Mossad also believed that plans were afoot in Cairo to construct, with foreign help, a kind of poor man's atomic weapon by placing cobalt and atomic waste in warheads. In fact it later turned out that stories about these new weapons at President Nasser's disposal were to say the least exaggerated. Isser was determined to run no risks.

It was when he dispatched two agents to Switzerland to threaten Germans working for Nasser, and they were arrested, that even the Israeli government began to think he had gone too far. David Ben Gurion was at the time intent on improving relations with West Germany in order to get financial support and weapons supplies, and had no intention of upsetting his long-term political aim by tolerating Harel's gangster methods abroad.

'Little Isser', the hard man, had by this time arrogated to himself too much independent authority, and was even beginning to have political ambitions. When reproached and told to go easy by the Prime Minister, who wanted to see evidence of Egyptian missile developments, Harel refused, and indignantly resigned his office.

It was not quite the end of his career, for in 1965 he was recalled to become special adviser on intelligence to the then Prime Minister. But in face of increasing signs that once again he was trying to re-establish himself as boss, that arrangement came to an end. Isser Harel was replaced by a much smoother and more intellectual spymaster, Meir Amit.

HARKABI, Major-General Yehoshaphat

An academic who fought as a company commander in the siege of Jerusalem in 1948, Harkabi served in Israel's Foreign Ministry until 1950, when he was recalled by the army and, after attending a school for battalion commanders, was invited to become deputy head of military intelligence. Untouched by the Lavon affair because he had fallen out with his boss, Benjamin Gibli, and had been sent to Paris on extended leave, he was brought back to be chief of military intelligence with the rank of major-general in 1955.

He was a great believer in the acquisition and analysis of knowledge, and preferred to obtain his knowledge by overt means if possible. He applied his academic brain to this problem, and established a research centre into Arab affairs whose evaluations have constantly given the Israelis an edge over their enemies.

However, he did not hesitate to use covert operations and to kill, if he thought it necessary. It was Harkabi who planned the bomb murders of the two Egyptian intelligence officers responsible for running fedayeen missions into Israel from the Gaza Strip and Jordan.

He came to grief when he ordered a practice mobilization of Israel's forces without telling the Prime Minister. The mobilization cost hundreds of thousands of pounds in lost production, and embarrassed Ben Gurion. Harkabi was forced to resign, and returned to the academic world as Professor of International Relations and Middle East Studies at the Hebrew University. There he quickly acquired a world-wide reputation for understanding the Arab thought-processes, and produced a series of books and pamphlets which are required reading for any intelligence agent — or anyone else — working in the Middle East.

In the Israeli tradition, Harkabi is still a consultant for the intelligence services. In 1977 this position was recognized when he was made adviser on intelligence to the Prime Minister.

HARO, Miguel Nassar

Chief of the Mexican directorate of federal security since 1977, he was revealed as an important source of intelligence to the American intelligence service when the CIA tried to do him a favour by blocking his prosecution before a San Diego court in 1982 on charges rising out of stolen-car smuggling operations.

He was described by American intelligence men as a great expert on subversion in Central and Latin America. His directorate was responsible for monitoring movements of agents through Mexico. The CIA were embarrassed that Haro's appearance in court might uncover their connection with him, and make the Mexican Government less co-operative. Miguel Haro departed from his job in 1982.

HARRIS, Tomas

Because of his close connections with Burgess, Maclean, Philby and Blunt, the quartet of British spies for the Soviets, this painter and art connoisseur who became a wartime secret agent qualified as an obvious candidate for investigation as the 'Fifth Man'. His father was English, his mother Spanish (hence the Iberian 'Tomas'), and early in the war on the recommendation of Guy Burgess he and his wife were installed at a training establishment for saboteurs in Hertfordshire known as 'Guy Fawkes College'.

Harris, according to Burgess, was 'a sort of glorified housekeeper because he and his wife were inspired cooks'. Later the Harrises kept open house at their agreeable establishment in Mayfair. Tomas graduated effortlessly from the role of cook to that of spy, as a promising recruit to the Iberian section of MI5 because of his inside knowledge of Spain and Portugal.

He specialized in misleading German agents through disinformation. It was Harris who helped Kim Philby to become head of the Iberian section of MI5, and this was one good reason for deeper investigation of his role in the great British spy dramas.

Furthermore, it became known that even before he began his military intelligence activities he had acted as a courier for Philby when he was ostensibly reporting the Spanish civil war for *The Times* newspaper. Harris is further suspected of helping Melinda, the wife of Donald Maclean, to fly to Moscow and join her husband after his defection. He is known to have introduced Anthony Blunt into MI5.

The final element in the mystery surrounding the activities of Tomas Harris was the manner of his death in a car accident in 1964. No satisfactory explanation could be found to account for the fatal skid and slide of his new French-built car on a Spanish road.

HARRISON, Sir Geoffrey

In 1968 the KGB attempted to compromise Sir Geoffrey, British Ambassador to Moscow, by placing in the mission an attractive maid named Galya, whose favours he was unable to resist. When she then told him that compromising photographs had been taken, and the only way to avoid exposure was for him to provide information to the KGB, he wisely informed a senior Foreign Office friend.

A counter-espionage officer of MI5 who questioned him back in London was alarmed to discover from the ambassador's confession that he had made love to Galya in the laundry of the residence. For if pictures had been taken there, it meant that the KGB was able to penetrate what was considered a well-guarded building.

Even after his confession the ambassador had written a love-letter to Galya, and when it was discovered he had to admit that he had a real love affair with her. He told security men that he had met Galya once on a visit to Leningrad, where she said she was visiting her brother, who just by chance had a flat near his hotel.

This was obviously a KGB entrapment set-up, and it had been there that they took pictures. No action was taken against the misguided ambassador, who later retired on full pension.

HARVEY, William

A refugee from the FBI, where he had fallen foul of Edgar Hoover, Harvey was quite unlike his smart graduate colleagues in the upper echelons of the CIA. He was a fat, drunken womanizer who liked to frighten people by playing with guns while he talked to them. Nevertheless, he displayed a certain maverick talent for undercover operations. He ran the Office of Special Operations, which was responsible for espionage and intelligence-collection in the early days of the Agency, then moved to Europe, where he was involved in the Berlin tunnel operation to tap Soviet military telephones. He later became head of Task Force W, the CIA's contribution to Operation Mongoose, the Kennedy brothers' plot to get rid of Castro by sabotage and subversion and, if necessary, by assassination, after the Bay of Pigs landings had failed. But Harvey was as blunt with the President and his brother, the Attorney General, as he was with everybody else, and after a series of brushes he was removed from Operation Mongoose and sent to Rome as chief of station in order to keep him out of the Kennedys' way.

By this time Harvey's drinking had reached a dangerous level. His work suffered, and so did relations with his colleagues. He was eventually recalled from Rome and given the task of making a report on security against bugging at CIA buildings around the world. Retired on medical grounds, he was called to give evidence about Operation Mongoose to the Church Committee. He died in 1976.

HAUGEN, Sven Erling

A loyal and patriotic oil-man approached by the Russians in 1974 with an offer to pay him for detailed technological and geological information about North Sea drilling operations. He at once made contact with the Norwegian secret service and agreed with their help to act as a double agent, providing the KGB with carefully 'sanitized' information. For seven years he continued to act in this role.

To the Russians he was known by the code-name 'Jan Hansen', while Western intelligence labelled him 'Arne'. This dossier, on which we were given information by Haugen himself in 1981, reveals in minute detail how the Russian secret service works on the ground.

Haugen was running a stand at the North Sea Exhibition in Stavanger, Norway, when Alexander Dementiev — a KGB officer working with the Soviet Trade Delegation in Oslo — strolled up and began asking about the Statfjord A platform then under construction. There followed a number of business lunches, after which Dementiev offered small presents, such as a bottle of vodka, and mention of the fact that his friends in Moscow could offer useful business in return for the more precise information they needed.

'If you play your cards right you could make a lot of money,' said Sacha (for by now the two men were on Christian-name terms). Dementiev, an uncouth and greedy agent, put high value on even items of seemingly minor interest provided they could be made to appear top-secret. When Haugen produced published documents the Russian bluntly told him, 'Get your secretary to type it out so that it looks more secret.'

The agent began paying for information — unaware, of course, that it was being carefully prepared as disinformation by Western intelligence. The usual sum paid was £1,000. Although Haugen had to sign for the full amount, the KGB man handed it over less his own cut of between 10 and 15 per cent, thus proving that Soviet agents sometimes cheat their own spymasters.

Demands for information became heavier, and concentrated on three areas: technical and geophysical aspects of the North Sea fields, Norwegian and British; exploratory and naval activity in the Arctic, especially by the United States; and details of off-shore oil-search on the China coast. The shopping list was written in English as the common language, and close study

of it showed that behind the lust for technical information was a desire to pinpoint targets, for the Soviet fleet in time of war. The Russians wanted not simply technical data for their own undersea research but also material which could be fed into their military computers for making tactical battle-plans.

The Norwegian double game continued until 1977, when it became enmeshed in another spy affair involving a Norwegian diplomat Fru Gunvor Haavik. Because of this affair Dementiev was expelled from Oslo with a number of other Soviet diplomats.

Haugen thought with some relief that this was the end of the affair. He had been well aware of the risks he was running, but felt it his duty to co-operate with his own intelligence service. 'You hear about such things. But somebody has to do something to stop them. They have to be stopped somewhere,' he said. Nevertheless, the strain was beginning to tell.

A year later the Soviet trade delegation called him again, passing on greetings from Dementiev and asking whether Haugen would like to go to see him in Vienna. Arrangements were made to meet a Soviet official in Oslo first, and it became apparent that the KGB was carefully checking on Haugen to make sure that he was not being followed, for the Russians wanted to reassure themselves that he was still *nash* (one of ours).

When he arrived in Vienna it was obvious that a heavy team of Soviet surveillance men were keeping watch. Haugen feared that a trap was being set for him when he was told to make his own way by taxi to the Soviet Embassy. He believes that the obvious presence of Russians there had been planned as a test of his nerve, and was relieved to be ushered into a more friendly room where drinks were being offered.

He was asked to assure the Russian that he had made no contact with the Norwegian secret service, and then Dementiev gave him £1,000 in dollar bills — less 10 per cent commission, naturally — and fixed their next rendezvous outside the Volksoper, where he was to appear carrying a copy of *Fortune* magazine.

After several meetings a new man named

Belozerov turned up and announced that Dementiev had been promoted and had to return to Moscow. Dr Arkady Belozerov, as he turned out to be, was short, plump and a well-dressed 47-year-old. His cover role was as secretary of the International Institute of Applied Systems Analysis set up in Vienna as a gesture of détente by President Johnson and Dzermen Gvishiani, son-in-law of Kosygin.

Belozerov was also a KGB colonel, and he took over the task of running the Norwegian agent — not as it turned out, very efficiently. Haugen was amazed by his bungling: when they arranged to meet at a restaurant it was closed. So they went to another, also shut down. When they eventually found somewhere to eat he took Haugen's papers and rushed out to a waiting car so that they could be taken away and photocopied. He could not find the car.

Dr Belozerov was particularly interested in China, and in his attempts to get ever more information about oil-drilling there he suggested that Haugen might set up a company in Hong Kong at Soviet expense in order to learn more. He also talked a good deal about himself and his career, revealing in an unprofessional way that he had recruited and 'run' an important person in Vienna, thereby providing enough detail for Western agents to identify that person.

With money he was tight-fisted. On one occasion he failed to bring a promised payment of $10,000, saying that it could not be handed over until the documents concerned had been examined. But he was very precise about information required. He even listed the index numbers of scientific papers on North Sea oil of interest to his service. He was clearly an intelligence officer working on behalf of the Soviet Committee of Science and Technology.

The Haugen saga ended in April 1981. The Norwegian secret service, which had kept other Western services informed, decided that they were unlikely to get further benefits after the exposure of Soviet diplomats in Oslo and the network in Vienna. A brief statement announced that T.A. Besidin, a trade delegation functionary, and the new contact in Oslo, was unwelcome in Norway,

and so were G. G. Petrov, and E. S. Mirinenko of the same organization, who had already left the country.

The announcement must have given a nasty shock to Belozerov in Vienna, who had made a rendezvous three days later with Haugen outside the Volksoper as usual. It was nevertheless a great relief to Haugen that he did not have to go there.

Two weeks later Arkady Belozerov made a statement in Vienna. 'I deny the charges completely,' he said, 'but the accusations may disturb the spirit of the Institute, therefore I have decided regretfully to offer my resignation.'

The international organization accepted the resignation and Arkady Belozerov and his family packed their bags and returned home to Moscow.

HAYHANEN, Reino

A professional KGB lieutenant-colonel with a good record until he learned English and was sent in 1952 on his first trip to the West to operate in the United States. It was New York which proved his undoing, for once there his sex life became active, there were quarrels with his wife and quite a bit of drinking, all of which led to what the KGB would describe as laxity in his duties.

This did not at all suit the agent he was supposed to work with, the efficient and enthusiastic Colonel Rudolph Abel, operating in New York as the spymaster of a potentially important spy ring. After Hayhanen had fallen down on the job during a brief absence of his boss, and had put KGB money into his own pocket to sustain his social life, Colonel Abel firmly suggested that he should return to Moscow.

He did set off for Moscow in 1957, but fearing what might happen when he got there, he slipped away in Paris to ask the CIA station chief for asylum. Hayhanen was flown back to America, where he betrayed Rudolph Abel, and identified Master Sergeant Roy Rhodes, who had spied for the Russians while employed at the US Embassy in Moscow in the transport section.

A grateful CIA subsidized his new life in the United States. Nothing more was heard of him until his death in a car accident in 1961 on the Pennsylvania turnpike.

HELMS, Richard

There is a certain irony in the fact that this most discreet man, to whom secrecy was a way of life, should have ended his career in a blaze of publicity. Books were written about him, a television series was based on his work and secrets he had so carefully guarded were revealed before a Senate committee.

He started his life trying to uncover secrets as a correspondent for the news agency UPI in Hitler's Germany, but switched to the management of newspapers before joining the Navy in the Second World War. His knowledge of Germany took him into the OSS, where he worked under Dulles. He was one of the few who survived President Truman's dismantling of that wartime intelligence organization, and continued to work in Germany, first for the Central Intelligence Group and then, when it was created in 1947, for the CIA.

Helms was one of the original Cold War Warriors of the CIA, yet a man of liberal thinking who saw at first hand what the Russians were doing in Europe and determined that they had to be fought by all possible means. He was therefore involved with the Gehlen Organization, and the frantic, often bloody, secret war for Europe which was fought out in the ruined alleys of Berlin. (Helms always hated John le Carré's spy books because they evoked only too well those desperate events in which he had taken part!)

It was during this period that secrecy became his watchword. Recalled from Europe to serve in Washington, he proved to be an able administrator, but because he did not approve of the flamboyant covert operations which were fashionable then, he seemed doomed to spend his career in the middle echelons of the Agency. But one after the other his seniors and potential rivals were removed from the scene, Lyman Kirkpatrick by polio, Frank Wisner by mental breakdown, Allen Dulles and Richard Bissell by the Bay of Pigs failure.

He succeeded Bissell as Deputy Director for Plans (Operations) in 1962, became Deputy Director of the Agency in 1965, and a year later was made Director. It was his misfortune that his appointment coincided with the growth of President Johnson's paranoia over the war in Vietnam.

It was an even greater misfortune that Nixon and Watergate followed Johnson and Vietnam. The trouble was that Helms was probably only a good number two. He needed to take orders from somebody, and so he took orders from the Presidents he served, too uncritically, obeying them even though he knew that what he was being asked to do violated the CIA's charter, as well as all the rules of discretion which he had so carefully nurtured over his lifetime in intelligence work.

The CIA was involved in the Watergate break-in, even if it was only by way of peripheral help to an ex-CIA man, but when Helms realized the extent of the potential damage to his beloved Agency he did his best to protect it, an action read by Nixon as treachery. And so, on 2 February 1973, after six years as DCIA, Richard Helms was fired. As a sop Nixon appointed him ambassador to Iran. But his troubles were only just starting. In the next four years he was summoned home from Iran no less than thirteen times to give evidence before various committees probing into Watergate and the CIA. He did his best to maintain secrecy, but most of the CIA's 'Family Jewels', details of the illegal and immoral operations, came tumbling out. And Helms's name was involved with most of them. Helms prevaricated, twisted and turned in his efforts not to divulge anything that would harm the Agency.

Helms had already gone too far. In 1973 he had told the Foreign Relations Committee — which as is customary were examining him on his fitness to become ambassador to Iran — that the CIA had never attempted to overthrow Salvador Allende's government in Chile. The new brooms at the CIA, busy sweeping up the Agency's past actions, found this to be untrue, and their report was passed to the Justice Department.

Four years later Helms, once so powerful, was found guilty of perjury, fined $2,000, given a two-year suspended sentence, and lectured by the judge: 'You stand before this court in disgrace and shame...If public officials embark deliberately on a course to disobey and ignore the laws of our land because of some misguided and ill-conceived notion and belief that there are earlier commitments and considerations which they must observe, the future of our country is in jeopardy.'

Helms, unrepentant, sure in the belief that he had done his duty to the Agency and his country, if not to the letter of the law, left public life.

In October 1983 the President presented Richard Helms with the National Security Medal, saying that the award of this, the highest decoration for intelligence work, was 'long overdue'. It marked the rehabilitation of the seventy-year-old former director of the CIA and was greeted with approval by those CIA agents who felt that Helms had been badly treated in return for his unswerving loyalty.

Helms, by then a political risk consultant on Middle East investments, said 'I suppose it has something to do with the swing of the pendulum. I have no feelings about remorse or exoneration.'

HERZOG, Chaim (President of Israel)

A cheerful extrovert and man of many parts, Vivian Herzog as he then was (and still is to personal friends), the son of the Chief Rabbi of Ireland, born in Belfast and Cambridge-educated, served in British Army field intelligence before going to Israel.

At the age of thirty he was chosen as head of the Israeli military intelligence service, where he worked for nearly three years in the crucial period after 1948. After serving as military attaché both in Washington and in Paris — posts reserved for high-flyers in Israeli intelligence work — he again became director of the military intelligence service in 1959.

In Paris, Herzog played an important part in cementing Franco-Israeli co-operation which was so important before, and after, the Suez expedition of 1956. A well-informed military commentator, both as a writer and as a

broadcaster, he moved also into politics, though in that field Israelis regarded him as something of a lightweight with an undoubted talent for public relations.

These were the qualities which finally ensured his election in 1983 as President of Israel. Thus he shared with that unlikely stable-mate Yuri Andropov the distinction of having become President of his country by way of a career in intelligence work.

HILLENKOETTER, Rear-Admiral Roscoe H.

Appointed in May 1947 as the first director of the new model Central Intelligence Agency, reluctantly established by the United States as the cold war got under way, he was an efficient graduate of the Annapolis Naval Academy who had served in intelligence with Admiral Nimitz's wartime Pacific Fleet. He was fluent in three languages, and had a reputation as an administrator.

It was one of his achievements that he restored smooth working in the Agency after the personality clashes and freebooting of the 'Wild Bill' Donovan days. But he was a cautious man, given to analysis of information which came in automatically, rather than an aggressive seeker-out of intelligence.

In 1949 a three-man committee was set up under Allen Dulles to report on the working of the CIA under Hillenkoetter's control which resulted eventually in the choice of General Walter Bedell Smith to replace the Admiral, with Allen Dulles as his deputy. The need to reorganize the agency was underlined in June 1950, when the North Koreans invaded the South and it became painfully obvious that the United States was sadly lacking in hard information on their military movements.

HINCHCLIFFE, Leonard Michael

He was an archivist in the British Embassy in Khartoum involved in a sad business of threatened blackmail by a Soviet agent there simply named as

'Andrei'. In a state of depression about the death of his ten-month-old child and the absence in London of his wife (who was having a baby), Hinchcliffe saw a good deal of a woman in the English community. Although there was no question of their having an affair, her companionship cheered him.

After his wife returned to Sudan he was amazed to get a telephone call from the Russian 'Andrei' saying bluntly, 'Does your wife know about your mistress?' Despite his innocence in this matter, Hinchcliffe was so scared of scandal and of upsetting his wife that he agreed to hand over the Embassy cypher key and to supply a number of documents.

Sentencing him to ten years in 1972, Lord Chief Justice Widgery said, 'You sold your country's secrets at a time when you were in a position of trust.' Then aged thirty-nine, Hinchcliffe had been paid almost £3,000. Had he not become worried about his meetings with Soviet agents, and distressed by his actions, he might never have come to trial. Finally he decided that the guilt was too heavy to bear and made a full confession to his Foreign Office superiors.

HIRSCH, Willi

It was in 1958, when he recommended espionage for the Soviet Union as a profitable business to a friend in Chicago, that this left-wing German brought up in the United States started getting into trouble. For the friend, William McCuag, reported to the FBI, and they used him as a double agent to catch Hirsch, and his Soviet contact Igor Melekh, a Russian translator at the United Nations who ran a spy ring.

Hirsch had been in the game since 1936 when he made a visit to Moscow. As a freelance journalist he travelled around the U.S. and managed to dig out naval secrets about Polaris and anti-submarine detection devices.

Melekh was expelled from the US in 1961, and Hirsch after a short spell in prison was exchanged for two US air force officers shot down over the Soviet Union. He reached Moscow, but died shortly afterwards.

HISS, Alger

The central and controversial figure in the great spy hunt of the late 1940s which came to be known as the American 'Dreyfus Affair'. Alger Hiss was a respectable lawyer of the American establishment whose credentials appeared to be impeccable to East Coast liberals of the time.

In the 1930s he had moved from law practice into government by way of service as clerk to the Supreme Court, and he eventually served in the State Department from 1936 to 1945, attending the Yalta conference. Despite that there were worrying items about his activities in the files of the FBI and of the State Department. For already the seedy journalist Whittaker Chambers, who was the later cause of his downfall, had denounced him and his wife for being members of the same communist underground to which Chambers belonged.

Despite some questioning of Hiss, and even after information from French intelligence appeared to support the allegations, no action was taken. Hiss denied all accusations.

The turning-point came when Igor Gouzenko defected from the Soviet Embassy in Ottawa and claimed that a Soviet agent whose name he did not know was an assistant to the US Secretary of State. It appeared that the man in question was Hiss, although no other evidence could be discovered.

It seemed that nobody wanted to believe that Hiss could have been guilty, so there was a feeling of relief when Hiss appeared before the House Committee on Un-American Activities and firmly denied that he had ever met Chambers, the man who was denouncing him. Despite that, Chambers was able to display an uncannily detailed knowledge of the Hiss household, where he claimed to have lived for some time.

After a confrontation Hiss had to admit that he had met Chambers, who went under another name at the time, and who had altered his appearance. In a 'Meet the Press' radio programme Chambers categorically stated, 'Alger Hiss was a communist and may be now.' Hiss promptly sued for slander, and Whittaker Chambers went further, with an outright allegation that Hiss was also a spy. The core of his case was that in the 1930s Hiss had taken home classified State Department papers which had been typed out by his wife Priscilla and handed over to Soviet agents. Whittaker then produced what came to be known as the 'Pumpkin Papers', papers including 65 microfilmed type-written sheets which had been hidden in a hollowed-out pumpkin at Chambers' farm.

The case turned upon these typewritten sheets and upon Priscilla Hiss's typewriter, which nobody was able to find. Despite the missing piece of crucial evidence, a grand jury indicted Hiss for perjury in saying that he had never met Chambers, and in denying that he had given him classified papers.

After a first jury had disagreed, a second one found Hiss guilty of perjury, for they decided that the copies of the State Department documents had emanated from Priscilla's typewriter. The machine had by now been discovered, and there was evidence that it had been in the Hiss household at the relevant time.

Alger Hiss now cast himself as a victim of what he called forgery by typewriter, and appealed. Despite that, he was sent to gaol. After his release for good behaviour four years later Hiss devoted himself to proving that he had been wrongly convicted. Divorced from Priscilla and remarried, Alger Hiss at the age of seventy-five was still loudly protesting his innocence in 1983.

HODIC, Dr Joseph

A Czech historian and former army officer sent to Austria in 1977 by the Czech secret service as a defector to spy upon exiles living there. He posed as a supporter of the Charter 77 groups and claimed to have been persecuted in Prague, which made it easy for him to win the confidence of fellow-expatriates abroad.

In 1981 he and his wife left Vienna for a summer holiday in Linz. But in July the Czech radio triumphantly reported, 'A highly skilled member of our secret service has returned home after successfully completing his mission abroad.'

They said that Colonel Hodic had discovered links between Czech exiles and Western intelligence services trying to destabilize Czechoslovakia. Shortly after his return to Prague more than a score of Czechs were arrested, and he was also blamed for the seizure of a French couple charged with smuggling in anti-communist material.

Despite that Bruno Kreisky, then Chancellor of Austria, declared that he was not convinced that Hodic had been a spy from the beginning. He believed that he might have been either taken back against his will or under pressure, in order to denounce exiles with whom he had been in contact.

HOFI, Major-General Yitzhak

The Israeli government blew the cover of General Hofi by announcing in the summer of 1982 that since 1974 he had been head of Mossad, its secret service. As befitted such a spymaster, his appearance before the judicial commission investigating the Beirut massacres in the summer of '82 was shrouded in security, as well as secrecy. General Hofi was the officer who had made clandestine contacts, and arrangements with the Christian phalangists in Lebanon led by the Gemayel family; and it was their private army which was held responsible for the massacres in the PLO camps in Beirut.

He had long experience of anti-guerrilla and terrorist operations, having served originally in Arik Sharon's notorious Unit 101 which carried out cross-border raids against Palestine fighters. After retiring from the army, where he was a Northern Front commander in 1973, he became head of Mossad and chairman of the co-ordinating committee for all intelligence activities.

In this function he was responsible for planning the operations involving a dramatic air attack upon Iraqi nuclear installations in Baghdad where the Israelis claimed that the Iraq Government was producing nuclear weapons.

HOLLIS, Sir Roger (Roger Henry)

Director-General of MI5 in the critical espionage period for Britain between 1956 and 1965, Sir Roger remained, even ten years after his death, the centre of controversy and divided opinions among the British and American intelligence community. The question which has not been conclusively answered is whether or not he was a mole acting on behalf of the Soviet Union.

When the matter of his loyalty was raised in 1981 Mrs Thatcher, the Prime Minister — who had not hesitated to expose Anthony Blunt — stated that Sir Roger had been fully investigated in the 1970s, but that no proof had been discovered that he was working for the Russians. Lord Trend, a former Secretary to the Cabinet, conducted that inquiry, and although he admitted that it was difficult to demonstrate positively a negative, he found the case against Hollis unproven.

In October 1981 Sir Martin Furnival Jones, who replaced Hollis as Director-General, and Anthony Simkins, the DDG, wrote to *The Times* declaring, 'We are wholly convinced of his innocence.' This was an unprecedented step for MI5 officials, but they had seen the results of earlier investigations.

Despite such powerful rebuttals, doubts about Hollis's loyalty still prevailed in the minds of some in-house informants who inspired Chapman Pincher, an experienced journalist and author of *Their Trade is Treachery*. He remained the main protagonist of the 'Hollis was a Russian agent' school of thought.

Their case goes back to almost the beginnings of Roger Hollis's career. The son of a bishop, he was educated at Clifton College, Bristol, and Worcester College, Oxford. At Oxford he had been a friend of notable communists such as Claud Cockburn, the Irish journalist and writer.

But after two years at Oxford he left without taking a degree, determined against the wishes of his family to travel. He went to Malaya and found a job with the British American Tobacco Company, which sent him to Shanghai.

Hollis's critics point up the fact that he was there in China at the time when the notorious Soviet agent Richard Sorge was operating. Also in Shanghai were Agnes Smedley, the American journalist and Comintern agent. In place there too was the formidable Ursula (or Ruth) Kuczynski, to appear eventually under the name Ursula Beurton, a Soviet agent who later turned up in Switzerland, and then in Oxford, at a time when Hollis was working for British security near there during the war. Of course, all this is purely circumstantial.

During his nine years in the Far East Hollis became ill with tuberculosis. BAT sent him for treatment in Switzerland, and he travelled by way of the Trans-Siberian railway and the Soviet Union. Even though medical treatment was a success, the company considered he should not be employed further and he returned to England.

In 1938 after being rejected by the Secret Intelligence Service, possibly on grounds of ill health, he succeeded in joining MI5, which was then expanding in face of the threat of war. It is claimed that he showed an excess of zeal to enter the service. Later he seemed to display less vigilance in his important mission to Canada in 1945 to debrief one of the early defectors, Igor Gouzenko. The task should have been Kim Philby's as head of the appropriate MI6 section, but he was busy in Turkey making sure that he was not exposed as a mole by Volkov, another defector.

Gouzenko himself later claimed that Hollis had not pressed him on the subject of his report of a talk in Moscow revealing that a British mole codenamed 'Elli' was one of the British agents of the KGB highly placed in military intelligence. It was suggested afterwards that Hollis was 'Elli', though it might easily have been one of the others since detected.

Hollis was also criticized for his handling of the security side of the Profumo scandal. Although Ivanov, a Soviet naval attaché, was implicated, the Director-General of MI5 was in no hurry to involve his service by informing Harold Macmillan, the Prime Minister. He justified himself by saying that it was no part of his duty to concern himself with the sex lives of cabinet ministers.

The subsequent Denning Report endorsed the Hollis view, but some ex-colleagues make the point that the Director-General was known in the office as 'Mr Inertia'; he was slow to take decisions, and in the words of one senior officer, 'He was the wrong man in the wrong job.' Being a rather shy and diffident man, he was not popular in the office, and his talents were not always highly regarded.

Under his rule MI5 did not have a good record. Its spycatching operations were not entirely successful, and depended heavily upon defectors whose information was relayed by the Americans. Even triumphs were spoiled by suspicion that in several cases Soviet controllers escaped while the lesser fry went to prison.

Deeper worries were exposed by the flight from Beirut of Kim Philby in 1963. Only five senior MI5 men knew about recent information which was to be used in an attempt to force a confession from him, yet before Nicholas Elliott, the interrogating officer, arrived in Lebanon, Philby's old Soviet case officer, Yuri Modin, had visited him with a warning of what was in store.

Hollis was one of the five in the know, and after an internal investigation had cleared his deputy Graham Mitchell, he accepted the fact that he too would have to be checked out. That in itself was in his favour, and no evidence was discovered to blame him.

Before that happened he had suffered the humiliation of having to fly to Washington to explain to American intelligence chiefs that because of doubts about internal security in MI5 all information known to that office would have to be treated with circumspection.

Sir Roger retired in 1965. He died in 1973.

One final possibility remains to haunt British intelligence. That is that KGB manipulators, whose expertise at sowing doubt and disinformation is undisputed, set up through false defectors trails which would point investigators towards Sir Roger in order to hide more deeply their real mole.

HOLT, Harold

A wave of indignant denials followed publication in 1983 of a book entitled *The Prime Minister Was*

a Spy, alleging that Harold Holt, the then respected Prime Minister of Australia, had spied for the Chinese, and that when he mysteriously disappeared in the ocean off Cheviot Beach he was taken away by frogmen to a Chinese submarine off-shore.

This improbable-sounding scenario was written by Anthony Grey, an accomplished journalist and former Reuter correspondent in Peking, but most of the information contained in the book apparently came from a former Australian naval officer named Ronald Titcombe.

Gareth Evans, the Australian attorney-general, declared, 'I can deny categorically that Harold Holt was ever investigated by the Australian Security and Intelligence Organisation. The whole tale seems to be out of fruitcake land. Dame Zara, wife of the late Prime Minister, put it more bluntly still by saying that the book had been blown out of the author's arse.

HOOVER, J. Edgar

The prima donna who ran the Federal Bureau of Investigation for half a century. A Washington man, ambitious, vigorous, he was only twenty-nine when he became boss of an organization badly in need of overhaul and liberation from political control. He devoted the rest of his life to his beloved FBI, hacking at the incompetents, promoting the efficient, and in the process making himself so indispensable that no President dared to fire him.

It was as a gang-busting and crime-fighting organization that the FBI became famous in the 1930s, and Hoover's agents won success in the era of Thompson guns and bootleggers. When he moved into the business of spycatching he kept to the old police methods, compiling the dossiers, preparing the court cases to get convictions, which is not always the most satisfactory way of breaking espionage rings.

This chunky, dynamic man, with slow eyes and a wealth of skill and experience in fighting out departmental battles, was at first less successful when he took the FBI from the war against crime into engagements with German spies during the war, and the period of hostile American neutrality which preceded it. The FBI was an investigative rather than an analytical agency.

In 1940 Hoover began a period of close co-operation with William Stephenson, of British Security Co-ordination with its headquarters in the Rockefeller Plaza, New York, which eventually had a staff of 2,000. Churchill and Roosevelt had agreed to this joint effort in Anglo-American counter-espionage. Before Pearl Harbor it had to be clandestine.

The British were grateful for Hoover's enormous efforts to help, but were critical of his methods. To their way of thinking he was still the heavy-handed policeman, too anxious for court-room success and good publicity for his agency.

They criticized him for failing to keep suspects under observation before arrests, in order to follow them deeper into spy nets. Yet it was Hoover who began to suspect instinctively that the British SIS had traitors within in the form of Maclean, Burgess and Philby, who were pursuing Soviet aims to split the Anglo-American collaboration.

Hoover mistrusted double agents, and in particular Dusko Popov, who worked for the Germans and the British. He disliked the man personally, and gravely underestimated Popov's advance warning that the Japanese might be about to raid Pearl Harbor.

Later Popov became indignant when Hoover claimed in a magazine article that it was his FBI which had discovered the secrets of the microdot, described by him as 'the enemy's masterpiece of espionage'. In fact Popov had been the first agent entrusted by the Germans to use microdots, and had dutifully handed over the information to the Allies.

Hoover fought tooth and nail against the setting up of the wartime Office of Strategic Services under William Donovan, which became the forerunner of the CIA. He jealously tried to keep counter-espionage and intelligence as functions of the FBI when President Roosevelt was persuaded of the need for an integrated and co-ordinated intelligence agency. This in turn brought him into conflict with Stephenson and his BSC, to which Hoover began denying facilities, in spite of the help it had given him in tracking down German spies in America.

After the war when the CIA was reactivated Hoover always kept its men at arm's length. He himself became obsessively concerned with Soviet activities in the cold war.

Convinced of the reality of a great conspiracy between American subversive lefties and Soviet agents, he devised a new system of counter-espionage. He set up counter-intelligence pro-grammes known as Cointelpro using wire-taps and even more dubious methods of countering domestic spies.

During the Vietnam War he turned his attention to anti-war protesters, then student radicals and Ban the Bomb crowds, and even civil rights enthusiasts. Hoover, a law-enforcer of the old school, refused at first to employ either women or Blacks, and became public enemy number one of the American liberal establishment, which branded him as an autocrat and a spy-spotting maniac.

In 1971 he was forced to abandon Cointelpro, but to the end of his career he defended his FBI. He kept it out of the Watergate scandal, and fought to the end to keep the United States free from Soviet machinations. He died in 1972.

HOUGHTON, Harry Frederick

This jaunty, hard-drinking sailor joined the Royal Navy at sixteen and, after twenty-three years' service, retired as a chief petty officer and went to live near Weymouth. There he had no difficulty in being taken on the clerical staff of a naval research centre, and was soon promoted to a plum job as 'writer' to the British naval attaché in the Warsaw embassy.

That was the beginning of his downfall. The easy life with foreign allowances and duty-free booze suited him well enough, but his natural greed was stirred by helpful information from an embassy colleague that there was also a fine chance of making money through the Polish black market. Soon he was in co-operation with a young blonde Polish girl named Karytzia who helped him, not only to make money by selling illicit coffee, but also to spend it agreeably on the animated Polish night life.

This suited Houghton very well, the more so as he was constantly rowing with Peggy, his English wife, who had little taste for life abroad.

Whether or not because of his extra-mural activities, Harry Houghton was sent back to England before the end of his tour of duty. Surprisingly in 1952 he was then given a responsible job in the Admiralty's Under-Water Weapons Establishment at Portland on the south coast.

While there he had met a jolly lady called Ethel (Bunty) Gee, a blacksmith's daughter who worked in the same establishment. He bought a caravan where they used to spend a lot of time when they were not out and about drinking and going on excursions together.

Four years after his return to England, Houghton got a telephone call from a Pole announcing himself as a friend of Karytzia, and who proposed a little business deal involving the export of penicillin to Poland. When that began to fail, he suggested a more remunerative line in spying, and put Houghton in touch first with a Soviet diplomat, and then with a man known as Gordon Lonsdale, who turned out to be a highly professional Soviet agent.

What he wanted was a supply of test reports on submarine-detection, for at that time the Royal Navy and NATO were well ahead of the Soviet Union in anti-submarine equipment. It was, said Lonsdale, 'an order', though he was happy enough to pay several hundred pounds for the material.

In order to persuade Bunty — who still worked in the research establishment — to co-operate more willingly, they hatched a plot to pretend that Lonsdale was in fact Commander Alec Johnson of the US Embassy.

It was in this fashion that Houghton became the key supplier of high-grade naval intelligence material to one of the most efficient of Soviet spy networks, operated by Lonsdale with the help of

Mr and Mrs Kroger, or Cohen, an American couple working for Soviet intelligence. This happy arrangement continued until 1962.

But some time before that Houghton had aroused suspicion. A naval security officer who knew him had seen Houghton in his big-spending role with Bunty in Dorset pubs, and began making inquiries about his life-style. How could a man on his modest salary and pension afford to spend so much on drink, a new car and a gramophone? It was also recalled that his now estranged wife Peggy had told her friends about finding a batch of Admiralty papers in a parcel at home. It soon became obvious that something suspicious was going on, and the Special Branch began keeping watch.

Investigations conducted by both MI5 and Special Branch led them both to Lonsdale and to the Krogers. Early in 1962 Detective Superintendent George Smith led a team to a spot near the Old Vic theatre in London where they arrested Houghton and Bunty Gee in the act of passing over to Lonsdale a shopping basket containing four Admiralty files and a quantity of undeveloped film in a sealed tin. When developed the film revealed three hundred photographs of naval ships and equipment including details of the atomic submarine *Dreadnought*.

'Your conduct was in many ways the most culpable,' said Lord Chief Justice Parker at the subsequent trial when he addressed Houghton. 'You betrayed the secrets of your country by communicating secret information about Her Majesty's Navy....' Fifteen years.

The same prison sentence was passed on Bunty — Ethel Elizabeth Gee. 'I am inclined to think that yours was the stronger character of the two. I think you acted from greed', was the Lord Chief Justice's comment on her. So ended the Portland Spy Ring.

Houghton and Bunty served ten years and when they were released they married. Houghton wrote a highly coloured account of the affair in *Operation Portland, the Autobiography of a Spy*, cheekily explaining that all his troubles began through 'chasing a bit of skirt behind the Iron Curtain'.

HOUSTON, Lawrence

The man whose job it was to get the CIA out of trouble when one of its operations went sour. Originally a Wall Street lawyer, he joined OSS and served in Cairo in 1945. According to Allen Dulles, his brief by 'Wild Bill' Donovan was that 'the main target for intelligence operations should now become discovering what the Soviets were doing in the Balkans rather than German operations in the Middle East. The German threat was receding, the Soviet danger was already looming.'

Houston afterwards became the CIA's General Counsel and as such was privy to most of its secrets. He negotiated the U2 contract with Lockheed, and he was heavily involved in trying to save the CIA's reputation when it came under investigation in the aftermath of Watergate. But he had to give evidence, and added to the account of CIA illegalities.

Among his tasks were organizing a pension for the widow of Dr Frank Olson, who jumped out of a tenth-floor window of the Statler Hotel in New York after being given LSD in a CIA drug-testing programme, and making sure there was no fuss over the death of several pilots who were under contract to the CIA and were killed at the Bay of Pigs. He retired in 1973.

HUNT, E. Howard

An excellent writer of spy thrillers for whom things never seemed to go right in the CIA. He was apt to fall foul of ambassadors and lose documents. He played an important part in the overthrow of Arbenz's government in Guatemala, but was fired as political action officer of the Bay of Pigs operation for refusing to obey orders.

Unlike most members of the CIA, he was extremely right-wing. He was also committed to being devious, the characteristic which eventually led to him achieving notoriety. When he resigned from the Agency in 1970 after filling a series of not very brilliant posts not very brilliantly he took early retirement, and joined a public relations firm.

Soon afterwards he showed up as a member of President Nixon's White House staff. He was the dirty tricks expert, and with the White House's backing he applied for and was given some limited technical help by the CIA. He was supplied with a wig, a device to alter the sound of a voice and false identification. However, he became too importunate and the help was cut off.

Hunt's chief job was burgling information for use against Nixon's enemies. It was he who organized the break-in at the offices of the psychiatrist of Daniel Ellsberg, the man who had fed the Pentagon Papers to the *New York Times*. These papers, the Defense Department's 'History of Decision-Making on Vietnam', seriously embarrassed the government.

The crunch came for Hunt when his team of burglars was caught breaking and entering the Democratic Party's campaign headquarters in the Watergate complex in Washington. Everything that stemmed from Watergate, the resignation of Nixon, the emasculation of the CIA, can all be traced back to Hunt, the compulsive but failed spy. He went to prison for his role in Watergate. He should have stuck to thriller-writing.

INMAN, Admiral Bobby Ray

An exceptionally professional American intelligence officer with high-rank experience in both signals and 'human' intelligence. After a career in naval intelligence he became at forty-six the youngest ever director of the National Security Agency. In 1981 he moved to the other side of the house, to become deputy director of the Central Intelligence Agency under William Casey.

A Texan with a still boyish face and a noticeable gap between his front teeth, he progressed to NSA by way of intelligence analysis as a naval officer.

keeping an eye on the development in the 1960s of
the Soviet fleet. After service as a naval attaché in
Stockholm and at Pacific Fleet headquarters
Admiral Inman returned to take up the NSA
post.

In this capacity he revealed his diplomatic skills
at dealing with Congress and in defending NSA
interests. He tactfully handled a crisis which arose
about the employment in the agency of
homosexuals. This was always a cause of suspicion
in intelligence organizations, and especially so at
NSA, because two of its analysts so involved had
defected to Moscow in 1960.

Admiral Inman agreed not to dismiss a declared
gay on the staff in return for his written promise
not to succumb to blackmail and an undertaking
that he would inform his family, thus removing
potential for blackmail. It was generally agreed
that his enlightened attitude enabled him to
arrange this business neatly.

It was shortly after that, and after Ronald
Reagan became President, that he was persuaded
to become deputy director of the CIA, though he
would have preferred the top post there.

In this post he sustained his reputation as a non-
political and professional intelligence officer,
acting as a watchdog ready to resist excessive zeal
among the Reaganite extremists. The four-star
admiral stood out against the leaking of
intelligence secrets for political purposes, as when
the White House publicized covert operations
against Nicaragua, to demonstrate that Reagan
was taking a hard line with Sandinistas.

After only fourteen months in office the
Admiral resigned on the grounds that he needed to
make money in private employment to pay for the
education of his teenage sons. Although he went
quietly, it was generally assumed in Washington
that there were clashes of opinion between him
and his boss, William Casey.

In particular it seemed that Inman resisted plans
involving the CIA in reorganizing counter-
intelligence which would have embroiled it in
domestic spying. He feared that questionable CIA
operations abandoned by the Agency after earlier
scandals might be reinstated, with a consequent
threat to civil rights.

IVANOV, Lieutenant-Commander Eugene

British intelligence first made the acquaintance of
this Soviet GRU naval intelligence officer when
his name appeared upon the list of Russian agents
in their London embassy obligingly provided by
Oleg Penkovsky, the double agent for the British
in Moscow. The list included personal details, and
showed that Ivanov was a keen communist, and
well connected in the Soviet privileged class by
way of his wife. She was the daughter of Alexander
Gorkin, chairman of the Supreme Court. Her
sister was also in London, married to the air
attaché.

What was even more interesting from an
intelligence point of view was that he had a
weakness for attractive women and was a bit of a
socialite, with a taste for lively parties. For such
reasons he seemed a man worth keeping an eye on
as a possible target for defection, or turning by
way of blackmail or entrapment.

Those whose business it was to keep a watch on
him were happy to find that not long after his
arrival in March 1960 he was visiting Stephen
Ward, at his London home. For not only was
Ward a fashionable osteopath but he was a
provider of attractive girls for his wide circle of
friends.

Using the name 'Woods', from the War Office,
an MI5 man took Ward to lunch, asking about his
Russian friend. Ward agreed to co-operate, and
later introduced Woods to what he described as
the most beautiful girl he had ever met —
Christine Keeler.

It was not long before the osteopath reported
meeting Ivanov at his own country cottage on the
Thames-side Cliveden estate of Lord Astor, with
whom he was also on good terms. He said Ivanov
had asked him to find out whether the British
government intended to approve the arming of
West Germany with atomic weapons.

He also mentioned that John Profumo,
Secretary of State for War, had also been at the
Cliveden house-party. So keen were British
intelligence on their Ivanov operation that when
they had Mr Profumo informed, they even
suggested the dangerous idea that the Minister

might help with the plot. Very sensibly, he rejected the idea firmly.

Ivanov managed through Ward and the influence of Lord Astor to make representations to the Foreign Office on his behalf during the Berlin crisis of 1961. Of course, an assistant naval attaché at the Soviet Embassy had no business to be making such *démarches*.

During the Cuban missile crisis in October 1962 Ivanov again tried to make contact with Sir Harold Caccia, head of the FO, to suggest some kind of behind-the-scenes negotiation. But by now that organization had been warned, and refused any such plan.

It was the end of Ivanov's career in British high diplomacy, for soon after that the so-called Profumo Affair was beginning to make its way into the headlines. It was also the end of MI5's hopes of trapping the GRU man.

Christine Keeler, who had been to bed with Eugene Ivanov as well as with the Secretary of State for War, was about to tell her amazing story in the papers. Warned of this dangerous development, Ivanov packed his bags and returned to Moscow in January 1963.

There was a postscript to the Ivanov story from behind the Iron Curtain. The Soviet double agent codenamed 'Fedora' reported to the FBI a conversation he had in Moscow with the former naval attaché. Ivanov boasted that he had installed a microphone in Miss Keeler's bedroom which recorded many secrets from the pillow. MI5 checked the room again and thought this unlikely.

So this was disinformation from 'Fedora'; or maybe Ivanov was simply bragging back home to the boys about his wild old times in London.

J

JOHN, Dr Otto

Among those present at a commemoration in Berlin in July 1954 to mark the tenth anniversar of the failed plot to kill Adolf Hitler was Dr Otte John. As an anti-Nazi working as legal adviser t Lufthansa, he had been involved in the plot. On of his brothers was brutally killed by the Nazis fo taking part in it.

By 1954 Dr John (who had himself escaped i the confusion after the plot by flying to Madrid had served for four years as director of interna security, the BfV, Bureau for the Protection of th Constitution. He had been the British candidat for this appointment, charged with acting agains Nazis and communists. After his arrival in Madri he had gone to Britain and worked for the wartim Black Propaganda service broadcasting dis information to the German army. Dr John' version of what happened to him in 1954 after th commemoration was that he went in the evenin to the house of a friend, a surgeon named D Wolfgang Wohlgemuth, had some coffee, an feeling drowsy asked to be taken back to his hote The next thing he recalled was waking in th presence of a formidable nurse and three Russian in a house in East Berlin on the communist side o the line.

His jacket and shoes were missing. The me interrogated him, and he eventually agreed t speak at a Press conference criticizing politica developments in West Germany. It was this stage managed appearance of so important an officia which caused such a sensation at the time.

Dr John declared that he resented th appointment of ex-Nazis and SS men in hig places, but he had said such things before in Wes Germany. His great mistake, speaking on communist platform, was to assert that thi statement was made in East Berlin, because h would never have been permitted to speak out i the West, which was palpably untrue.

He compounded the error by broadcastin similar remarks, and adding that it had becom impossible for him to continue in his office. If tha were so he could perfectly easily have announce his resignation in Bonn and explained his reason there. What caused offence was that he was doin so in East Berlin.

The mystery of Dr John's apparent defection o

as he thought of it, his kidnapping — and it has to be remembered that kidnapping to the East was by no means uncommon at that time — continued for almost a year. Then he arrived back in East Berlin, after a stay in Moscow and on the Black Sea, in December 1955. At the Press Club he told a Danish journalist that he wanted to return, and together they drove over to West Berlin, where John was arrested.

At his subsequent trial he was sentenced to four years in prison despite his protestations that he had been kidnapped, and that he had only agreed to speak publicly at the press conference in order to remain free enough to make his eventual escape. Dr Wohlgemuth, who was an East German agent, did not attend the trial, but simply wrote to say that Dr John had asked to be taken over the border.

Opinions about the motives behind this affair are still divided. Otto John was known as an amiable and sociable person by no means noted for extremist views. Neither before nor after did he show any great taste for espionage, and even when he was running the BfV, he confined himself to reporting on activities rather than becoming involved in counter-espionage plotting.

In his own book, written in 1968, he expressed the view that he had been kidnapped because of his wartime connection with Kim Philby, the British double agent. During John's time in Madrid Philby ran the Iberian section of the Secret Intelligence Service and was determined, in the interests of his Soviet masters, to thwart attempts by the anti-Hitler plotters to make a separate peace with the Western Allies.

In 1954 Philby had not yet been exposed, and Otto John was not aware of his double-agent role. However, he reported that the Russians often questioned him about Philby. In hindsight, this gave him the impression that they were not at all certain about the loyalty of their man in SIS.

The most convincing fact in favour of Dr John's version of his experiences is that he did take the opportunity to return to Western Germany. After his release from prison he played no further part in public life.

JOHNSON, Sergeant Robert Lee

When this dim and drunken US army NCO stationed in Berlin, a man with no future and plenty of grudges and resentments, made contact with the KGB by way of his Austrian wife in 1952 only a patient and imaginative Soviet state security officer could ever have considered that he would eventually turn into a prize agent. Johnson himself thought that if he defected he might become a big radio star for the Russians!

They had other long-term plans, which brought a rich reward in espionage material. For the time being they were content to train the sergeant in spycraft, pay him and take delivery of minor photographed material from the American army's HQ, where he worked in Berlin.

As a bonus Johnson also brought in a fellow-NCO, Sergeant James Mintkenbaugh, a 35-year-old friend who was a secret homosexual. He too came in useful to the KGB.

Indeed, it was Mintkenbaugh who reactivated Johnson four years later, by which time he had returned to the US after the vicissitudes of Service life, and had left the army. On KGB orders he rejoined and got himself posted to Paris — not to Shape, as they had hoped, but by chance to the Armed Forces Courier Station at Orly airport, Paris.

This was a number one target for Soviet espionage which had long been considered impregnable. It was a kind of strategic post-office for ultra-secret written communications between the Pentagon and US army commands in Europe. It was heavily protected with steel doors, multiple locks and armed guards, of whom Johnson, the weak link in the chain, was now one.

When he reported his posting to his Paris contact 'Viktor' there was jubilation in the KGB, and they planned an extremely efficient and well-co-ordinated scheme involving whole teams of specialists to exploit the fact. Johnson was first ordered to get wax imprints of the keys to the high-security vault. Then he was equipped with an X-ray device specially shipped in from Moscow Centre to identify the locking devices and combinations.

Once he was able to get into the vault 'Viktor' told him to volunteer for unpopular weekend guard duty. On Saturday nights he was alone in the Orly establishment for several hours, which gave him time to remove the packets of documents, and hand them over to a KGB contact near by.

Within three hours, before the guard was relieved, the Russians drove the packages to the Soviet Embassy, where a special team of experts photographed them before returning them for replacement in the vault before dawn. In all, Sgt Johnson carried out seven such raids, the last one being in April 1963.

That time he blundered by going to sleep while waiting for the return of the KGB officer with the packets which had been photographed. He missed the outside rendezvous, but the Russian agent put the packets in his car, from which he recovered them, and replaced them with only minutes to spare.

The KGB, particularly anxious that the thefts should not become known to the Americans and highly satisfied with their haul to date, called off operations for the time being. What they had got from the sergeant-spy was invaluable — US contingency plans for international crises, force dispositions, cryptographic materials and estimates of both Soviet and NATO strengths and weaknesses.

A Russian defector to the United States reported that such was the delight of the intelligence service at the high-class information they had taken that papers were shown to Chairman Khruschev. Technically, the operation had been conducted with enormous skill and brilliant co-ordination.

The wretched Johnson was posted back to the US in the following year and worked at the Pentagon, but nothing more could match what he had accomplished for the Soviets already. His Austrian wife Hedwig — partly because of constant worry about the dangers of spying — was undergoing psychiatric treatment. She was also making life hell for her husband.

Acutely depressed himself by constant domestic threats and nagging, he disappeared in October 1964, taking a drunken bus ride to Las Vegas. FB men investigating his disappearance questioned his wife, and listened with amazement to he incoherent account of his espionage adventures.

Eventually Johnson, broke and miserable, gave himself up to the local police. Both he and Sergeant Mintkenbaugh were tried and sentenced in July 1965 to twenty-five years in prison. Seven years later Johnson's son Robert returned from army service in Vietnam to visit his father in prison and stabbed him to death — for personal reasons he explained. Johnson was then fifty-two.

KACHENKO, Dr Vladimir

Soviet state security officers in London used particularly dirty trick to recover this 25-year-ol Russian scientist who had been legitimate working at Birmingham University with un classified research on a low temperature physic project. He attracted attention by going to th Soviet Embassy in the early hours of the mornin of 16 September 1967.

Several hours later he went back, and was see by MI5 watchers leaving the Embassy, an walking along Bayswater Road. Four Embass officials, including a known KGB officer name Shischkin, pursued him in a car. They caught u with a screeching of brakes, and snatched th scientist and took him back to the embassy 'fo treatment'.

For them to act so publicly in a London stree something important must have been at stake This was not the only drama of that Saturda morning, for soon a convoy of Soviet diploma cars was heading for London Airport, and th dazed Dr Kachenko was bundled aboard Tupolev flight for Moscow.

Near the end of the runway its pilot was ordere

to hold, and seven London police cars surrounded the aircraft. Special Branch officers who boarded the flight found Dr Kachenko was barely conscious, but he said he wanted to talk in private, so he was removed and taken to an MI5 safe house.

Dr William Sargent, the eminent British psychiatrist who examined him, found a puncture mark on his arm, but as he did not know what drug had been pumped in he advised against further treatment, especially as the scientist's condition was deteriorating. He also found indications of schizophrenia.

This placed British security officers in a quandary. Because the doctors did not know what antidote to prescribe, it seemed more than likely that Kachenko would die. They had been outsmarted by the KGB, which had administered the original drug and were now in a position to make propaganda out of the death of a Russian while he was held by the British.

Dr Kachenko had to be returned to the Soviet Embassy, and he was at once flown to Moscow. Nothing more was heard of him, though his wife — no doubt on KGB orders — accused the British of attempting to kidnap her husband.

KALININ, V. G.

The unknown spy about whose life and death the only publicly recorded facts were those set out in a brief item in only one Soviet newspaper, *Izvestia*. His first names were not recorded, and no mention was made about who he was spying for, or why.

His name is a common one; he was the Mr Smith of the USSR. His only claim to fame was that he became in February 1975 the first Russian espionage agent to be officially identified since Soviet security arrested, tried and executed Oleg Penkovsky twelve years before.

Izvestia, a journal not noted for investigative reporting, simply stated: 'It was established that after being recruited by foreign intelligence, Kalinin was engaged in collecting and transmitting to its representatives information constituting state and military secrets.'

When he was arrested they found secret information ready for sending, coding equipment and other espionage materials. He was tried by the Supreme Court for treason and spying, found guilty and shot, though not a word has survived of the no doubt stern words of the judge.

No proof was ever offered of any connection with the CIA, the SIS, or the Red Chinese intelligence service. No claim was ever made by any service that V.G. Kalinin had worked for them. Not a single diplomat was expelled after his arrest; not a single military attaché packed his bags to go on unexpected leave.

It just did not suit the Soviet authorities to say more on the life and times of V.G. Kalinin, except that his mother had denounced him, and we do not know why. He remains the unknown spy of the espionage wars.

K'ANG Sheng

The founding father of the Red Chinese intelligence service, who constructed it during the long years of the communist struggle against the nationalist regime of Chiang Kai-shek. The son of a well-to-do bourgeois merchant in Shantung, he became a communist at Shanghai University, and went off to Moscow in 1933.

Russian-trained in espionage, and almost as much at home in Moscow as in Peking, he was among the first to launch Maoist doctrinal attacks upon the 'revisionists' when the China-USSR rift first opened in 1960.

K'ang Sheng was well equipped from his earlier experiences to begin routing out Soviet agents and their Chinese contacts from his organization, quaintly known at the time as the Social Affairs Department. He exposed the Russian use of maps specially prepared by the KGB to sustain their territorial claims on the Chinese border.

Perhaps his greatest achievement was in a peculiarly Chinese form of intelligence work, the luring back home to China of overseas scientists studying in Soviet and Western universities. He compiled the dossiers on missile engineers and nuclear scientists, and devised the means to either persuade or bully them into working to create Chinese nuclear weapons, and the means to deliver them.

By 1962 this oriental spymaster with thirty years of experience in the espionage business had achieved high office in the Chinese communist party under Mao. Then came the Cultural Revolution, during which he faded from public view.

KAO Liang

Simultaneously a foreign correspondent — 'a most illustrious' correspondent, as New China News Agency called him, and a government agent — Kao Liang lived rather grandly and ostentatiously in Africa. Later he appeared in 1971 as a member of the Chinese delegation to United Nations in New York, when his country first became a member. He was always ready to oppose the Soviet Union.

For years before that he had been watched carefully on his wide-ranging travels through the third world by agents of both the American CIA and the Soviet KGB. In 1960 he was expelled from India for plotting, and a few years later they turned him out of Mauritius.

In between times Kao Liang became immensely active in Zanzibar, and was known for his diverting and lavish parties when based in Dar es Salaam, capital of Tanzania, where the Chinese were busy expanding their influence in 1961. He was always a popular figure in Africa, and not only because he disposed of lavish funds for influencing friends in favour of China.

However, his task was by no means purely social. He spied upon Soviet activities in Africa at a time when the Chinese were trying to keep them out of that continent. And like all Chinese secret agents he had to point in the other direction as well, in order to counter American and European plots in Africa.

KASTNER, Professor Hermann

One of the rare examples of a cabinet minister who was also a spy. The Professor was a liberal German brought into the East German communist government as a propaganda move. He became deputy prime minister, though unknown to the communists he supplied West German intelligence with government papers from 1949 until 1953.

His wife, who as 'Frau Minister' with special privileges was allowed to cross to West Berlin in the official government car to make frequent visits to her doctor, was his courier. Professor Kastner even managed to preserve excellent relations with the Russian commander-in-chief, General Chuikov.

Indeed, it was his friendship with the Soviet top brass which protected him as he came under increasing suspicion. Finally after the defection of a West German double agent, General Gehlen, head of West German intelligence, decided that it was too risky to leave him in place.

Plans were made for him to leave, and after his wife had been reassured that she could take her jewels with her they were smuggled by Western agents through two deserted buildings into West Berlin in 1953 and flown to Bonn.

Professor Kastner died of a heart-attack in 1957.

KEELER, Christine

The woman in the tangled case of politics and espionage centred around John Profumo, the war minister, and Eugene Ivanov, the Soviet spy in the 1960s. She was a show-biz girl turned call girl, working on behalf of Stephen Ward. At the time she was eighteen, and was described by a British intelligence officer as the most beautiful woman he had ever seen.

She was bathing naked in a swimming pool at the Cliveden estate of Lord Astor when she first met John Profumo, who was attending a weekend party there. It was not long before they made love, and the Profumo Affair was launched.

But Stephen Ward, with whom she lived, had other plans for her, in his ever grander ambitions to demonstrate how useful he was being to the British intelligence into which he was convinced he had been recruited. He nudged her into love-making with Eugene Ivanov, the jolly Soviet state security officer masquerading as assistant naval attaché.

He asked her if she could find out what were the intentions of the British Government about arming the West Germans with atomic weapons. She was obviously intended to discover such things from John Profumo, though in fact she did not.

In fact Christine did not take such things very seriously at all. 'When Stephen told me he was working for MI5, I just laughed,' she said later.

Her lively friend Mandy Rice-Davies from the same set, who later became proprietor of a Tel Aviv nightclub, made a famous remark after Lord Astor denied having met them — 'He would, wouldn't he?'

KEENAN, Helen

When she unexpectedly resigned from her job as a shorthand typist in the Prime Minister's office at 10 Downing Street in 1967 this 22-year-old girl from Halifax aroused suspicion by giving as her reason that she found the work boring. Most of the girls there found it fascinating and enjoyed the glamour of Downing Street, and an alert Special Branch officer decided to question Helen.

She told him the real reason for wanting to leave was that she had been passing copies of Cabinet minutes to a man named Norman Blackburn whom she met at the Zambesi Club. He told her that his father was in business in Rhodesia (now Zimbabwe) and that it would be useful for him to have any papers about talks then going on between the British government and the break-away white regime of Ian Smith.

Blackburn was promptly arrested, and said that he had received papers on three occasions before Helen Keenan became alarmed. He was a professional intelligence officer attached to the South African Intelligence Service then known as BOSS, and dealt with a Rhodesian Special Branch case officer on neutral ground in Dublin.

In July 1967 Blackburn was sentenced to five years in prison and Miss Keenan got six months. For a while the British security services were more circumspect in their hitherto friendly co-operation with the South African Service.

It was also the first direct experience of espionage for Harold Wilson, the Prime Minister. Because the spying had taken place within his own office, he became sharply conscious of South African operations in Britain, and remained especially touchy on the subject.

KERR, Sir Archibald Clark

A wartime British ambassador to the United States, later elevated to the peerage as Lord Inverchapel, who did much to strengthen the American belief in English eccentricity. He arrived from Moscow bringing with him unannounced his Russian valet, an odd little man in vaguely Cossack clothes.

Stalin had offered the ambassador a farewell present of his choice, and Sir Archibald replied that he did not suppose he would permit him to take his Russian valet to Washington. 'Why not?' replied Stalin, mischievously amused.

Among those less amused were Donald Maclean, then spying for Stalin within the British Embassy, who took a priggish view; and J. Edgar Hoover of the FBI, whose agents were laboriously sorting through even menial staff at the Embassy in an elimination process to get at the big one they knew was there. The security men were simply speechless.

The valet made a number of enemies, partly because he insisted on poking about in various parts of the building, including the Registry, to the great annoyance of Maclean. After a few months Sir Archibald was persuaded to arrange to part with his manservant, not because there was any evidence that he was spying, but because disapproval was general.

Sir Archibald after his retirement died in 1951.

The valet was last heard of opening a fish-and-chip shop in Rothesay, Scotland which he had set up with a legacy from Sir Archibald, so that he was

saved from the fate of returning to his native
Soviet Union.

KING, Captain John Henry

The first British spy working for a foreign Power
to be caught in the opening days of the Second
World War. He had been named by an early Soviet
defector, Major-General Walter Krivitsky, as one
of their men in the Foreign Office, where he
worked in the coding department.

He was arrested red-handed on his way to
deliver a secret message to a Soviet contact at a
tea-room in the Strand, London. At his trial in
camera at the Old Bailey in October 1939 he was
sentenced to ten years' imprisonment.

KIRKPATRICK, Lyman B.

An ambitious Central Intelligence Agency officer
who at one time seemed to stand a good chance of
becoming Director. He was a big, confident,
former football player who was struck down with
polio while on Agency business in Asia. He
eventually returned to duty in a wheel-chair, but
the moment for promotion had passed.

He succeeded only to the extent that he became
Inspector-General in 1953, which gave him
unrivalled opportunities to impose his own ideas
by looking into any part of the organization which
interested him. When he seized such opportunities
it caused ill-feeling. His strongly critical report of
the CIA involvement in the Cuban invasion
disaster at the Bay of Pigs, and of the officers
concerned in its planning and execution, provoked
deep resentments. The Agency was already in a
state of gloom and depression about its failure,
and to many the report seemed unnecessarily
harsh.

After nine years as inspector, Lyman Kirkpatrick became comptroller as well, the third most
important man in the hierarchy. In that capacity
he stayed on for another two years until he
resigned once he felt convinced that he would
never become director. He went to teach political
science at Brown University.

KISHAK-COHEN, Shulamit

This mother of seven in Beirut was a most unlikely
choice even by the standards of the Israeli
intelligence service to run a Lebanon spy-ring. At
her trial before a Lebanese court the phrase-
making prosecutor insisted on describing her as
'the Mata Hari of the Middle East'. However,
although she was undoubtedly an attractive and
elegant woman, it might have been more
appropriate to describe her as the Jewish mother
of espionage.

The child bride in an arranged marriage with a
much older member of the Jewish community in
Beirut, she drifted into espionage through chance
and circumstance. Born in Jerusalem, she found
herself living in the neighbouring Arab-Christian
state at the time when Israel was just establishing
itself in the late 1940s.

In the first place, and to the dismay of her
merchant husband, she helped to bring ashore to
Beirut an important anonymous Jew from a
Greek ship, and arrange for him to be smuggled
into Israel. An active and intelligent woman, she
became involved in performing the same service
for large numbers of refugee Jews from the Arab
countries.

She took up refugee-smuggling rather as
middle-class American ladies might engage in
social work, while simultaneously she devotedly
raised her large family and was for ever busy
preparing all those anniversary rituals and special
ceremonies so beloved by Jewish families.

From refugee work she slipped effortlessly into
providing Israeli intelligence with State and
political documents and information from
Lebanon and Syria. She accomplished this
through her ever-widening social contacts with the
high, and low, society of Beirut, where most
commodities — including loyalty and secrets —
may be bought, provided the price is right.

Under her code name — 'Pearl' — she made
frequent visits to Israel, where she learned the
basic elements of fieldcraft. After the Lebanese
border became more difficult to cross she
journeyed by way of the Istanbul aerial
interchange, swopping passports on the way.

In between Bar Mitzvahs and Sabbath preparations she worked hard at extending her ring of informants and protectors. A good deal of money was spent in purchasing favours and information, and at one stage the Israelis financed the establishment of the Star nightclub in Beirut as a useful meeting-place.

Eventually an ambitious young Lebanese Deuxième Bureau officer penetrated the ring. Shula Cohen, as she was generally known, came to trial, and was sentenced to death by hanging. This was finally commuted to seven years' imprisonment. After the Six Day War in 1967 she was exchanged for Lebanese captured in the fighting, and her remaining family in Beirut were allowed to emigrate to Israel. Back home she set up a flower-shop near the King David Hotel in Jerusalem.

KISLYTSIN, Filip Vasilevich

During his stay in London as a cypher clerk in the Soviet Embassy, London, from 1945 to 1948 he was in reality a high-ranking KGB man, who handled material provided by Guy Burgess, the British spy. When he went back to Moscow Centre, Kislytsin was in charge of intelligence from London agents.

In 1952 he again appeared in public, this time as a Second Secretary in the Soviet Embassy in Canberra, Australia. There he mismanaged the affair at Sydney airport in 1954 when Mrs Petrov, wife of a defecting colleague from the Embassy, Vladimir Petrov, was hustled aboard an aircraft by KGB 'heavies'. This caused a near-riot among indignant Australian spectators. She was later rescued. Not long afterwards Kislytsin returned to Moscow, where they no doubt blamed him for bungling the Petrov affair.

Vladimir Petrov himself told his debriefers later that Kislytsin had boasted to him about his London exploits. He had reported that 'the clerks of the Soviet Embassy were almost fully employed encyphering it so that it could be radioed to Moscow'.

KLUE, Warrant Officer Joseph

A South African NCO on the staff of the London embassy ordered to leave in December 1982 after another agent, and a burglar hired by him, had been sentenced for plundering documents and files from the offices of anti-apartheid black African organizations.

His agent, Peter Caselton, a Briton who had spent time in Africa, recruited a London burglar named Edward Aspinall to carry out the raids for £500 a time. Both of them were sentenced to prison — Caselton for four years and Aspinall for eighteen months.

It was the burglar who exposed the existence of this spy-ring by confessing to the Special Branch after he had been arrested for drunken driving. What their trial did reveal were the lengths to which the South African intelligence service was prepared to go to discover details of activities by the London offices of ANC, the African National Congress, and SWAPO, the South West Africa People's Organization.

Within a year Caselton had received more than £58,000. He had also worked through another known South African intelligence officer, Major Craig Williamson, who in 1980 succeeded in infiltrating the International University Exchange Fund, a Geneva organization helping students and anti-apartheid groups. He even managed to become deputy director of the fund before being discovered.

KNOBBE, Heinz

Minister and chargé d'affaires for the GDR in London, he was exposed in 1983 as East Germany's 'Resident' in Britain. An affable member of the diplomatic corps, among whom he had spent five years, his major espionage task was to mastermind the infiltration of international organizations by East German civil servants, who were then ordered to spy on and recruit fellow-members.

Knobbe was 'blown' by Gunther Mitschke, an East German who defected from his post at the

International Maritime Organization, and told everything he knew about Knobbe. One of the most interesting aspects of his story is what it revealed about the life of East Europeans in Western countries. They are spied upon by their compatriots, bullied into fulfilling espionage missions, virtually imprisoned in their homes without being allowed to travel, except in the company of other couples, and being forced to hand over professional pay-packets to their embassies in return for a subsistence allowance. Any failure to fulfil their allotted tasks or any sign of dissent led to a visit from the Embassy's 'heavies'.

KNUTH, Maria

An attractive German actress in 1951 who joined the so-called 'Kolberg Ring' of Soviet spies in Berlin run by a former Polish cavalry officer, Colonel Gregor Kowalski. She came into espionage by way of her lover, an art historian, Heinko Kunze, and it was her task while working in his antique shop to lure British and American officers, so that they could be blackmailed.

The ring as it grew more ambitious set up a villa love-nest near Cologne and an apartment in Frankfurt. Ironically, Kunze, a former army officer, became the first victim. He committed suicide, distressed by the knowledge that his mistress was being turned into a spy-whore.

Kowalski and his masters were specially anxious to get information about plans at the time for the re-establishment of a German army, and this came to the ears of the Gehlen Organization, the embryo West German intelligence service, who placed in his path a double agent — Dr Petersen, who claimed to be working in the office of Chancellor Adenauer.

He became the bait for Maria Knuth, telling her of his doubts about the need for German rearmament, and promising to supply information about it. British and American intelligence officers joined with the West Germans in providing false information, while Maria's activities were monitored.

Finally, it was officers from the British MI5 who arrested Maria Knuth in a Cologne post-office where she was collecting a *poste restante* letter from Colonel Kowalski. The ring was broken, though the Polish colonel escaped in 1952. A German federal court sentenced Maria to only three years' imprisonment, as she was known to be suffering from cancer. She died two years later in the prison hospital.

KOKHLOV, Captain Nicolai

The first Smersh agent from the KGB execution squad to defect to the Americans, while on a mission to West Germany in 1954. He had orders from Nikita Khruschev to kill Georgi Okolovich, a leader of NTS, the anti-Soviet émigré organization with headquarters in Frankfurt. He had been carefully trained as an assassin, and was equipped with a miniature weapon firing poison pellets.

Once in Frankfurt, Captain Kokhlov, an experienced wartime guerrilla leader as well as a KGB agent, changed his mind. He went to his compatriot in the NTS and said that he wanted to surrender, and was then turned over to the Americans.

Kokhlov also identified two fellow-agents on similar missions in West Germany, and they were arrested. After he had made a lecture tour explaining the bloodcurdling activities of Smersh, the KGB hit back in September 1957 by poisoning him. For many weeks he hovered between life and death before American doctors alerted by Okolovich, the intended victim of Kokhlov, discovered that the poison was in fact radioactive thallium. He was treated, and survived.

In 1981 Igor Okolovich was still in touch with him and reported that he had news of his doing parapsychological work in California.

KOZLOV, Major Alexei

A tough-looking KGB officer arrested in 1980 by South African intelligence on what they claimed he had told them was his third mission to southern Africa to evaluate the effectiveness of black nationalist guerrillas in that part of the world. He had previously served in West Germany.

Two years later he was released in a complicated exchange in return for a South African soldier named Johann van der Mescht, who had been held for four years after his capture by left-wing guerrillas in Angola. The arrangement, which also included the release of seven other Western prisoners held in Africa, showed the extent of Soviet influence on left-wing irregulars in the south of the continent.

KRIVITSKY, Major General Walter

The first high-ranking KGB spymaster to defect to the West, he arrived in 1937 with a mass of information about the workings of the organization. This Polish Jew, originally named Ginsberg, forlornly tried to break through the atmosphere of disbelief and warn of Soviet penetration of Western society. Director of Russian spy networks in Western Europe with headquarters in Paris, he sought refuge in France after being summoned home to Moscow following the murder by a Soviet hit-team of Ignace Reiss, his colleague in Switzerland.

In the United States where he went next, Krivitsky was interrogated, and provided detailed information about Soviet espionage. It was the American journalist ghosting his book who drew the attention of the British Ambassador to his evidence about British spies.

Krivitsky then went to London to denounce three highly placed British spies. Two of them, he claimed, had penetrated the Foreign Office. He provided circumstantial descriptions of one and named another. He also knew about another British-Soviet agent who had posed as a journalist for a London paper in the Spanish civil war.

Had his information been assiduously followed up it might have led to the unmasking of the Cambridge group of spies. As it was, in the early days of the war, British intelligence was content that his visit led to the arrest and conviction of

Captain John Henry King of the Foreign Office coding department, who was working for the Russians.

The unfortunate Krivitsky was found shot dead in his hotel room in Washington in 1941. Although a verdict of suicide was given, it is almost certain that he was killed by a Soviet assassin.

'KROGER', Peter and Helen

When this agreeable 'Canadian' couple presented themselves in the London suburb of Catford in 1955 looking for a nice furnished house to rent there seemed to be no reason for unease or suspicion. Peter was a quiet, thoughtful man with grey hair; his wife was a rather noisy transatlantic extrovert.

They had chosen to live in Britain because of Peter's health, and so that he could make his living as a dealer in rare books from a room in the Strand. They did not mention to the neighbours that he specialized in works on sado-masochism and torture. They were also KGB specialists in deep-cover operations.

After a while the friends they had made locally were sorry to hear that this sociable pair were leaving the district because they had found and bought a good-sized bungalow — better for the books — at 45 Cranley Drive in Ruislip to the west of London.

Soon it became the centre of pleasant social gatherings, and among the visitors was a confident man, introduced by Helen as 'our young Canadian friend, Gordon Lonsdale'. He often spent the weekend with the book-dealer and his wife.

Helen was one of those women given to popping in on the neighbours, and she was often to be found drinking tea in the kitchen with Mrs Search across the road in Courtfield Gardens. They were good neighbours, and when Mr and Mrs Search celebrated their twenty-fifth wedding anniversary in 1957 Mrs Kroger presented them with a box of silver spoons.

It came as quite a shock to the Search family

when in November 1960 they received a telephone call from the local police, followed by a visit from Jim Skardon of MI5. He did not tell them very much except to say that a question of national security was involved, and he would like to have permission for two of his watchers to spend the weekend in the suburban house in Courtfield Gardens to watch out for a wanted man whom they suspected came to the district.

Jim Skardon showed Mr Search, who was an aircraft engineer, a photograph of Gordon Lonsdale, but Mr Search had never seen him. That was just the beginning of a long operation which kept a team of girls from the British security service in Mrs Search's kitchen, and in her daughter's bedroom overlooking the Kroger bungalow. They were there for two months, and the quiet Ruislip family suddenly found that the world of international espionage had moved into their cluttered drawing-room.

The trail which led to the modest house in west London had begun when Michal Goleniewski, a Polish intelligence officer, arrived in Washington, and during his debriefing reported that there was a British naval spy for the KGB who had once worked at the British Embassy in Warsaw. British intelligence identified him as Harry Houghton, a retired chief petty officer, and by keeping watch on him they discovered Gordon Lonsdale. They then had followed Lonsdale to the Kroger bungalow in Ruislip.

For two months MI5 watched the suspects, and on the first Saturday in January 1961 Special Branch police officers arrested Houghton, with his girl friend, 'Bunty' Gee, as they were passing secret papers to Lonsdale near the Old Vic theatre. Detective Superintendent George Smith promptly signalled, 'Lock, stock and barrel' and drove straightway to Ruislip.

Peter Kroger opened the door, and the police officers told him they were investigating a robbery in the district. Once inside they got down to business with questions about Lonsdale, and then arrested the Krogers. When Helen asked if she might stoke up the boiler before being taken off to headquarters they prudently searched her hand-bag first. It contained a cypher message, three

microdots mounted in microscope slides, and a five-page letter in Russian dated that day.

A thorough search of the house uncovered an array of espionage equipment, a device for reading microdots, a Ronson lighter with a code message in it, and onetime cypher pads on quick-burning paper which gave several Moscow Centre call signs. The police also found quantities of money and several false passports, both Canadian and New Zealand.

More detailed investigation, which lasted a whole week, revealed the presence of a high-power radio transmitter equipped for sending in rapid bursts. There could be no doubt that the quiet Krogers were manning a communications centre for sending naval secrets stolen by Houghton to Moscow. Years later in 1980 new tenants in the bungalow digging in the garden found yet another Soviet transmitter.

Examination of the Krogers' fingerprints by the American FBI proved conclusively that the people known as the Krogers were in fact an American couple, Morris and Lona Cohen. They had suddenly disappeared from their apartment on East 71st Street, New York, on the day that the FBI arrested Julius and Ethel Rosenberg, who belonged to a Soviet network in the United States which had passed atomic secrets to Moscow. After a sensational trial the Rosenbergs went to the electric chair in 1953, but their close associates the Cohens were warned in time to make their escape.

The American dossiers showed that Morris Cohen had been born in 1910 in the Bronx, the son of East European immigrants. He became a university communist before going off to fight in Spain. Before joining the US army he married Lona, an immigrant communist like himself. Even before the war they had both begun spying for the Soviet Union.

Well provided with a stock of forged passports, they travelled widely in all parts of the world between their disappearance in 1951 and their arrival in London four years later. By then they had assumed the identity of Peter and Helen Kroger, the names of two people who in fact had died some time before in New Zealand.

When they were sentenced to twenty years in

prison the Lord Chief Justice described them as professional spies, though he did not believe that they were the directing minds in this case. In fact the Kroger-Cohens were released in October 1969 in exchange for Gerald Brooke, a British lecturer imprisoned by the Russians for distributing subversive literature in the USSR. The Russians deliberately held him and mistreated him in order to have in their hands a pawn to trade against the Krogers.

By sleight of hand the Russians were able to claim that the Krogers were in fact Polish citizens, and by this means prevented them from being deported to the United States, where the FBI would have been waiting. So they returned first class to Warsaw, and Peter's last words (which displayed a talent for the English vernacular) were to British journalists on the flight. 'Ta-Ta', he said, 'and say goodbye for me to all the lads in Parkhurst.'

Normally when Russian spies go in out of the cold nothing more is heard. But in this case, thanks to the information provided by Peter McGill — a Scotsman working in London as a floor-layer who had struck up by chance an entirely innocent friendship with the Krogers — it was possible to peep through the Iron Curtain.

During his eight years in prison Kroger wrote to McGill, who had kindly visited him there, and later invited him to Lublin in Poland. He spoke of the pleasures of the garden and of the cherry harvest 'at home', ready for distilling into brandy to celebrate their 'return'. Only once did this friendly neighbourhood spy write about espionage, and that was to say: 'Every man to his trade, and this is mine.'

Back in New York one of his old classmates was astonished when he heard that Peter Kroger was a spy. They had always called him Uncle, and he said, 'Nobody could ever think of "Unc" Cohen being a hot shot espionage agent.'

After a few months in Poland the Kroger-Cohens sank from view. They were by then getting on in years, and it is quite likely that they used their undoubted talents for deep-cover work in the West to instruct a new generation of KGB sleepers for work in the field.

KROTKOV, Yuri Vasilevich

A Georgian from Tbilisi with lifelong connections with the KGB by way of his father (who painted a popular picture of the notorious Beria), he became a sort of freelance agent specializing in the techniques of trapping Western visitors and residents into compromising situations. As a tall and presentable dramatist and film writer who talked easily on cultural subjects, he was popular with the foreign community.

He was also noted for having available a ready supply of what the service (poetically, for once) calls 'swallows' — namely, attractive KGB helpers willing to oblige in return for favours. He recruited them from among his showbiz friends in the film set.

In June 1956 he was selected to mount the long-drawn-out seduction operation planned at the top to compromise French diplomats, including the ambassador, Maurice Dejean. Krotkov made friends with Madame Dejean, though he failed in his amorous advances. He contrived outings and social gatherings, including one at the specially loaned dacha of the KGB boss, General Serov. The French diplomats anxious to make friends with real Soviet people did not realize that the personnel were specially provided.

The plot succeeded in entrapping the ambassador but came to grief when Colonel Louis Guibaud, the air attaché (who was compromised with a woman) shot himself rather than betray his country.

His death greatly affected Krotkov, who felt responsible for it. On a visit to London in charge of a visiting group of Soviet authors and artists in 1963 he slipped away and made contact with British intelligence. To them he revealed the whole plot, and details were promptly passed to the Americans and the French. He later testified before the US Senate Internal Security Committee.

KRUMMINS, Zigurd

At the age of seventeen this Latvian boy joined the German army simply to fight against the hated

Russians, and in 1945 ended up in a British prisoner-of-war camp in Germany. Scouts from the Secret Intelligence Service spotted him there, and after a course in radio in England he volunteered for a cold-war mission in the Baltic countries.

In 1952, together with a compatriot named Janis Plos, he was landed in Estonia by a British trawler on a clandestine mission. Once there he made contact with partisan groups carrying out sabotage operations against the Russian occupying troops, and succeeded in making contact by radio with his British base.

He was able to operate for nearly two years before being captured by Soviet security troops. At Riga he was sentenced as a traitor and a spy to fifteen years.

Nothing more would have been heard of him had it not been for the fact that in 1960 he was by chance placed in the same cell in Vladimir prison as Gary Powers, the American U2 reconnaissance pilot shot down over the Soviet Union. He told his story to Powers, and when the American was released on exchange Krummins still had six years to serve.

KUCZYNSKI, Ursula Ruth

A professional, though still mysterious, spy for the KGB, she was the daughter of a German Jewish professor of economics who settled in England and taught at Oxford University. The first sighting of her in the world of espionage was when she appeared in Shanghai in the thirties with her first husband, Rudolph Hamburger, who was also a Soviet agent.

In 1935 he was arrested and detained by the authorities there, but Ursula escaped to Switzerland with her two daughters and made her home in Montreux. Three years later Alexander Foote, who became radio operator for the wartime Soviet spy ring codenamed Lucy, met her in Geneva, and was recruited into the organization she was then establishing.

He had first made contact in North London with her sister, Birgette, and she passed him on. In 1940 the KGB ordered Ursula to Britain, and she

lived in Oxford. It seems that during the war she operated a spy radio there, furnishing secret material and assessments, some of which were provided by her father, who was well connected in government circles.

Foote described her as a 'demurely dressed woman with black hair, good figure and better legs'. Her obvious attractions did not, however, prevent him from denouncing her as a communist spy when he returned to Britain after the war.

In August 1947, the same year that Foote returned home, MI5 and police officers went to question her in a village near Chipping Norton where she lived with her second husband, Leon Beurton. As an excuse they claimed that they were investigating her bigamous marriage, though she denied that she was still married to Hamburger. However, she did admit to having been a Soviet agent, while claiming that she was one no longer.

The security men had reason to regret later that they had not pressed their investigations and had accepted her word, for by this time she had played a role in reactivating Klaus Fuchs, the atom spy. On his return from the United States he had hesitated for a while before getting in touch with his Soviet controllers, but eventually he was sent to report to Ursula. On two occasions he had dealings with her before going to work in America on the atom bomb project, once in 1941 and once in 1943, when she told him how to contact Harry Gold in New York.

It has been suggested that Ursula Kuczynski was the case officer for a number of British agents, and even that she had been in touch with Sir Roger Hollis, eventually the head of MI5, who was investigated as a possible double agent. He too had lived abroad in both China and in Switzerland, though he denied that he had ever met her.

What is known for certain is that after the MI5 call at her home Ursula — now Beurton — and her husband left for a holiday in East Berlin from which they never returned. Ursula was last heard of a few years ago living in East Germany, by this time in her seventies. The Kuczynskis were a curious family of spies. Not only did the professor help his daughter, who was a Soviet agent, but also the other daughter Birgette apparently spied for the cause, as did her brother Jürgen, who also finally returned to East Germany.

KUZICHKIN, Vladimir Andreyevich

A comparatively young major in the KGB at thirty-five, this Moscow University historian and student of oriental languages and fluent speaker of Farsi, arrived in Britain in October 1982 after quitting his cover post as consul in the Soviet Embassy in Teheran. Because he is such a recent arrival in the West, bringing gifts of intelligence and seeking asylum in return, not a great deal has yet emerged from his testimony, though it was put about by British intelligence that he was a big fish.

Certainly the effects of his information about affairs in Iran, where he had moved about freely, and specialized in close contact with Iranian communists, were immediate. Hundreds of members of Tudeh, the communist fringe group there, were arrested, and many were executed.

In May 1983 the Ayatollah Khomeini regime announced that the Tudeh party was officially dissolved, after its secretary-general Noureddin Kianouri had confessed to having been a Soviet spy since 1945. More Iranians were rounded up, and the government ordered eighteen of the forty Soviet diplomats in Teheran to leave within forty-eight hours, for spying and contact with traitors.

This encouraged the belief that in order to get Kuzichkin out of Teheran — a difficult place from which to arrange a defection — British intelligence had done a deal with the Iranian Government. In return for providing them with his information about Soviet activities in their country, they helped him to fly out to Paris, after which he was brought to London. This would also have had the advantage of allowing the British to do a good turn to the Iranians, in return for possible later favours.

Vladimir Kuzichkin had disappeared in Teheran in July 1982, leaving his car outside Iranian intelligence headquarters. He had served in Iran since 1977, and this posed the question of whether he had in fact been working as a British double agent for some time.

On his arrival in Britain he was taken for prolonged debriefing to a safe house in Sussex, and the CIA was also brought in to question him about matters of interest to them. Ever since the affair of the American Embassy in Teheran, and the seizure of hostages there, the United States has had to rely heavily upon British and other Western sources for intelligence from Iran.

Only a limited amount of Kuzichkin's information became public — in for example an article by him in *The Sunday Times* of London, which mostly concerned the problems of corruption and possible civil strife facing Yuri Andropov, then Soviet leader. He correctly predicted in advance Andropov's moves against corruption and to tighten labour discipline.

The question remains, how much information was he able to provide about KGB networks in Europe and in the Middle East? It was certainly after his arrival in the West that Britain, France and Belgium smartly expelled a number of Soviet diplomats and trade-mission officials in their countries, but no connection was made officially.

Experience with assessment of defectors' information proves that KGB officers are often well informed about the activities of colleagues operating far away from the countries where they themselves are stationed. Kuzichkin worked for the S Branch of the KGB, which has control over officers running networks of 'illegals' in foreign countries. Such men gain a good deal of worldwide information through office gossip with colleagues on their visits to Moscow, who over a vodka or two are happy to boast about their achievements in the field.

LACOSTE, Vice-Admiral Pierre

In yet another reshuffle in the direction of French espionage services the Admiral became the first naval officer in France ever to head the external intelligence organization, the DGSE, in November 1982. The prime task of this experienced officer was to provide high-grade intelligence reports on the Middle East and the Mediterranean region. Also at a time when the socialist government had decided to increase French influence in Latin America, with a view to becoming a principal supplier of military equipment to that area, the Admiral was required to improve intelligence-gathering potential in that part of the world.

The appointment of a 58-year-old naval officer to carry out such tasks was welcomed by the French intelligence community, upset by earlier political interference with their duties. He replaced Pierre Marrion, an outsider called in by President Mitterrand.

LAVON, Pinhas

The most tortuous and long-running of all the Israeli scandals of politics and espionage revolved around this old youth movement and trade union militant who in 1954 had become an incompetent Defence Minister at the age of fifty.

A group of plotting special forces officers and Israeli secret service men, convinced that they had the backing of Pinhas Lavon, launched a mad and ruthless operation in Egypt which ended in disaster for those involved. At the time the Israelis were alarmed by the increasing power of Egypt's new ruler, President Gamal Abdul Nasser. As they saw it, the British were aiding him by being about to withdraw their troops from the bases in the Suez Canal Zone. The Canal had already been closed to Israeli shipping.

What was even more distressing in Tel Aviv was the fact that the Americans, their principal allies under General Eisenhower, seemed to be favouring President Nasser. Quite properly, the then Israeli government was attempting by diplomatic means to persuade the Anglo-Americans that they were misguided in this policy.

At the Ministry of Defence and at intelligence headquarters wilder actions were in preparation. Military intelligence under Colonel Benjamin

Gibli thought they might help by launching a series of terrorist bomb attacks on British and American government and business offices in Cairo and Alexandria and blame them on the Egyptians. By this unlikely and devious means they hoped to persuade the Americans and British to turn against Colonel Nasser.

Even if the operation had succeeded it could hardly have influenced Anglo-American actions at the time. As it was, those carrying it out were blundering and amateurish, and easy game for the shrewd Egyptian director of counter-intelligence, Colonel Osman Nouri.

Of the group of eleven — mostly composed of Jews living in Egypt — one man known as Paul Frank was a traitor. Only he and the operational chief, Colonel Dar, escaped; two were executed in January 1955, and one committed suicide, while the rest were imprisoned. The only result of the plot was the further suffering of Egyptian Jews.

With almost British understatement, General Moshe Dayan referred to it as the 'security mishap' and wrote later that he had warned an officer of the special forces unit to be wary of Lavon's eagerness to activate it. Even though the details remained a secret much stronger words were used in government circles in Tel Aviv.

Pinhas Lavon, who knew little about defence matters, was generally blamed. So was the Defence Ministry, though Mossad apparently washed its hands of the affair. When questions were asked in parliament and a secret investigation was held Colonel Gibli, who gave the launching signal, declared that he had verbal orders from Lavon. But Lavon stated that the officer had acted on his own initiative.

A two-man committee of investigation produced a report which remained secret at the time. Its cautious and neutral tone served no purpose but to split politicians and Ministers into rival camps, divided by fierce arguments, and as pressure mounted Pinhas resigned in February 1955. David Ben Gurion came out of retirement to take over the Defence Ministry.

Even that was not the end of the affair. More details emerged with the arrest and trial in 1957 of Paul Frank, the betrayer of the terrorist group, and this revived the scandal with political repercussions.

Finally in 1960 Pinhas asked to be exonerated of blame, claiming that new evidence had come to light. Ben Gurion refused this, though he did order a new inquiry by General Chaim Laskov, the chief of staff.

Still the affair would not go away, even when a committee of seven Ministers looked into the plot again. They concluded that it was impossible to determine what were working conditions in the Ministry of Defence in 1955, though there was nothing to show that Lavon had given orders for the operation which had been carried out without his authorization.

Pinhas Lavon held no further public office. He died in 1976.

LAZIN, Viktor

When this Second Secretary at the Soviet Embassy in London was given his marching orders in August 1981 he achieved the doubtful distinction of being the first Russian diplomat to be expelled since the mass clear-out of 105 spies from Britain in 1971. He had been caught red-handed trying to pay money, but the identity of the person he was intent on luring into an espionage ring has never emerged.

There were several versions at the time, but the Foreign Office remained remarkably discreet on the subject. One form of the Lazin story was that he had tried to recruit a well-known American businessman, another that he was suborning a British civil servant. He was a KGB officer specializing in technology and scientific affairs, a field in which the Russians became very active in the 1970s.

A London double-glazer later claimed that he had played a part in exposing Lazin's activities by placing a bug at a conference in the Soviet trade mission. London neighbours of Lazin in Kensington also revealed that it was an open secret in the neighbourhood that British security men had been keeping watch on his house from a nearby apartment.

In retaliation for the expulsion the Soviets ordered John Gordon, the British cultural attaché, to leave Moscow.

LEE, Andrew Daulton

At a time when the Americans were making great efforts to develop new and ever more complex space and electronics espionage devices Soviet intelligence, always anxious to probe such developments, had two pieces of extraordinary good fortune.

One Briton and two Americans well placed to help volunteered to feed highly secret information without the KGB having to make any effort at all. Geoffrey Prime, then in the Royal Air Force, left a note in January 1968 with a Soviet officer at a Berlin checkpoint offering his services.

In April 1975, while Prime was moving into top-secret work at Government Communications Headquarters at Cheltenham, an American with a bushy moustache named Daulton Lee stepped into the Soviet Embassy in Mexico City and handed an envelope to the first official he noticed.

'Enclosed is a computer card from the National Security Agency crypto system' was the message. 'If you want to do business, please advise the courier.'

It was an offer no KGB man could resist. For Daulton Lee was able to reveal to them that his partner in this sales enterprise was Christopher Boyce, a 22-year-old Californian dropout who despite his lowly position as a $140 a week clerk, could put his hands on the most sensitive material. Boyce worked in the code-room of the Special Projects Office of TRW, the builder of the latest spy satellites.

Although physical security on the establishment was tight, Boyce was one of the six people cleared to enter the code-room known as the Black Vault. Inside was the equipment for scrambling telephone calls to CIA headquarters at Langley, Virginia, and special crypto machines for the automatic coding of written messages backward and forward. It was one of Boyce's tasks to change the cypher key settings each day, for the transmission of messages between secret stations controlling spy satellites. There were also messages about new satellite developments and projects.

Equipped with the most discreet of Minox cameras, Boyce began photographing key cards and quantities of messages, exposing occult secrets.

The task of Daulton Lee, son of a prosperous Californian doctor, who had graduated to espionage by way of peddling marijuana, was to fly down to Mexico (which he knew well from his previous enterprises) and deliver the material to the Soviets there. The Russians had only one complaint. That was about the technical quality of the photographs. So, to remedy this, they arranged for Daulton Lee to fly to Vienna for a two-month course in technique. About the same time the KGB also flew Geoffrey Prime the English spy to the same city, which appears to be a favourite place for them.

For more than a year the American partners delivered huge quantities of material for which the Soviets paid large sums of money. Then in 1976 Boyce became certain that Daulton Lee was cheating and handing over to him only a small part of this money. So he himself made the journey to Mexico City for the first time, and got on with the Russians even better than his junky friend.

One more delivery was promised for a payment of $75,000. The partners in an orgy of spy photography were to deliver the secrets of TRW's project to construct a covert satellite network so that the CIA could operate in 'denied areas' of the world. It was code-named 'Pyramider'.

Early in 1977 Daulton Lee with hundreds of negatives in his pocket again flew to Mexico. But he was late in arriving, and could not make contact with his KGB minder, Boris Alexei Grishin.

It was then that he made the fatal mistake. Badly needing money for a fix, he forgot everything he had been taught on the crash course of espionage in Vienna. He went to the Embassy and hurled through the railings the cover of a dictionary with the letters KGB written on the inside.

Mexican police on duty at the Embassy,

thinking Lee must be a terrorist, grabbed him and took him to the police station, where they discovered the Minox films. Within days he was handed over to the FBI, and he and Boyce were separately charged with espionage.

At their trials much was made of the disillusionment of these two American dropouts in the wake of Vietnam, and the Watergate and CIA scandals. But it seemed clear that it was lust for money rather than anxiety about the capitalist system which impelled them into treachery.

Because of the gravity of their betrayal, they received exemplary sentences. Daulton Lee, the instigator of their acts, got life imprisonment, and Boyce forty years.

LEVCHENKO, Stanislas

Son of a Russian general, and well connected in Moscow. After an extensive course in Japanese language and a quick course in journalism, intended to make it possible for him to convince other journalists that he really was one, Levchenko arrived in Tokyo in 1975. He was ostensibly the correspondent of a notably boring Soviet trade union publication, *New Times*.

His real task, so he declared later before a US congressional committee of investigation, after he had fled to the CIA in 1979, was to cultivate politicians and journalists. According to his own rather fulsome account of his successes, he had a ring of some two hundred persons and was paying out to individuals up to $2,000 a month.

'Japan is a spy's paradise,' he reported. That may well be true, for Japanese law does not award sentences of more than twelve months even for military and government servants who practise that trade.

Levchenko's political conquests appear to have been largely in the Japanese socialist party, though the people that he named have denied being spies. He himself claimed that he could identify others, but did not want to do so in case they committed suicide. But a Japanese government spokesman who did not appear to take the allegations very seriously suggested that the KGB had been lobbying, rather than recruiting spies.

In fact the Levchenko revelations made remarkably little impact upon Japanese political life, and it may well be that the defector was a touch over-anxious to display his own importance.

LI HUNG-shu

A Chinese agent spying on behalf of the rival communist power, the Soviet Union. He was caught in January 1974 handing a secret report to KGB case officers from their embassy in Peking, and collecting from them a radio transmitter.

The only information about the man himself came from the Chinese authorities, who claimed that he had been trained in Moscow by Soviet military intelligence. In December 1973 he received a coded telegram ordering him to make contact with V.I. Marchenko, First Secretary of the Russian Embassy in Peking.

He made his way into China overland, collected secret information about conditions in the Chinese provinces bordering the Soviet Union, Mutankiang and Chiamuszu, and then took a train to the capital. Once there he exchanged messages with the Russians over a miniature radio and fixed a live drop by night near a bridge outside Peking.

But security forces and the people's militia had been alerted, and as the Russians left their car a red flare was fired, and they rushed the party. Li Hung-shu with his suitcase radio legged it for the nearest commune, but was caught. Needless to say, he admitted all, though none of the Chinese statements about the affair mentioned his fate.

The five Soviet diplomats were expelled at once. The Russians naturally retaliated. They arrested and later expelled a Chinese diplomat, Kuan Heng-kuan. The Chinese counter-claimed that he had been pulled off the Trans-Siberian express while travelling home at the end of a six-year posting.

LIDDELL, Captain Guy

A practised old hand in the game of espionage and counter-espionage, his career with the British MI5 began in 1919 and not only spanned the inter-war years but continued into the post-war period when British intelligence was so mole-ridden. During the Second World War he ran B division of the service, specializing in counter-espionage.

Though a first-class officer and amiable, friendly and patient, he was passed over for promotion to head MI5 and became Deputy Director-General in 1946. Clement Attlee, the Labour prime minister, mistrusted the intelligence community and brought in Sir Percy Sillitoe, a police officer, to run MI5. As they said at the time, 'He has put in a rozzer.'

Despite that, Guy Liddell soldiered on until 1953, when he was appointed chief security officer at the Harwell Atomic Energy Centre, a sensitive post. This move helped to dispel rumours and suspicions brought about by his close association with both Guy Burgess and Anthony Blunt, the British spies for Russia.

If he had a fault it was in the choice of his friends. He continued to chat unsuspectingly about security matters with Blunt after the latter left the service in 1945. Although he himself was not a homosexual, he seemed to have quite a few close acquaintances who were.

Throughout his career he kept a diary which in due course he handed over to MI5 on retirement. He died in 1958.

LINNEY, Brian Frederick

The greatest risk of eventual exposure for providers of secret information to case officers is that their identity may be known to other officers who defect, taking with them their memories and files. It was because a Czech defector had spoken in the United States that this British electronics engineer, then aged forty-two, came to be arrested in Worthing, and finally to be sentenced to fourteen years in July 1958.

Linney had met Colonel Prybl, the Czech military attaché, at a reception, and after being invited with his wife to a concert he agreed to supply secret files from the aerospace company in Shoreham, Sussex, where he worked. When questioned by British intelligence later he admitted his guilt, and said that he had met Prybl nine times and received from him £500.

LITTLEJOHN, Keith and Kenneth

The two brothers from Birmingham, both with criminal records, claimed in 1973 while standing trial in Dublin for their part in a bank raid that they were both working for British intelligence. It was their mission, they said, to make contact with the criminal fringe of the Irish Republican Army.

It was further revealed that Keith, the younger brother, had made use of Lady Onslow, a charitable visitor to the Borstal institution where he had served time, to get in touch with a government minister. Kenneth Littlejohn, the elder brother, offered information to Geoffrey Johnson Smith, junior minister at the Defence Ministry, and then met officials.

The trendy, tough-looking Littlejohns had gone to Ireland and set up a fashion boutique called Whiz Kids Ltd, and for twelve months led a busy and ostentatious social life in Dublin. It seems that they also considered it part of their intelligence-gathering task to rob banks. In 1972 warrants were issued against them by the Republic of Ireland on charges of stealing £67,000 from the Allied Irish Bank in Dublin.

At their trial they were sentenced respectively to twenty and fifteen years in prison, and it was at this embarrassing stage for the British government that they claimed they had been recruited by MI6 to infiltrate the IRA.

Under political pressure, Mr Carr, the Home Secretary, had to admit that the brothers had indeed been working for British intelligence. But he denied that they had been given any kind of immunity from arrest on law-breaking charges.

Suspicions were voiced in Ireland that the Littlejohns might also have been responsible for bomb explosions in Dublin planned as provocative acts. It was after these outrages that the Dublin government strengthened its anti-terrorist laws.

According to Nigel West in his authoritative book about MI5, *A Matter of Trust*, Sir Maurice Oldfield, head of MI6, gathered his staff to refute the allegations of the Littlejohns that they had been employed to rob banks and to carry out assassinations.

No evidence has ever emerged that the brothers were able to produce any useful information about IRA activities. They seem to have been too busy with their own interests, though they may indeed have been in touch with Irish bank-robbers. The affair served only to cool relations between London and Dublin, and to reduce co-operation between their police forces for a while.

LONG, Leo

Another graduate from Anthony Blunt's nursery of spies at Cambridge in the thirties. He was not activated by Blunt until he joined MI4 at the War Office in 1941. From his evidence it appears that Blunt was far more involved in active espionage than he admitted publicly.

The two men used to meet in London pubs, and Long would hand over information gleaned from agents operating in Europe for Blunt to pass on to the Russians. This information included reports of troop movements, with comments by British intelligence on the progress of the war. It also included some Ultra information from Bletchley.

Long said that he gave up working for the Russians in 1943, when he joined the D Day planning staff. After the war he joined the civil administration in occupied Germany, and Blunt sought him out once again and asked him to renew his spying activities, for Long was in a position to pass on invaluable information as the cold war developed. But Long insists that he refused.

Long expected to be exposed when Burgess and Maclean, fellow-members of the Blunt ring, defected to the Soviet Union, and investigations were made into their background and friends. However, he was not tracked down until 1964, when the American Whitney Straight — who had been involved with the left wing at Cambridge — named him and Blunt to the FBI. It was Straight who revealed to British intelligence that Blunt was the 'Fourth Man'.

After Blunt had confessed he advised Long to do the same, and make 'a clean breast of things.' Long, burdened with a guilty conscience, did exactly that, and although he was not officially granted immunity from arrest, no proceedings were taken against him.

He made a public confession in November 1981, only when it became obvious that he would be exposed in the great newspaper hunt for Blunt's accomplices after Blunt himself had been named as a traitor.

Long said then, 'I feel deep regret and remorse. I have lived in anxiety for years, not because this would become known to the security service (who have known about it for years), but that it would be exposed to the world.'

'LONSDALE, Gordon'

It was as a friendly, pleasant, well-dressed Canadian businessman who radiated self-confidence that Gordon Lonsdale stepped on to the London scene in 1955. He seemed to have plenty of money, and lost no time in installing himself in a smart apartment near Regent's Park. He meant to see Europe as well, and there was plenty of talk about his business interests. With a view to expanding them eastward he even signed on for a while as a Chinese-language student at the School of Oriental and African Studies.

He was always ready to talk about his activities to his circle of friends, which was quickly reinforced with a number of girl-friends — for as Mrs Kroger, a fellow-Canadian, said of him, he was definitely one for the ladies. Lonsdale began trading in juke-boxes, then bubble-gum machines, where he met with failure in attempting to export them to unwilling Italians.

A bit of a setback, that was, and for a while he had to take a more modest apartment. Even so, he kept up his playboy activities, and was undoubtedly a social success. All of which shows how carefully and professionally he was working himself into cover, ready for his main task, which was naval espionage.

For in fact he had been carefully groomed by the KGB to slip into London life, in order to take over as controller of those most valuable spies, the members of the Portland Ring, with Harry Houghton, the old naval petty officer, as the information-provider. Posing for the purpose as a US Navy commander from the Embassy in London, he often met Houghton to give him orders and to receive material for onward transmission to Moscow, via the Krogers.

From the Soviet point of view it was too good to last, for even a skilled agent like Lonsdale was not immune from the bungling behaviour of Houghton. By 1960 the meetings were being quietly observed by the men from MI5.

While Lonsdale was away on one of his foreign trips the Special Branch seized the opportunity to have a look at the case and deed-box which he had been observed to deposit at the Midland Bank. They found such spy items as a specially adapted camera for filming documents and his personal papers. The security people gave him time to lead them to the communications centre of the network at the Krogers' house and then waited for another Houghton meeting.

Finally they arrested Lonsdale with his top-secret package near the Old Vic theatre in London. With the cool approach of the old pro, he promptly declared, 'To any questions you might ask me the answer is: "No." So you needn't trouble to ask.'

When the spy nest was looked at later a very different Gordon Lonsdale emerged. For the police discovered a freshly written and warmly affectionate letter from him to his wife in Moscow, in reply to ones newly arrived from her and his children, one with a PS reading, 'Daddy, come home quickly.'

To beloved Galyusha he had written 'I know very well what loneliness is. From the age of ten, for the last twenty-nine years, I have only spent ten years among my own people. I didn't want this and I didn't seek it. It just turned out that way.'

There is, it has to be admitted, a certain pathos about the lonely, double-sided life which has to be led by a spy in the field. But because Lonsdale firmly refused to answer questions the investigators had to await help from the FBI to piece together the story of his life.

The real name behind the cover was that of Konon Trofimovich Molodi, born in Russia, the son of a well-known scientist. At the age of seven he was sent off to be educated with an aunt living at Berkeley, California, and at sixteen, in 1938, he had to decide whether to become an American citizen or return to the Soviet Union.

Back home he served with the Red Army in the war, and moved into the KGB. After training and field work, he made his appearance in 1954 in Canada to take on a new identity, that of Gordon Arnold Lonsdale, a genuine Canadian of East European descent who had disappeared in Finland during the War. So equipped, he spent a year in Canada to get his accent right and set out for London.

At the trial he was sentenced to twenty-five years, after being described by the judge as 'a professional spy'. In the manner of judges he went on to comment, 'It is a dangerous career and one in which you must be prepared, as you no doubt are, to suffer, if and when you are caught.'

Lonsdale-Molodi smiled. And he was right to smile, for within a few years an arrangement was made to exchange him for the unfortunate Briton Greville Wynne, imprisoned for his part in the Penkovsky affair in the Soviet Union. The traditional swop through the Berlin check-point took place.

Back in Moscow, and with some literary help from Kim Philby, the British defector to the Soviets, he published a fanciful version of his activities entitled *Spy*, which was later made into a Soviet film.

In October 1970 a brief announcement from Moscow recorded that K.T. Molodi had died of a heart attack while picking mushrooms. It emerged that he held two high decorations, the Red Star and the Red Banner.

LOTZ, Wolfgang

One of Israel's most successful and audacious spies. His father, a German theatrical director,

was a Gentile, but his actress mother was a Jew. She fled from Germany before the Second World War and took him to Israel. Speaking perfect German, and with Aryan features inherited from his father, he joined the British Army in the Middle East and was used to interrogate prisoners of war from the 115th Division of Rommel's Afrika Korps.

After the war he joined Haganah, the Israeli underground force, and then when Israel achieved independence he became a major in the Regular Army. The value of his German background and wartime experience was recognized by the Israeli intelligence branch, and he was sent back to Egypt disguised as a former member of the German division whose record he knew so well.

Posing as a German of independent means, he set up a stud farm and cultivated equestrian enthusiasts in the Egyptian hierarchy. He spent money freely, and gave lavish parties. Although he spent much more than his paymasters wished, the results were spectacular.

Through him Israeli intelligence gained insight into the thinking and behaviour of the Egyptian High Command. He was also involved in the terror campaign against the former Nazi scientists who were working for Nasser, in which letter and parcel bombs were sent to the scientists to force them to flee Egypt. In the end it was Lotz's success which proved his undoing. He used too often the radio transmitter hidden in his bathroom scales, and Egyptian radio-detection vans eventually pinpointed its location.

He was tried in July 1965 and found guilty. But despite interrogation he was able to maintain his German façade, and instead of being executed as an Israeli spy he was sentenced to life imprisonment.

Even that was cut short after two years, for it was his name that headed the list of prisoners whose return was demanded by the Israelis in exchange for some 500 Egyptian officers captured in the Six Day War. Lotz returned to Tel Aviv with his German wife, who had also been imprisoned. Still a bon viveur, he wrote a book about his experiences. It was called *The Champagne Spy*.

But the champagne soon went flat after his

return to Israel. His German wife, Waltraud, died and the riding-school he had started failed. He went to the United States, and another riding-school failed there. In 1978, with only $1,000 left, he went to Germany and took a job in a Munich department store. His second wife had left him, his Mossad compensation money was gone; and he complained that all they paid him was a pension of $200 a month.

LOUIS, Viktor

Although he is customarily referred to in Western newspapers as a colonel in the KGB, and is undoubtedly the most travelled man in the Soviet Union as a purveyor of information and leaks, the truth is that Viktor Louis is not a spy, and holds no rank in the state security service. A mild-mannered man with glasses and a sharp and witty tongue, he is a successful entrepreneur who dabbles in journalism when it suits him, and in this capacity is used by lobbies in the Soviet system, such as the KGB, to put out information for Western consumption.

Born in 1928, he studied law and languages at Moscow university, and shortly after the end of the world war was arrested while working as a translator at the Brazilian Embassy. He spent nine years in various Soviet labour camps.

With skill, courage, a great deal of luck, and some protection from the fact that he married an Englishwoman, he has built up during twenty-five years a way of life in Moscow which proves that Soviet society does not necessarily enforce equal misery for all. His success is built around the fortunes of *Information Moscow*, his publication which lists the names and addresses of foreigners and foreign organizations in Moscow, together with key Soviet telephone numbers in a capital still without telephone directories.

Viktor Louis has also worked as a journalist for a wide range of European and other foreign newspapers. He has dabbled, furthermore, in the grey area of supplying unofficial news and information to the West, through involvement in projects which may well have been inspired and

directed by the KGB. The tip-offs which he produces are seldom wrong, and he has provided stories for Western journalists, not all of which pleased the Soviet authorities in content or presentation.

The main criticism of Viktor Louis is that he peddled works to the West at the instigation of the KGB. For example, he offered an early draft of a book by Svetlana Alliluyeva, Stalin's daughter, and the taped memoirs of Nikita Khruschev. It may be that the KGB was involved for purposes of disinformation, but Louis himself can recognize a good property when he sees one.

There is hardly a country in the world which he has not visited on a Soviet passport which allows him to leave the USSR whenever he feels like it. It is possible that on his return from such journeys abroad he provides information about people and organizations he has been in touch with for the benefit of the Foreign Ministry, the KGB or for military intelligence.

But it might equally be that he prefers to spend his spare time directing work to build a new wing to his elegant dacha with its swimming-pool and tennis court, or amusing himself with his several exotic cars. He has style in a country which lacks it, and Winston Churchill's remark that Russia was a riddle wrapped in a mystery inside an enigma might equally apply to Viktor Louis.

LOUK, Mordechai

He provides an object-lesson in how not to be a spy. A Moroccan Jew who emigrated to Israel, he became fed up with his military service in 1961 and, feckless in Gaza, deserted to the Egyptians, who promptly imprisoned him.

There he attracted the attention of Cairo intelligence officers, who saw him as a good-looking, intelligent and multilingual Israeli whom they might put to good use. From his prison cell the idea of becoming a secret agent looked pretty attractive, and he readily agreed to take a course in espionage.

That done he was dispatched to Europe with the mission of cultivating Israelis there, and sniffing out Mossad agents. The cautious Egyptians kept him on low pay, around $150 a month, and constantly challenged his expenses, which was reasonable because the material he produced was disappointing.

Using a Moroccan passport in the name of Joseph Dahan as well as his Egyptian one, he circulated through France, Germany and Switzerland, after the Egyptians had methodically established his cover on a visit to Damascus. In 1964 he was ordered to re-base in Naples, making sorties into Germany and Switzerland.

But short of money (partly because of his love affairs with a number of Italian women) he complained bitterly to his Egyptian diplomat case officer in Rome, Selim Osman El Sayad. By this time the Egyptians were deeply dissatisfied with Louk's activities, and at a meeting in Rome they snatched him.

Their plan was to ship him back to Cairo for punishment, and the method was to place him in a tin trunk under diplomatic seals to be placed in the animals' hold of an Egyptian airlines flight to Cairo. But when Customs officers at Rome airport examined the trunk — probably after a tip-off from the Israeli secret service, which had been keeping an eye on Louk — they heard thin cries for help from inside it.

As the mystery of the man in the trunk slowly unfolded and Louk's identity was revealed, the Italian Government expelled two Egyptian diplomats including El Sayad, and handed over the apprentice spy to the Israeli authorities.

In November 1964 he was flown back to Tel Aviv after making a fulsome statement at the airport, 'I want to thank the Italian police for saving my life. I want to apologize to my country and to my wife.' Back home he was sentenced to thirteen years' imprisonment, and after his release he went back to work as a carpenter.

LUEDKE, Rear-Admiral Hermann

Chief of the logistics department of Shape (Supreme Headquarters, Allied Powers in Europe). He shot himself at a hunting lodge in the Eifel mountains in October 1968, on the eve of his arrest on charges of spying for the Russians.

Great alarm was expressed among Western military leaders, for the Admiral had cosmic clearance for access to NATO papers. Strict secrecy has surrounded the case ever since, but a lengthy investigation was carried out to try to discover how much damage he might have done.

His suicide was the first in a series of such acts among senior German officers and officials. The following day a friend of the Admiral, Major-General Horst Wendland, deputy chief of the BND, West German intelligence, shot himself in his office at Pullach, headquarters of the Gehlen organization.

His death was followed by two more, a Ministry of Defence colonel shot himself, and a senior official at the Ministry was found drowned. The Federal government announced that only the death of the Admiral was connected with intelligence matters, but few believed the statement.

The truth was that after the Soviet invasion of Czechoslovakia which ended the Prague Spring a number of high-ranking Czech intelligence officers made their way to the West. Among them was Major Ladislav Bittman, who had claimed that the Admiral and the others who subsequently killed themselves were Soviet moles within West Germany.

LYALIN, Oleg Adolfovich

When police constables Shearer and Paterson went after a Hillman car driving erratically along Tottenham Court Road, London in August 1971 they can have had no idea that they were blundering into a tense spy drama. The inebriate at the wheel, who refused to be breathalysed and was therefore taken to the station, was Oleg Lyalin, a 34-year-old Russian from the Soviet trade mission in Highgate.

This personable young man with wavy hair and a small moustache was not at all happy when after a night in the cells he appeared before the magistrates and was released on bail of £50 paid by the Embassy security officer. For although he did not enjoy diplomatic immunity under his trade mission cover, he was a KGB officer.

Furthermore, he was a KGB officer who had done a deal with the British security services who had recruited him earlier that year. In return for information he was ready to supply MI5 had offered him a new life, together with Irina Teplyakova, the blonde secretary he was sleeping with, free from their respective spouses.

The drunken-driving charge might upset the whole applecart. MI5 too were worried, and lost no time in responding to Lyalin's prompt plea for help. As soon as he left the Marlborough Street Court he was whisked to a safe house for debriefing.

What he was in a position to reveal was of the highest importance. It led to an international scandal, as well as to political uproar in Britain and the departure of no less than 105 of his former KGB allies from Britain.

For Oleg Lyalin was attached to one of the most alarming departments of the KGB, Department Five, which is responsible for sabotage and assassination. It is also the most secretive.

When the traffic police in London arrested him by accident they were in fact taking in an agent who in the autumn of 1971 was providing the British authorities with details and documents about such activities, together with plans for infiltrating agents for the purpose of sabotage. One of Lyalin's personal tasks had been to prepare schemes to put out of action the British and NATO radar station at Fylingdales on the Yorkshire moors. It had been installed at a cost of £45 million to provide early warning of any Soviet nuclear attack.

Although the Russian stated that sabotage plans were only to be put into effect in time of war, there was little to prevent them going ahead at any time the Russians thought fit. Here was clear evidence that Soviet personnel posing as diplomats and trade mission officials were engaged in preparations for warlike acts.

Two weeks after Lyalin had been granted asylum, the Attorney-General, Sir Peter Rawlinson, announced in Parliament that the Russian had held a post of importance in the KGB

division whose mission included the organization of sabotage within the United Kingdom. He added that Lyalin was in fear of his life, 'enhanced by the fact that the duties of his department of the KGB also included the elimination of individuals judged to be enemies of the State'.

For the Conservative government in which the Foreign Secretary was Sir Alec Douglas-Home, the Lyalin defection proved the final straw after a long period in which the KGB seemed to have treated the country as its own backyard. The government promptly expelled no less than 105 Soviet diplomats and officials.

Although the Kremlin riposted by expelling 18 Britons from the USSR, their main preoccupation was the damage which their man in London might now be doing to their international networks. For Department V men were active elsewhere in Europe and in North America.

In a panic, and fearing that other Western countries might follow the British lead and order mass expulsions, Leonid Brezhnev, the party leader, and Yuri Andropov, then head of the KGB, took crash action and ordered their under-cover sabotage and assassination officers to get back to Moscow as soon as possible.

By so doing a number of them blew their cover. Valeri Kostikov hastily left Mexico City, a diplomat-agent disappeared from Montreal, and others stationed in Paris, Bonn and Athens beat a hasty retreat. Whatever else he had done, Oleg Lyalin had caused high alarm at KGB head-quarters and in the Kremlin.

In London the police Special Branch quietly made a number of arrests of British citizens, including Siroj Abdoolcader, a Malaysian, and two Cypriot tailors who had been involved in the Lyalin network. They all pleaded guilty.

A curious aspect of the affair was that while the Russians trembled, the Americans admired, and the Europeans assessed; the British Labour Party launched sarcastic attacks upon the bold action taken by the government in expelling so many Russians. Harold Wilson, leader of the Opposition, was particularly scathing in his references to Lyalin, and anxious about the effect upon Anglo-Soviet relations.

He even went so far as to accuse the Conservatives of an election ploy. His supporters threw doubt upon the evidence of Lyalin, and they played down his seniority in the KGB.

McCARTHY, Senator Joseph R.

The hectoring Senator from Wisconsin, the originator of the term 'McCarthyism' which gave the world a new phrase of abuse. In 1950, horrified by revelations about Soviet agents in the United States, and even more so by the communist takeover in China, he launched the notorious campaign of persecution against 'communists in government' which included persons of all shades, from pink to deepest red.

Senator McCarthy's allegations and revelations, as he hauled victims before the Un-American Affairs Committee, set in motion a wave of spy hysteria in the United States comparable only to that which existed in the Soviet Union about Western spies.

He would dearly have liked to launch a campaign of investigation into the Central Intelligence Agency, but when he moved in that direction he was up against an equally hard professional, for Allen Dulles was the newly appointed Director, determined to prevent it from being harmed by McCarthy and his men.

Dulles put Lyman Kirkpatrick and Richard Helms in charge of his defences, and conducted his campaign on two levels. He got rid of those who could be considered security risks — one brilliant man had to go because he was a homosexual with a record — and he defended those guilty only of McCarthyite smears.

Two men in particular came under fire. One was Cord Meyer, a former Marine officer who had lost an eye fighting the Japanese on Eniwetok Island.

After the war he had become president of United World Federalists, convinced that peace could only be achieved through world government, and was active in the American Veterans Committee. Attempts by the communists to seize control of these organizations led him from the dream of world government into the CIA. When McCarthy picked on him Meyer fought back with a 100,000-word account of his life, demonstrating his opposition to communism and his belief in the American system.

One of his arguments reads strangely today. He pointed out that he had opposed the election of Ronald Reagan, then president of the Screen Actors Guild, to the planning committee of the American Veterans because he felt that Reagan was 'too radical'.

Meyer was suspended, but his firm defence and friends in high places won him reinstatement, and he eventually became one of the most powerful men in the CIA. Nevertheless, his McCarthy experience had scarred him, and he turned from his liberalism to become one of the most rigid of the Agency's anti-communists.

Another of McCarthy's CIA victims was the young William Bundy, then an analyst working in the Agency's Office of National Estimates. McCarthy attacked him because he was the son-in-law of the liberal Dean Acheson, who McCarthy accused of 'giving away' China to the communists, and because he had contributed to Alger Hiss's defence fund.

McCarthy said that he was going to summon Bundy to appear before his Senate Sub-committee on Governmental Operations. However, Dulles, fearful that this would give McCarthy the opportunity to rampage through the Agency's secrets, refused point-blank, and eventually McCarthy backed down. Bundy later became an Assistant Secretary of Defense under President Johnson.

Dulles was helped by President Eisenhower, who when McCarthy threatened a full-scale investigation of the CIA announced that a special committee, headed by General Mark Clark, would examine the Agency. McCarthy was pre-empted.

Clark's report recommended the establishment

of a Congressional watchdog committee to supervise the CIA, and the appointment of a Presidential committee to 'periodically examine the work of the government foreign intelligence agencies'. It is interesting to note that if these recommendations had been acted upon with any vigour they might well have saved the CIA a great deal of grief twenty years later.

Another revealing sidelight on this affair is that in the summer of 1952 David Schine, one of the Senator's brash inquisitorial team of Cohn and Schine, whose activities made America a laughing-stock around the world, was called up to do his military service. McCarthy brought enormous pressure to bear to have him given an immediate commission, but failed with all three Services. Cohn then went to General Bedell Smith shortly before Smith retired as Director CIA and asked him to accept Schine in the Agency. Smith refused, pointing out that it was hardly proper for McCarthy to demand such a privilege from an organization he was investigating.

McCarthy's influence declined greatly after 1954. He died in 1957.

MACLEAN, Donald Duart

'He is six foot four, blond, with beautiful eyes, altogether a beautiful man,' was how the enraptured American girl called Melinda saw the young diplomat Maclean whom she was about to marry.

'Large, flabby, white whale-like body' was how Guy Burgess, his fellow-spy and the man who introduced him to sodomy, saw the same man.

Maclean, son of a notable politician who was Scottish and Presbyterian, was really in love with Russia from his time at Cambridge University onward. He even considered going to work there until his Soviet recruiter in London discouraged him, and convinced him that he could serve the communist cause better by pretending to renounce it, and then joining the Foreign Office.

In due course he came to hate America, which hurt his American wife. Sarcastically he spoke of 'our bloody Yankee friends'.

He did take pains to become an ideal functionary, at least so far as his superiors in the Foreign Office were concerned, though his contemporaries were much more aware of his drunken orgies, quarrels and priggish arguments and fights. The Soviet masters who directed him were content to wait for results until he achieved a position of importance, from which he could supply them with intelligence material. Just to make sure that conscience did not deter him in working for them after the war, the Soviets had a blackmail weapon. Guy Burgess had obligingly taken some photographs at one of his orgies showing Donald in bed with another man.

It was when Maclean was posted to Washington in 1944 as First Secretary in the British Embassy that he became most useful to the Kremlin. As British representative on the Combined Policy Committee for Joint Atomic Development with the Americans and Canadians, he was in a position to supply important documents on nuclear planning.

He also made full use of a non-accompanied pass to the headquarters of the US Atomic Energy Commission, and was a frequent and studious visitor there after office hours. Maclean delivered wholesale the results of his espionage activities on regular twice-weekly visits to the Soviet consulate in New York for transmission to Moscow.

Roy Medvedev, the Russian historian, believes that Maclean passed on to Moscow a Korean War instruction from President Truman forbidding General McArthur to carry the war into Chinese territory. Until Stalin passed this on, Mao Tse-tung, the Chinese leader, fearing American invasion and possible use of atomic weapons, had hesitated to intervene in Korea. This document gave him the green light.

The same source is convinced that the reason Stalin was so little impressed by President Truman's announcement at Potsdam conference about the atomic bomb was that he already knew the details, thanks to Maclean and Philby. There is no doubt about the high importance of Maclean's espionage activities to the USSR.

But even by 1949 American intelligence officers of the CIA, which was being refurbished at the time, had good reason to suspect Maclean. They discovered his misuse of the Atomic Energy Commission pass and cancelled it. It also seems likely that they had information from an unnamed British double agent working with Maclean on atomic espionage.

But decisive information came from crypto-analysts, made suspicious by the high volume of traffic out of the Soviet consulate in New York. Fortunately for them, a Soviet cypher clerk blundered and began transmitting Maclean material in a simpler code reserved for lower-grade material, and this was recognized by the Americans.

With the help of British code-breakers they made more headway still. Heavy transmission coincided with Maclean's bi-weekly visits to New York, and messages revealed that the source was the British Embassy, and that the agent had a wife who was pregnant. All this evidence pointing straight at Maclean was garnered for future use by James Angleton of the CIA, though the British were extremely reluctant to believe that the respected First Secretary was in fact guilty.

Kim Philby knew that Maclean was under suspicion and warned the KGB, but so keen was the Kremlin appetite for the material he was supplying that they insisted on keeping him in position for as long as possible, regardless of the risk. Philby was aware of all this from his Soviet source well before Maurice Oldfield, later head of SIS, told him in September 1949 that there was a spy in the Washington embassy.

Under great pressure, Maclean began to disintegrate, becoming ever drunker and more quarrelsome. He was pulled out of America and sent for a spell in Cairo, where things got even worse. Then after a partial recovery from nervous breakdown, he went back to work as head of the American department at the Foreign Office in London in 1951, still under the protection of his foreign service friends who believed he could do no wrong.

The end of the spying saga came in May 1951 when, warned by Philby with the help of Burgess and Blunt, that he was about to be interrogated by MI5's best man William Skardon, he fled the country in company with Guy Burgess.

Donald Maclean survived the debriefing and interrogation of Russian KGB colleagues which might well have proved his undoing, for Stalin was still in control, and quite capable of liquidating agents who had been caught out, or who might be suspected of disloyalty. It is an ironic fact that most of the enthusiastic recruiters who had brought the British traitors to communism eventually perished in Stalin's purges.

Maclean was more fortunate, and lived on to enjoy the privileges of a state security officer with the KGB rank of colonel, a comfortable apartment well stocked with foreign books, and a dacha outside Moscow.

He was known as 'Mark Petrovich Frazer', and the Soviet historian Roy Medvedev met him in the 1960s chatting with Soviet dissidents. He had discovered that Moscow was not the workers' paradise he had naively imagined it to be in his youth.

By the time of his death in 1983 Maclean was a lonely man, at the age of sixty-nine living more or less in retirement, despite his title of Foreign Ministry adviser. Melinda, who followed him to Moscow, had taken up with Kim Philby and then returned to America; his family were dispersed, and he spent most of his time quietly gardening at his dacha, still an alcoholic but no longer in the frantic manner of his youth.

He spied for love of the Soviet Union. He was not paid, though finally they rewarded him as a pensionary of the KGB. In his will dated 1948 he left £5,000 — his frozen London bank-account — to Melinda.

McCONE, John

He was the first director of the Central Intelligence Agency to make use of the brand-new office designed for his predecessor Allen Dulles in the specially built headquarters at Langley, Virginia. Dulles had left in disgrace in November 1961, a few months after Cuban rebels backed by the CIA had failed miserably to overthrow Castro.

John McCone was more fortunate in his dealings with the continuing crisis in American relations with Cuba. While he was at the head of the Agency it displayed its intelligence skills, by discovering in detail the Soviet build-up of missiles threatening the United States from Cuba. This put President Kennedy on firm ground when he took strong action to force their withdrawal.

This success helped the new director in his task of restoring confidence in the Agency. He served as director from November 1961 until April 1965. By the end of his time there the CIA was deeply involved in Vietnam operations.

McMAHON, John

Unlike the British SIS, the CIA not only acknowledges its existence but allows its senior officials to be named. John McMahon, the deputy director of the CIA, appeared before the House of Representatives Permanent Committee on Intelligence in July 1982, and after suitable editing his evidence was published. It consisted of the most detailed exposé of the KGB's 'Active Measures' around the world. He estimated that the Russians were spending between $3 and $4 billion a year on these measures — forgeries, disinformation and covert propaganda.

Among the examples he produced was a forged letter from President Reagan to King Juan Carlos of Spain, purporting to advise the King that several of his close advisers were opposed to Spain joining NATO. Posted to Spanish journalists, the purpose of the forgery was to 'complicate US-Spanish relations by making it appear that the US was interfering in Spain's internal affairs'. McMahon commented, somewhat resignedly, 'Whatever ends justify the means.' During his evidence McMahon made a plea for more men and more money to counter the KGB campaign. According to the latest figures, those requests have been granted.

MAENNEL, Captain Gunther

For more than a year before he sought refuge in West Germany in 1961 this officer of the counter-intelligence branch of the East German state security service had been acting as a double agent for the CIA. When he was originally turned by a Gehlen Organization man he agreed to stay on in East Berlin in return for a $20,000 bonus and an assurance that if things went wrong he would be pulled out.

The Americans kept quiet about his arrival in the West in order to confuse the other side. He produced a whole package of surprising information about traitorous senior German officers working for NATO and in the West German defence ministry.

Further alarm was produced when during his debriefing Captain Maennel revealed that there was a double agent working at the Pullach headquarters of General Gehlen's organization. Although he could not name the man, his description fitted Heinz Felfe, head of counter-espionage at Pullach, and led to Felfe's arrest.

Captain Maennel also had information of interest to the British. Armin Grosz, one of his colleagues, had set up a network in London in 1958–9 with a man known as Eric Hills, under cover as trade-union officials. They had been in touch with the Krogers and with Gordon Lonsdale, all arrested in the 1961 Portland spy case. Both East Germans escaped to East Berlin after the London arrests.

Another revelation from the same source led to the arrest and sentencing to twenty years in prison of Captain Joseph Kauffman of the USAF, who had supplied East Germans with information about radar installations in return for cash payments. After his posting to the US base in Greenland he informed about U-2 spy plane operations.

MAHEU, Robert

A shadowy former G-man who was used as a free-lance by the CIA for certain covert — and usually dirty — jobs. According to the Church Commission's Assassination Report, the head of the operational support division of the CIA's Office of Security (who was unnamed), and Colonel

Sheffield Edwards, the CIA's Director of Security, got in touch with Maheu and told him that the Agency would pay $150,000 for a contract killing of Castro.

Maheu agreed, and went to the Mafia to provide his killers. The Mafia had their own reasons for wanting to kill Castro, because he had kicked them out of Cuba and shut down their profitable gambling and drug operations. Maheu worked through a Mafioso called John Rosselli who in turn brought in the notorious Sam Giancana and Santos Trafficante. It came to nothing, but caused the CIA a great deal of embarrassment when the story was told.

Even more embarrassment was caused when it was alleged that President Kennedy and Sam Giancana had been sharing the favours of the same woman, Judith Exner. In a bloody footnote to this affair Rosselli, who had testified before the Church Commission in 1975, was found shot dead and stuffed into a 55-gallon drum in Dumbfoundling Bay in August 1976, and Giancana was shot dead in June 1975, a few days before he was due to appear before the Commission. The Mafia manages its own killings more efficiently than the CIA.

Among Maheu's other 'dirty tricks' was the production of a pornographic film of President Sukarno of Indonesia, using an actor to impersonate him. Given Sukarno's legendary reputation as a womanizer (which was regarded with some pride by most Indonesians), this operation would seem to have been, not only dirty but counter-productive.

MARCHENKO, V. I.

It must have been a pretty nasty moment for the First Secretary of the Soviet Embassy in Peking, when on a cold January night in 1974 he sat crouched behind the wheel of his Volga under a bridge over the Paho river, to see a red flare explode above, and find himself surrounded by Chinese militiamen. The game, as they used to write in the old spy novels, was up.

Marchenko, his wife, their interpreter and two

other diplomats had made their perilous night journey to contact a Chinese agent, Li Hung Shu, and to collect his secret reports. They were also to hand over to him a suitcase marked with the slogan 'Serve the people!' containing a radio transmitter.

But Red Chinese counter-intelligence men — whose task in following foreigners in Peking is not, it has to be admitted, very difficult — were watching. They were not fooled by the fact that Marchenko and his party were wearing padded Mao jackets and Chinese anti-cold-germ masks in an attempt to disguise their Russian-ness.

They were all hustled off and held incommunicado for four days before being put on a flight to Moscow, accused of being involved in 'the dirty game' of espionage. It must also have been distressing for good communists — and no doubt they were state security officials as well — to hear themselves charged with being counter-revolutionaries who were, in the Chinese Government's words, 'trying to subvert the dictatorship of the proletariat in China'.

There was little goodwill between the two states practising rival brands of communism after the Russians withdrew technical help to China in 1960, and this was followed five years later by the first of the border incidents which soured relations even further. The lot of a KGB officer trying to discover secrets of what was going on along the Chinese border was not a happy one.

MARENCHES, Count Alexander de

The Count, a huge man known for his boisterous ways and occasional burst of temper, lost no time in resigning as head of the French intelligence service once François Mitterrand won election to the Presidency of France in 1981. It was, he decided, no position for a right-winger like himself to hold under a socialist President who in the course of his chequered political career had been more spied upon than spying.

Besides, there is a long tradition in France that heads of the secret service do not long survive a change of regime; and an equally venerable custom that such persons rapidly remove the most sensitive political files before an incoming administration can get its hands upon them.

De Marenches had served for ten years, having been appointed by his old friend President Pompidou with a mission to clean up the SDECE, the intelligence service, after the scandals of the 1960s, one of which had attempted to smear the President. It was also his task to improve relations with the American and British services of which he had wartime experience, in the wake of Gaullist hostility to his former allies.

The French secret service chief knew George Bush of the CIA very well. He had been a guest of President Reagan at the White House, where his bilingual skills had been useful. Neither of these social achievements seemed likely to over-impress François Mitterrand.

In any case, the SDECE was not a happy ship as the new Presidency began. The intelligence organization had been plotting against Qaddafi of Libya without much success. As a result Colonel de Marolles, head of information-gathering, had resigned early. There had been two unexplained suicides on the staff.

Count de Marenches was promptly replaced by an Air France executive brought in from outside to apply management techniques to the SDECE, but he met with no greater success, and was soon replaced.

MARION, Pierre

When François Mitterrand became President of France he began reorganizing the French secret services in line with his own socialist philosophy of how such things should be done. Although names were changed, the old structure remained. Military intelligence is divided into internal and external branches, while counter-espionage is handled by a fundamentally police organization, the DST.

As new head of the external service formerly known as the SDECE, but renamed in 1982 DGSE (Direction Général de la Sécurité Extérieure), the President chose an outsider who was a personal friend of his Defence Minister, Charles Hernu. Pierre Marion, an Air France executive untarnished by the world of spies, was thought to be a suitable person to reorganize external espionage.

Although M. Marion, a 61-year-old, began making enthusiastic use of his talents for business administration to weed out high-ranking espionage professionals appointed by earlier governments, the experiment did not succeed. He did achieve some progress in reorganization, and in developing the capacity of the service to gather economic and scientific information, but under his direction the DGSE proved itself incapable of providing fast and good material on the war in Lebanon and in coping with a wave of terrorism in France. It was put about that President Mitterrand rudely described one sheaf of intelligence reports as being 'no better than press clippings'.

After Pierre Marion had made determined attempts to co-ordinate with the DST internal branch by discovering its secrets — which are often denied to colleagues in the overseas branch — the Cabinet accepted his resignation in November 1982.

He was promptly replaced by Vice-Admiral Pierre Lacoste, who became the first naval officer in France to hold the post.

MARKELOV, Valeriy Ivanovich

A 32-year-old Russian translator at United Nations took the extraordinary step (considering his trade) of indicating that he did not understand English when brought before a New York court in 1972. He had been caught in a Long Island restaurant receiving classified documents about the US Navy's F-14A fighter from an engineer employed by Grumman Aerospace Corporation who was working with the FBI.

He had worked at the United Nations for several years, and during the two years that the FBI had been on his trail he had no less than eleven meetings with the engineer who supplied him with secret information. The Soviet agent had given his 'stringer' a copying machine and cameras.

Released on bail, Markelov went on living for a while in New York, until in May 1972 he was allowed to return to the Soviet Union and the charges were dropped.

MARKOV, Georgi

A talented Bulgarian writer living in exile in London with his attractive English wife Annabel, he was murdered on Waterloo Bridge while waiting for a bus, as punishment for broadcasting the truth about his homeland on the BBC and Radio Free Europe. Markov was especially well informed about the corrupt life at the top in his native Bulgaria, and he hated the regime of this most Stalinist of the Eastern Bloc countries.

His killer was never traced, but the device he used, an umbrella which fired a pinhead platinum pellet containing ricin — a poison made from castor oil plant — was clearly the handiwork of the KGB Technical Operations Directorate.

It is more than likely that the assassin who approached Markov and then apologized for jabbing him with the umbrella was from the Bulgarian security services, for similar though unsuccessful attempts were made about the same time to kill Boris Korczak, a Polish suspected double agent, in Virginia, and Vladimir Kostov, a Bulgarian exile in Paris. The Bulgarian service has an ugly record for killing those who antagonize the regime. They are also known to have killed a Bulgarian rocket technician in Vienna and the editor of an émigré newspaper.

However, the Bulgarians could not have used the sophisticated poison pellet invented by the KGB without at least the tacit approval of the Russians. The poison takes some time to work, and leads to cardiovascular collapse. For this reason an unsuspecting doctor might simply assume that death was through a heart-attack, and it is possible that other assassinations have passed unrecorded for this reason.

MARKS, Dennis Howard

An Oxford graduate involved with an international drug-ring which smuggled quantities of cannabis concealed in rock-band electronic gear. He was arrested in Holland in 1973, and disappeared while awaiting trial. It then became known that he had furtive links by way of an old Oxford friend with British intelligence.

Superintendent Fairweather of the Thames Valley police was ordered to investigate this aspect of Marks's career. Extracts from his report later appeared in the *New Statesman*, the left-wing London magazine, and the Superintendent in a state of anxiety and depression — partly caused by fear that he might be prosecuted under the Official Secrets Act — killed himself.

In 1981 Marks, a clever 36-year-old Welshman, who according to the judge had lived on his wits for years, was acquitted on one drug-smuggling charge but sentenced to two years for passport offences. Then in February 1982 he pleaded guilty to involvement in an international drug-smuggling ring in the 1970s, and received a three-year prison sentence.

The prosecution revealed that Marks had voluntarily returned to Britain after his original arrest in Amsterdam and disclosed his role as an MI6 informer. Lord Hutchinson QC, who defended Marks, said that he had worked under cover for the intelligence service and had helped them to track down a notorious Provisional IRA gun-runner named James McCann.

It seems that Marks worked for MI6 only for a while, after his Oxford friend Norman McMillan (who had later joined the Foreign Office) asked him to help. He had come across McCann in Germany while the Irishman was involved in drug and arms smuggling.

Little more has emerged in the way of details about this obscure affair, but a family friend of the Marks family at Port Talbot in Wales said after the trial that Marks was never the hippy type. 'He believed he was doing something for his country. I accept absolutely that he was recruited to try and find out who was behind the trafficking.'

MAROLLES, Colonel Alan de Gaigneron de

At the age of fifty-nine he resigned in September 1980 as head of most important section of the

French intelligence service, the one which organizes the 'product', after serving there for only a year. Tactfully he said that he was leaving for technical reasons, but as he was the fifth officer to hold the position in ten years, it was suspected that he left after policy rows.

The Colonel, a graduate of the French military academy of St Cyr and a paratroop officer, had always been known for his zeal in the service, and before moving to his last appointment he had headed the action department of SDECE. It was thought at that time, in 1977, that he had helped President Sadat of Egypt to prepare military measures against President Qaddafi of Libya which led to a border confrontation.

Members of the Western intelligence community believed that he continued to urge plans for the overthrow of Qaddafi, including the encouragement of formation of a Libyan government-in-exile. In August 1979 there were disturbances in Benghazi, and in these the hand of the SDECE was seen. But French plotting achieved nothing.

Colonel de Marolles had kept a keen eye on events in North Africa, and was particularly anxious for France to counter destabilization attempts by the Libyans, both there and in Africa. He was an active officer, and frequently flew abroad to keep in touch with field operations.

MARSHALL, William Martin

A chapter of errors ended the secrets sales of this 24-year-old ex-army signaller who had joined the Diplomatic Wireless Service, and was persuaded to spy while serving at the British Embassy in Moscow. By chance an off-duty MI5 watcher getting off a bus in April 1952 recognized Pavel Kuznetsov, a GRU man from the Soviet Embassy, sitting on a park bench with a man who seemed to be drawing sketches.

He followed the sketcher back home and discovered he was William Marshall. Eventually watchers and Special Branch men waited in hiding behind bushes ready to arrest the Russian and his contact in a park near the Thames.

It was at this stage that an element of farce intruded, for the watchers had been observed by a local resident who telephoned the police, and suddenly the spycatchers were surrounded by a squad of uniformed police. While explanations were being made Kuznetsov tried to slip away. As the two were arrested he protested loudly, and said he had never met Marshall before.

Marshall confessed, and in June 1952 was found guilty of passing secrets. The jury recommended leniency, and he got five years.

MAY, Alan Nunn

Because there was nothing particularly remarkable about him, even those who thought that they knew this lonely little man found him difficult to describe. A clever scholarship boy from the Midlands who made his way to Cambridge University to become an academic physicist, he was not really part of the smart, show-off crowd at the University at the time — the Burgesses and Macleans and Blunts.

The one thing he had in common with them was a belief in communism, and the anti-fascism so predominant before the Second World War among the intellectuals. Unlike the bolder spirits who went off to fight (and some to die), in the Spanish civil war, Alan Nunn May was content to make a routine pilgrimage to Moscow, where he saw what he wanted to see.

Despite his open sympathies with Russia and communism, this promising though not top-flight scientific researcher was taken from his university post to join what was discreetly called the Tube Alloys project. At the Cavendish Laboratory in Cambridge they were working in the 1940s on atomic energy, and the possibility of an atomic bomb. It was all very hush-hush, and before he joined Nunn May had to sign the Official Secrets Act.

It is still not known for certain whether at this point he was in touch with Soviet intelligence, but when atomic research was moved to Canada for greater wartime safety, and to make co-operation with the American project easier, it was not long before Colonel Zabotin, the GRU man in Ottawa, got in touch with him. From the fact that Moscow also furnished the password, 'Best regards from Mikel', it seems that some contact had already been made.

For two and a half years after 1943 Nunn May moved regularly between Chalk River, where a heavy-water pile was established, and Montreal. He also made a number of visits to the American project at the Argonne Laboratory in Chicago. Indeed, the American security men noticed that he had been there more often than any other British physicist. They refused his next application.

Working through Pavel Angelov, a GRU lieutenant, Nunn May's task at first was to supply information about atomic energy and uranium. Despite his reluctance, the Soviet agents insisted, as is their normal practice, in paying him a modest 200 dollars and two bottles of whisky, but that meant that they had the receipts needed to bind the spy to his masters.

When Nunn May informed them that his official duties were coming to an end in Canada they asked for one last favour, and he provided them with a report on the New Mexico trial of the first A-bomb. He also supplied a tiny sample of uranium 235. As an extra, he let the Russians have details of the electronic anti-aircraft shell which was so useful in the war against Japan.

Content with their latest haul, the Russians then set about making arrangements to contact Dr May when he returned to London. However, their plans were upset by the unexpected arrival in the Western camp of Igor Gouzenko with a quantity of incriminating documents about the atomic spy ring which made clear Dr Nunn May's part in it.

Neither the Canadians nor the British were keen to arrest the young physicist, for the Gouzenko files pointed in many directions and they did not want to lose a chance of catching a whole ring of spies by premature revelation of the extent of their new knowledge. For the time being they were content to keep him under observation as he flew back to London and watch over his movements there.

In fact, according to Nunn May's version of events he was having doubts. The war was over, he was back at London University, and according to a later statement he put on record that 'I decided

to wash my hands of the whole business.' That was his explanation for not having kept an appointment with his new Russian control in London when the British police finally arrested him in March 1946.

He admitted the facts, justifying himself by declaring, 'The whole affair was extremely painful to me and I only embarked on it because I felt this was a contribution I could make to the safety of mankind. I certainly did not do it for gain.'

It was a defence which did not stand up in court at the Old Bailey when he was charged under the Official Secrets Act with passing on information useful to an enemy. He pleaded guilty.

When his defence lawyer, Gerald Gardiner, KC, pleaded in extenuation that the information had only saved time for foreign scientists engaged on atomic research, and that the Russians were then allies of Britain, even the Attorney-General intervened to say that 'there is no kind of suggestion that the Russians are enemies or potential enemies'. That was the mood of the time.

Nevertheless, Mr Justice Oliver, who sentenced Nunn May to ten years' imprisonment, rejected his justification about the spreading of scientific knowledge. He spoke of 'the crass conceit' and wickedness of deciding to reveal the country's most precious secret.

But in scientific and in left-wing circles there was a protest movement to condemn what was called the harshness of the sentence. At that stage the extent of Russian espionage in the West had not yet made its impact upon public opinion.

In fact the scientist won full remission for good behaviour and was released from Wakefield Prison after less than seven years in 1952. He returned to Cambridge, where his Viennese-born wife, Dr Hildegarde Broda, was living with their son. Ten years later he went for a while to the newly independent African state of Ghana as Professor of Physics at the university there.

MENZIES, Major-General Sir Stewart

King George VI once ventured a jokey conversation with Menzies after he had been appointed head of the Secret Intelligence Service in 1939 by asking what would happen if he asked the name of our man in Berlin. The reply was that his lips were sealed.

'Supposing I were to say, "Off with your head?"'

'In that case, Sir, my head would roll with the lips still sealed.'

Menzies was that kind of man, upright, rather old-fashioned — the product of Eton, Sandhurst, and the Brigade of Guards. When he retired in 1953 there was some fuss that his name and job had been mentioned in public. He happily told the *Evening Standard* that he did not think that the revelation affected national security; but he added that he was not at all certain how fellow-members of his county Hunt would take it.

He was a clever man, a man of keen instinct, well connected in high places. Though some of his remarks gave the impression to those who did not know better that he was playing the silly ass, he was a shrewd and effective spymaster. Menzies had the difficult task of running the intelligence service throughout the war under Churchill, who was by no means an easy chief.

When the great scandals of Burgess and Maclean and then Philby created waves of indignation Menzies was still at the head of the service. Naturally, he was blamed by many, and criticized by all. (He retired prematurely the following year.) Yet his record was by no means all bad. He personally had gone to Poland in 1939 and secured with Polish help the Enigma code machine, and it was the breaking of German codes which contributed more to Allied victory than any other act of espionage during the war. He was well aware of the importance of the code-breaking operations at Bletchley, which was loosely under his control.

General Gustave Bertrand, the French intelligence crypto-analyst, described taking the British copy of the machine to London on 16 August 1939, and handing it over at Victoria station in person to Menzies dressed: *'en smoking, avec rosette de la Légion d'Honneur à la boutonnière. Accueil triomphal!'*

Sir Stewart was an admirable administrator, good at departmental manoeuvring, and he was well liked by government ministers for his discretion and economy. Churchill once remarked that the good thing about him was that he ran his service on pennies.

Within the service he appears to have been a rather lonely figure. Life was not made any easier for him by the constant bickering between his two senior colleagues, Colonels Dancey and Vivian, each of them ever ready for jealousy should he seem to favour one rather than the other.

MERKULOV, Vladimir

A KGB career man specializing in the fashionable activity of that organization — not hard spying, but the paying out of money to encourage Soviet-style peace movements in Western countries. He had served for four years as Second Secretary in the Russian Embassy in Copenhagen before his detection and expulsion by the Danish authorities in the autumn of 1981.

With the help of a local author who used money provided by him, he launched a campaign to make Scandinavia a nuclear-free zone. Merkulov was known to have sponsored other attempts through publications to discredit NATO, and to organize black propaganda aimed at the governments of countries in the Western alliance.

MITCHELL, Bernon F, and MARTIN, William H.

The defection of this young and clever Californian cryptologist to the Soviet Union in 1960, together with his old Navy friend William Martin, caused an espionage panic and scandal in the United States comparable only to that provoked in Britain by the flight of Burgess and Maclean. Both these men worked for the National Security Agency, the centre near Washington which deals with electronic espionage world-wide.

Until they appeared at a press conference in Moscow to reveal some of the secrets they had already passed on in detail to Soviet intelligence, few people in the West were aware even of the existence of NSA. The pair also drew attention for the first time to GCHQ, the British sister organization of NSA, and revealed that NSA analysts were intercepting communications of no less than forty countries, both friendly and neutral.

The treachery of Mitchell and Martin, and the subsequent inquiry, revealed grave weaknesses in security at the heart of the most secretive of all American intelligence organizations. Homosexuality was involved, as it was in several British cases, and after the inquiry a purge of gays was conducted at NSA. Some twenty-six people were fired on grounds of 'indications of sexual deviation'.

But what on earth had persuaded Mitchell and his friend Martin to choose life in the Soviet Union? There was nothing particularly devious about their early life. The only oddity turned up by the polygraph lie-detector test on Mitchell when he applied to join NSA was to do with what he called 'sexual experimentations' with dogs and chickens on the farm in his teens.

He had been a bright boy, studious and good at school. So had 'Ham' Martin, and that is why when they did national service in the navy they went into the security branch and met at an intercept station in Japan.

Back home later and going on to university, the pair kept in touch. Martin had stayed on in Japan an extra year as a civilian in the US army security agency there. As keen mathematicians and with some intelligence experience, they both looked like ideal recruits when they were interviewed for jobs at NSA.

Vetting and security checks offered no difficulty, and in January 1958 both of them began work at the Agency, applying their mathematical skills to cryptography. They seemed content enough, but what began to worry them and raise 'doubts' was the knowledge they acquired at work about so-called ferret flights by US aircraft.

America was making flights along the borders of, and sometimes over, the territory of the Soviet Union, in order to spy out normally inactive radar equipment, capture the signals and return them to

NSA for analysis. An EC-130 Hercules aircraft had been shot down on one such mission in 1958 over Soviet Armenia, with six of the crew killed and eleven posted missing.

In an attempt to learn more about the fate of the crew, and in order to refute a Soviet statement that the plane had just crashed, the State Department released a transcript of voices of Russian MiG pilots actually shooting it down.

This was what especially worried Mitchell and Martin. They were so carried away by fears of a world war by accident that they went to give inside information to a Congressman who had raised questions.

Disappointed with his reaction, they decided that the American way of life was not for them, and began seeking inspiration in, of all things, Soviet propaganda magazines such as *Soviet Life*, which naturally presented a pretty idealized picture of life in the USSR. Both of them were militantly anti-religious, and this was another characteristic which tempted them towards Soviet life.

In the summer of 1959 they decided to defect and began making quiet preparations which lasted a whole year. Martin took up an NSA scholarship, and while on a further university course in mathematics also learned Russian. The two men made a clandestine visit to Cuba, where they got in touch with Soviet officials before returning to NSA.

Having arranged three weeks' leave in the summer of 1960, and telling colleagues they were off to visit their parents, Mitchell and Martin flew again to Havana by way of Mexico City. From there the Russians put them aboard a Soviet ship sailing for the USSR.

It was more than a month before NSA noticed that they were missing. When security men searched their homes they discovered a carefully prepared letter of explanation of their defection. It was a jumble of high-minded criticisms of the role of NSA and naive sociological talk about capitalism and its wickedness.

Reacting as government departments frequently do when shocked by news of spies in their midst, the Pentagon lied, saying that neither Mitchell nor

Martin had access to classified defence documents. John McCormack, the Democratic leader in Congress, was better informed, and promptly went on the attack, declaring that the affair marked one of the worst security breaches in American history.

There was no doubt that they had taken valuable cryptographic information. Indeed, inquiries by the Un-American Activities Committee revealed that the pair while still at work had specially sought out information about the U-2 high-level reconnaissance mission of Gary Powers, who was later shot down over the Soviet Union in May 1960.

Mitchell and Martin were triumphantly produced at a Moscow press conference to denounce in detail ferret and spy plane missions launched by the Americans.

The amount of detail gloatingly retailed by the Soviet media made it clear that the Americans must have revealed a great deal more in debriefing sessions with KGB officers. Among other details publicly announced were the NSA connection with GCHQ in Britain, intercept programmes affecting America's allies and neutral nations of the Middle East, and the location of listening stations.

Detailed inquiries into the defection began in the United States. The Un-American Activities Committee blamed homosexuality, though there was some evidence that Mitchell at least was in fact bisexual.

Ex-President Harry Truman roundly declared that both of them should be shot. In fact their punishment took a different form. Both Mitchell and to a lesser extent Martin (who had changed his name to Sokolovsky and married a Russian girl) soon became disillusioned with Soviet life. When Mitchell made inquiries about the chances of returning to the United States he was stripped of his American citizenship, and all his attempts to return home have so far been rebuffed.

MITCHELL, Graham Russell

The entry in *Who's Who* outlining the life of Graham Mitchell — Winchester and Magdalen College, Oxford; recreations, yacht-racing and chess — also records 'attached War Office, 1939–63'. That is the polite British code for declaring the open secret that he was a senior officer in the security services.

In fact he ended his career at retirement in 1963 as Deputy Director-General of MI5, the internal counter-espionage organization, after seven years in that post. He had joined the service at the age of thirty-four, after working in the research department of the Conservative Party and as a magazine journalist.

Graham Mitchell rose to high rank in the service during the most difficult years of MI5. It was a time of humiliating failure after failure. Burgess and Maclean escaped to Moscow, so did Kim Philby. The security services had minimal success with double agents, and even their successes in spycatching were marred by deep suspicions that on each occasion Soviet case officers controlling British spies had escaped.

There were also suspicions that a highly placed mole remained within the organization, warning his Soviet friends in advance of intelligence moves. After the Philby defection, and further revelations about it from the Russian defector Golytsin, the service decided on a detailed inquiry.

According to Nigel West in his history of MI5, *A Matter of Trust*, it was decided that only four officers could have known details of the mounting evidence against Philby before his flight from Beirut in 1963, including Sir Roger Hollis, Director-General of MI5, and one secretary.

In the summer of 1963 a small team of officers began a detailed investigation of their colleague Graham Mitchell, keeping him under scrutiny in his office on a clandestine TV, having him followed by watchers, and combing through his records and his waste-paper bin. It was by no means the first time that an intelligence service had applied its counter-espionage methods to one of its own men, for in the nature of their secretive work officers are often involved in suspicious-looking activities. But the MI5 one was exceptionally thorough.

No evidence against him was ever discovered, and he retired normally in the autumn of 1963 to a quiet life in the country. Only the circumstantial putting of two and two together to make five had ever pointed to him as a mole. In 1982 when the *Sunday Times* asked Graham Mitchell about the investigation he said, 'I felt hurt and shocked.' But he realized his colleagues were only doing their duty.

After the investigation (code-named Peters) morale in the service was low, and continuing doubts in the organization led to suggestions that the mole might have been the Director-General himself, Sir Roger Hollis.

MIYANAGA, Major-General Yukhisa

The discovery in 1980 that a major-general, together with a lieutenant and a warrant officer, in Japanese military intelligence, had been spying on behalf of the Soviet Union caused alarm. It was the first time that serving army officers had been arrested for espionage.

They had been paid up to £1,000 each for documents handed over to Soviet military attachés, and one of these Russians, Colonel Yuri Kozlov, left Tokyo hastily as soon as the arrests became known. The information they passed over was to do with intelligence organization in Japan and about troop movements.

The general, who was aged fifty-eight and had recently retired, kept a diary recording his instructions from the Russians. He confessed, and Japanese security men using his information were able to decode new instructions to him after his arrest, which provided them with useful information.

Japanese law is not harsh on spies, and the general received the maximum sentence of only one year.

MORROS, Boris

The man who brought the cinema into espionage. Russian talent scouts spotted him, this movie man who became musical director of Paramount, when he went to visit his old parents — who lived in Leningrad — back in 1934.

He later set up his own film company, and was reactivated by the Russians, to use it as a cover for the formation of a spy ring in the United States. Some of its members became better known than Morros himself — for example, Jack Soble, and his brother Robert Soblen, who had adopted a slightly different transliteration of the original Lithuanian family name.

Soble helped with the recruitment of the much more important pair the Krogers, who were finally detected in London through their connection with the Portland spy ring in 1961. The Morros movie ring acted as couriers, and gave back-up to more professional Soviet agents, though they achieved little themselves.

However, Boris Morros himself began to have doubts about his nefarious activities for the communists in 1947, and went to confess all to the Federal Bureau of Investigation in Los Angeles. They signed him up as a double agent to work against Soviet spies, and sent him on contact-making trips to Europe.

When Jack Soble fled in a panic to Canada after the execution of Lavrenti Beria, the supreme Soviet spymaster in 1953 Morros was sent on an unsuccessful mission to persuade him to return to the US. But by now the whole spy group was in confusion, and its members dispersed in various directions.

Soble, who had much earlier helped to plot against the exiled Trotsky, was finally arrested in 1957, while his brother Soblen remained free for another three years. When they were all indicted Morros gave evidence against them. Soble was sentenced to seven years in prison; Soblen made a dash for Israel, was turned back, and committed suicide in London in 1962.

Morros died the following year.

MUNSINGER, Gerda

A determined East German lady spy for the Soviets in West Germany. Undeterred by the refusal of a Canadian visa (because the Royal

Canadian Mounted Police accurately described her in 1952 as a spy, a prostitute, a thief and a smuggler), she managed to slip in three years later using the name of a US army sergeant whom she had meanwhile married and divorced.

She got to work at once, making her charms available to suitably well-connected persons, and when she applied for Canadian citizenship in 1960 her sponsor was Pierre Sevigny, associate Minister for National Defence.

But the application again drew the attention of the RCMP, who once more reported that she was a security risk. Gerda Munsinger went back to East Germany, but already the affair was developing into one of those spy and sex scandals so popular in Western countries.

When the Liberal government came under attack for another spy affair the Conservatives hit back by bringing up the Munsinger case, and Lester Pearson, the Prime Minister, ordered an official inquiry.

It found that because of the Gerda connection Pierre Sevigny had been a security risk, though there was no evidence that he had passed secret information. Although a number of politicians emerged the worse for wear, it did not seem that Ms Munsinger had in fact done any very useful work on behalf of the Soviet Union.

NECHIPORENKO, Oleg Maksimovich

The moustachioed, black-haired and Spanish-speaking man from Moscow installed in the Mexico City embassy of the USSR to help organize an uprising of Mexicans against their government. He has been described as the KGB's best man in Latin America.

Nechiporenko may have been the son of Spanish communists who fled to Russia after the civil war, or the child of a Soviet father and Spanish mother. Be that as it may, he spoke impeccable Spanish in many dialects, was a haughty fellow, and frightened even his KGB colleagues, whom he treated as inferiors.

His main task was to recruit students from Mexican universities for further training in subversion at the Patrice Lumumba University in Moscow, which specializes in processing third-world sympathizers and potential agents.

Together with four other agents, he was expelled from Mexico in 1971 after Mexican security had broken the plot to activate the Revolutionary Action Movement, whose leader, Gomez Souza, he had personally selected.

NIKOLAYEV, Boris Serafimovich

Identified in the Thai press as the KGB's 'Resident' in Bangkok, his cover job was permanent Soviet representative at the Economic and Social Commission for Asia and the Pacific (ESCAP). An economist, he previously served in the London embassy as a senior economic counsellor, and as a lecturer in world economics at Moscow's Diplomatic Institute where diplomats and KGB officers take courses before being posted abroad.

As Bangkok Resident, he was boss of the most important and active KGB and GRU network in South-east Asia. Bangkok in fact has a touch of wartime Lisbon about it. The secret services of all the big Powers use it as a listening-post for what is going on in the area. It is comparatively easy for agents to operate there, and the Russians find it simple to pose as Western business-men and tourists.

The trouble for the Russians is that Thailand is altogether too pleasant and easy-going, and the attractions of the massage parlours and the bar girls have proved altogether too much for a number of Nikolayev's men. So many have been declared *persona non grata* by the Thais, or flown home in disgrace by the Russians themselves, that it has become embarrassing even to the KGB, hardened as it is to the constant deportation and defection of its agents.

NINIO, Marcelle

When Colonel Abraham Dar, an experienced officer of Israeli intelligence, arrived in Egypt in 1951 posing as a British businessman, to rebuild an Israeli spy network there after early ones had been rolled up by the Egyptians, one of his first recruits was this young French Jewess, Victorino (known as Marcelle), who lived in Alexandria.

She was twenty-four years old, an attractive Olympian athlete girl, and they became lovers. Through her many friends in Egyptian high society, she was able to provide useful information, and also to help the Colonel to recruit more agents.

That was how she came to be involved in the most disastrous of all Israeli espionage operations, the 1954 plan to plant terrorist bombs in British and American offices in Egypt in a ludicrous attempt to turn those countries against President Nasser. She suffered greatly for it.

When the plot was betrayed by another Israeli agent, Paul Frank, the network was quickly rounded up by Egyptian counter-intelligence, though Colonel Dar managed to escape.

Marcelle Ninio, unsure what to do when she heard that things had gone wrong, went to see Max Bennett, the top Israeli undercover man in Egypt. Egyptian security men who had her under surveillance burst into the apartment, and caught him transmitting to Tel Aviv by radio.

Tortured and constantly interrogated, Marcelle twice tried to kill herself, the second time by jumping from a window. In the autumn of 1954 she was sentenced to fifteen years, and spent fourteen of them in Egyptian gaols before being repatriated in a prisoner exchange in 1968 after the Six-Day War.

Back home in Israel, she was treated as a national heroine. She married Colonel Eli Boger in December 1971, at a rather grand wedding ceremony, attended by Golda Meir (then Prime Minister) and by top generals and intelligence officers.

NOSENKO, Yuri Ivanovich

Among the most equivocal of KGB defectors to the West, Major Nosenko presented himself to the Americans in Switzerland in 1964, and despite three years of interrogation the CIA has never been able to make up its mind whether he was genuine or a plant. Did he defect, or was he pushed, on orders from above?

The reason for doubt springs not only from the fact that it can be proved that many of his statements were false, but also because of his connection in the Soviet Union with Lee Harvey Oswald, the man who murdered President Kennedy. Nosenko was deputy director at the American section of the VIIth Department of the KGB, which had dealings with American visitors to the USSR.

In that capacity he had to inspect Oswald's application for Soviet citizenship during his stay in Russia in 1959. According to the Nosenko scenario, the KGB had put down Oswald as unstable and unreliable, and had given orders that on no account should he be recruited for any kind of work on their behalf.

When it emerged that the assassin of the President had visited the USSR, and moreover had a Russian wife, the Kremlin was terrified that it might be assumed that they were implicated. Judging other people's behaviour by their own, they assumed that these facts would convince the Americans that the KGB had been plotting assassination because of the Russian connection.

The arrival of Nosenko at an appropriate moment, eager to explain that the KGB had nothing to do with Oswald, faced the CIA with a dilemma. The fact that he was in America to make this point must mean one of two things. Either it was true that the Kremlin considered Oswald a loner, and wanted to reassure the United States by dispatching Nosenko as a false defector for the purpose; or they were trying to hide something.

Some argued that the Kremlin could have

transmitted its assurances of innocence by other means. It was certainly unprecedented for them to hand over a senior intelligence officer on a one-man deception mission. But the Kremlin often does move in a mysterious and devious way, its wonders to perform.

On the other hand, it soon became apparent that Nosenko had not been carefully prepared for such a mission. He was easily caught out on detail, and yet the importance of the mission would surely have forced the KGB to prepare him carefully for the interrogation they knew he would have to face.

Whichever way the Nosenko defection is assessed, it does raise the question whether or not Oswald was associated with the KGB. It seems extremely unlikely that at that stage the Russians would really have planned to kill the President of the United States. But if they had decided upon such an enterprise, fraught with risks and dangers, would they have chosen such a man as Oswald?

Besides his instability, he had a known record on American security files; he was a man totally unsuitable for such a task. The likelihood is that if such a desperate assassination plan had been hatched the KGB with its immense resources would have chosen an anonymous professional killer with experience and the ability to cover his traces.

Nosenko himself gave an account of the high-level panic in Moscow when it was learned that Oswald had spent time in the USSR. They dispatched a special military aircraft to collect his dossiers, fearing that despite the edict that he was not to be employed by the KGB, some lowly officer in an outlying station might have commissioned him unawares for some task. No such evidence was discovered.

During his debriefing Nosenko gave the Americans many details about the activities of the KGB against foreigners in Moscow. Among the more diverting was his account of a big operation to raid the Swedish Embassy.

Careful preparations had been made by a woman agent for the seduction of the night watchman. A reconnaissance had also revealed the presence of a fierce guard-dog.

As the time approached for the raid the KGB girl lured away the guard while another agent was detailed off to silence the dog by feeding it with meat. As the twelve-strong squad of safe-pickers and break-in experts went about their work the dog duty man urged them to hurry, saying 'He is eating meat by the kilo!'

NOURI, Colonel Osman

One of the most effective of Egyptian counter-espionage officers, he was head of intelligence in Cairo in the 1950s. A faithful servant of President Nasser when he first came to power, the Colonel established close links in Syria and Iraq, where his agents took part in plots against governments disliked by the Egyptians.

He also set up networks in Europe. He himself visited Pullach, headquarters of the West German intelligence service run by General Gehlen, who was at that time helping (as he put it) to inject expertise into the Egyptian service.

Osman Nouri proved an apt pupil, and was happy to co-operate with some of the ex-Nazis in Gehlen's service. He was the officer who broke the ill-conceived Israeli plot in 1954 to make terrorist bomb attacks in Cairo and Alexandria. He achieved this by paying 40,000 Deutschmarks to an Israeli spy named Paul Frank, to act as double agent and betray the plotters. Nouri arrested eleven conspirators, allowing Frank to escape to Vienna, where he remained in contact with him.

The Colonel later played a notable role in the Egyptian invasion of Yemen to overthrow the Imam. He was a ruthless intelligence chief, and his men did not hesitate to use torture and brutality to secure confessions.

Later he became Egyptian ambassador to Nigeria and used intelligence skills to thwart Israeli influence in Africa.

NUT, Lieutenant-Colonel Bernard

Gendarmes found the body of this colonel in the French counter-espionage service sprawled in the snow by his parked Peugeot 305 on a mountain road in the French Maritime Alps in February 1983. Six feet away, they discovered a Smith and Wesson .357 Magnum which had fired three shots.

The colonel had died from a bullet in the back of the head, and although the authorities stuck to their theory that this was a case of suicide, there was no note. What did emerge was the fact — unsuspected by his neighbours, who thought that Bernard Nut, a quiet family man, was an engineer — was that he had in fact been active on behalf of the Alpine Affairs Bureau of French security.

The south of France is a critical area for espionage. In the foothills of the Alps are electronic intelligence-gathering stations, French nuclear missiles are based on the Albion plateau there, and near by is the nuclear submarine base at Toulon.

Soviet Bloc agents are frequently active in the area, which is easily accessible from the Italian frontier. The French colonel's death was linked with an announcement a few days before of the arrest of a KGB officer named Viktor Pronin, who had been working under cover as an Aeroflot official in Rome, and who had microfilm of Western defence plans on him.

There was also the suggestion that he had helped the Italians to uncover the Bulgarian connection in the attempted assassination of the Pope in 1981. Although it is most unusual for secret services to carry out revenge killings, this case aroused suspicions, for Colonel Nut had spoken of a rendezvous the evening that he disappeared, and it seems more than likely that he was murdered.

OLDFIELD, Sir Maurice

The man appointed to become head of the British Secret Intelligence Service in 1973 was a 57-year-old bachelor who after his time at Manchester University had spent a lifetime in intelligence work. The entry under his name in *Who's Who*, as is customary in Britain, was vague about his career, giving away only hints to the well-informed.

He was listed as a counsellor in the Foreign Office. His address was Over Hadden, Bakewell, Derbyshire, and his recreation was noted as 'farming'. Yet, for thirty-four years the man who had risen to the rank of lieutenant-colonel in the Army had tended acres of secret information, and had gained a great reputation in the international circles of espionage. He had served in the Far East, in Singapore, and had headed the SIS station in Washington.

After his period as deputy head of SIS in London, during which time he supported moves which led to the mass expulsion of Soviet spies from London, he took over the organization at a difficult time. A bespectacled man with chubby face, a cheerful manner and a lively sense of humour, he was tough, though opposed to violence. Indeed, it is unlikely that he had any experience of the rough stuff of espionage.

He retired with a knighthood in 1978, but was then appointed as Co-ordinator of Security in Northern Ireland, where the Provisional Irish Republican Army was actively engaged in terrorism. He was well suited to co-ordinate military and police intelligence in the task of keeping law and order.

Sir Maurice died in 1981 after he had gone into full retirement.

OSBORN, Richard

The interesting fact about the routine announcement in Moscow that this First Secretary from the economics section of the US Embassy had been caught red-handed in May 1983 was that it contained a technical mystery. For the KGB claimed that Osborn had been arrested while transmitting messages from a radio to a Marisat communications satellite.

No comment was forthcoming from the

Americans, but if this method was in fact being used it marked a new development in espionage techniques, and that indeed may be why the KGB was so keen to announce its detection. They added no further details, except that Osborn had notes written upon paper which quickly dissolved in water. Together with his wife, Mary, and his two children, he was expelled from Moscow.

It was the first such expulsion of an American diplomat since 1978, when a woman diplomat named Martha Petersen was said to have been caught taking a message from a dead-letter box, and was declared *persona non grata*.

OWEN, Will, MP

A 69-year-old ex-miner who became Member of Parliament for Morpeth in Northumberland and an agent for the Czechs. According to the confessions of Joseph Frolik, the Czech security service defector, he had been recruited during a visit to Prague in 1957 sponsored by the communist government. Frolik further claimed that he had been a useful source of British information, for which he was paid.

Owen was appointed to the Defence Estimates Committee in 1960, and served on a sub-committee dealing with Admiralty matters. He firmly denied to MI5 officers that he had received any cash from Colonel Jan Paclik and Robert Husak of the Czech Embassy in London, but later admitted lying, and said that he had received a total of £2,300.

In 1970 he resigned his seat in Parliament after more evidence became available through another defector. At his trial that year, which lasted for thirteen days, he defended himself by claiming that although the Czechs had blackmailed him, he did not have access to any military information not generally available. He was found not guilty on all the eight charges brought against him.

After the trial Will Owen, secure in the knowledge that he could not be tried again on charges of which he had been cleared, agreed to be interviewed by British security in the presence of another Labour MP, and spoke freely to them.

PAQUES, Georges

The most fascinating feature of the spy scandal at NATO headquarters of the North Atlantic Treaty Organization in 1963 was the personality of this urbane French intellectual, a teacher who had become a senior government servant, and the curious nature of his motivation. When he was arrested at his opulent Paris apartment near the Bois de Boulogne that summer he was deputy head of NATO's press and information department.

Paques had passed over to the Russians quantities of highly secret intelligence material, both political and military. So far as the Soviets were concerned he was an extremely valuable agent, reporting to the counsellor, no less, at their Paris embassy; at his trial in 1964 the French court pronounced him guilty of treason, with a sentence of imprisonment for life.

Despite that, Paques himself, though admitting the facts of the case and acknowledging that he had supplied the Russians with information, insisted that what he had done he had done for France. For he had a vision of France as a key partner in a great utopian socialist Europe of the future, which he believed he could help to create.

'I have never been a Soviet agent', he boldly stated in court. Indeed, from the evidence it further emerged that he believed that he could supply secret information to the KGB without becoming a Russian agent.

Early in his espionage career this remarkable spy had coldly refused to be instructed in spy photography, or to take pictures of the documents he was willing to supply. That would have been vulgar and unsuitable in his eyes, for it would have made him into a lowly agent, when he saw himself as a high-powered 'negotiator', acting in the cause of world peace to prevent misunderstandings between the super-Powers.

Quite what the Russians made of all this has unfortunately never been recorded. But his case officer (if one may use the phrase in the circumstances) Vasili Vlassov, counsellor at the Soviet Embassy, must have had a pretty unenviable task explaining things to his hard-nosed colleagues in Moscow.

In the long campaign of the well-placed French functionary, he handed over details about NATO contingency plans at the time of the Berlin crisis of 1961, when the East Germans first built the wall to divide the city. Armed with the knowledge that the West intended no firm action, the Eastern Bloc was able to ignore verbal protests.

Paques had also provided the Kremlin with details of American radar installations in Turkey. He had done this, he said, in order to convince the Russians that the Americans really had removed a number of obsolete missiles, which otherwise they might not have believed.

Yet at his trial (which was the first spy case to reach the French security court established by General de Gaulle) Paques was able to insist, 'Russia does not mean anything to me. Marxism is nothing to me.' He was proud that the Russians had flattered him by saying that his help with information about the Berlin crisis had helped Nikita Khruschev to act with moderation.

In the words of the French prosecutor Maître Caron, 'His arrogance was boundless.' Georges Paques explained that the small sums of money he had accepted from the Russians had been taken simply to convince them that the information was genuine. He told the court that he had a rich wife, and that the £40 or so a year he received was of no significance.

It emerged that Georges Paques — described by the friends who rallied round him as brilliant, rather cynical, a *bon vivant* and good company — had been in touch with the Russians since his time in Algiers just after the end of the world war. But he only became really useful in Paris in 1958, when he was appointed as an official to the joint chiefs of staff department of the French defence ministry.

In the same year Vasili Vlassov returned to Paris as Soviet Embassy counsellor, and had frequent clandestine meetings in the Paris Métro and in other public places. The Soviet diplomat had been disappointed to hear that he was leaving the Defence Ministry, and then suggested that he should move into NATO.

Vlassov revealed his own professionalism as the net began closing in upon his contact, who was put under surveillance in 1963; for he failed to appear at a number of rendezvous arranged between them. It was at that point that even Paques began to think that he was KGB rather than a diplomat. After the arrest Vlassov was discreetly ordered to leave by the French government.

Officers of DST, the French counter-intelligence service, had begun investigating the career of Georges Paques on the basis of information from Anatoli Golytsin, a KGB colonel who defected to the United States in 1962. He had specialized in probing NATO secrets, and was able to supply copies of documents signed by Georges Paques, which he had provided from the files in Paris.

Georges Paques, the spy who thought he was not a spy, and who believed he might use the KGB to promote his own ambitions as a man of influence, was fifty when the security court sentenced him to life imprisonment. His sentence was later reduced to one of twenty years.

PATHÉ, Pierre-Charles

In one of the exceptional cases in which court action has been taken against what is called 'an agent of influence', the French arrested and convicted this 71-year-old journalist. He was the son of Pathé, the cinema pioneer. For twenty years he had been connected with the KGB, but as the DST arresting officer put it to the State Security Court, 'He is not a spy, he is a KGB freelance.' They had mostly used him as a channel for publication in his political newsletter of material favourable to the USSR, for analyses of political developments in France, and for items of information about people in public life.

In fact the Russians who used him were obeying the Andropov order to win support abroad for the USSR by disinformation. The reason for the arrest and subsequent five-year sentence on Pathé was that the French government and its security services wanted to teach the KGB a lesson, and demonstrate that they were aware of the new tactics.

Perhaps they were influenced also by memories of the trapping in Moscow of Ambassador Dejean, when Soviet intelligence took blackmail pictures of him with a Russian girl. The KGB had intended to use him too, not to pass over secret papers but as an agent of influence close to General de Gaulle.

Technically, M. Pathé was proved guilty of dealings with a foreign Power because he had received from Russian agents up to 100,000 francs in payment for his services. He also supplied lists of French people sympathetic to the Russian cause, and was asked for personal details about an officer in the French intelligence service.

Although the old gentleman defended himself by saying that the list he handed over to the Russian at a café in 1979 was simply a list of subscribers to his newsletter, the court was convinced that he had been up to mischief in the field of disinformation — or as the French put it, *l'intox* — intoxication, that is, poisoning of opinion by false rumour.

A year after his conviction Pierre Pathé was pardoned by President Mitterrand and released from gaol because of his advanced age. But the point had been made.

PAVLICHENKO, Vladimir Pavlovich

Denounced as a veteran KGB agent at the United Nations in New York in 1971, Pavlichenko nevertheless had his contract as Director of External Relations in the Office of Public Information there renewed for another two years shortly afterwards. He was then a powerfully built 48-year-old linguist who had been in the post for five years.

He originally went to the UN as a translator in 1953. US security officers believed that it was his main duty to cultivate scientists at various international meetings.

Pavlovich travelled extensively on the American continent. He first visited Canada to attend the Pugwash scientific conference organized by Cyrus Eaton, the American industrialist. Although he was not known to have any scientific qualifications, he went as head of a delegation from the Soviet Academy of Sciences to the Toronto international assembly on nuclear weapons.

When he was named in a *New York Times* article as an agent he described it as a slander. The Soviet Union huffed and puffed, demanding that the US should take measures to stop the American press trying 'to evoke anti-Soviet hysteria'.

But a well-placed defector, Peter Deriabin, insisted that he had worked with Pavlichenko at Moscow headquarters in the old days in what was later called the First Chief Directorate. It is well known to the CIA and FBI that a high proportion of the swollen Russian contingent at United Nations works for the state security organization.

PENKOVSKY, Colonel Oleg

Of all the Soviet citizens who provided the West with intelligence information, the best-informed, highest-placed, most courageous and indeed the noblest of them all was Colonel Oleg Penkovsky. He was a spy of conscience who helped to give espionage a good name.

A much-decorated artillery officer of the Red Army — in which he served during the Second World War as commander of the 41st Guards Anti-Tank Regiment — he had graduated from the Frunze military academy. As a full colonel at forty, he was chosen for service with the GRU, the intelligence directorate of the General Staff.

After a spell of field-work as assistant military attaché in Ankara, Turkey, he returned to GRU headquarters and took a nine months missile course at the Dzerzhinski artillery academy. He seemed an ideal Soviet man, a party member and an enthusiastic officer on the way up. He was married to Vera, the daughter of Lieutenant-General Varentsov, Army Group artillery commander under whom he had served.

It was his growing disillusion with the hypocrisies and failures of the Soviet Union which pushed him into another course of action which he considered justified as a Russian patriot, rather than as a communist party loyalist. He particularly hated Khruschev, who was ruling and rampaging at the time in the Kremlin.

In particular he feared that Khruschev might be the cause of the world blundering into a nuclear war. In his papers published later he wrote, 'In Moscow my life has been a nuclear nightmare. I know the extent of their preparations ... the plan to strike first at any cost ... I must defeat these men.'

These deep convictions prompted him to supply military information which might help to prevent disaster. In fact his high-level briefings on Soviet military preparedness did greatly assist President Kennedy in outfacing Khruschev in the Cuban missile crisis of 1962. Through Penkovsky he knew that despite their bluster the Soviets were not strong enough in rocketry to start a war. Khruschev had to accept the American President's demand that the missiles he had placed in Cuba must be withdrawn.

Penkovsky gave details about the missiles placed in Cuba by the Soviets which included not only their range and the procedures needed to make them operational but also their rate of re-fire. This was essential for decision-making in Washington. When President Kennedy considered plans to bomb the rocket sites he wanted to know how long it would take the Russians to be ready for a second launch if the first bombing failed to take them out completely.

Penkovsky's first contact with the West was made in late 1960 through Greville Wynne, a British business-man with wartime experience of clandestine work who was in Moscow to arrange for a Soviet trade delegation to visit London. He simply told Wynne that he was in possession of facts which must be made known to the West.

To prove the point, he handed over a sealed envelope giving full details about himself, together with top-secret material to demonstrate the depth of his knowledge. Shortly after, in April 1961, Penkovsky himself led the delegation to London, staying at the Mount Royal Hotel near Marble Arch. Every night after his compatriots had gone

to bed he went to a specially organized suite for detailed debriefing by British and American intelligence officers. They were astonished by the depth and breadth of knowledge of this well-placed member of the Soviet military privileged class, which as a professional himself he was able to pass on succinctly.

Careful arrangements were made for him to continue the service after his return to Moscow. He wrote later in the apocalyptic style later made familiar by Solzhenitsyn, 'A new alliance was created ... God will help us in this great and important work.' Back at his flat overlooking the Moscow river, 'Alex', as he was now code-named, used his new Minox camera to photograph quantities of secret papers and manuals. He handed sixteen rolls of film to Wynne on his next visit to Moscow. They were duly passed on to Ruari Chisholm, the clever SIS man at the British Embassy, for onward transmission to London.

When Wynne was in Moscow, or when Penkovsky was allowed to visit London and Paris, it was relatively simple to hand over material. More dangerous and complicated arrangements by drop, and apparently casual meetings with diplomats, had to be contrived in Moscow.

During two winter meetings with Mrs Chisholm, wife of the diplomat, Penkovsky's practised eye noted the presence of the same small brown car with the registration number SHA 61.45. There could be no doubt that his activities were arousing the suspicion of the KGB, the 'Neighbours' as they were known to GRU officers — and the 'neighbours' were always ready to prove their vigilance in ferreting out disloyalty in a rival service.

There were other signs of KGB activity. Penkovsky learned that they were trying to discover the burial-place of his father. This too was ominous because he had been born in the Caucasus, son of an officer in the Tsarist army who fought against the communists in the civil war, and, if it could be proved that he was not dead but treacherously in exile, it would be taken as evidence against 'Alex'.

Despite the very real danger Penkovsky made it clear that he considered it his duty as a soldier to stay, as he put it, in the front line at a crucial time of international tension. But in London plans were already being made to rescue the valuable informant from the Soviet Union if need be.

One idea was to have him and his family picked up by a submarine in the Baltic, but a more favoured plan was to get specially made caravans into Leningrad as part of a convoy being set up by Greville Wynne as a mobile trade exhibition. It became obvious how perilous such an enterprise would be when Wynne visited Moscow to make arrangements.

The Peking restaurant, where he was to meet 'Alex', was most obviously under KGB surveillance, and Penkovsky arranged another rendezvous at Sheremetyevo airport early the following morning. At that meeting he gave Wynne another intelligence packet and pulled his GRU rank to get him out on an earlier flight, fearing that the British business-man might be arrested. Not content with that bold step, he complained to his superiors about KGB insolence in spying on a GRU officer.

Despite that the hunters were closing in, and by the time that Wynne finally got to Budapest, trying an alternative plan to move his rescue caravan to Moscow by way of Hungary, Penkovsky had already been arrested. Wynne too was seized and taken to Moscow.

The show trial took six months to prepare, and the authorities were determined to go the whole way in exhibiting the depravity and disloyalty of Colonel Penkovsky. They even brought on two witnesses to prove that Penkovsky had once drunk wine from the shoe of a girl, for it is always important in Soviet trials to show that traitors have adopted rather out-of-date corruptions of the West. To clinch the matter in anti-semitic Russian eyes, the witnesses of such horrors were Jewish.

Colonel Penkovsky, as is customary in Moscow trials, made a full and detailed confession giving an accurate account of what had happened. He was also made to confess to the basest qualities, moral decay brought on by heavy drinking and 'certain inherited characteristics' — no doubt from his Tsarist officer father.

Even though reduced to such a desperate state, Penkovsky did everything he could in his evidence, to minimize the part played by Greville Wynne. He made it clear that it was he who had approached Wynne, and that the British business-man had no knowledge of the contents of material handed to him.

Lieutenant-General Gorni, the prosecutor, stressed that as a result of moral decay Penkovsky had become an agent of imperialist intelligence services. He condemned both the CIA which 'like a giant octopus extends its tentacles into all corners of the earth' and the old-established British intelligence service, 'no less insidious and astute in its methods'.

There was no doubt about the verdict — Oleg Penkovsky was found guilty of high treason, and sentenced to death and his personal property to be confiscated. A few days later *Izvestia* announced that he had been shot, adding for good measure that when his appeal was rejected 'There was not a trace of the grand manner he had assumed in court. He met his death like a despicable coward.' That is difficult to believe.

Such comments showed that everything possible was being done both to discredit Penkovsky and to minimize the importance of the fact that an ideal Soviet man of high position had for more than eighteen months leaked the closely guarded secrets of the Kremlin to outsiders. Here was a spy whose information had put the West at an advantage in the Cuban crisis and in the Berlin crisis. He had shaken the Soviet hierarchy to its foundations.

When after Penkovsky's death his collected writings were published in Britain and the United States, the Soviet government indignantly protested, and claimed that they were a fake.

What the Russians had failed to mention during the trial was Colonel Penkovsky's modest ambition: that eventually the British would offer him a knighthood, so that his reward would have been to become known as Sir Oleg Penkovsky. Curiously enough, it was a vanity he shared with his opposite number Kim Philby, the British spy for the Kremlin. Philby's desire to become 'Sir' was prompted by ironic motives, and he had to be content with general-officer rank in the KGB instead, rather than as well.

PETROV, Vladimir and Evdokia

A survivor from the old espionage service in the Soviet Union before it became known as the KGB, Petrov was an experienced agent who had come into the business by way of service in the navy as a cypher expert. He had done well, and was a major in the KGB when he arrived in Canberra in February 1951, nominally as consul.

Within a few months the Australian Security Intelligence Organization, knowing his history, had put him in touch with one of their men, Dr Michael Bialoguski, a Polish refugee used to acting as a communist sympathizer. They soon became friendly, and Petrov frequently complained about his ambassador, whose wife quarrelled with Mrs Petrov, and talk turned to defection.

Petrov, by now alarmed at the idea of being recalled to Moscow — especially after the downfall of his old boss Lavrentia Beria — began making arrangements to buy a farm in Australia. Australian intelligence had a tape recording of him arranging on 5 April 1954 for completion and defection.

The date was chosen because Petrov knew that his replacement was arriving on that day. In due course he left the Embassy with a pile of documents.

What he had not told the Australians was that his wife Evdokia Petrov was also a senior KGB agent, and for that reason he had not talked to her of his defection plan. When news of his disappearance broke she was held under guard at the Embassy.

When the Russians drove Mrs Petrov to Sydney airport for the first stage of her flight under escort back to Moscow there was a near-riot. Indignant Australians angrily surged forward as she was led by two guards towards the BOAC Constellation. The guards panicked and roughly pushed Mrs Petrov, which incensed the crowds further.

Before the flight reached its first stop in Darwin a Russian-speaking stewardess had talked to Mrs Petrov when she went to the lavatory. She was given newspapers which printed appeals from her husband to join him. Eventually she told the crew that she too wanted to stay in Australia and the captain alerted Darwin.

Police officers came aboard there and disarmed the two Soviet heavies, who both had Walther automatics. Petrov and his wife were reunited, and later that year testified before the Royal Commission investigating Soviet espionage in Australia. They were able to reveal that a spying offensive was under way.

They also provided useful information for British intelligence on details of the Burgess and Maclean defection.

PHILBY, Harold Adrian Russell ('Kim')

The Soviet spy who during and after the Second World War inflicted more damage on Western intelligence operations, and was responsible for the death and disappearance of more loyal field men, than any other secret agent. For nearly thirty years he supplied quantities of secret information to the Soviet Union, and when they finally rescued him after his ultimate detection the Russians marked their appreciation of his services by promoting him to the KGB rank of general.

Kim Philby (so nicknamed after the boy spy hero of Kipling's story) was also the longest surviving of the Cambridge group recruited in the 1930s to mole their way into positions of influence. In the 1980s, and now aged over seventy, Kim Philby was still labouring in Moscow on behalf of his Soviet friends.

In Moscow it was widely held that President Andropov, himself an old KGB man, relished Philby's advice on his favourite subject of disinformation. Philby was also remarkable among his generation of traitors for not being a homosexual. Nobody blackmailed him into espionage; he volunteered for it, almost as though the chase, and the quest, and the secret life were ends in themselves.

Indeed, it can well be argued that this stocky,

independent man was a born spy. His father St John Philby was a cantankerous adventurer and traveller, who after leaving the civil service of the old Raj in India took to Arabia as the friend and confidant of desert monarchs. Kim was born in India, lived in the Middle East in early life and as he himself wrote later did not feel English, or indeed of any nationality. For him patriotism was not a quality which came naturally.

At Cambridge University in the early 1930s he came in contact with the infamous trio Burgess, Maclean and Blunt, and they all gravitated to the University red cell. It was not long before Philby was spotted for more serious and covert work. From the discussion groups of communist dons he quickly graduated as a leg man to Samuel Cahan, the Soviet resident director in London. It was a meeting with this Russian officer in a London safe house, probably in 1933, which began the long chain of events which transformed him into a top spy.

That was the year in which he left Cambridge, and before long he made his first sortie into Europe, on a motor-bike to Vienna. There under strict supervision of his new masters he became deeply involved in the complicated and violent street-fighting politics of pre-war Vienna. This provided his first taste of the rough stuff, and the experience also furnished him with his first wife, Litzi, the daughter of a Jewish Austrian who was herself a keen communist.

Back in London he took no overt part in politics but went to work quietly for a respectable weekly magazine. From there he went off to report as a freelance on the civil war in Spain, choosing the fascist side in order to improve his cover. He made a bit of a name for himself, was taken on by the London *Times*, and in 1939 went to France as a correspondent for that newspaper, covering the phoney war.

When he returned to London the smart set from the universities were busy enrolling themselves in various special units and in the rapidly expanding secret services. To get into the SIS by way of the newly formed Special Operations Executive was as Philby later confessed 'much easier than I had thought'.

He took an agent's course, and this well-built young man proved an apt pupil in unarmed combat and suchlike skills. Soon he found himself running a subversion and sabotage group consisting of Poles and other Europeans who had fled to England, and some of whom he was later to betray.

From there Kim — 'The son of old St John Philby, you know,' and therefore considered an ideal man for bizarre enterprises — moved, to the delight of his Soviet controllers, into counter-espionage, where he ran an Iberian sub-section. One useful consequence from a Kremlin-eye view was that before long he was in close touch with the Americans from the Office of Strategic Services who came to Britain to learn their trade. They were the nucleus of what developed into the CIA.

So far as the British intelligence service was concerned, the first big mistake in the Philby case was to retain his services after the war as a regular. For that enabled him to continue his upward career, enjoying ever greater possibilities of providing the Soviets with important material.

To their great satisfaction, he was now entrusted with the Russian desk of MI6, where he could not only supply information about British and American operations but could also suppress information damaging to the Russians.

When Konstantin Volkov, ostensibly Russian consul-general in Turkey, informed the British Embassy that he knew of English spies in high places in London Philby tipped off the KGB and delayed his recovery and interrogation, to give the Russians time to dispose of Volkov. The unfortunate Volkov was shipped back to Russia to an unpleasant fate.

Unharmed by an event which might have led to his exposure, Philby's career continued satisfactorily. In 1946 he received the OBE for wartime service, ridded himself of his Austrian communist wife by divorce and married Aileen Furse in London.

Three years later he achieved the summit of his promotion by being appointed to Washington as the SIS representative with the duty of liaising with the CIA. As a hard drinker and amusing talker he got along well enough with most of his

American colleagues. But James Angleton, a veteran of OSS who had known and harboured suspicions about Philby in the old days in London, kept him at arm's length, even when they lunched together. He was now head of CIA counter-intelligence, and it has been suggested that he ran a double agent who was keeping him informed about Philby's activities.

In particular, Angleton suspected Philby's role in the Albanian affair. This was an operation begun in 1946 by the British to help Albanian exiles mount guerrilla operations and a coup against the newly established communist regime there. Later the CIA joined the operation, which failed because every time that guerrillas were parachuted in, communist security troops were waiting to attack them. Up to three hundred lost their lives, and Philby was the man responsible.

SIS and CIA mounted another operation, parachuting in Ukrainian exiles who disappeared without trace. With callous humour Philby later wrote, 'I do not know what happened to the parties concerned. But I can make an informed guess.' Their exiled Ukrainian leader, Stefan Bandera, was murdered by a KGB assassin in Munich.

While Philby was still in Washington there were post-mortems on the Albanian affair, attended by himself, and by Angleton, who felt more and more convinced that Kim was the man to blame. He did not voice his suspicions to the British, preferring to pursue his schemes for cornering the other British spy in Washington at the time, Donald Maclean.

Meanwhile in his official position as liaison man operating in the British Embassy with limitless access to papers, Philby was providing a mass of material for his Kremlin bosses. In fact his very presence there was enough to undermine every move by the Anglo-American intelligence community, for everything became known to the Russians in advance.

Among other pieces of information he had access to was the fact that investigators were closing in on Donald Maclean, who was by then back in London. To warn him of the danger Kim unwisely used his other and less reliable friend,

Burgess, who returned to London to pass on the message. Clumsily, Burgess not only warned Maclean but also fled with him, thus automatically throwing suspicion on Philby, with whom he had stayed in Washington.

Although he was named in Parliament by Marcus Lipton, MP, as the guilty 'third man' in the case, and then interrogated at length within the SIS in London, Philby did not break and nothing could be proved against him.

Despite his forced resignation and the suspicion which now surrounded him, Philby continued as an MI6 freelance in Beirut under cover of being the joint correspondent there of the Observer and of the Economist. He became a public figure of sympathy, many people feeling that he had been driven out of his post by McCarthyism, and was now down on his luck.

He was to be seen in the shabby Normandy Hotel drinking with fellow-journalists, and doing a passable imitation of a correspondent in the field. He ran off with Eleanor, the then wife of Sam Pope Brewer of the New York Times, and later married her.

But by this time his long run of good luck and skilful manœuvring was coming to an end. In 1962 Nicholas Elliott from SIS volunteered to fly to Beirut and confront him with hard evidence of treachery.

He was unable, however, to corner the old spy and persuade him to return to London for further interrogation. By now Philby realized that new information against him was available. There had been many changes at SIS, which was putting its house in order, and fresh defectors had come over to provide more damning evidence.

Late in January 1963 on a stormy Lebanese night Kim Philby failed to turn up for dinner with his wife at the apartment of a British diplomat. He had fled by way of the Soviet trade mission to Moscow, and it is in keeping with the life-style of this still enigmatic spy that to this day it is not certain whether he left by sea or made his way overland up into Soviet Armenia.

Unlike the other British defectors to Moscow, Philby settled down there happily enough, loaded with Soviet decorations to replace the Order of the

British Empire of which he had been deprived. When Eleanor went to visit him there she found that Melinda, Donald Maclean's wife, had moved in with him. Later he married a Russian woman, with whom he was still living in the 1980s.

His political views do not seem to have changed. In his book, *My Silent War*, he wrote, 'There is still an awful lot of work ahead; there will be ups and downs ... But as I look over Moscow from my study window, I can see the solid foundations of the future I glimpsed at Cambridge.'

To that statement Vladimir Sakharov, who fled to the West much later, added an interesting postscript: 'Contrary to what was believed in the West, Philby was no retired intelligence agent when he reached Moscow. In fact, from the moment he arrived in Moscow, he had become an important member of the KGB's inner circle.'

Sakharov even believes that Kim Philby played a part in the rise to power of President Andropov.

PHILLIPS, David Atlee

An actor turned journalist, Phillips had his first taste of undercover work after he was shot down while serving as an air gunner in a Liberator bomber. Captured by the Germans, he became a member of his camp's escape committee, and after a year made his own escape to the American lines.

He was recruited by the CIA while running a shoestring newspaper in Chile, and took to espionage as if he had been born to it. He was one of the men behind the coup that toppled Jacobo Arbenz in Guatemala, which succeeded mainly because of his skilful use of black propaganda over a secret radio station. He did a similar job for the Cuban Bay of Pigs invasion, but that time he failed. In his book *The Night Watch*, he put the blame for failure on President Kennedy for cancelling the vital air strike on the day of the landings, and on the CIA for allowing the operation to escalate from a small-scale landing of guerrillas to a full-scale military invasion.

He was head of the Chile Task Force which tried to prevent Allende being elected, and he was chief of station in the Dominican Republic, where he was heavily involved in President Johnson's successful intervention to secure a friendly government in 1965. He served in eight countries, and ended his CIA career as head of the Western Hemisphere division dealing with Latin America as GS 18, the highest rank a CIA officer can reach unless he becomes Deputy Director or Director of the Agency.

He might have risen even higher, but heartsick at the way the CIA was being reviled in the wake of Watergate he resigned in 1975 in order to fight what amounted to a one-man campaign in support of the Agency. He turned his considerable energy and skill into writing, broadcasting and lecturing — often to hostile college audiences — and editing *Periscope*, the magazine of the Association of Former Intelligence Officers. He sought direct confrontations with men like Philip Agee, the ex-CIA operative who revealed the names of CIA agents serving abroad. He was particularly bitter about the men he held guilty of the murder of his friend Dick Welch, who was gunned down in Athens when his identity as Athens station chief was revealed along with his address by a Greek newspaper. Atlee Phillips' conclusion was that despite all its troubles the American intelligence set-up 'will survive'.

PICARD, Maurice

As some men love women, or wine, this high-ranking French Government servant had a passion for secret documents. In the words of one of those connected with his eventual conviction for leaking state papers, 'He always had something to sell.'

His taste for espionage developed early through contacts not only with German officers from the occupying force in France but also with the Russians. He claimed that his father had been a friend of Admiral Canaris, the wartime German intelligence chief.

It was because of his disappointment at being passed over for promotion in the French prefectorial administration that he decided to take his revenge by acting against the Vichy government in occupied France. His method was strange, for he decided to accomplish this by denouncing a local resistance group. Even that did not prevent him from being considered finally as a member of the Resistance — 'I was only 10 per cent a German agent,' he said.

After the war, as he rose in rank to become Prefect of one important *département* of France after another, he made contact not only with General Gehlen's new intelligence service in Pullach but also with the KGB. Finally, after he became head of the French civil defence organization, he was frequently in touch with Sergei Kuznetchev, counsellor of the Soviet Embassy in Paris from 1959 to 1964. Picard was able to supply useful military information.

But even the Russians became suspicious of the multiplicity of his activities. Maurice Picard was acting as a double agent for the Spanish intelligence service in providing information about communists on the Franco-Spanish border, and then in denouncing their activities to the Russians. He sought out Eastern Bloc diplomats, and even tried to make contact with the British and Americans.

In 1968 he was sentenced to seven years in prison. He was released a year later after powerful friends had intervened on his behalf.

PONOMAREV, Boris Nikolaevich

One of those septuagenarian heroes of the Soviet Union who has been plotting in the cause of world revolution in high places for a lifetime. At one point, in 1967, it looked as though he would become head of the KGB, but Yuri Andropov, the younger man, got the appointment instead.

He was a friend of Stalin, active in the old Comintern days before the war, and heavily engaged in the treacherous operations which ended in the invasion of Czechoslovakia, and the betrayal of Dubcek in 1968. As head of the international department responsible for control of non-ruling communist parties in the West, he played an important part in issuing directives to

the KGB and GRU for clandestine operations in support of those actions.

In October 1976 he visited London, and was the centre of hostile demonstrations organized by people well aware of his record. Although he met left-wing Labour members of parliament, an effort was made to prevent him visiting the House of Commons, as a person who clearly did not believe in democracy.

Not used to such treatment, he looked surly and ill at ease, rather like a provincial bank manager in his dark suit and with brushed forward hair, who intends to complain bitterly that things are not quite as they were portrayed in the tourist holiday brochure. 'The communists always remain the party of socialist revolution,' he had insisted, and was rather put out to find that workers in the West were not as ready as he had hoped to welcome Soviet subversion.

PONTECORVO, Bruno

'Goodbye, everybody. — Bruno' was the message on a holiday postcard from Italy addressed to Harwell, the British atomic research establishment, by the most cheerful and extrovert of those involved in the early atomic spy scandals. And that for several years was all that was heard of Pontecorvo, who had until that moment been touring his native Italy on a carefree holiday with his wife and children.

That was in 1950. It was not until five years later that the mystery was solved, at any rate partly, when as Comrade Bruno Maximovich and clutching a Soviet identity card, Pontecorvo was paraded at a press conference in Moscow. There he announced that he was working at the grandly styled International Centre of Research in the Peaceful Use of Atomic Energy in the Russian city of Dubna.

What never has emerged is quite why this brilliant Italian scientist, a handsome, friendly and outward-looking tennis-player of a man, had chosen to defect to the Soviet Union at the time when he did. The son of a prosperous Jewish family, he had moved to pre-war France to work with the Joliot-Curies. From there he made his way to the United States and worked with American atomic researchers before joining the British team on that side of the Atlantic, and becoming a British citizen.

Although he worked on projects which gave him access to a number of secrets, no evidence has ever been produced that he spied for Russia in the networks of foreign and domestic atomic spies. The Gouzenko papers from the GRU office in Ottawa made no overt mention of his name.

The only shadow of a doubt cast by them was a reference to someone codenamed 'Gini' and described simply as a Jew, which may or may not have been Pontecorvo. He was certainly not much interested in politics, and was by no means one of the left-wing sympathizers of the time.

There were several communists in the Pontecorvo family back in Italy, and indeed after the Fuchs affair Bruno went to the Harwell security officer to tell him that one of his brothers, Gilberto, was a party member. In the light of what had happened recently this did make him slightly suspect, and account for the fact that he thought seriously about leaving the secret establishment to take up an offer of open academic research at Liverpool University.

He was a man who constantly sought after new jobs, both academic and governmental, and he made it clear that he was ready to change nationality for the purpose almost as willingly as he exchanged posts. It is far from certain whether, when he left England on holiday, he intended to return or not.

Certainly his plans changed fairly abruptly after a meeting with Gilberto in Rome. Soon after he left his car and bought tickets for himself, his wife and family to fly to Stockholm, paying for them with hundred-dollar bills. Instead of leaving the flight there, not far from the home of the parents of his wife Marianne, they flew on to Helsinki, where a car was waiting at the airport to drive them to Soviet territory.

By that time any atomic secrets still in Pontecorvo's possession would have been out of date, and in any case the Soviets had already caught up the British, and indeed were in some respects well ahead of them. Even so, they were content enough to get the professional services of a Western scientist of international reputation, known as an innovative worker full of ideas. The alternative explanation for their aid in his flight eastward is that they feared that he might be questioned in the West, and would still be able to provide information about Russia's atomic spies.

When Pontecorvo appeared at his Moscow press conference, he stuck strictly to the party line and cheerfully talked about science in the service of human progress and not of war. He said he had chosen to work in the field of high energy.

In 1978 Italian academics invited Pontecorvo to Rome for celebrations in honour of his old teacher, the physicist Professor Enrico Amaldi. To their surprise the Soviets gave him a temporary exit visa. He would only say, 'I have never worked on a bomb.'

To mark his seventieth birthday in 1983, it was announced that Pontecorvo had been awarded the Order of the October Revolution for his work in developing the physical sciences.

POPOV, Dusko

A playboy spy whose success with beautiful women was matched only by his skill at espionage and daring in the field. This led to the theory that he served as a model for James Bond, the hero figure created by Ian Fleming. When the point was put to Popov he answered, 'I rather doubt that a Bond in the flesh would have survived for more than forty-eight hours as an espionage agent.'

The son of a wealthy Yugoslav family, he hated the Nazis, but by working for them contrived to be sent to Britain, where he offered his services to the Secret Intelligence Service. Code-named 'Tricycle', he became part of the Double XX system run by Sir John Masterman, which specialized in turning German agents and using them to plant false information.

Retailing German secrets to the British and passing on prepared information to the Germans, Popov became a classic double agent. One of his successes was in getting early information about the V-1 flying bombs. He also played a part in unmasking 'Cicero', the valet to the British ambassador in Ankara who took secret information from the Embassy safe and passed it to the Germans.

Although Popov was most useful to the British, he was less successful with the Americans. J. Edgar Hoover, the opinionated boss of the FBI, did not approve of him or trust him. With a code-name like 'Tricycle', he said scathingly, 'he had a liking for bedding two girls at a time'.

What that had to do with his skills in espionage was not clear, but it is certain that Hoover did not believe Popov's hints that the Japanese were about to attack Pearl Harbor, and his American career ended in mistrust and failure.

After the war he worked as a lawyer in France, and wrote a book about his experiences. He died at Opio in the south of France in August 1981 at the age of sixty-nine.

POPOV, Lieutenant-Colonel Pyotr Semyonovitch

This GRU (Soviet military intelligence) officer offered his services to the Americans in Vienna in 1952 simply by leaving a note in the car of a US diplomat. His most helpful piece of information was a list of the code-names of Soviet agents operating in the West, which set an agreeable puzzle for the cryptographers and researchers.

The following year, however, after spending some leave in Moscow he was re-posted to East Germany, completely cut off from his CIA case officer. Once again he had to resort to his old and dangerous trick of leaving a letter, this time with an officer of a visiting British military mission. He dutifully passed it on to the MI6 man in West Berlin at the time, who happened to be George Blake, later convicted as a British traitor in the service of the Russians.

It was at first assumed, after this fact came to light, that when Colonel Popov was arrested back in Moscow this was the reason. But there might have been another cause of Popov's downfall, for when he got back in touch with the CIA he warned them that he was dispatching a woman 'illegal' to

New York. The FBI made such a performance of watching her that the girl became terrified and rushed straight back to base. It seemed that the KGB might have assumed that Popov of the GRU was responsible.

It was not until October 1959 that the Colonel was arrested in Moscow, taken red-handed together with his CIA case officer, Russell Langrelle, while handing over messages on a bus. A later defector claimed that the unmasking was the work of KGB watchers who had kept Langrelle under surveillance on dead-letterbox duty and were waiting for him to meet his agent.

Colonel Popov was executed, according to one report, by being thrown into a furnace watched by GRU colleagues, *pour encourager les autres*.

This seems a fanciful version of what finally happened to him. It is much more likely that he was shot. This was a case of one mole in the British service — Blake — betraying another mole working for the West within the Soviet GRU. But for six years Popov had provided Western intelligence with valuable information about the regime he hated, and for a while he was particularly well placed in East Berlin as the officer responsible for choosing Soviet agents and then arranging their infiltration into the non-communist world.

POWERS, Francis Gary

A victim of high-altitude spying over the Soviet Union in 1960 in pre-satellite espionage days. With the help of the USAF, the Central Intelligence Agency, in face of the extreme difficulty of operating agents on the ground in the closed society of the Soviet Union, launched its U-2 programme to spy from above on warlike installations and troop movements.

Gary Powers, an Air Force captain who had trained as a fighter pilot, was briefed when he took off in May 1960 from Peshawar, Pakistan to fly over Russia to Norway, that the Russians had nothing capable of hitting him at 68,000 feet. That proved there was poor information about technical developments, for high over Sverdlovsk his U-2 was hit by a missile and badly damaged.

After parachuting to safety he was arrested, tried as a spy and sentenced to three years in gaol, and seven in a labour camp. He served only two years before the Russians used him as a pawn to secure the release of their valuable 'illegal' Rudolph Abel, who had been caught by the Americans.

The U-2 incident gave Khruschev a fine opportunity for rampaging propaganda, and terrible threats to bomb US bases if the U-2 was used again. President Eisenhower was caught wrong-footed because no cover story was available, except the lame excuse that Powers might have wandered over Russia by mistake. Finally, there was nothing for it but to admit the truth, though the President himself had not known about this flight — justified though it was.

Khruschev made full use of this unexpected bonus to break up the Paris summit, and to storm about France where the Great Power leaders were gathered, ranting about the wickedness of the Americans. In fact he was relieved not to have to go through with the summit, for he was already in trouble with the ruling clique at home, and could hardly have emerged from it with credit.

There had been U-2 flights before the Powers incident, and there were many more of them after it; and the Russians knew it. After his return Powers was subjected to a court of inquiry which considered whether to bring charges against him for failing to push the destruct button on his plane before bailing out. Powers, having heard about the fate of several Nationalist Chinese U-2 pilots who had pushed the button when their U-2s had 'flamed out' over China and had been destroyed with their aircraft, decided not to risk it. He also failed to use the suicide pin charged with shellfish toxin and hidden in a silver dollar.

There were those in the CIA who thought Powers should have killed himself instead of allowing himself to be captured. However, no charges were brought and, belatedly, in 1965 he was awarded the Intelligence Star, the CIA's highest award. In 1970 he published his best-selling memoirs. But fate caught up with him seven years later when he was killed in a helicopter crash while working as a pilot for a Los Angeles television station.

PRAEGER, Nicholas

He was a second-generation spy who ought to have known better, and a sad retribution awaited him. Nicholas Praeger was born a Czech, and his father, who worked in the British Embassy in Prague, took up British nationality in retirement, thus enabling Nicholas to get British nationality.

But unknown to the British the old man had worked for Czech intelligence all the time that he had been in the Embassy. The young Nicholas was not only fascinated by the country of his forbears, but also became an admirer of the communist way of life.

During 1959 he went to visit Czechoslovakia, and the intelligence service recruiters were waiting for him. He was a tempting and willing target who made no secret of his political leanings, and who by this time was serving in the RAF as a sergeant in a radar-development unit.

Lieutenant Husak took him over and introduced him to a girl who later became his wife. She too helped with his recruitment, which was not difficult. He returned to England as an active agent code-named 'Marconi', soon to be joined there by his fiancée.

First-hand evidence of what happened then comes from Josef Frolik, a Czech intelligence agent working in London at the time who later defected. Frolik reported that Nicholas Praeger (he changed the spelling to Prager in Britain) informed his control, a man named Malek, that he could sell to him complete plans of Blue Diver and Red Steer radar-jamming equipment. It was to be used by the British V-bomber nuclear force to evade detection.

To make sure that the photography was good they equipped 'Marconi' with a Polaroid and told him to pose as a camera buff at his workplace. Despite the fact that careful arrangements had been made for him to leave the precious pictures at a drop, Praeger ignored such refinements of caution, and simply went round to the Czech

Embassy and handed the secret material over. The intelligence men were horrified at such risky and unprofessional procedure.

It even gave Frolik himself a nasty turn. The Czech general staff were not very impressed with the material, or at least they affected not to be. But when it was passed over to the KGB they took a different view, saying that it was the best yet from the Czech service, and forwarding a telegram to Praeger saying that he would be highly rewarded. That was in 1961.

Praeger went on spying for another ten years before he was arrested. 'Now he was pale and shaken', wrote Frolik. 'But I felt no pity for him. He had entered espionage knowing exactly what it was about.'

He served only six of the twelve-year prison sentence imposed in June 1971 before being paroled. Then his suffering really began. As a naturalized citizen, he was stripped of British nationality and the government issued a deportation order. But no country would take him, and the Czech spymasters he had served well refused him refuge.

Stateless, and classified as unemployable, the wretched spy could not even go to see his wife and their son, by then living in West Germany. On security grounds, West Germany refused him re-entry after only one visit. He died in 1981, just twenty years after his great espionage coup, and at the age of fifty-two.

PRIMAKOV, Gennady

In March of 1983 (which was a busy year for the detection of spies), the British ordered the expulsion from London of this assistant air attaché. Speculation that a defector had provided an up-to-date order of battle of KGB men in the West was strengthened by the fact that Sergei Ivanov, a Second Secretary in the Soviet Embassy in London, and Igor Titov, a correspondent of *New Times*, a notorious nesting-place for Soviet security service men, were also turned out of London.

A month later the Russians announced the reprisals which are customary on such occasions, by declaring that Squadron Leader David Williams, an assistant British air attaché and Anthony Robinson, Moscow correspondent of the *Financial Times*, were spies, and should leave the USSR at once. Once again everybody denied having been involved in such activities.

The next British move in the sequence of espionage events was to turn out Anatoly Chernayev, a 35-year-old second secretary and labour attaché at the Soviet Embassy in London. That was in April 1983.

By the end of that month at least sixty-two Soviet agents had been detected and returned to base from non-communist countries in the first part of the year. This showed a significant increase over earlier years. During the whole of 1982 the comparable figure was forty-nine, and the year before only twenty-seven Soviet agents were expelled.

PRIME, Geoffrey

The first British traitor in the new age of electronic communications espionage was remarkably different in origin and upbringing from the élite university boys who took service with Stalin's KGB. Geoffrey Prime was born just before Hitler's war into a modest and unhappy Staffordshire family.

Despite the horror of being sexually assaulted by an adult relative, and nothing much in the way of education, he developed into a clever boy at a local technical school and escaped from the Staffordshire home by joining the RAF. This gave him a chance to go on a Russian-language course which brought him a posting to RAF Gatow in West Berlin. In the course of his duties he began learning German, and moved to Service interception work on Eastern Bloc military communications.

His Russian improved. He was promoted to corporal, then sergeant. It was at this stage that Prime, lonely and socially inadequate, began thinking that the Soviet regime was rather a good thing, presumably in the mistaken belief that communists were on the side of the under-dog.

Quite suddenly he made his decision, and at a Berlin check-point handed a note to a Red Army officer to say that he wanted to make contact. He volunteered for treachery, and the young airman was soon in touch with his two Soviet manipulators, Igor and Valya, promising to give them whatever they wanted.

During his short apprenticeship he photographed some RAF papers and informed about Russian codes which had been broken. His twelve years in the RAF were almost done, and no doubt with Russian encouragement he decided to use his Service training to get a linguistics job in London with the highly secret GCHQ, British Government Communications Headquarters.

It was the descendant of the British code-breaking organizations of the two world wars. Prime's first job in it was the translation of communications intercepts in London for onward transmission to the organization's centre at Cheltenham.

Between getting the job in July and joining the office in September 1968 he went back to East Berlin for a course in espionage methods. He was given the code name 'Rowlands', and returned to London equipped with a complete spy kit, most of it contained in a special leather briefcase with a false bottom, revealed by undoing two screws in the handle. In it also was a bundle of banknotes amounting to £400. Some of that was used to buy a good short-wave receiver and a reliable tape recorder, the other essential tools of his new trade.

He dispatched his material by microdots and the up-to-date versions of the spies' old stand-by invisible ink messages and sometimes made 'drops' to be collected. They got in touch with him through short-wave broadcasts of spaced groups of figures.

Not long after his first marriage (which turned out badly) the message from the East instructed him to go to a hiding-place by a lake near Esher, in Surrey. There he found a welcome package of money and a thank-you note for his services so far. Then there was a panic when Prime lost his supply of one-time pads which were needed to

translate his controller's messages. He took a risk, and at about the time that he had his second positive vetting wrote a plain-language message in invisible writing to the East German address.

The Russians responded and re-equipped him with what is called a 'live drop' — that is, one carried out by an agent. In fact, two agents called on Prime's sister and left a parcel containing another leather brief-case complete with pads and money.

By this time Geoffrey Prime was an old hand in the British service in Sigint, signals intelligence, and was ready to be promoted to more important work. In 1975, before being transferred to the establishment at Cheltenham, he was given a briefing on a new category of information which he would be called upon to handle and translate there, which required a special security clearance.

Under long-standing arrangements Cheltenham was part of an intelligence-sharing arrangement with the American National Security Agency, and both were now receiving material from a recently launched new type of spy satellite named Rhyolite, which could monitor all manner of conversations and electronic written messages in the Soviet Union. An even more advanced model, Argus, was almost ready for service.

Excited by this development, Prime promptly passed on the good news to his masters, who arranged for him to fly to Vienna with his material, and rewarded him with a modest few hundred pounds. The Russians were already being kept up to date about impressive technical developments by way of the self-recruited American spies in California, Boyce and Daulton Lee, who were at this time providing details about satellite-construction. Now they wanted to know about the intelligence product of the satellites from Prime.

Both of Prime's careers were prospering. On the one hand the Russians said that if he had to defect to them he would be made a KGB colonel; on the other the British promoted him to be section head, which allowed him to get his hands on ever more sensitive material.

In 1977 he married for the second time, to Rhona Ratcliff, a divorcée with three sons in whose house he had been lodging. In the same year he seemed anxious, and for a time thought seriously of defecting to Russia. It may be significant that he was having these doubts not long after the conviction of the two American spies in the same field as himself, who were sentenced respectively to life and forty years' imprisonment.

He may well have been tempted to take up the offer of defection with KGB field rank, in fear that the Boyce-Lee trail in California might be his undoing. Twice he booked flights to Helsinki, and twice he could not quite steel himself to do it. Finally, instead of retiring from the Soviet service he chose to resign from the Cheltenham establishment, though as a parting gesture he took five hundred photographs of secret documents with him.

In fact he seems to have been rather out of touch with the KGB for over two years before they made contact in April 1980 and again summoned him to Vienna when they took him for a three-day boat cruise on the Danube. It is not known whether they too had feared that he might be compromised by the American business or whether they lost interest when he resigned from his GCHQ job. But in any case, on the Danube trip they paid him for his left-over material and urged him to return to Cheltenham.

The following year Prime was again ordered to Berlin by the Russians, who were keen to reactivate him, and in a meeting at Potsdam they gave him £4,000, the largest sum they had ever paid for his services.

But by this time the wretched Prime had other troubles on his mind. He was a paedophile, and in this other secret life he had an obsessive passion for small girls. For the purpose of selecting victims, and unknown to his wife, he kept a card index of names and addresses of more than two thousand young girls taken from local newspapers. He even logged further details of telephone calls to them, and then followed up prospects by visiting houses hoping to find the children unprotected.

He made one such sortie just before going to see his spymasters in Vienna, then a more serious assault the following year. Finally, in April 1981,

he threatened a girl with a knife. She screamed, and he fled in terror.

The West Mercia police had been working for a long time on the case, and after this incident they got a description of the man good enough for a reasonable photofit and details of Prime's car. Two detectives called at the Prime house and interviewed him. Although badly shaken, he denied all knowledge of the assault, but the officers agreed that he bore a remarkable resemblance to the photofit.

Later, the nervous Geoffrey Prime told his wife about his obsession, and then in full confession went on to tell her about his spying as well. Yet when he went to the police he mentioned only the assaults, and it was not until Rhona, his wife, felt it her duty to inform the police about his espionage activities that a full investigation into that part of his life began.

In November 1982, at the end of his trial at the Old Bailey, Geoffrey Prime was sentenced to 38-years' imprisonment, thirty-five for spying and three for the sexual offences. It was not until after he had been tried that the British intelligence service had its chance to question Prime in detail. Earlier investigation had been left to the police, because it was feared that Prime might go back on his confession if questioned by military intelligence before the trial, and that would have meant discussion in court of highly sensitive secret material.

As the customary public and press outcry which always follows a new story of treachery in Britain subsided, the intelligence services in Britain and America began the difficult task of assessing the damage done to Allied communications intelligence. The judge had said, as judges often do, that the harm done was 'incalculable'. Caspar Weinberger, the US Defence Secretary, believed it was a serious breach, but not a catastrophe.

There had been a good deal of transatlantic talk about how shocked the Americans were at the laxness of British security which might tempt them to break off information-sharing. What in fact emerged from the Boyce-Lee case was that security seemed to be no better in NSA installations.

The truth is that in Western societies it is impossible to give total protection to such secretive places. The National Security Agency sent a delegation to London to help with the interrogation of Prime, headed by Benson Buffham, a former Deputy Director with experience of the British side of the operation. As a result of their joint investigations the British and Americans made moves to standardize security procedures.

Under American pressure the British finally agreed to resort to the polygraph lie-detector as a back-up to positive vetting. In this field the Americans are by no means perfect, for although in their establishments civilians must be polygraph-tested, service personnel are not bound to be so tested, on the grounds that they are posted and do not join.

After Prime the fear remained, bred by memories of the third, fourth and fifth men scandals of an earlier generation, that moles still remain undetected at GCHQ.

PROFUMO, John

What began as a minor scandal over the indiscreet sexual relationship between this Minister for War and an attractive call-girl named Christine Keeler slowly developed into the notorious Profumo Affair, which helped to bring down the Conservative Government of Harold Macmillan in 1963. It was the connection of Miss Keeler and Stephen Ward, the society whoremaster with a stable of girls, and Lieutenant-Commander Eugene Ivanov, a GRU officer and assistant naval attaché at the Soviet Embassy in London, which gave the case a security link.

John Profumo, Harrow and Oxford, came from a notable Italian family settled in London, and in 1940 became the youngest Member of Parliament. He had a good war, and ended up as a Brigadier, before going into business and entering politics.

He married the actress Valerie Hobson, and in 1960 became Secretary of State for War. He appeared to be at the beginning of a glittering political career when at the Cliveden country house of Lord Astor he came across the beautiful Christine Keeler bathing naked in a swimming-pool. Shortly afterwards they began an affair which was to make Miss Keeler famous, and bring disgrace upon Mr Profumo.

Through Stephen Ward, a fashionable osteopath in whose house she lived, Christine Keeler also met and slept with Commander Ivanov, the Soviet spy. All three were present at parties in Cliveden, some of them attended by Profumo.

News of the War Minister's arrival on the scene reached MI5, the counter-intelligence people, by way of their contact with Ward, who was providing information about Ivanov. That was on 10 July, and three weeks later Sir Roger Hollis, the director-general, informed Sir Norman Brook, the Cabinet Secretary, who warned John Profumo in August about intelligence interest in his connection with Ward and Ivanov.

The War Minister was alarmed, and mistakenly assuming that MI5 also knew of his affair with Christine Keeler, he wrote to her, breaking off relations. In fact the service, in a state of turmoil, was busy searching for moles within its own organization, and did not know of this aspect of things at the time.

Rumours did, however, begin circulating. George Wigg, a Labour Party expert on defence and security, received an anonymous telephone call in November 1962. 'You want to look at Profumo,' said the caller, darkly. It has since been suggested that this call was inspired by the Russians, who through reports from Ivanov knew what was going on. Clearly there was a chance for them to exploit their knowledge to muddy political waters.

However, what really began the process of revelation was an unrelated incident in December 1962 when two West Indians tried to shoot a way into Ward's flat in Wimpole Mews in an attempt to get at Christine Keeler. She appeared as a witness when one of them called Edgecombe appeared in court. This obviously attracted the attention of the newspapers. Christine Keeler received offers for her story, and began talking.

The news retailed by Ward to Commander Ivanov alarmed the Soviet agent, and he made hasty arrangements to return to Moscow. He was already compromised because he had asked Keeler, through Ward, to get information for him about West German rearmament.

John Profumo's sources were slower, but when he heard about Miss Keeler's indiscretions he went to MI5 in an attempt to get the story about his affair with her hushed up. As they were satisfied that no secrets had been passed, they were not interested, saying that a Minister's private life was no concern of theirs.

In the absence of Harold Macmillan abroad, his Principal Private Secretary, Timothy Bligh — who had been informed by the *Daily Mirror* about their story involving Profumo — was taking considerable interest. He too consulted the intelligence men. He then met the Minister and accepted his denial that he had slept with Christine Keeler.

As the newspapers took up the story rumours were beginning to fly thick and fast. John Profumo thought that the time had come to make a statement, and on 22 March he made the mistake of telling the House of Commons that there had been 'no impropriety whatsoever' in his relations with Christine Keeler. It was a lie, and an error of judgment which was to cost him dear.

By now Harold Wilson, Leader of the Opposition, and his adviser George Wigg, scenting scandal which might damage the government and increase their political chances, were in full cry. Naturally, they picked upon the security aspects of the case and demanded further investigations.

Reluctantly Harold Macmillan — who had no taste for either sex scandals or espionage — agreed to consult MI5. They washed their hands of it, saying that no further advice about security concerning Mr Profumo was needed.

Further parliamentary pressure was applied by the Opposition. They were by no means satisfied, though Mr Macmillan accepted the intelligence view that although Ward was said to have asked Christine Keeler to find out the proposed date for the arming of West Germany with atomic weapons, she had not provided it, and therefore there had been no threat to security.

In June the unfortunate War Minister felt compelled to announce his resignation from Parliament and from the Government. When the Opposition pressed their demands for an inquiry Mr Macmillan appointed a judge, Lord Denning, to carry out a full investigation.

Public opinion reproached John Profumo for lying to the House of Commons, and for his indiscretions, but nobody believed that he had betrayed military secrets to the Russians. Although the Denning report absolved the government from blame on the security question, the affair had revealed political ineptitude, in an affair separately exploited for their own respective ends by the Labour Party in Britain and by Moscow Centre in the Soviet Union.

In the summer Harold Macmillan resigned, and at the elections Harold Wilson's Labour Party came to power with a small majority. Mr Macmillan, in his famous Edwardian style, insisted that the affair was caused by Profumo getting into 'a silly scrape with a woman' at a 'raffish' party at Cliveden. Perhaps history will come to a similar conclusion.

Profumo abandoned politics and occupied himself with social work in expiation of his errors. In recognition of these good works he was awarded the CBE in 1975.

QADDAFI, Colonel Muammar

'The most dangerous man in the world' was President Reagan's description of the eccentric Libyan leader who in the course of his political life has certainly stirred up trouble in many parts of the world. The young army officer who plotted his way to power by coup d'état in 1969 became paymaster for scores of terrorist groups considered by him to be national liberation movements. Although over the years he became more cautious in handing out money, he could never resist a plot.

His own military intelligence service may not be very successful in the business of providing information, but is nevertheless remarkably adept in plotting abroad. Using lavish funds provided by Libya's oil income (for a country of only three million people!) they have planned assassinations and attempts to overthrow governments in almost every Arab state and many African ones.

In 1981 it was even claimed by the American government that the Libyans had organized hit-teams to kill President Reagan. Libyans themselves were not spared either; the security services acted quickly against any citizen suspected of trying to overthrow 'Brother Colonel', as Qaddafi likes to be known.

Amnesty International, the London-based civil rights organization, reported in 1982 that 'routine, systematic' use of torture by the Libyan intelligence service was becoming more frequent. Hundreds of arrests had been made within the country, and there was a series of executions.

Abroad, Qaddafi hit-squads sought out and murdered a number of Libyan exiles in Europe and in America.

The most feared officer in Libyan security is Major Sayed Qaddafadem, a cousin and confidant of the leader. He travels frequently to Western Europe, and is always kept under surveillance on such visits. He often works from headquarters in Libyan embassies, and has been known to co-operate with the Syrian secret service in tracking down dissidents. When he appears in a country Libyan exiles run for cover.

Colonel Qaddafi remains the most enigmatic of Arab leaders. In private conversation he is mild and reasonable, displaying great charm; but on a public platform he rants for hours, pausing sometimes to hurl abuse at audiences not sufficiently diligent in listening to his words. To build up his security forces at home he hires foreigners with expert knowledge. Among his highly paid recruits was Edwin Wilson, a renegade ex-CIA American, later sentenced to thirty years in the United States for his illegal dealings with Libya. Qaddafi's most notorious mercenary was Carlos, the Venezualan assassin who instructed the Libyan hit-teams before falling out with Major Qaddafadem.

In April 1984 one of his gunmen opened fire from the 'People's Bureau' in London's St James's Square on an opposition demonstration, killing WPC Yvonne Fletcher and wounding eleven demonstrators. After a six-day siege Britain broke off relations with Libya.

RABORN, Admiral William T.

As a naval officer William Raborn had been a success. He had a great deal to do with establishing the American underwater Polaris missile force. However, as the executive head of the American intelligence service he was a resounding failure. He had been selected for the office by President Johnson in April 1965, not because of his naval achievements, but because he had given firm support to the new President in his election campaign, and better still, he was a fellow-Texan. His brief fifteen months in office revealed what a mistake it can be to make political appointments in the world of espionage.

He caused comment on the occasion of the swearing-in ceremony when President Johnson insisted that, together with the senior officers in the CIA, he should be in a group photograph at the White House. As was his habit from the old days at sea, the Admiral replied as he frequently did, 'Aye-Aye, sir'. The cameras clicked, and there for all to see was the assembled might of the most secretive men in America, for all the world, friends and foe alike, to recognize.

Geopolitics were somewhat outside the range of the Admiral's intellectual guns, and soon

Washington was buzzing with tales of his gaffes. It was even claimed that at a briefing he once inquired what was the staple food of the Chinese. Years after everybody else he caught on to the idea that China and the Soviet Union were engaged in some kind of quarrel, and was reported to have asked a bewildered Agency (which had been preparing detailed studies on the subject from the beginning) to produce a paper on this interesting subject.

At their headquarters in Langley, Virginia, intelligence men unkindly said of him when he finally resigned that the only lasting effect he had on the CIA was the banning of white bread in the cafeteria. For he had that deep concern about brown bread and bowel movements so common among naval officers, regardless of nationality.

RADO, Sandor

A Commissar in the Hungarian Red Army when it staged its abortive coup in Budapest in 1919, Rado, who had trained as a cartographer, scored an enormous success with his 'DORA' network, which serviced the Soviet Union from Switzerland during the Second World War. The depth and extent of his precise military information and the speed with which he answered questions, especially about the German order of battle and its intentions, both surprised and delighted the Russians.

Some of his material was so detailed and up to date that they could hardly believe it; but time after time he was proved correct. It was claimed that he was being given this information by a group of anti-Nazi officers on the German High Command. Much later it became apparent that he had been fed information gathered by the British from Ultra, the decoding unit at Bletchley, which had broken the German Enigma code and enabled Britain to read the German military radio traffic. Nevertheless, while Britain was anxious to help the Russians defeat the Germans, it had no intention of telling them about Enigma. Rado was therefore chosen as a safe conduit for Ultra information to the Russians.

It was passed on through Alexander Foote, the British communist who was Rado's wireless operator, and it was of enormous value to the Russians. Possibly the greatest of DORA's coups was the news that Hitler was preparing to launch the greatest armoured assault the world has ever seen at Kursk. It was planned to destroy the Soviet army.

Because of Ultra information giving the order of battle and the German tactical plans passed on by Rado's group, the Russians were able to prepare for the onslaught, and eventually break the power of the German panzers.

When the Swiss, under German pressure, closed down DORA towards the end of the war Rado fled to France. He was ordered to make his way to Moscow, but like so many other communists serving abroad, feared the recall order meant that he was marked for liquidation. He was in fact in danger because the Russians wanted to know precisely how and why DORA had closed down, and he was suspected of treachery.

Foote was also recalled to Moscow, but when their aircraft reached Cairo Rado refused to continue the journey, and went underground in Egypt. The Russians, claiming that he was a deserter from the Red Army, forced the British to send him on to Moscow. His apparent defection enabled Foote to clear himself, but Rado disappeared, and it was reported that he had been executed after a secret trial.

A number of books recount the story of his execution, but in fact he survived imprisonment, and after Stalin died he was accorded full recognition for his work. In 1955 he returned to Budapest and taught geography at the University until his retirement. He died, aged eighty-two, on 20 August 1981. His real name was Alexander Radolfi.

RAFAEL, Sylvia

A chic and attractive woman agent of Mossad in ski pants and sweater who got far more publicity than was suitable for the part she played in the unsuccessful attempt to kill Ali Hassan Salameh, intelligence chief of Black September squad responsible for the Munich Massacre. Sylvia was one of the ten-strong hit-team which went to Lillehammer, Norway, in July 1973, wrongly identified their target, and shot dead a Moroccan waiter named Ahmed Bouchki.

The actual murderers managed to escape, possibly with the unofficial assistance of sympathetic agents in Norwegian intelligence, but Sylvia Rafael and a colleague called Abraham Gehmer, using false Canadian passports as Mr and Mrs Roxburgh, were arrested. Because they had clumsily written down the ex-directory telephone number of the Mossad 'legal' at the Israeli Embassy in Oslo, two other members of the gang were caught at his apartment.

Sylvia and her pretended husband were both sentenced to five and a half years, though they served only twenty-two months. While in prison she sent a facetious get-well card to the public prosecutor signed, '005½ The Spy who Came in From the Cold'. She also kept a diary, extracts from which were later published in the newspapers.

When she returned to Israel they put out the flags in her kibbutz and offered flowers, a curiously public homecoming for a secret agent whose operation looked rather amateurish.

RENNIE, Sir John

Having spent almost his entire career as a professional diplomat, he was the surprise candidate chosen by Michael Stewart, Foreign Secretary in the Labour Government, to become head of the Secret Intelligence Service in 1968. He had started work with an American advertising agency, and entered the Foreign Service after wartime duties in New York with the British government information service there, set up to counter pro-German propaganda.

In the Foreign Service his most notable success had been as head of the information and research department, established in the early stages of the cold war to alert public opinion to communist and Russian machinations.

During Rennie's spell at MI6 headquarters in London his son was imprisoned for drug offences. It was during the court case that Rennie's position as head of SIS first appeared in newspaper reports.

Rennie was a sensitive and likeable man, with a reputation as a painter, having been hung at the Royal Academy as a young man. He served with SIS until his retirement in 1973, when Maurice Oldfield succeeded him. He died in 1981 at the age of sixty-seven.

RINALDI, Giorgio

An unlikely-sounding spy from Italy, a parachuting enthusiast and professional stuntman. Working with his wife, Angela Maria, an attractive woman who was fifteen years older than himself, and who had an antique shop in Rome, he masterminded an international ring of Soviet agents and informers providing field intelligence about American and NATO military installations and bases.

Rinaldi made a number of ostentatious secret trips to the Soviet Union, where he had the customary course in espionage methods. He was tactlessly friendly with a Russian officer in Italy, and suspicion about him built up because, although the antique shop was in money trouble, he never seemed short of cash.

Angela Maria looked after communications with Moscow. They were both arrested in 1967 and awarded long prison sentences, shortly after the arrival in the West of Svetlana, daughter of Stalin. It was believed that the Rinaldis had been making preparations for an attempt to kidnap her when she reached Switzerland, and indeed one of their people was arrested crossing the Alps into Switzerland.

Italian security also caught Yuri Pavlenko, a GRU air attaché in Rome, as he picked up messages from a drop. He and his wife were expelled. In the subsequent rolling up of the network Soviet legals and local agents were expelled and arrested in Cyprus and Greece. Others were traced in several European countries and in Morocco.

The case proved how easy it is for Soviet intelligence to get information from multinational military bases with large locally recruited staffs.

RITCHIE, Rhona Janet

The promising career of this attractive and vivacious woman, after she left an academic post to enter the Foreign Service and became First Secretary at the British Embassy in Tel Aviv, ended sadly when she was convicted under the Official Secrets Act for wrongfully communicating confidential information. She was given a nine months' suspended sentence.

Miss Ritchie had made the mistake of having an affair in Israel with a personable young intelligence man at the Egyptian Embassy, named Rafaat El-Ansary. He was gleefully described in the Israeli press as the 'Don Juan of the Nile', who built his career on diplomacy and espionage through sex.

The pair made no secret of their attachment, and were constantly seen together on the Tel Aviv and Jerusalem cocktail circuit. Rhona Ritchie was a popular and sociable woman who became famous for organizing the one and only kosher Burns night dinner in Israel. A smart dresser, she attracted attention at a 'night at the circus' fancy-dress ball by appearing in fishnet tights.

She was a lively and intelligent person. Her only fault was that she took to showing her Egyptian lover Embassy telegrams which he had no right to see. One of them concerned the formation of the multi-national force to police the Sinai withdrawal.

She was not a spy, as her defence counsel at the Old Bailey took pains to point out. She was guilty of an error of judgment and of an indiscretion, though it has to be remembered that it is not always easy for diplomats to decide what they may reasonably reveal to other diplomats from friendly countries, or indeed to journalists.

What seems remarkable in the Rhona Ritchie affair is that the British ambassador failed to prevent one of his senior officers from getting into this kind of trouble. A well-informed diplomat should have been aware of her attachment for the Egyptian, and ought to have taken appropriate action before any harm was done.

There was nothing clandestine about the love-affair, yet it seems that not until the Israeli Government alerted the Embassy after Miss Ritchie's promotion to First Secretary had the British appreciated the dangers. The Israeli intelligence service keep watch over foreign diplomats accredited to Israel, and Mossad certainly knew a great deal about Rafaat El-Ansary. For them it was still something of a novelty even to have an Egyptian Embassy in Israel.

While Miss Ritchie resigned from the Foreign Office and returned to Scotland, her Egyptian lover was promoted and posted to Vienna.

ROOSEVELT, Kermit ('Kim')

'He was a courteous, soft-spoken Easterner with impeccable social connections, well-educated rather than intellectual, pleasant and unassuming as host and guest. An equally nice wife. In fact, the last person you would expect to be up to the neck in dirty tricks.'

That was the judgment on this Central Intelligence Agency officer of the old brigade made by Kim Philby, the British spy, who shared a common nickname with him. It was contained in a letter to the British author Leonard Mosley, who had written to Philby while researching his book on the Dulles brothers. In addition, Philby claimed that five years before Graham Greene had coined the expression for the title of his novel he had dubbed Kermit Roosevelt 'The Quiet American'.

Roosevelt's most notable coup in intelligence was in Iran. The Prime Minister, Mohammed Mossadegh, with the help of the local Tudeh communist party and of the Soviet Union, had overthrown the Shah and nationalized the Anglo-Iranian petroleum company. He was about to arrest the Shah.

The CIA ordered Roosevelt to mount a covert mission with a budget of two million dollars to restore the Shah to his throne. He already had experience, as a former chief of the agency department concerned with what they called 'unconventional operations', and he put it to good use.

Army officers were instructed in the tactics of coup d'état, such as how best to seize a radio station. Then Kim Roosevelt set about stirring the Teheran mob to street demonstrations, recruiting for the purpose an unlikely though colourful Iranian wrestler known as 'Ahmed the Brainless'.

His tactics succeeded, and he received personal thanks from President Eisenhower as well as the secret award of the National Security Medal. This was slightly resented by the British, who had themselves played a part in the manœuvring, but received none of the credit for its success.

Roosevelt specialized in Middle East affairs, where he had failures as well as successes. One mishap occurred when he attempted to seize the Buraimi Oasis (claimed by both Oman and Abu Dhabi) on behalf of the Saudi Arabians. In a minor skirmish the British-officered Trucial Oman Scouts routed the Saudis on behalf of their Gulf allies, and Roosevelt, after failing to win by bribery, withdrew.

He was also active in trying to cement American friendship with President Nasser of Egypt in the 1950s. Roosevelt arranged to give the Arab leader a bullet-proof Cadillac, but President Nasser refused it as being too ostentatious for him, though he did accept a more modest Pontiac.

Then the CIA man sent one of his officers, Miles Copeland, with a bribe of six million dollars. But Nasser was a man of modest requirements, and not easy to bribe, and he spent the money on building a rather ugly tower near the Nile, known to the citizens of Cairo as the 'CIA Tower'. At the American intelligence agency it is always referred to as 'Roosevelt's Erection'.

Kermit Roosevelt left the CIA in 1958 to become vice-president for governmental relations with Gulf Oil, a post he occupied until 1964, when he joined a Washington public relations firm as a partner.

ROSENBERG, Julius and Ethel

Heads were broken on the Paris boulevards when the Rosenbergs went to the electric chair in 1953; demonstrating mobs marched noisily through the streets of American and European cities. Their case had become a *cause célèbre*, agitating the consciences and letter-writing abilities of that army of the 'wise and good' composed of clergymen and liberal public figures. The Russians and the communists in whose interests Julius and Ethel had acted lent a helping hand and hypocritically denounced 'American fascism'.

Thirty years later the war of words between the upholders of law and order, and the partisans for ever digging out 'new' facts to support their belief that the Rosenbergs were innocent was still being fought out. The release of FBI documents under the Freedom of Information Act revived the old acrimony.

Certainly the trial of the Rosenbergs was not an inspiring one. Evidence against Ethel was slender, and it does seem that she was arrested and prosecuted in order to put pressure upon her husband to confess. In espionage cases the Roman law maxim that confession is the queen of evidence prevails over Anglo-Saxon custom, because in the nature of things secret activities are extremely difficult to prove.

The prosecution case turned upon the evidence of two witnesses, Harry Gold a professional Soviet agent, and David Greenglass, the brother of Ethel Rosenberg. It was considered at the time unsavoury that Greenglass should denounce his own kith and kin; yet thirty years later when the wife of Geoffrey Prime, the British electronic-information spy, denounced him to the police she was considered patriotic and conscientious.

A deal was done by which the wife of Greenglass escaped prosecution in return for the evidence her husband gave against his sister. Judge Irving Kaufman did perhaps behave unwisely by discussing the sentence with the prosecution in the course of the trial.

There were doubts about whether the death penalty was appropriate, and whether it should have been carried out. However, all processes of law were observed, the appeals failed, and finally, the newly elected President Eisenhower rejected a plea for mercy.

The spirit of the times no doubt had its effect. America was deeply shocked by revelations about the extent of spying, and the use of American nationals by the Russians at a time when the Soviet Union was a wartime ally, and when the US was supplying that country through Lend-Lease with the weapons of war. By the time that the Rosenbergs came to justice the Korean War was raging, Czechoslovakia had been seized, and there was a tendency to exaggerate the effects of their espionage, and even to blame them for the Korean War.

However, thirty years later when the FBI documents were released they proved how scrupulously the Bureau had gone about its investigation. There was no longer any question of the frame-up which had been alleged by Rosenberg supporters. An admission that Ethel and Julius were not totally effective in providing the Russian spymasters with all the secrets of the atomic bomb does not affect the fact that they were spies on behalf of the USSR, and that Julius in particular did everything in his power to provide high-class espionage material.

Both the Rosenbergs were children of Jewish immigrants brought up in New York. Julius, with his prominent glasses and small black moustache, came from an orthodox religious family who hoped he might become a Rabbi. Instead he chose Marxist-Leninism, and at City College in New York, where he took a degree in electrical engineering, he became a card-carrying, hard-line Stalinist militant. Ethel too shared his political faith when he married her on graduation.

In 1943 Julius quietly moved out of open party activity to prepare himself for work as a full-time agent under the orders of Anatoli Yakovlev, a KGB officer in New York, operating from the Soviet consulate. His tasks were at first quite minor ones such as collecting reports probably left in 'dead drops'. He then began to recruit people known to him, including David Greenglass, his communist brother-in-law.

The basis of the prosecution of Rosenberg was

that he had sent his sister-in-law to ask Greenglass (by then serving as a soldier at the atomic research base in Los Alamos) to provide secret material about the early A-bombs. Greenglass also fed information to Harry Gold, which was in turn routed through the Soviet consulate.

In fact Julius Rosenberg, working out of his modest apartment, became what is known as a 'principal agent', recruiting and handling agents on behalf of his case officer Yakovlev. His recruiting methods were by no means inspired, for he tended to keep it within the family and in his immediate circle of friends.

Whether in fact Ethel was recruited as a real agent is open to doubt. At all events, she certainly co-operated with her husband, for they were a close and loving couple, and she must certainly have been aware of his activities.

Greenglass went to New York on leave on New Year's Day 1945 and handed to Rosenberg a sketch of the lens mould which detonated the bomb. He had also supplied to the Soviets a rough sketch of the bomb itself. The pro-Rosenberg faction has since made great play of the fact that the drawing was fairly primitive and useless, and that anyway the British traitor Klaus Fuchs had already given the Russians a more detailed one. Even so, the rough sketch may have helped to confirm how the bomb worked.

Without access to KGB reports, in a country which has not even dreamt of such freedom of information, it is impossible to assess the extent and quality of information supplied by the Rosenbergs, in relation to that from Fuchs, Dr Nunn May, and those in Colonel Zabotin's Canadian network. What is certain is that when President Truman at Potsdam told Stalin officially about the existence of the powerful new weapon Stalin was not surprised.

To the very end, while awaiting their execution the Rosenbergs insisted — and often insisted grandiloquently — that they were totally innocent.

As the network established by Anatoli Yakovlev collapsed several minor members of it made a run for Mexico. Among those who got clean away were Morris Cohen and his wife, two New York Americans who had been connected with it and with the Rosenbergs. Renamed Peter and Helen Kroger, they surfaced again a few years later in deep cover in London, where they handled communications as 'illegals' for the British naval secrets network.

The Cohen case raises the question what might have happened to the Rosenbergs had they escaped from the United States instead of staying to plead their innocence. Would they, like the Cohens (Krogers), have turned up later in Britain or Australia as 'illegals' with a new name and cover story?

S

SAGUY, Major-General Yehoshua

A handsome professional soldier with thirty years' service in the Israeli army, mostly in intelligence work. He was dismissed as director of military intelligence following the Israeli inquiry into the massacre of hundreds of Palestinian men, women and children by Phalangists at the Sabra and Chatilla refugee camps in Beirut in September 1982 when the Israeli army was in control of the area.

The inquiry strongly criticized the General for his failure to prevent the slaughter. It accused him, after examining his evidence, of a conspicuous lack of concern. He had failed in his duty as director of the intelligence arm of the Israeli army by neglecting to keep informed about what was happening.

Lebanese Christian militia who were known to have a vendetta against the Palestinians were encouraged to engage in a mopping-up operation in the refugee camps of their enemies, after the Palestine guerrillas had been evacuated from the city. Israeli intelligence could not conceivably have been unaware of the fact that Christian troops would run amok in the camps, for Lebanon has a long history of sectarian massacre. It was for his failure to prevent the dreadful tragedy of Sabra and Chatilla, and his seeming indifference, that the Israeli government dismissed this intelligence general.

SALAMEH, Ali Hassan

A dashing and cosmopolitan Palestinian fond of silk shirts and smart suits, and the well-trained senior intelligence officer of Fateh, the Palestine guerrilla and terrorist organization which used to operate from Beirut. He played a prominent role in many operations in Europe during the 1970s on behalf of Black September, a special terrorist group master-minded by Abu Iyad.

They were responsible for the kidnapping and final death of eleven Israeli athletes at the Olympic Games of 1972, which came to be known as the Munich massacre. This was the outrage which prompted Mossad, the Israeli intelligence organization, to move revenge squads to Europe under the awesome title 'Wrath of God' with orders to murder Arabs responsible for it.

One such attempt to kill Salameh at Lillehammer in Norway was carried out by a blundering Israeli hit-team in July 1973 which wrongly identified and shot dead a Moroccan waiter at a local health farm, named Ahmed Bouchki. Salameh knew he was on the hit-list, and had used informers, and possibly an Israeli double agent in Switzerland, to mislead Mossad on his whereabouts and lure them to Scandinavia.

The son of Sheikh Hassen Salameh, a Palestinian notable killed by an Israeli bomb at his HQ in 1948, Ali Hassan was well trained in intelligence work. In 1968 he went on a six-weeks' course in Cairo run by Egyptian intelligence, the best in the Arab world. He also had connections with Saika, a Syrian-run guerrilla outfit, and had benefited from Soviet training during a visit to Moscow in 1972.

Mossad continued pursuit of Salameh, wounding him on one occasion, before they finally succeeded in killing him with a car bomb in Beirut in January 1979.

SALINE, Guennadi

First Secretary at the Soviet Embassy in Dublin who was expelled by the Irish Government in September 1983 for spying activities together with a known KGB officer, Viktor Lipassov and his wife. Evdokia, the wife (or perhaps simply the KGB 'wife') of Lipassov was also a state security official, who made use of her relative inconspicuousness to move around outside the limits imposed upon diplomats.

The Dublin trio had been using the neutral Republic of Ireland as a clearing-house for NATO information: Aeroflot has some twenty flights a week routed through the Shannon international airport. The other advantage of Dublin was that for travel to the United Kingdom no passports are required, and this made it a useful meeting-place for Soviet agents.

There were also suspicions that Soviet diplomats had crossed into Northern Ireland, and that they might have been in touch with Provisional Irish Republican Army people. Lipassov was an old hand at the 'legal' game; he was expelled from Denmark in 1972.

SCHLESINGER, James

The reign of James Schlesinger as director was nasty, brutal and short. He was put in charge of the Central Intelligence Agency on 7 February 1973, at the time of its greatest humiliation as a result of the Watergate break-in the previous year. His mission was to cut the Agency down to size and to reveal its misdemeanours.

He was an outsider to the intelligence community, and his main knowledge of it was academic and administrative. Two years previously, as assistant director of the Office of Management and Budget, he had made a detailed study of the community, taking an accountant's-eye view of its activities. He made a managerial assessment that its technical information was a great deal better than its political information.

Schlesinger succeeded a professional, Richard Helms, who had graduated to the CIA from the old wartime OSS. White-haired, craggy-featured and academic in appearance, James Schlesinger smoked a pipe and favoured tweed suits. He was far from the popular image of a CIA chief.

Confident in the knowledge that President Nixon had placed him in office to turn the place upside down, he got to work at once, moving into Helms's office, which he had enlarged, and declaring that he had no need for the services of the former Director's secretary. When the departure of Helms was speeded up he was convinced that Schlesinger had ordered this move, though in fact it appears that the order came from the President.

He wanted to cut down on the clandestine services, but the principal result of his tenure of office was the brutal clearing out of the old guard. He regarded the Agency as a gentleman's club, and roundly declared, 'I am no gentleman.'

That indeed proved to be the case. He himself selected hundreds of officers for the axe, and got rid of more than two thousand in waves of sackings. The general principle was that anyone with more than twenty years' service must go.

Naturally, the old hands were deeply resentful, and feelings were so strong at headquarters that the Director arranged for additional bodyguards to protect him in and out of the office. When his portrait took the place reserved for it on the walls it was monitored by a special TV device as a protection against any angry agent who might be tempted to deface it. The only recorded incident was of a woman who approached the official picture to thumb her nose at it.

As the scandal of the Watergate affair grew Schlesinger sent out a directive ordering every employee with knowledge of such events to come forward with anything to show that the CIA had exceeded the limits of its charter. Denunciations flooded in. They were the basis for the eventual report about what came to be called 'the Family Jewels', with revelations about bugging, dirty tricks, and plots to assassinate Trujillo, Ngo Dinh Diem and Castro.

These revelations opened the floodgates of seemingly endless allegations about the wickedness of the CIA which ruined its reputation for years, and for a while destroyed its effectiveness. The brief and bitter directorship of James Schlesinger over the Agency came to an end in July 1973, when he moved to the Defense Department after only five months. He was replaced by William Colby.

SCHWIRKMANN, Horst

The KGB took revenge upon this highly skilled West German technician in counter-audio and debugging in a particularly unpleasant fashion after he 'swept' the West German Embassy in Moscow and unearthed numerous microphones. Whenever he found one Schwirkmann fed high voltage into it, giving a nasty shock to the secret listeners.

However, what really irritated the Soviet security service was that he discovered a new electronic toy which they had carefully installed in the Embassy code-room. This gadget broadcast to the Soviet HQ messages as they were typed for automatic cyphering, but before they were cyphered.

It enabled the KGB to read all the most sensitive messages going out of the German mission. They were also able to use it to help break diplomatic codes by comparing cyphered messages with their intercept *en clair*.

To hit back the Technical Operations Directorate used one of their nastiest inventions, an injection of nitrogen mustard gas. The unfortunate Schwirkmann was jabbed in the behind with this mixture one Sunday morning in 1964 while making a tourist trip to the Zagorsk monastery outside Moscow.

Doctors at the US Embassy recognized the symptoms, and after long and extremely painful treatment the German expert survived. Obviously the KGB, probably acting on their own initiative, meant to assassinate him.

The West Germans demanded an apology and refused to go ahead with a summit conference with Khruschev until they received it. By the time that the Russians expressed regret Khruschev had been overthrown.

SCOTT, Edward

The Czechoslovak intelligence service set a very simple trap when they installed Irena Peckova as housemaid in the residence in Prague of this British diplomat, then serving as head of Chancery in the Embassy there. The surprising thing is that such a senior diplomat should so readily have succumbed to her charms. In 1956 the affair began, and he often went to her apartment near the Embassy.

When his entrapment came to public attention in 1981 Mr Scott expressed mild regret and gave the impression, furthermore, that Irena had not been all that attractive. Be that as it may, the fact that he was sleeping with the maid gave Czech agents their chance to apply pressure, and by the late 1950s he was meeting with them, both in Prague and later in London.

Edward Scott told security officers that he had never handed over documents, nor did he reveal secrets. According to his account, he simply discussed various subjects with them. However, it is well known that Eastern Bloc services play a long-term game in trapping diplomats, and do not necessarily expect immediate espionage results. The whole point of such operations is to get a hold over officers who may later rise to important positions in a diplomatic service.

The Scott case only came to the attention of British security in 1969 through the confessions of Joseph Frolik, a Czech intelligence man who fled his country, and revealed activities against the British of Czech agents. By then Scott had contrived an exit visa for Irena Peckova to go and live in Vienna as a refugee, thus placing himself under a further obligation to the communist authorities.

After the *Sunday Times* had published details in 1981 of Scott's improper behaviour Mrs Thatcher, the Prime Minister, declared that when he had confessed in 1969 it had seemed that on the evidence available, little damage had been caused to the national interest. As a result Scott took early retirement.

SEJNA, General Jan

This highly placed Czech officer, who as Deputy Minister of Defence had attended numerous meetings of Warsaw Pact high-level committees, was able to reveal many aspects of Soviet planning when he defected to the US in 1968. His most remarkable revelation was the extent of Eastern Bloc preparations for sabotage in the West, and not necessarily only in time of war.

In a magazine interview he explained that the Warsaw Pact had already implanted, in both Europe and North America, sleeping organizations of saboteurs who were ready for action at an appropriate moment. One plan put forward, according to his evidence, was for the sabotage of the London underground railway system at a time of serious political crisis. The second part of the scheme was for agents to organize mass demonstrations, and then accuse the British Government of provocatively bringing the railway to a standstill in order to prevent them.

It seemed at the time that such devious plans were unlikely though the later defection of such an important and credible officer as the Russian Oleg Lyalin confirmed the information of the Czech general.

SEMICHASTNY, Vladimir Yefimovich

The youngest man ever to be chairman of the KGB, he served in this post from November 1961 to April 1967. He was a protégé of Alexander Shelepin, his predecessor, and came to the KGB through the same route: the ranks of the Young Communist League. His appointment confirmed that the KGB was once again under the control of the party after the Beria era, when it competed with it for power.

Semichastny was responsible for a number of embarrassing incidents which did not please his political superiors. It was he who sanctioned the arrest as a spy of Professor Frederick Barghoorn of Yale University when he was visiting Moscow in October 1963. The plot was to use the American as a hostage to bring about the release of Igor Ivanov, a Russian spy caught red-handed in New York. But what the Russians did not know was that Barghoorn was a personal friend of President Kennedy, and after the President had established that he was in no way involved in espionage he held a press conference and demanded the release of the innocent professor. The Kremlin was humiliated and forced to release the scholar. Semichastny was eventually replaced by a quite different character, Yuri Vladimirovich Andropov.

SEROV, General Ivan Alexandrovitch

'Somehow I found it hard to believe that this cold, hard man with bloodstained hands could show so much warmth to those near to him.' That was the judgment of Colonel Oleg Penkovsky, the Russian military intelligence man who was also a British agent, on Ivan Serov, whom he knew very well.

According to the Colonel, Serov was at that time his boss in military intelligence, having already served from 1954 to 1958 as head of the KGB under his patron, Malenkov. Descendant of a peasant family, he had made his way up the bureaucracy by way of the Red Army, to enter the KGB, where he made a name for himself deporting thousands from Eastern Europe. Indeed, he is believed to have ordered the Katyn Forest massacre in which the Russians killed 15,000 Polish officers.

At secret service work he was less effective. Because he failed to detect in advance a 1958 plot against Khruschev, he ceased to head the KGB.

Two years before he had a rough time in London where he was sent to organize a State visit by Khruschev and Bulganin. A spirited attack by the British press, which knew his record well, called him 'Ivan the Terrible' and 'The Butcher', and forced his prompt recall.

Despite this, he was determined that his wife and their daughter Svetlana should sample English pleasures, and sent them to London on a private visit in 1961. Colonel Penkovsky on a trade mission to London escorted them shopping, and took them to restaurants and night clubs. Both mother and daughter were delighted, and invited the dashing colonel to their dacha, where they boasted of all-the-year-round strawberries and their own beehives.

Such family intimacy with Penkovsky (who was later shot for treason), proved the undoing of old Serov, who had served the Soviet state so loyally and brutally earlier, by smashing the Hungarian uprising in 1956 when he seized its leaders at a banquet. After the Penkovsky affair nothing more was heard of him.

On his famous visit to London Serov created a sensation in British intelligence circles by asking for KGB facilities in Hong Kong, so that the Russians could monitor events in communist China. Request refused.

SHAMIR, Yitzhak

'The most exciting and often the most dangerous of my life' was the only public comment made about his ten years' service from 1955 in Mossad, the Israeli intelligence service, by the 67-year-old Israeli Foreign Minister who succeeded Menachem Begin as leader of the Herut Party and Prime Minister in 1983. Although it has never been officially confirmed, it is generally believed in Israel that he was European chief of the intelligence service, operating from a secret headquarters in Paris.

Like Mr Begin, he was born in Poland. He had played a violent part in the underground war which preceded the birth of the state of Israel. As leader of the Stern Gang, responsible for notable assassinations in 1948, he was detained three times by the British, and each time escaped.

This small, wiry man, quiet and affable in his later years, was once an adept at disguises. One of his specialities was to pose as a blind man in dark glasses.

SHELEPIN, Alexander Nikolayevich

Khruschev's nominee, promoted to succeed Serov after the downfall of 'The Butcher' in 1958. Shelepin was an unusual choice because he had virtually no experience of the secret world. He had risen through the party to become head of Komsomol, the Young Communist League, an influential post in which he controlled some 20 million youngsters. He scored a great success in his propaganda work among the disillusioned young people following Stalin's death.

He remained with the KGB until 1961, during which time he was credited with publishing an anti-CIA booklet called *Caught in the Act*. He also tried to refurbish the KGB's domestic image, telling the 1961 Communist Party Congress: 'We are happy that the state security organs have fully liquidated distortions in their work and violations of Socialist legality. Decisive measures of the Party's Central Committee and the Soviet Government have finished with this, finished forever....'

This did not, of course apply to the KGB's operations outside the Soviet Union. He personally received Bogdan Stashinsky, the KGB killer who had assassinated two Ukrainian émigré leaders in Western Europe. Shelepin read out the official citation awarding Stashinsky the Order of the Red Banner for carrying out an 'important government commission'.

Shelepin took care, learning from Serov's misfortunes in London, to maintain a low profile. Perhaps the measure of his success was that when he left the KGB he did not do so to go to prison or to be shot but to another government job in charge of the Soviet Union's so-called trade unions. But his star, once so bright, waned when Khruschev fell from power, and he slipped down the bureaucracy until he is now believed to be running the Russian equivalent of the Forestry Commission. 'All he has left', says one former friend, 'are the cuttings books of stories which have appeared about him in the West.'

SHEVCHENKO, Arkady

The highest-ranking Soviet official ever to come over to the Western side. When he defected with CIA help in 1978 he was able to provide, as an expert on disarmament, high-level insight into Soviet policy-making and negotiating ploys. He was a high-flier, a protégé of Andrei Gromyko, the Soviet Foreign Minister, placed in the influential United Nations post of Under Secretary-General in New York with an annual salary of nearly £50,000.

Shevchenko was keen on money, and having taken the plunge to disobey orders to return to Moscow he negotiated with his UN chief, the then Secretary-General Dr Waldheim, for a large cash compensation settlement. His reasons for abandoning the career he had built in the Soviet hierarchy were complicated. He developed a taste for American life, but also this 47-year-old Russian (who had once been spotted as a possible future Foreign Minister) believed that he was not highly enough appreciated by the Kremlin.

His wife and daughter returned to Moscow. His son, who had a job with the Soviet delegation to the Geneva disarmament conference, was hastily put aboard an aircraft for home.

So alarmed were the Soviets by the first news of Arkady Shevchenko's disappearance that they claimed the American intelligence services were guilty of 'this detestable frame-up'. He was able to provide the CIA with details of KGB men infiltrating the United Nations organization both in the US and elsewhere, for he himself had run a very tight Soviet ship within the international organization.

Because of his high rank, he also knew a good deal about earlier defectors such as Nosenko, and the man named 'Fedora', about whom the Americans remained suspicious.

SILLITOE, Sir Percy

It was because he was an outsider to the intelligence world that the Labour government appointed this long-serving police officer — the 'honest copper' — as head of the British counter-intelligence organization MI5 in 1946. He took over on the day that Alan Nunn May, the atom spy, appeared on espionage charges at the Old Bailey, and it was a clear sign that Sillitoe was in for a rough ride.

His career had started in the South African, and then the Rhodesian, police, after which he returned to Britain and became Chief Constable for several big cities including Glasgow, where he built a reputation as a gang-buster. In that respect Sillitoe was the British equivalent of J. Edgar Hoover of the FBI, who went into spycatching from the war against criminals.

Within MI5 the professionals were at first wary of their new policeman boss, in particular because they suspected him of the senior policeman's vice — a taste for publicity. He shocked the community with his entry in *Who's Who*, which gave his address as War Office, Room 055. He actually gave press conferences and travelled under his own name.

This practice led him into trouble when the flight of Burgess and Maclean plunged the intelligence world into turmoil in 1951. It was decided in June of that year that he must go to the United States to explain this dreadful lapse in security to the American allies, and in particular to Hoover, who was far from sympathetic.

The mission got off to a bad start because Sillitoe and his colleague Arthur Martin arrived at Heathrow airport under their own names and were spotted by reporters. *The Daily Express* indeed published a picture of them.

There was the big, burly policeman in his crumpled suit clutching an airline bag which (though this was not known at the time) contained 'doctored' papers intended to convince the Americans that British security was not to blame for what had happened. The professionals were not amused.

Worse was in store for Percy Sillitoe, for J.

Edgar Hoover, quite rightly, was convinced of the guilt of another British agent of the Russians, Kim Philby, who had been MI6 liaison man in Washington, and whose immediate withdrawal from that post he had demanded.

It was not surprising that Sillitoe later wrote about his early days in charge of the counter-espionage men, 'I found it difficult to find out precisely what everyone was doing.' He did not really like secrecy, and his heart was in the right place when he said that he would rather spies did escape undetected than that MI5 should turn into some sort of secret-police organization.

He had the misfortune to be head of the service during the difficult years between 1946 and 1953, when one spy scandal succeeded another, and when the Western security services were only slowly coming to realize how widespread were the Soviet networks operating at the start of the cold war.

It had been his plan to retire quietly to run, as he put it, a sweet-shop in Eastbourne on the south coast. He was in fact persuaded by De Beers to go off to South Africa to track down diamond-smugglers, a task which he found more congenial.

SINCLAIR, Major-General Sir John

Nicknamed 'Sinbad' because he had served in Royal Navy submarines before going into the Army, where he eventually became director of military intelligence, he was appointed Director-General of the Secret Intelligence Service in 1953. His career came to an early conclusion because of his responsibility for the Crabb affair in 1956.

The 'let's have a go' crowd in MI6 and naval intelligence could not resist the opportunity provided by the arrival in Portsmouth of the Russian cruiser *Ordzhonikidze*, bearing the joint Soviet leadership Bulganin and Khruschev on an official visit to Britain. They dug out of retirement a gallant old commander, 'Buster' Crabb, to frogman under it and take a look.

It was an operation which went badly wrong. Crabb was spotted, and most likely killed by the Russians, his headless body being discovered

months later. The Russians seized upon the chance to make a strong protest accompanied by heavy anti-British publicity.

The SIS had to call in the services of the rival MI5 to fetch Crabb's possessions from the Sallyport Hotel in Portsmouth, where he had stayed with one of their own men. Pages were torn from the register.

Sir Anthony Eden, the then Prime Minister, under pressure both from the Opposition and from the Russians, got into a terrible state. He had to apologize to the Russians, and found it necessary to inform the House of Commons that 'What was done was done without the authority or the knowledge of Her Majesty's ministers. Appropriate disciplinary steps are being taken.'

General Sinclair, although exonerated by the subsequent official inquiry, was forced into early retirement, and was replaced by Dick White, the head of MI5. Yet he had been an experienced intelligence officer, best remembered for improving administration within the SIS by regularizing contracts and conditions of service for his staff. The Crabb affair reinforced the belief that he had been less expert in keeping control over his agents.

SKARDON, William

A shrewd and thoughtful ex-detective from the Metropolitan Police with long and successful experience in MI5 at the less glamorous end of the espionage trade, he was regarded by colleagues as the best in Britain. 'Jim', as they always called him, was essentially a law-and-order man who saw it as his duty to work against wrongdoers.

For that very reason he held the men from MI6, the offensive arm of the British service, at arm's length. He looked upon them as a crowd of brigands, and in the 1950s when traitors kept appearing in their ranks he even referred to MI6 as 'the enemies' (for it had been the custom of the service to speak of them as 'the friends').

His best-known achievement was the series of interrogations of Klaus Fuchs, the British atomic spy, in 1950. In this detailed questioning, and using his deceptively gentle technique, Skardon contrived to persuade Fuchs to make a full confession, and that is the essence of spycatching in democratic countries. It is almost impossible in some cases to furnish the kind of proof which police officers would need to secure a prosecution.

It is said that Skardon never tried to bully the person under interrogation, and he would certainly never have resorted to brutal methods. By clearing up small points, as he put it, he managed not only to get the confidence of the man he was questioning but also to expose lies and destroy subterfuges.

Skardon was involved in all the important British spy cases of the time. He had been about to question Donald Maclean, but the weekend before that Maclean fled with Burgess to Moscow after he had been warned. It has been claimed that one reason for his sudden departure was the fear of a session with Skardon.

He never had a full opportunity to deploy his undoubted talents upon Kim Philby, though Philby was certainly aware of his skill, for during his MI6 days in Washington he had full reports on the Fuchs interrogation.

In 1952 MI6 strongly suspected Philby of being a double agent, but decided to subject him to a kind of unofficial trial in which Helenus Milmo QC, a former intelligence officer turned barrister, questioned him in the role of prosecuting counsel. He was unable to break Philby, who never gave an inch, and made full use of his stutter as a defence mechanism.

Jim Skardon had only a brief chance after this failure to try his own method of questioning on Kim Philby when he drove back with him to collect Philby's passport. He visited him briefly several times, and Philby wrote later in his own book, 'He was much more dangerous...'

This was by no means the end of Skardon's career. He was promoted to control the watchers, the counter-intelligence teams which keep spies and their controls under surveillance, and in 1960 deployed the teams which ran to earth the Portland Spy ring probing naval secrets.

The Russian agent, Gordon Lonsdale, was followed from a rendezvous with his suppliers, Harry Houghton and Bunty Gee. The trail led to a suburban house in west London, in Cranley Drive, Ruislip, the home of Mr and Mrs Peter Kroger.

Driving around the area, William Skardon chose a corner house occupied by Mr and Mrs W.S. Search which overlooked the Krogers' bungalow and would be ideal for use by watchers. Then began one of the most delicate tasks undertaken by him, for he had to persuade Mrs Search to allow his people to use a spare bedroom in order to spy upon neighbours with whom they had become friendly, and who often visited them.

Skardon did not explain further than to say at first that they believed a wanted man came to visit the Krogers, and needed to keep watch over the 1960 November weekend. In fact counter-intelligence women were in the house for much longer. It was not until early January 1961 that they were able to arrest Lonsdale and to be sure that the Krogers were the Russian agents through whom he was passing his material to Moscow from the house in Cranley Drive.

Skardon needed all the tact and gentle persuasiveness for which he was famous to overcome the growing doubts and fears of Mrs Search, and to prevent her from alerting the Krogers — not out of any disloyalty, but because of her own anxieties about the double role forced upon her household, which included a teenager daughter preparing for examinations.

This delicate domestic situation which needed careful handling is an object-lesson in the difficulties faced by spycatchers in Western countries, who need to go about their duties with enormous care and tact when members of the public inevitably become involved.

William Skardon after his retirement moved to the south coast of England, where his hobby was playing bowls.

SMITH, General Walter Bedell

Director of CIA from October 1950 to February 1953, he had a distinguished and varied record. He was General Eisenhower's Chief of Staff in the invasion of Europe, and then became US Ambassador to Moscow from 1946 to 1949.

Bedell Smith — inevitably nicknamed 'Beetle' — was unlike the smart young men who had staffed OSS and moved to CIA. He was a poor boy who was commissioned in the army in France during the First World War. He was a thruster, and rode roughshod over those he felt were incompetent. He used his toughness of mind in knocking the CIA into shape when it was split by the factions left behind when President Truman wiped out the OSS.

The other move he made which had a profound and lasting effect on the Agency was to bring Allen Dulles back to espionage as his deputy and then his successor. Before he eventually picked Dulles he had tried to persuade his English friend, General (later Sir) Kenneth Strong, who had been Chief of the Intelligence Staff at Eisenhower's headquarters, to take the job, but Strong refused.

Despite being in constant pain from stomach ulcers (which made his temper notoriously short), Smith left Dulles an organization which was not only united but running smoothly on well-ordered lines. When he left the Agency to become Under Secretary of State for Political Affairs — a move which was suspected by some to have been organized by John Foster Dulles, Allen's brother — he was remembered, if not with affection, certainly with awe and admiration.

He was also remembered by the British SIS, for when Kim Philby — then acting as SIS liaison officer with the CIA in Washington — tipped off Maclean that he was about to be arrested, and the CIA's suspicions about Philby became certainties, he wrote to Sir Stewart Menzies, the head of SIS, telling him that Philby was no longer welcome in Washington, and that all connections between Philby and the CIA had been severed.

SNEPP, Frank

He joined the CIA as a political analyst in order to avoid being called up for the Vietnam war. When he was safely ensconced in the European Division some of his wittier friends filled in an application on his behalf in which he supposedly pleaded to be sent to Vietnam. The application was immediately accepted, and Snepp found himself in Saigon on behalf of the CIA.

Much to his surprise, he enjoyed the work and became an expert in Vietnamese affairs. His first tour lasted from 1969 to 1971, and then in 1972 he was sent back specifically to break by interrogation an important North Vietnamese prisoner, Nguyen Van Tai, head of the communist counter-espionage and terrorist network in Saigon.

Snepp worked on him for months, and claims he was close to success when the Vietnam ceasefire came into force in February 1973. Snepp was taken off the case, but Van Tai remained in prison until 1975, when North Vietnamese tanks were advancing on Saigon. Snepp revealed in his book *Decent Interval* that rather than risk allowing him to be rescued to turn his own talents on his erstwhile captors, he was taken up in an aircraft and thrown out 10,000 feet over the South China Sea. Snepp says this was done at the suggestion of a 'senior CIA official': he himself was in no way involved.

Snepp exchanged the role of interrogator for that of analyst and remained in Vietnam to the bitter end, being one of the last to be helicoptered off the roof of the US Embassy.

He was awarded the Medal of Merit by the CIA, but failed to get anybody to accept his version of what caused the American defeat in Vietnam, and grew increasingly bitter, until he resigned to write his exposé book.

Because of this he was regarded in some quarters of the CIA as disloyal. He carefully avoided naming people whose lives and careers might be endangered. *Decent Interval* is not just about the CIA; it is about the State Department, the army, the government and Vietnam. Snepp was regarded as one of the victims of an ignoble episode.

But as with Agee, the CIA had no intention of letting Snepp off the hook. In a series of battles through the courts, the Agency accused Snepp of breaking his contract. First the Agency won. Then Snepp won. Finally, the Supreme Court ruled in 1979 that he had broken his contract.

He was ordered to turn over the $100,000 he had earned from the book and told that he could not write any more about the CIA without first clearing with the Agency.

SOBELL, Morton

One of the American atom spies working under the code-name of Stone, he was sentenced to thirty years' imprisonment in the trial which in 1951 ended in the death sentence for the Rosenbergs. Sobell had previously fled to Mexico with his wife Helen, but had been extradited, and taken into custody by the FBI. Six years later at the trial of the Russian master-spy Colonel Abel a link was established between Abel and Sobell by Reino Hayhanen, Abel's drunken aide, who had defected to the West rather than go back to Moscow. Hayhanen told the court that he had been sent to Bear Mountain by Abel in 1955 to dig up $5,000 to give to Helen Sobell for 'Stone's' legal costs. Hayhanen dug up the money, but kept it for himself. After the trial Abel joined Sobell in Atlanta Federal Prison, where the two men played chess together before Abel was exchanged for U-2 pilot Gary Powers.

SOLOMON, Mrs Flora

Because she considered that newspaper articles written by Kim Philby (when he was working as a correspondent in Beirut, after leaving the intelligence service) to be anti-Zionist and pro-Nasser, Mrs Solomon denounced him as a KGB agent.

Mrs Solomon, of Russian ancestry, settled in London before the war. At one stage she employed Philby's second wife, Aileen, and knew Kim Philby. After her outburst about him being a KGB man she was introduced to a senior British counter-intelligence officer. She was able to tell him that Philby had confessed his role to her, and had asked for help.

The information which she was able to provide at this late stage, in 1962, provided a basis for the detailed interrogation of Philby by Nicholas Elliott in Beirut.

SORENSON, Theodore C.

Special aide to President Kennedy, and a leading knight of Kennedy's so-called 'Camelot' court in Washington, Sorenson was nominated to succeed George Bush as Director CIA on 23 December 1976. He was a moralist who wanted to reform the Agency: 'I'd like to get rid of the dirty tricks image of the CIA, the idea of trying to do people in or mess people up.'

It was a strange appointment, and came under immediate attack from all sides. The AFL-CIO (the 'American TUC') were opposed to it, and so were the conservatives. He was specifically attacked on a number of points: he had taken classified material from the White House files for his book on the Kennedy administration; he had been a conscientious objector to military service; he had helped Teddy Kennedy attempt to explain away Chappaquiddick; his law firm represented Iran and Zaïre; he had had no experience in intelligence.

So fierce was the opposition that he withdrew on 17 January 1977 in the face of what he described as 'scurrilous and unfounded personal attacks'. The affair was seen as a setback for President Carter and a sign that Congress intended to assert itself in the field of foreign affairs.

SORGE, Richard

The most brilliant and successful spy of the Second World War, this Russo-German had been with the GRU since 1929. Through the excellence of his high sources in Tokyo, both German and Japanese, he was able to inform the Kremlin in advance about events of capital importance. Furthermore, this intellectual among spies, a Doctor of Philosophy who was also vigorous and highly sociable, was able to analyse political and military events as well as to report them.

His first posting was to China, where he built up a number of contacts of great use to him later. Although he had been a communist party member from his early days in Hamburg, Sorge contrived before going to Japan to join the Nazi party, and his farewell dinner was attended by no less a person than Dr Goebbels.

He established himself in Tokyo as a journalist, correspondent of the influential paper *Frankfurter Zeitung*. With such credentials he was a welcome visitor to the German Embassy. He became a firm friend of Major-General Ott, the military attaché who was later ambassador, and eventually the two breakfasted together daily to discuss current developments.

Through his Japanese journalist contacts from the old days in China, Sorge was soon extremely well connected in Japanese military and political circles. Thus he was admirably placed to report to Moscow Centre on the activities of Germany and Japan, two principal adversaries of the Soviet Union.

He correctly informed the Kremlin that Japan after long hesitation had decided to attack in South-East Asia rather than against Soviet territory in the Far East. This vital piece of news made it possible for the Red Army to redeploy whole divisions from that region back westward to play their part in the counter-attacks after the siege of Stalingrad.

Like his colleague Leopold Trepper, head of Soviet intelligence in Europe, he was able to warn Russia in advance about German plans to invade, which were ignored by Stalin. Finally, on the eve of his arrest, he dispatched a message that the Japanese were about to attack Pearl Harbor.

One remarkable feature of his career in espionage was that he never used false papers and never resorted to a cover-name. He was always known by his true name, Dr Richard Sorge, Nazi journalist. It was a remarkable achievement that he survived undetected for over six years in Japan, a country with rigid censorship and under tight military and police control.

He worked throughout with the same team of five, four well-connected Japanese and one top GRU radio operator-technician named Max Klausen. It was his firm rule never to recruit new agents on the spot.

Just how wise that decision was is proved by the fact that through a sub-agent who was recruited by one of his five suspicion about him was finally aroused. One of his agents was arrested, and it became obvious that soon he too would be exposed.

He made plans to leave but delayed his departure — almost as though his was a fictional spy story — because of his infatuation for a Japanese dancing-girl. What he did not know was that she was working for Colonel Osaki, head of Japanese counter-intelligence.

She reported to the Colonel that on their way to his house Sorge had thrown away a torn piece of paper. This last message before Sorge's arrest read: 'Japanese carrier air force attacking United States Navy at Pearl Harbor probably November six ...'

There is no evidence whether or not the message got through to the Kremlin. Certainly there was no sign that President Roosevelt ever received it from that source.

Richard Sorge was not executed until November 1944. Not until twenty years later did the Soviet Union recognize his services by making him a posthumous Hero of the Soviet Union and by putting his picture on a postage stamp.

SOUPERT, Dr Jean Paul

Picked up by the Belgians while acting as a courier and industrial spy for the East Germans, this elderly Swiss-born, naturalized Luxemburger was turned to become a double for the British, French and West German security services.

He was sixty-nine when he made his one and only public appearance in Britain as a witness at the trial of two British employees of Kodak who, since no military secrets were involved, were charged under the Prevention of Corruption Act. Both the anonymous MI5 witnesses for the prosecution and Dr Soupert were pilloried by the defence. This was conducted by Jeremy Hutchinson QC, who was able to demonstrate that Soupert had been promised £5,000 to give evidence by Kodak. Both the accused were acquitted.

Various Western services had been watching Soupert since 1960, and when the Belgian Sûreté de l'Etat pulled him in he made a full confession and agreed to become a double. His story was that he had written to an East German academic in search of a job, and after being invited to East Germany had agreed to supply information about Western industry. As an industrial chemist he was well qualified to do this.

They taught him spy photography, and instructed him in the use of dead-letter boxes. One of his methods was to conceal microfilm in a tube of toothpaste, which he would hide behind the radiator in the lavatory of a train bound for East Berlin. He then got off the train before it reached the frontier, leaving the film to be recovered at the destination. He was issued with a spy kit briefcase and a book with a secret compartment in its cover.

He was in fact a professional, and made numerous missions as a courier carrying quantities of material. Once caught he had no hesitation in working for the Belgians and MI5, who used him to trace British communists working for the Eastern Bloc. He also blew another active agent in Europe, a man called Herbert Steinbrecher, who among other activities was spying on the French version of Concorde, then in the early stages of development.

SOUSTELLE, Jacques

A Radical archaeologist specializing in the Inca civilization, Soustelle became enmeshed in espionage at the age of thirty when he joined General de Gaulle and his Free French forces in wartime London. In 1944 he took over direction of the General's intelligence bureau, and ran it from Algiers.

It was an appointment which had far-reaching consequences on his career and life. He was made Governor-General of Algiers in the 1950s, and fell under the spell of the place. He wanted Algeria to remain French, and using his experience in intelligence work he plunged into the plots by French settlers and army officers to prevent Algeria becoming independent. These plots led to the return to power of General de Gaulle in 1958. At one stage Soustelle, under surveillance, escaped from his Paris apartment concealed in the boot of a car to join the faction in Algiers demanding 'Algérie Française.'

Like so many others, he was disappointed when de Gaulle, having been recalled to power to stop the threatened civil war in France, turned his back on the French settlers, and made Algeria independent. Soustelle eventually abandoned politics and returned to archaeology.

SPRINGHALL, Douglas Frank

A former commissar with the International Brigade in the Spanish civil war, he became national organizer of the British communist party. He was used as a link man by the Soviet Embassy intelligence team in their early dealings with the newly recruited Cambridge University spies.

During the war he was arrested and sentenced to seven years in prison for espionage. He had persuaded a woman clerk in the Air Ministry to pass over technical information about work on early jet engines.

The communist party expelled him, not so much because of his activities as because it was considered indiscreet of the national organizer to get mixed up in espionage publicly. This happened at a time when Russia was generally seen as a brave ally against Hitler. The party hoped to win new members in this emotional atmosphere, and did not want to spoil its appeal with suspicions about spies.

STASHINSKY, Bogdan

A good-looking Ukrainian, he was pressed into service as an apprentice 'illegal' after the Russians had caught him travelling on a train without a ticket. After special training they sent him to West Germany as a courier and agent. Because he showed promise the KGB promoted Bogdan (then aged twenty-five) to their killer squad, which specialized at the time in particularly unpleasant forms of chemical warfare assassination.

His first target was Lev Rebet, a Ukrainian émigré living in Munich, and the chosen weapon was a tube spray gun. A detonator exploded a small ampoule of prussic acid, and when the vapour hit its victim at close range it killed him, producing the symptoms of death by heart-attack. Stashinsky was instructed that he would not be harmed by the effects of the spray when he fired it, provided that he remembered to take a special pill beforehand, and immediately afterwards inhaled the contents of another ampoule. To prove that the gadget was fool-proof they had him try out the procedure on a dog in the Berlin woods.

He carried out his first mission successfully in 1957. He ambushed Lev Rebet on a staircase leading to his Munich office. The autopsy pronounced that Rebet had died of a heart-attack.

Stashinsky's second mission was to kill Stepan Bandera, another leader of the Ukrainian anti-Soviet movement, also in Munich. But by this time the KGB recruit was beginning to have doubts, and at first made excuses. On the second attempt, and under pressure from his masters, he again used a spray gun and killed his victim.

As a reward for these acts he was awarded the Red Banner and a promise of promotion. However, at this stage in his career he met and married a sensible and strong-willed East German girl called Inge. She was horrified by his confessions and persuaded him to escape to the West, where he surrendered to the American authorities in West Berlin.

At his trial by a West German court he revealed the full story and managed to win the sympathy of the court with his detailed confession. He was sentenced to only eight years as an accomplice to murder.

The case was important in that it demonstrated how a branch of the Soviet state security service had institutionalized murder. Soviet authorities were so horrified by Western reaction to the revelations about their murder technique that although they still considered that assassination was sometimes necessary, orders were given that people must in future be liquidated only in special circumstances.

STEINBRECHER, Herbert

It was in a small hotel among the tourist traps and strip joints of Place Pigalle in Paris that officers of the French DST counter-espionage unit moved in to arrest this craggy-faced East German spy in 1965. In his pocket was a packet of sweets, and when the bon-bons were cut open technicians at the laboratory discovered pieces of microfilm concealed in their sticky centres.

The identity of this 32-year-old East German from Leipzig with a good background in technical engineering had been disclosed by another industrial spy, Dr Jean Paul Soupert, a Luxemburger turned by Belgian security. He had already completed thirty missions in Western Europe. His speciality was the Anglo-French Concorde then being developed, and in order to prepare for his latest mission he had taken a job in a French aircraft factory.

When they pulled him in he was about to leave for Toulouse, the base of Sud Aviation, builders of Concorde, where he intended to set up a spy network. The French State Security Court sentenced him to twelve years' imprisonment.

He was less fortunate than another Concorde spy in France, Sergei Pavlov, the Paris manager of the Soviet airline, Aeroflot. Pavlov ran a network which had penetrated the Sud Aviation factory. After two years in France he was simply expelled and put on a flight to Moscow.

STEPHENSON, Sir William

The quiet Canadian, best known for his work under the code-name 'Intrepid' as co-ordinator of Anglo-American intelligence during the Second World War. Stephenson started out in the great game as a pilot in the Royal Flying Corps, when after being shot down and taken prisoner by the Germans he escaped from a POW camp and produced a report on conditions in Germany which attracted the attention of British intelligence.

Between the wars, as a patriotic business-man with a keen interest in scientific development, he combined business and private espionage in Europe. He was quick to see the dangers of Hitler's rise to power, and to help frustrate his plans he provided Winston Churchill with detailed reports on German preparations for war.

Stephenson was equally active in Scandinavia in operations intended to deny the Nazis access to Norwegian heavy-water supplies for atom-bomb development. One of the first to realize the full danger of atomic weapons in enemy hands, he helped to make sure that scientists like Dr Niels Bohr, the Danish physicist, did not fall into German hands.

His most important intelligence contribution to the war-effort was to organize with the blessing of President Roosevelt joint Anglo-American operations which hinged upon close and at first secret co-operation between the Federal Bureau of Investigation and BSC, British Security Co-ordination, the organization established by him in New York.

As 'Little Bill' he worked closely with 'Big Bill' Donovan, the American founding father of the Office of Strategic Services, which later developed into the CIA. The two men had known each other for more than twenty years, and worked closely together on the organization of resistance forces in Europe.

After Pearl Harbor, when America came into the war against Japan and the Axis, Stephenson was less involved in Nazi spycatching in the United States. He worked closely with the British Special Operations Executive, which controlled resistance operations in Europe.

Perhaps the best known remark of Stephenson came when he was explaining to President Roosevelt how the British intended to get back into Europe, then under Nazi control. 'If I were a worm and wanted to get into this orange, I would go on walking around it until I found a hole. I might have to walk round it until the orange went rotten and a hole appeared. But I would get into

this orange in the end — provided I did not starve first.'

William Stephenson was knighted in recognition of his services, and after the war returned to business and became adviser on industrial development to the Canadian government. A biography of him was in fact entitled *The Quiet Canadian*, while there were other books about him called *A Man called Intrepid* and *The Two Bills*.

STOESSEL, Walter

The US ambassador to Moscow in 1975 who became the victim of radiation poisoning as a result of unconventional methods used by the KGB against the American Embassy building. High-intensity rays were beamed at the windows of the diplomatic mission to affect the communications system.

Dr Kissinger, who was Secretary of State at the time, described the affair as being of such complexity and sensitivity that he did not believe it should be discussed in public. He added darkly; 'We have made unilateral efforts to reduce any dangers.'

Mr Stoessel recovered from the illness when he returned to Washington. The incident is remarkable for the revelation of how complicated the techniques of eavesdropping and counter-eavesdropping have become. Although the purpose of the Moscow rays has not been revealed, they might have been used either to activate electronic devices or to neutralize anti-bugging equipment installed by the Americans.

STONEHOUSE, John, MP

When John Stonehouse was named in 1970 by the Czech security defector Joseph Frolik as a victim of entrapment by Czech security officers in Prague he was serving in the Labour Government as Minister for Posts and Telecommunications. Questioned by the Prime Minister on the allegations, he denied them, and no further action was taken.

In 1976 Mr Stonehouse was sentenced to seven years on charges of theft and fraud after contriving his own disappearance. Later he turned to writing for a living and produced *Ralph*, a thriller which described an entrapment and blackmail operation carried out by East Germans.

STRAIGHT, Michael Whitney

His sins were those of omission, for although he did not commit the final one of betraying his country it was, as he made clear in his autobiography of self-justification, a close-run thing. For this wealthy, cultivated, literary person from a well-connected American family was a friend and for a time a political sympathizer with Britain's best-known spies, Burgess and Anthony Blunt. Yet being an indecisive man, he could never bring himself to denounce them until it was almost too late.

He arrived in England in 1926 with his mother Beatrice Straight, the widow of a financier with liberal views, and four years later went up to Trinity College, Cambridge, to read economics. Romantic and impressionable, the young Straight found himself in a hotbed of academic communist intrigue. His tutor was Maurice Dobb, a leading member of the British communist party; he was soon visited by the proselytizing James Klugman, and the poet John Cornford.

So he joined the communist cell of his rather smart college and later made a dutiful trip to Leningrad, with among others Anthony Blunt. He also joined the Apostles, a curious secret society originally founded by Tennyson and his brother, and now composed of young men who believed themselves to be very clever and extremely nice.

It was in 1937, after the death of his friend John Cornford (who had gone off to fight in Spain) that Anthony Blunt summoned Straight to his elegant rooms in Trinity. Playing on his grief, Blunt made it clear that the Communist International considered it was Straight's duty to leave Cambridge and go to work in, and spy upon, Wall Street. He pleaded in vain to be released from such an obligation, but convinced that his appeal had been rejected by 'the highest circles in the Kremlin', he faked a nervous breakdown and went to New York.

But first he was given a few tips on field work by a Russian. He was advised, for example, to use public telephones in order to avoid detection.

Back in Washington, the American who had no need actually to earn his living was taken on as an unpaid volunteer at the State Department. There he busied himself writing papers on such subjects as the economy of Hitler's Germany.

Before long a Soviet contact man who announced himself to be 'Michael Green' got in touch, bringing greetings from Cambridge friends, and asked him to supply interesting documents. Straight wrote later that the only documents he did hand over were those written by himself, including one attacking the Nazi-Soviet Pact.

Although he did not call them — for he had no wish to become embroiled — the Soviet agents kept calling him. He was further alarmed by the interrogation of General Walter Krivitsky, a defector who informed the Americans about Russian spy networks.

Guy Burgess, on a visit to the US early in the war, looked up his old Cambridge friend, and by asking Straight to put him in touch there with 'our friends' made it clear that it was Burgess who had dragged him into contact with Russian agents. Straight replied that he would not, and could not. In 1942 Straight joined the US Air Force and served as a bomber pilot.

However, even after the War he was not free of the communist entanglement. On a trip to England in 1949 he saw Anthony Blunt and Guy Burgess, who asked whether he was still with them. He was not, he said.

After a further meeting with Burgess in Washington early in 1951 Straight became indignant at the thought that Guy, working on Far Eastern affairs, might have betrayed secrets to the Russians about British and American plans in the Korean War.

It was not long after that when Straight read of the flight to Moscow of Burgess and Maclean. He felt he ought to do something, and made a half-hearted attempt to inform the British authorities, though he was reluctant still to implicate his old friend and hero, Anthony Blunt.

Finally Straight found himself face to face with an ugly choice when President Kennedy offered him the chairmanship of the Advisory Council on the Arts, a job which he very much wanted. He could not take it without an FBI security clearance, and that might bring to light unpleasant facts about his political past.

Reluctantly, therefore, he decided to unburden himself by confessing all to an FBI agent. It was a decisive step so far as the British security service was concerned, for the FBI dutifully passed on to them the vital information about Guy Burgess, and about Blunt, who until then had not been decisively implicated in espionage.

Arthur Martin of MI5 pursued the questioning, and Straight was able to tell him that Burgess had drawn Blunt into his network, and that he believed that another man named Leo Long had also been involved. In 1964, after Arthur Martin had obtained a confession from Blunt, he arranged a confrontation between the man and Straight.

In a brief private conversation beforehand Straight revealed that Blunt had said to him, 'We always wondered how long it would be before you turned us in.' If Straight had been able to make his mind up earlier it would have saved the United States and Britain from a great deal of harm inflicted upon them by the Soviet network.

Although Western intelligence was now, and at last, in possession of the facts, they did not emerge publicly until the publication in 1979 of *The Climate of Treason* by Anthony Boyle, and the subsequent naming of Blunt as the 'Maurice' of that book by Mrs Thatcher.

After the public disgrace Michael Straight, partly in order to excuse himself for his own tardiness in coming forward with information only he could provide, told his side of the story in his book *After Long Silence*.

STRONG, Major-General Sir Kenneth

A British Army intelligence director who achieved the singular distinction of being invited to become Deputy Director of the American Central Intelligence Agency in 1950. He had served as chief of intelligence to General Eisenhower at SHAFE, the wartime Supreme Headquarters, Allied Expeditionary Forces in Europe.

When General Walter Bedell Smith returned from his post as US ambassador in Moscow to become head of the CIA, depressed by the lack of information about Soviet intentions, he approached his old friend General Strong with the offer to join him. Strong, who had by that time served for two years as head of the freshly formed Joint Intelligence Bureau at the British Ministry of Defence, was strongly tempted.

He finally turned down the offer because it would have been necessary for him to renounce his British citizenship and to become a naturalized American. He also anticipated that his appointment as a foreigner in Washington would lead to suspicion of divided loyalties which would make his position difficult.

Instead General Smith appointed a wartime American intelligence officer, William H. Jackson, who had become a New York banker.

SUTTERLIN, Leonore

The mission given to Heinz Sutterlin, a German agent of the KGB, was not simply to seduce but to woo and marry an agreeable though plain 35-year-old secretary in the West German Foreign Ministry in Bonn named Leonore. He had been chosen for his undoubted romantic good looks and appropriate age, and he went into action at once by arriving at her apartment in 1960 bearing a bunch of roses.

Soon Leonore became Frau Sutterlin. In order to please her husband, and then so as not to lose him, she began bringing home at his insistence quantities of secret documents for him to copy and pass on. He tried unsuccessfully to get her a new job as secretary to the Federal Chancellor, Willy Brandt, but despite this setback the papers rolled in until Sutterlin's case officer, Lieutenant-Colonel Eugene Runge, went over to the CIA in 1968 and reported that the Sutterlins had supplied him with no less than 2,900 documents, one-third of them top-secret. He boasted that the KGB was reading such papers even before the West German Foreign Minister.

After his arrest Sutterlin confessed. His wife stoutly protected him with denials until they told her that in his confession he had said that he married her on KGB orders, not because he loved her. This was too much for the unhappy woman to bear, and she hanged herself in her cell.

This was just one of the sad cases in which the KGB deliberately exploited the fact that as a result of the world war there were in Germany very many lonely, unmarried women often with responsible jobs. From 1954 until his arrest four years later they employed a German named Carl Helmers, a sixty-year-old businessman who came to be known as the 'Red Casanova', for his skill at luring such women simultaneously into bed and espionage.

SWIESTRA, Captain Rudy J.

He was in command of a USAF ferret aircraft, a Hercules EC-130, shot down on 2 September 1958 while flying an electronic intelligence mission along the Soviet-Turkish border. In all there were seventeen people on board, a number of them radio experts, most probably employed by the National Security Agency. The aircraft went down over Soviet Armenia, and the Russians reported that six of the crew died. No hard news of the fate of the other eleven has ever come to light.

So concerned was the US government about the disappearance of the eleven who according to one report parachuted down, that President Eisenhower himself made several desperate attempts to persuade the Russians to reveal what happened.

Eventually the Americans gave to the Russians their own highly secret and conclusive evidence that the aircraft had been shot down by MiG fighters. The tape was then made public. The National Security Agency was against these steps being taken, for the tape blew NSA cover, and revealed not only intercept capability but also the fact that the EC-130 was flying over Soviet territory.

The transcript records the MiG squadron leader from a base near Yerevan, capital of Armenia, saying he could see the US aircraft on his side of the 'fence', the Turkish border. 'Attack!' he ordered and began firing at a height of 30,000 feet. Then he said, 'The target is falling.'

Despite this the Russians stuck to their version that the plane had simply crashed. One possible explanation is that they were embarrassed to admit that American technology was capable of finding such detail about their air-force operations.

Captain Swiestra's mission was to fly along the border so that the electronics technicians on board could pinpoint Soviet radar and ground-defence installations as they came into action. The Americans stuck to their version that his aircraft flew along the border. Whether he strayed over the Soviet Union accidentally or because he had orders to probe deeper is not known.

Similar ferret missions were frequently flown over Chinese and North Korean as well as Soviet territory in the late 1950s and 1960s. A number of aircraft were shot down in the course of such hazardous missions. Two years after the EC-130 incident a U-2 high-level spy-plane piloted by Gary Powers went down over Sverdlovsk, and Khruschev used this as a pretext to call off the East-West summit conference in Paris.

THYRAUD de VOSJOLI, Philippe

After spending nearly half his 25-year-long career as an officer in the French intelligence service, the SDECE, and acting as its liaison officer with its American counterpart the CIA, de Vosjoli found himself facing two crises. He had always worked closely with the Americans, and indeed had gone out of his way to do them good turns with intelligence from Castro's Cuba. Then General de Gaulle, the new President of France, began to distance himself from the American alliance.

The Gaullist defence policy of facing all points of the compass, west as well as east, involved loosening the ties between French and American intelligence services in the early 1960s. In Paris de Gaulle insisted that the many CIA men should register with the Interior Ministry, rather than with the Foreign Ministry. In the United States French intelligence officers were to spy upon their allies.

This did not at all suit Thyraud de Vosjoli (who despite his aristocratic name had joined the service as a senior NCO), for his career had been built on transatlantic co-operation. Suddenly Franco-American relations were worsening, not helped by the fact that Dick Helms of CIA had rather publicly been in contact with Jacques Soustelle, who was closely linked with French generals in open revolt against de Gaulle in Algeria.

To complicate matters further, the Russian defector Colonel Anatoli Golytsin of the KGB arrived in Washington in 1962 with information about treason in Paris. He exposed Georges Paques, a senior French official at NATO. He also claimed knowledge of a Soviet network, code-named Sapphire, at work within the SDECE itself, and even went so far as to claim there was a mole on General de Gaulle's personal staff.

President Kennedy wrote personally to the French head of state about this matter, and senior intelligence officers were sent to Washington to interrogate Golytsin. He convinced them that the KGB appeared to know far too much about the workings of SDECE.

British and American newspapers began publishing stories about a 'French Philby' in Paris. French newspapers, and particularly the satirical *Canard Enchaîné*, suggested that the Soviet mole was Jacques Foccart, a trusted adviser of de Gaulle who had helped him with intelligence affairs since the days of the Free French. Foccart sued, cleared his name, and was awarded damages of £6,000. The Presidential office dismissed the stories as 'absurd'.

Because of his position in Washington, Thyraud de Vosjoli found himself involved in all these affairs, the more so through his connection with Leon Uris, who wrote *Topaz,* a best-selling fictional spy thriller using the affair, in which Golytsin appeared as 'Boris Kuznetsov'. The hero of the book was a dashing French intelligence officer in Washington.

When Thyraud was ordered back to Paris in September 1963 he resigned from the service, in protest, he said, against corruption within the SDECE. He also drew attention to the infiltration of it by 'foreign services'. To those who mockingly called him a French defector to the US, he firmly denied that he was, or ever had been, any sort of double agent, and claimed that he was simply distressed by the state of affairs within the service.

In 1972, at the age of fifty-one, he was living in Miami. During that year he was awarded damages of £138,000 by a Los Angeles court against Leon Uris in a dispute over the contract they had signed sharing profits from the *Topaz* novel. Thyraud de Vosjoli had claimed that the novel was based on a manuscript he wrote after resigning from French intelligence.

TONDI, Alighiero

A Jesuit father and professor of theology discovered making unauthorized sorties into the secret records department of the Vatican intelligence service, reputed to be among the most thorough in the world. He was a secretary to Monsignor Montini, who later became Pope Paul, and for this reason a discreet inquiry into Tondi's activities was made by a French priest who had wartime intelligence experience in the Deuxième Bureau.

He investigated the fact that on numerous occasions when priests from the Vatican were carrying out missions in the Eastern Bloc countries it was obvious that their presence had been signalled in advance to the local intelligence service. The Vatican was also alarmed that details of papal dispositions, especially of its finances, had been leaked to the Italian communist party in advance.

Alighiero Tondi, who had entered the priesthood in 1936, admitted that he was associated with the Italian communist party, and had attended courses at the Lenin University in Moscow. From 1944 onward he provided information directly to Palmiro Togliatti, the party's secretary-general.

In the early 1950s, after the inquiry, he was expelled from Vatican territory. He then married Carmen Zanti. He travelled a great deal, and at one time in 1956 was adviser on religious affairs to the East German leader, Walter Ulbricht.

Tondi later announced that he had been pardoned by the Pope on the grounds that he was working for peace and reconciliation.

TREHOLT, Arne

Norwegian special branch officers were at Fornebu airport, Oslo waiting for Arne Treholt, the dapper and bespectacled senior diplomat when he arrived there on 20 January 1984. He had told his wife that he was flying to Paris, but the security men knew that he was on his way to Vienna for a rendezvous with an experienced and high ranking KGB officer named Gennady Titov.

In the brief-case of the 41-year-old diplomat were top secret documents, some of them relating to government discussions during the recent visit to Oslo of the US secretary of state George Shultz which Treholt, in charge of Norwegian foreign ministry press operations, had helped to organise. The Norwegian government later announced that Treholt had confessed to spying for the Soviet Union for fifteen years.

During that period he had begun a promising political career and served as a junior minister during negotiations with the Russians about fishing rights and delimitation of the Berents Sea, potentially oil-bearing. Officials feared that Norwegian government intentions and negotiating positions were being leaked in advance to the Russians.

Arne Treholt, who had a taste for high living and for backing horses, turned to a diplomatic career, working at United Nations before returning home to attend the Norwegian Defence College. In his new role he had access to quantities of confidential papers, including NATO documents. Indeed General Hamre, a former chief of staff, declared after the arrest that Treholt was in a position to reveal information rendering some Norwegian and NATO contingency plans useless.

It was not immediately clear how Arne Treholt had begun working for the KGB, but there were suggestions that his life-style used up more money than he was earning, and newspapers hinted at scandals in his sex life. But it was also known that as a young journalist he had taken a stance strongly critical of the United States, especially over Vietnam, for he was one of the 1960s generation. He was well known for his left-wing views.

Norwegian security men were aware of the presence in government circles of a 'mole', for they had been warned by a KGB defector who was unable to name him in 1977. While Arne Treholt was still serving at the UN in New York he aroused the suspicions of Norwegian Special Branch men, who asked the CIA and FBI to help keep watch on him. Surveillance revealed that he was a keen jogger, and that he was meeting his KGB contacts while on training runs in Central Park.

Nevertheless, it was not until the summer of 1983 that firmer proof of his activities was forthcoming in the form of photographs taken by Western security men of Treholt meeting with top Soviet agents. Among them was his case officer Gennady Titov, already a veteran of KGB espionage who had served in London and had been expelled from Oslo in 1977.

After the arrest of Treholt the shocked Norwegian government riposted promptly by expelling from Oslo three Soviet diplomats and two trade delegates, including Leonid Makarov, described as the KGB 'resident' in Oslo who outranked even the ambassador. Nine days later they also turned out a Soviet executive named Igor Granov.

Arne Treholt held a more elevated position than

any of the thirty other Norwegians unmasked as Russian spies since 1945.

TREPPER, Leopold

Of all the frustrations suffered by spies in the field, none can be more exasperating than the discovery that accurate information about forthcoming enemy military events, painfully gained and transmitted, has been ignored back home. That was the fate suffered by Leopold Trepper, a Polish Jew who was the conductor of what the Germans called the *Rote Kapelle* ('Red Orchestra') network of Soviet spies in Europe operating against the Nazis during the war.

His first espionage scoop was to provide early warning of Hitler's attack upon the Soviet Union in June 1941. The Kremlin did not believe him. A year later he radioed from Brussels that the German thrust against the Caucasus would be made in the spring of 1942.

Trepper was a technician of espionage, and using both communists and Jews who were only too willing to work against the Nazis, he built up a formidable network of well-informed people ranging from railwaymen to business-men and the occasional aristocrat, such as the White Russian Baron Vasily de Maximovich.

Trepper had turned to communism — 'because I am a Jew' — back in the 1920s. He emigrated to Palestine, was expelled by the British during the Mandate, and in the 1930s went to the Soviet Union, where he was given a complete espionage course. He returned to Europe as head of Soviet intelligence there, to replace Walter Krivitsky, one of the early Soviet defectors to the West.

It was in 1938 that he arrived in Brussels with little enough time to build a network from scratch before the war began. Trepper became Jean Gilbert, a Belgian industrialist, in an international raincoat business with offices everywhere, which served as useful cover. His organization was soon producing a wide range of information.

In occupied Paris, Trepper — who as a spymaster led from in front — mixed with the highest German circles, while at the same time keeping his links with the French communist party. Through his effective low-level contacts he not only produced the date for the planned invasion of Russia but identified German divisions about to be transferred to the Eastern Front.

The increasing volume of the music of his radio transmissions from many operators — that was the origin of the name 'Red Orchestra' — led to his detection. Hitler formed a special Red Orchestra Commando to seek him out. Trap after trap failed, but finally they got him through his dentist, and he was seized — literally in the chair — in November 1942.

After his arrest he displayed his cunning professionalism by affecting to believe in and co-operate with the German plan to go on communicating with Moscow Centre as though nothing had happened. They claimed that the High Command wanted to keep a channel of communication to be used for eventual peace negotiations. Trepper also managed through the French communist party to inform Moscow what he was doing. Then he escaped from the Germans and joined the Resistance.

After the liberation of Paris he flew to Moscow in Stalin's personal aircraft. There he did not receive a hero's welcome, but was thrown instead into the Lubianka. He had had the temerity to suggest that his work had not been taken seriously, which irritated Stalin, and so he was accused of working with the Germans.

A very tough and expert gentleman, was Leopold Trepper. He spent ten years in Soviet prisons, and was not able to return to his wife and three sons in Poland until 1957. Then he was written out of the official Soviet history of the Red Orchestra.

Even in Poland his troubles were not at an end. Depressed by a wave of anti-semitism there after the Six Day War, he decided that he wanted to go to Israel. Finally, and after an international protest campaign against the refusal of the Polish government to let him leave, he reached Jerusalem in 1974, and ended his days there, dying at the age of seventy-seven.

TUOMI, Kaarlo

A Soviet agent who started at the bottom, recruited by the KGB to spy on fellow-workers at the school where he taught English at Kirov, north-east of Moscow. He was trapped into doing that when security men caught him stealing bread rolls.

He was considered a promising recruit for more serious work because of his command of English, and the fact that he had been born of an immigrant family in the United States. That family, which was enthusiastically communist, had returned from Michigan to the Soviet Union in 1933.

No effort was spared in training Tuomi during a three-year course in Moscow so that he could operate in the United States without attracting attention. He even had individual tuition from a Russian woman brought up in the States, and was subjected to an intensive study course of American films.

Eventually, equipped with a complete and well-researched 'legend', a false biography, and papers to go with it, he was dispatched to New York in 1959 after an introductory run-in to capitalism in Europe. Despite all that the FBI spotted him, and did a deal which converted Tuomi into a useful double agent during the crises of the early 1960s.

Finally, on the eve of being recalled to Moscow by the KGB (who were still unaware of his contacts with the FBI), he decided in 1962 that he wanted to change allegiance and stay on in the United States.

TURNER, Admiral Stansfield

A former destroyer captain who was Commander-in-Chief, Allied Forces Southern Europe, when his erstwhile naval classmate President Carter, searching for someone to replace his rejected nominee, Ted Sorensen, picked him to become Director CIA in March 1977.

A man of somewhat pawky humour — he had a dog called Hornblower, and hung a sign saying 'Superspook' on the door of his office lavatory at the CIA. He was a man of considerable intellect, a Rhodes scholar and President of the US Naval College from 1972 to 1974. He was also a man of fierce ambition, and he ran the CIA with a rod of iron.

He was determined to have a lean young organization, and in what became known as the 'Halloween massacre' he fired 820 Agency employees. Many of them were long-serving senior men, who had served under Dulles and Helms. Turner explained, 'If I don't take away some of the people from the top who are all fifty years old you won't have a clandestine service in five years. It's been run like a family business for the last thirty years.'

Henry Knoche, his deputy, a professional intelligence analyst, resigned over policy differences. Morale at the Agency was at rock-bottom, but Turner moved a number of naval officers into top jobs and quelled the incipient mutiny. He had, moreover, the complete support of President Carter, who expressed his 'sincere and complete confidence in Admiral Turner'.

In addition to destroying the 'Eastern' establishment in CIA, Turner also waged a war against the other intelligence agencies, demanding the appointment of an intelligence tsar over the whole community, and in August 1977 Carter acceded to part of his demand, putting him in charge of all intelligence operations and budgets except those of the FBI.

There seemed to be no stopping the Admiral. He was succeeding in moulding the Agency into the form he wanted. President Carter, who genuinely wanted an effective CIA, loosened some of the restraints imposed after the post-Watergate inquiries. An advertising campaign for recruits was a great success.

However, Turner had become too closely identified with the President. He was viewed as a political appointee, not a career 'superspook', and when Carter lost the Presidential election in 1980 Turner lost too. President Reagan fired him, and replaced him with William Casey. The Admiral's dismissal was greeted with mixed feelings at the Agency. While he inspired no affection, he had certainly commanded respect.

Ulmer, Alfred

A former journalist, he was one of the OSS originals working out of Italy at the end of the Second World War. Kept on by the new CIA, he was station chief in Athens during the height of civil war, when the CIA successfully prevented the communists from taking over Greece.

He then became head of the Deputy Director of Plans' Far Eastern Division, and had the misfortune to be put in charge of the Agency's attempt to overthrow President Sukarno of Indonesia by supporting a group of rebel officers. It all ended in humiliation for the United States on 18 May 1958 when Allen Pope, one of the CIA pilots supporting the rebellion, was shot down in his B26 and captured after dropping his bombs on a church and killing most of the congregation.

Allen Dulles called off the operation, and shortly afterwards Ulmer was sent to Paris as station chief. It was an agreeable enough job, but obviously Ulmer's path to the top of the CIA pyramid was now blocked. He had, however, made friends with an up-and-coming shipowner, Stavros Niarchos, during his tour of duty in Greece, and in 1962 left the Agency to join Niarchos's company in London.

VASSALL, William John

An obvious homosexual with a taste for fine clothes and social life, who himself boasted that men said of him that he had 'come-to-bed eyes'. He should have been spotted as a potential security risk before he went to Moscow in 1954 as a clerk in the office of the British naval attaché. The KGB was quicker to assess him, and before long a Polish clerk working in the Embassy took him to a boozy party where he was involved in homosexual capers, and soon produced the photographs to prove it. By 1955 he was firmly in the 'trap', and stealing classified information.

Undetected, he returned to London the following year as a modest clerk in the Admiralty, currying favour and making himself useful as a dogsbody, which made it possible for him to get his hands on confidential papers he had no right to see. This vicar's son had trained as a photographer during his national service in the RAF, and was content to snap away on behalf of the Russians.

He was ordered to lie low in the aftermath of the Portland Spy case, but before long he resumed normal service. Nobody in London seemed to notice anything odd about the fact that the obliging young clerk with a modest salary was living it up, and putting money in the bank — £3,000 in one year — which was a considerable sum at the time.

It was only when the intelligence service discovered that the Russians were in possession of information which could only have come from inside the Admiralty that inquiries into his activities began. He was arrested in 1962, and documents were found in his rooms. He was sentenced to eighteen years in prison, Lord Chief Justice Parker speaking of his 'selfish greed'.

Twenty years later Captain John Moore, editor of *Jane's Fighting Ships*, the standard work on the world's navies, suggested that Vassall's information aided the Russians to develop the Soviet Union's first helicopter carriers, the *Moskva* and the *Leningrad*. While Britain was working on plans for *Invincible* class carriers, 'the KGB had their own agent within the Admiralty'.

The Vassall affair revealed unbelievable laxity on the part of British security services. Similar conclusions had been drawn by the Radcliffe Committee, set up to inquire into procedures after the George Blake spy case. It recommended stricter vetting procedures for those employed in sensitive posts.

A tribunal of inquiry set up to investigate the Vassall affair in 1963 wasted a great deal of time on what the Press had written about it. It did serve to demonstrate how little regard was paid to security at the British Embassy in Moscow.

Vassall himself was released from prison on parole in 1973. Further revelations about the penetration by the KGB of British security have led to the uneasy suspicion that Vassall was deliberately discarded by the Russians in order to draw attention away from continuing spies in London whom they considered even more important.

VASSILIEV, Major Vladimir

He figured only too prominently, being a GRU (Soviet military intelligence) officer working under diplomatic cover at the Beirut trade mission, in a melodramatic plot to secure a French-built Mirage 111 jet fighter in August 1969. As an encore seven years later, while playing the role of assistant air attaché at the Soviet Embassy in Ottawa, he was quietly expelled by the tolerant Canadian government for spying again.

An insignificant sort of man, he nevertheless acted in the Beirut plot more like an agent in a television serial than a real-life one. He made contact through a Lebanese intermediary and on behalf of his boss, Alexander Komiakov, with a Lebanese Air Force fighter pilot.

The deal they offered was $2 million in return for the Mirage, which was to be flown to a Soviet base in Azerbaijan after the pilot had pretended to crash into the Mediterranean. Unfortunately for them, the pilot chosen, Lieutenant Mattar, was a loyal officer who at once informed the Lebanese Deuxième Bureau, an intelligence service with an excellent reputation.

Vassiliev and his colleague compounded their original error of judgment when security troops burst in upon their plotting rendezvous by opening fire on them. Both the Russians were wounded in the affair, and were eventually sent back to Moscow.

KGB disinformation men helped to cover the grotesque failure by claiming that it was a Western provocation. They also put heavy pressure on the government of the small Middle East state to hush up the whole business.

VIVIAN, Colonel Valentine

What is best remembered about this amiable and capable SIS officer who was its director of security is that he was the man who recruited Kim Philby into the British intelligence service. To friends who knew him as 'Vee-Vee' he announced at the time, 'I've got a bright young man for us — Philby, the *Times* war correspondent. Used to know his father in the old days.'

For Colonel Vivian, like so many other officers then, had come into intelligence through service with the Indian Police, which was noted for its skill in the old British Raj. He had met St John Philby, Kim's father, when he was a British official in India.

It is easy with hindsight to blame Vivian, but at the time, early in the Second World War, he believed that as the intelligence service rapidly expanded to deal with difficult and complicated matters it was necessary to get into the service a new type of officer. He recruited a number of university boys, incurring the scorn of his traditionalist rival in the service, Colonel Dansey, as well as journalists, writers and artists. Colonel Vivian referred to them jointly as 'my intellect-uals', and hoped that they would leaven the lump of less imaginative armed forces officers and former colonial policemen, in order to increase the efficiency of the service.

Despite his conventional appearance, lean, monocled and rather elegant, Colonel Vivian was no fool; and in a service torn, as intelligence services frequently are, by fierce rivalries, he worked hard to mould together the new combination of scornful intellectuals and officers who disapproved of them.

It was his misfortune that his brightest star turned out to be Philby, the clever and ruthless traitor betraying his country to the Russians. It must be remembered that so many young men of the time had flirted with communism in their dislike of fascism that it was considered normal, though it was expected that university leftism would mature into more moderate political faith later.

Philby betrayed Colonel Vivian in house politics as well as in greater matters, for in order to ensure his own rise in the service he denounced Lt-Colonel Felix Cowgill, the loyal and devoted officer who was his immediate superior, for disloyalty to Vivian, and eventually Cowgill left the service.

VOGEL, Wolfgang

This East Berlin lawyer is the bring 'em back alive best friend of captured spies from the Soviet Bloc. He began his swop-a-spy career by arranging — in conjunction with the New York lawyer James Donovan — for the Soviets to release Gary Powers, the U2 pilot, in return for their professional spymaster Rudolph Abel, whose life had been spared by an American court.

He then went on to negotiate two further exchanges loaded in favour of Soviet professional spies. The British released Gordon Lonsdale in return for Greville Wynne; and then handed over the Krogers to secure the freedom of Gerald Brooke, an innocent British lecturer whom the Russians had grabbed specially for the purpose.

That is the danger of such exchanges. There is no rule of law or public opinion in Soviet territories to prevent the Russians from making unreasonable arrests to enable them to recover some KGB professional detected in the West.

Next to nothing is known about the early career of Vogel, except that after the war he chose to go to university at Jena and Leipzig in East Germany. He practises as a lawyer in East Berlin, enjoying the successful and affluent life.

WALLENBERG, Raoul

A young and idealistic Swedish diplomat accredited to his country's embassy in Budapest during the last stages of the Second World War, who disappeared in 1945. His principal mission was to help refugees, and he is credited with saving tens of thousands of Jews persecuted in Hitler's Europe. He is revered in Israel as a 'Just Gentile'.

He vanished in January 1945 after being summoned to the headquarters of the occupying Red Army in Budapest. His friends at the time did not know whether he was the prisoner or the guest of the Russians.

It has since emerged that the Soviets suspected him of being an American spy because he had at his disposal large sums of money from the United States to help with his work for the refugees. A former officer in the Russian 18th Army then living in Israel reported in 1981 that Wallenberg had been seized because they did not believe that he was simply involved in relief work.

The official Russian story is that he died in July 1947 in the Lubyanka prison in Moscow where he had been wrongly detained by Abakumov of the KGB, whom a Smersh squad later discredited and shot. Despite a number of reported sightings of Wallenberg after that date, it is still not known for certain whether he is dead or alive. He would have been seventy in 1982.

WARD, Stephen

Through his practice as an osteopath Stephen Ward, an ebullient name-dropper and professional hanger-on, had a knack of making friends in high places. He also ran a stable of attractive call-girls, which served to increase his popularity.

He came to public attention by way of his key involvement in the Profumo Affair, for it was through him that John Profumo, the Secretary of State for War, met Christine Keeler, who was living with the osteopath. He was also friendly with Lord Astor, on whose estate at Cliveden he had a cottage, and for whose weekend parties there he provided attractive girls.

British intelligence officers made contact with him because they discovered that Lieutenant-Commander Eugene Ivanov, a GRU officer serving as an assistant naval attaché at the Soviet Embassy, was visiting his apartment in Wimpole Mews, West London. Hoping to use Ward and his girls in order to entrap Ivanov into turning double agent, or to defect, they made contact through an MI5 man using the name 'Woods'.

Ward, who was a vain and ambitious person, was only too happy to work with the intelligence service. Indeed, he was under the impression that he had been recruited into it, and openly boasted the fact. He soon began urging Christine Keeler into bed with the Russian.

He reported that at Cliveden he had been asked by Ivanov to discover whether the British intended to permit the arming of West Germany with atomic weapons. He also told MI5 that Profumo and his wife had been at a Cliveden party, where he had met Ivanov.

Ward became very friendly with Ivanov, under whose influence he had fallen, and was getting ever grander ideas of his role. The British had intended to employ him as a whoremaster, but in the summer and autumn of 1962 he began using Lord Astor and other connections, to make high-level contact at the Foreign Office on behalf of Ivanov during first the Berlin crisis and then the Cuban missile crisis.

He was obviously becoming a security risk to the British by acting out the part of a double agent. When scandal began to erupt publicly through a shooting incident at his mews house after two West Indians tried to reach Christine Keeler she began to tell her story to the newspapers. Quite a story it was, for she had had affairs with both a British Minister and a Soviet spy, under the aegis of Stephen Ward.

There was question of prosecuting Ward under the Official Secrets Act, but by then Ivanov had fled to Moscow, and such a case would not have had much chance of succeeding. Instead the Metropolitan Police began proceedings against him for living off immoral earnings.

It was at this stage in May 1963 that Ward resorted to high-level blackmail. He was received by Timothy Bligh, Principal Private Secretary to Macmillan, and threatened to reveal that John Profumo had lied publicly about his relations with Christine Keeler, unless the police dropped their case against him.

The deal was rejected, and in August 1963 Ward was convicted of living off immoral earnings. At the trial, still striving to make an impression, he embarrassed the security service by revealing the name 'Woods' used by the MI5 case officer. But the whole thing had been too much for the unhappy man; everybody condemned him, and on the day he was to be sentenced he took an overdose of Nembutal and died.

WEBER, Ingeborg

One of the most successful agents of the East German intelligence service, the real name of this woman arrested in Bonn in February 1970 was Liane Linder, and her rank was lieutenant-colonel. By then, aged forty-five, she had been operational for twenty years, and specialized in getting intelligence about uranium fuel for nuclear reactors.

Her cover was to work for a West German publishing house, while she ran an efficient communist spy-ring. Her activities were directed at a number of NATO countries.

Only two years after her arrest she was allowed to return to East Berlin in a complicated exchange deal arranged by the East German lawyer Dr Wolfgang Vogel, who specializes in such matters. Another woman spy, Irene Schultz, a former secretary of the West German science minister, was also freed by the West Germans in return for the liberation of no less than a hundred people arrested in East Germany for political offences.

WENNERSTROM, Colonel Stig Eric

A spy for the connoisseur, this one. A stiff-necked, handsome, cool and elegant Swedish air force officer who outranked himself in his own lifetime, being only a colonel in his own service, but an honorary major-general in Soviet military intelligence. That was not all, for this extraordinary officer from a Service family was not just a double but a double-double agent.

According to his own confession he got his taste for espionage while busy learning Russian in pre-war Latvia. His clandestine career began with work on behalf of his own country while he was air attaché at the Swedish Embassy in Moscow.

Even then he could not resist passing on useful information to Nazi Germans about the Soviet Union. That, of course, was before the German invasion of the USSR.

Then the Russians recruited him to spy on his own country, and he was happy enough to provide them with full information about the air defences of Sweden. As a result of this, complete reorganization became necessary at great cost.

When he was posted to Washington as air attaché he supplied his Russian controllers with copious information. The Americans suspected nothing, for they were under the impression that he was friendly, and he had indeed provided them with secret information about the USSR, after they had discovered through the Gehlen Organization that he had supplied German intelligence with espionage material.

The only people this multi-purpose agent did not supply were the British. Yet before the war it seems he came close to being recruited by a British agent in Latvia.

During his fifteen-year stint Stig Wennerstrom spied most enthusiastically for the Soviet Union. The GRU military intelligence rewarded him handsomely by paying out some $100,000 — plus expenses, of course.

This cool traitor must have convinced himself that his pleasant though complicated life could continue for ever. He had never needed to go in for back-street espionage, carrying out his treacherous duties in the pleasant world of air attachés *en poste*, in gentlemanly and well-appointed embassies and government buildings.

Yet even in Sweden, where it is thought exceptionally wicked to consider tapping the telephone of a suspect, and where counter-espionage officers work on a very tight rein for fear of offending against civil liberties, suspicion began to grow that the Colonel was not what he seemed.

It is another unlikely feature of the Wennerstrom story that he was finally exposed, not by counter-intelligence, but by a part-time maid who worked for the family. Mrs Carin Rosen could not understand why the Colonel should spend so much time locked in one room of the house, nor why there were stacks of crisp kroner notes in a filing cabinet she happened to see open.

However, she did not like to bother the police about such things, and anyway she could not find any entry in the telephone book for 'Spy Police'. She hesitated for three or four years, and finally it was the police — who had been equally reluctant to cause offence by questioning the domestic staff — who called her. Mrs Rosen was greatly relieved, and willingly handed to them two small packets she had found concealed under a plant-pot, which turned out to contain film of secret documents.

Wennerstrom made an extremely long confession, justifying himself only by claiming that he had spied in the cause of peace. At his trial in 1964, which shocked and outraged Sweden, he was found guilty and sentenced to life imprisonment.

WHELAN, Lieutenant-Colonel William Henry

The highest-ranking officer in the United States army so far found guilty of spying for the Russians. He was a staff officer at the Pentagon tempted by Soviet offers of money for secrets, and between 1959 and 1961 he received $5,000 in return for information supplied.

The Colonel confessed in 1966 and was sentenced to prison for fifteen years.

WHITE, Richard Goldsmith ('Sir Dick')

In the course of a career in British intelligence which spanned thirty-two years Dick White, as he was always known, enjoyed the reputation of being a thorough-going professional. He was remarkable for the fact that after being director of MI5 for three years he was appointed to the other branch as director of the Secret Intelligence Service for another twelve years.

Unlike his predecessors in that office, he was not a military man but a career officer in intelligence, who joined the service in 1936 fresh from Christ Church, Oxford, followed by studies at two American universities, Michigan and Southern California. At one stage in his time at MI5, during an unhappy period while it was run by Sir Percy Sillitoe — a former police officer of whose methods he did not approve — he considered resigning.

It is well that he did stay on, for he did more to modernise both branches of the intelligence service than any other officer. He reformed the structure of recruitment and discipline within both MI departments, and restored their efficiency after the scandals caused by traitors and moles within the ranks.

It was after the Crabb affair (when MI6 used a retired naval frogman to investigate a Soviet warship visiting Portsmouth) that its then head, Major-General Sinclair, retired early as a result of the embarrassment suffered by the Prime Minister, Sir Anthony Eden. Eden appointed in his place Dick White, partly to display his anger at the actions of the other branch of the service.

It was when White took over MI6 in 1956 that he discovered that his recommendation that Kim Philby — brought home under deep suspicion from Washington — should never be employed again had been ignored. MI6 had arranged for him to go to Beirut posing as a journalist.

White — who had known Philby for many years, and had personally interrogated him in 1951 — felt certain that he was indeed a Soviet agent, though he could not prove it, or force a confession. His hand was further weakened by the newspaper scandals and questions in the House of Commons which led Harold Macmillan, the Prime Minister at the time, to state publicly that there was no evidence against Philby.

Finally it was White, when further and conclusive evidence did emerge, who sent Nicholas Elliott to Beirut to force a confession from Philby. He had hoped to frighten him into returning to Britain to face charges, but in fact Kim Philby fled to Moscow with Russian help.

After years of effort he had failed to nail the traitor in the service, and it was a disappointment to him, though he remained convinced that he had rightly decided against trying to bring Philby back by other means.

The final stages of his time in control of the intelligence service were full of difficulty. After the exposure of Anthony Blunt there were new suspicions about the continued presence of moles, especially about Sir Roger Hollis, who had succeeded Dick White as head of MI5. The latter thought it right to set up a committee of investigation, after which Mrs Thatcher declared that there was no proof of disloyalty.

WIGG, Lord

The old soldier and ennobled barrack-room lawyer who kept an eye on security matters for the Labour Party and advised Harold Wilson on the subject. It was he who broke the Profumo affair in 1963, and by emphasizing its security aspects helped to bring down the Macmillan government.

As a reward he became Paymaster-General in the new Labour administration with a wide brief to watch over intelligence matters. He never greatly trusted British intelligence officers, considering them a snobbish and upper-class lot.

However, he remained vigilant for signs of Soviet activity in Britain. When the KGB sent sex pictures of Commander Courtney's peccadillo in Moscow to a select number of MPs he was convinced that, apart from wanting to ruin the Commander's career, they were warning other parliamentarians of the fate in store for them. He remained convinced to the end — though he could not prove it — that the KGB was blackmailing at least one of his senior colleagues in the party.

Lord Wigg died in August 1983 aged eighty-two.

WILDPRETT, Wolfgang

An East German cigarette-smuggler recruited by the KGB's assassination squad in 1954 to kill Vladimir Poremsky, a leader of NTS, the Frankfurt-based organization of Russian exiles whose anti-Soviet propaganda and activity so worried the Soviet Union in post-war years.

Poremsky himself told the story of what happened then. 'They had given this Wildprett a Walther P38 and a newspaper picture of me, and told him to come to Frankfurt.

'At Christmas in 1954 this Wildprett (who was no fool) came to me and he said, "I'm here to kill you, but I don't trust them. If I kill you, then they will tell me to murder somebody else. Then one day the police will arrest me, and put me in prison with a big pile of Deutschmarks I can't spend."

'So he didn't kill me,' said Poremsky. 'I like Wildprett, and I still see him sometimes; in fact I went to his wedding.'

WILSON, Edwin

A tough renegade officer of the Central Intelligence Agency who became a millionaire by setting up a private intelligence and arms-marketing operation with its own 'safe' houses and headquarters in London. He dealt in particular with President Qaddafi of Libya, and recruited other former CIA men to work with him.

In the summer of 1982, when the Libyan leader himself was becoming suspicious about his activities, the CIA lured Wilson, aged fifty-four, back to the United States by way of Santo Domingo. He was arrested on arrival at Kennedy Airport, New York.

A court at Alexandria, Virginia, convicted him in December of that year in one of four criminal trials arising from his dealings in Libya. It

sentenced him to thirty years in prison, and fined him £200,000.

Edwin Wilson had worked inside the CIA for sixteen years, and had also been in naval intelligence. At his trials a number of attempts were made to persuade the court that he had been working on behalf of the CIA during his Libyan dealings. These claims were rejected, and none of the sensational evidence which his lawyers had threatened to produce was ever brought before the court.

What remained unexplained was Wilson's continuing contacts with people within the Agency after he had left. However, it seemed clear that he had persuaded some ex-colleagues that his operations had CIA blessing.

Eugene Tafoya, an associate of Wilson's who admitted working as a courier for him, was gaoled for two years in January 1982 for assault and conspiracy in the shooting of a Libyan opponent of Colonel Qaddafi, who lived in America. Tafoya was a former soldier in American special forces.

While still serving the earlier gaol sentence Wilson was convicted in November 1983 of trying to persuade fellow-prisoners to murder two US federal prosecutors, a business associate and five prosecution witnesses involved in his earlier trials. He was sentenced to twenty-five years on these charges, and fined the equivalent of £50,000.

WISNER, Frank G.

The archetypal cold-warrior whose exploits became a legend in the CIA. A Mississippian who became a Wall Street lawyer, he was one of the wartime OSS originals, working from Bucharest and Istanbul with great success. It was he who pinpointed the Ploesti oilfields in Romania for the American bombing raids from Egypt.

His switch from hating the Germans to hating the Russians was early and complete. He advocated a switch in OSS targeting to the new enemy, but like so many others, he was forced out of intelligence work when President Truman disbanded OSS in 1945. Like his friend Allen Dulles, he went back to his legal practice.

Wisner became bored and went back to Washington as Deputy Assistant Secretary of State for Occupied Areas, a job which gave him room to practise his real trade of intelligence, and then in 1948 he was made Assistant Director of the Office of Policy Co-ordination, created to fill the gap left by OSS and to fight the 'vicious covert activities of the USSR'.

One of his innovations was the establishment in 1949 of Radio Free Europe, which has been a thorn in the Russians' side ever since. He it was who helped to develop the Gehlen Organization. At this time he had almost a free hand in Europe, working with enormous energy and ebullience to counter the Russian attempts to subvert country after country.

He became well known as an expert in dirty tricks, and he regarded his mission as nothing less than a crusade. When General Bedell Smith reorganized the CIA and pulled the OPC into the revamped Agency Wisner found himself serving not only under Smith but also under Dulles. His enthusiasm was unchecked.

He was in person portly and balding, and with a somewhat pompous manner of speech, yet his operations nevertheless demonstrated a cynical and cunning brain. He is credited with having fed Stalin the story that the American communist Noel Field was in fact a CIA agent. The KGB promptly arrested Field, who had gone to live behind the Iron Curtain, along with everybody who had known him during his refugee work in Europe during the war. As these included many of Eastern Bloc leaders, the wave of arrests devastated the new communist countries. The purge swept across Eastern Europe. Some 150,000 people were arrested, most were tortured, many were shot.

The Soviet empire was thrown into turmoil. Wisner considered he had scored a great victory. From then on he was involved in most of the CIA's more hair-raising operations, concentrating on his dream of preparing forces in the satellite countries to rise and overthrow their Russian masters when the time was ripe. He was one of the planners behind the attempted coup in Albania which was betrayed by Kim Philby. Wisner and Philby knew each other well and kept up a superficial pose of cameraderie, drinking heavily together, but never really liking one another.

Wisner was involved in the Berlin telephone-tap tunnel; the acquisition of Khruschev's de-Stalinization speech; the successful coup in Guatemala, and the unsuccessful one in Indonesia. He was CIA's Deputy Director for Plans from 1953 to 1958. It was during this period that the strain of his work and of his personal crusade began to have an obvious effect. He broke down in 1956 when the Russians destroyed the Hungarian uprising and shattered his dream of an anti-communist uprising in Eastern Europe. He spent some months in hospital before returning to work, but a year later he had a complete mental collapse and spent another six months undergoing treatment.

Richard Helms took over Wisner's position, and when the latter came out of hospital he was sent to London as chief of station, where it was thought he could do a useful but not particularly stressful job. Even that did not work. Wisner resigned from the Agency in 1961, a man who might have been Director of the CIA but was destroyed by his own inner demons. He committed suicide in 1965.

WOLF, Lieutenant-General Markus Johannes

The golden boy of the Eastern Bloc intelligence services, trained by the KGB at all the best schools of espionage in Moscow, a graduate of the Liebknecht Academy, and a favourite of Yuri Andropov, later leader of the Soviet Union. Born in Germany, he was taken to Moscow in 1933 when his family fled from the Nazis.

He returned to East Berlin in 1945 as a KGB agent in the guise of a journalist named Michael Storm and reported the Nuremberg war criminal trials. A burly six-footer, it was not long before he emerged as a major-general at the age of twenty-eight, in charge of operations and counter-espionage at East Germany's Ministry of State Security.

General Wolf had completed his intelligence education on diplomatic missions; he served in

Helsinki as Dr Kurt Werner. He has a taste for travel, and has been seen in Aden, capital of the People's Republic of South Yemen, where the East Germans control security, and fill a prominent neo-colonialist role. It has been suggested that he played some part in attempting to destabilize the monarchy in Saudi Arabia.

There is no doubt about his many successes in infiltrating East German agents into high positions in the West, while his vastly increased use of women has already been referred to, in the Introduction. Gunther Guillaume, personal aide to Willy Brandt, was one of his 'arrangements'. Western intelligence men rate him as a formidable opponent. In contrast to many spymasters in the East, he is well liked by his own men, and keeps up morale by sending congratulatory messages on family occasions.

WOLLWEBER, Ernst

When after a lifetime of espionage and sabotage on behalf of the cause this huge caricature of a German communist, fat, bald and frightening, took over as East Germany's Minister for State Security the stage was set for a battle of the giants. For the task of Moscow's favourite security chief (appointed in 1953, after his predecessor had failed to prevent the East Berlin riots) was to match and destroy the Gehlen Organization in West Germany.

While these two heavyweights of international espionage slugged it out in Berlin the Soviet KGB, and the American CIA, stood on the sidelines in awed support. Though entirely different, they were well matched. On the one side the crafty Gehlen, an army officer, intelligent and experienced in war; on the other the uncouth docker and seaman, so enlarged by communist party good-living that they called him 'the walking pancake', a Comintern agent who had sunk more ships by sabotage than most countries' navies.

Using double agents, snatch squads and murderers, Wollweber inflicted heavy damage on the Gehlen intelligence service, making hundreds of arrests. In the end Gehlen, who had men planted high in East German government and in Wollweber's own office, was able to strike back.

Born in the Ruhr, the young Wollweber helped to organize a mutiny in the Kaiser's navy in 1917 before hijacking a trawler, and making his way to the Soviet Union to applaud the Revolution. After a thorough training in Moscow as a spy and agitator, he travelled the world between the wars sabotaging capitalist ships, taking over for communism the World Federation of Trade Unions, and manipulating the International Seamen's Union. He and his agents caused millions of pounds' worth of damage to British and French ships.

He became a member of the Reichstag for the German communist party before Hitler's seizure of power in 1933. He fled to Russia and then he helped to build a Soviet spy and sabotage network in the Baltic.

As head of the Comintern based in Denmark he had to flee from there when the Germans invaded in 1940, transferring his operational base to Stockholm, where he concentrated in organizing the sabotage and sinking of German ships until his arrest and expulsion to the Soviet Union.

He surfaced again in Germany after spending the war in Russia. In 1946 Wollweber became 'Director-General of Shipping and Transport' in the Soviet-occupied zone of Germany, though in fact Moscow had given him a much wider brief.

Training-schools for communist agents among international seamen were set up by his directorate, where his old speciality of sabotage at sea was high in the curriculum. Many of the post-war fires and explosions — aboard British ships in particular — could be traced back to the Wollweber groups.

Then in 1953, after only a brief spell as a Minister for Shipping in East Germany, the old war-horse was given his big chance at the age of fifty-five, when his friend Walter Ulbricht charged him with state security in command of the police, the SSD or Staatsicherheitsdienst after the dismissal of Wilhelm Zaisser.

Eventually the old revolutionary overreached himself in machinations against his own First Minister, Otto Grotewohl; and then against the

East German communist boss, Walter Ulbricht himself. Suddenly in 1957 he was thrown out of the Central Committee, and the espionage organization he had created was left in ruins. He died ten years later.

WYNNE, Greville Maynard

Back in 1960 East-West trade was beginning to be a fashionable activity as people started talking about the thaw in relations with the Soviet Union. Among those looking eastward with a view to promoting British exports was Greville Wynne, a bouncy enthusiast who had studied electrical engineering at Nottingham University.

He had made his original entry into Europe with the British Army at the end of the Second World War, and knew his way around. He had also been in army intelligence, and according to his own account, it was a wartime friend who had gone into professional intelligence who first suggested that he might think of expanding his business contacts in Eastern Europe.

It therefore came about that Greville Wynne found himself visiting Moscow in search of a market for electrical equipment, and in touch with the State Committee for the Co-ordination of Scientific Work, the official Soviet body concerned with foreign trade. He suggested the idea of promoting trade by arranging for a Soviet delegation to visit London, and the idea was taken up.

In the course of all this Wynne met a friendly Red Army colonel named Oleg Penkovsky. Soon they were on good terms, and it was all 'Grev' this and 'Alex' that, so Greville Wynne was therefore happy to find that the leader of the delegation was to be the good colonel, the more so as his London friends were particularly intrigued by that officer.

When Wynne made unfavourable comments about the delegation Penkovsky said that he needed to go to London to pass on important facts to the authorities there. The Colonel promptly gave Wynne a package with top-secret information and full details about himself.

At that meeting in the baroque National Hotel,

Moscow, Greville Wynne had become the chosen vehicle for the passing over of high-class information from a well-placed Soviet GRU officer. It was an intelligence coup of great importance.

Though other channels were organized by British and American intelligence, Wynne continued to see the Colonel on his occasional visits to Moscow, and indeed received material from him. Because of Penkovsky's high rank in the GRU military intelligence it was quite some time before the rival KGB began to confirm their suspicions about his activities.

However, by 1962 it became obvious that Penkovsky was in trouble, and plans were prepared to get him out before it was too late. Inevitably Wynne became involved, as managing director of Mobile Exhibitions Ltd. The idea was that Wynne should go to Moscow and get permission for his display caravans to visit Leningrad from Finland. Two of them had been specially fitted out so that the Russian could be taken across the border hidden in the caravan.

On arrival the British agent met Penkovsky for dinner at the Peking restaurant, and it was obvious that KGB men were everywhere, keeping observation on them. Penkovsky told him to leave at once, and they arranged to meet at Sheremetyevo airport next morning. Courageously, Colonel Penkovsky pulled rank to get his friend on an earlier morning flight, and moreover handed him a package of material.

The Helsinki caravan plan had to be modified, so it was arranged that Wynne would take his trailers to a Bucharest trade fair and then to Budapest, in the hope that they could then go on to Moscow. However, when Wynne left an opening party in Budapest he was seized by two men in raincoats who held off his driver at gunpoint. He was flown to Moscow and thrown into the Lubyanka, where he spent six months in dreadful conditions.

Wynne's gallant rescue effort was in any case in vain. Unknown to the British intelligence service, Penkovsky had been arrested several days before his arrival in Budapest.

At a show trial in Moscow both Penkovsky and

Wynne were found guilty, the Russian of treason (which carried the death sentence), and the Englishman of spying, which earned him three years in prison and five more in a 'correctional labour camp'.

They deliberately treated Wynne badly, consigning him to an ancient special-punishment prison in an effort to speed exchange arrangements for a Russian spy held in Britain. Lack of food and bad conditions affected his health. In April 1964 he was flown out of Moscow in ignorance of what was happening, until he realized on landing that he was in Germany.

At the Berlin check-point Wynne recognized the smiling figure of Gordon Lonsdale, for whom he was being exchanged.

Mr X

This hides the identity of a young Oxford graduate recruited by MI6, and subjected to a rugged training exercise in Northamptonshire. Details of his carefully contrived arrest and mock trial came to public attention later, in an article in the *Observer*.

X had been ordered by his trainers to go on a secret mission to Northampton and collect a package in clandestine conditions. After he had carried it out he was deliberately picked up by a policewoman out of uniform acting as a provocateur.

Genuine police officers later stopped their car, 'discovered' a quantity of cannabis in it, and carried out a mock arrest. X spent an uncomfortable and anxious night in a police cell. He was then taken into a genuine court, with the clerk of the court pretending to be a magistrate.

Presumably X learned a lesson from this elaborate charade and became more aware of the perils of being a secret agent.

YAKOVLEV, Anatoli

A GRU case officer, an 'official', who ostensibly served as Soviet consul-general in New York at the end of the war. He was the man who ran the American atom bomb secrets network in the United States.

He used Julius Rosenberg as an agent, and also ran the old professional Harry Gold. Although his network succeeded in providing highly important atomic information for Soviet scientists to work on, he made one fatal mistake which led to its collapse.

Yakovlev was running two clandestine operations, one through Rosenberg and the other through Harry Gold. No doubt under pressure to get speedy results, he used Gold not only to visit his prime supplier of information, Klaus Fuchs, the British scientist in the US, but also to act as courier for information from Rosenberg's man, David Greenglass.

As a result, when Fuchs was finally arrested and interrogated he was able to expose both operations. For Yakovlev it was the end of the affair, and he beat a speedy retreat to Moscow.

YAKUSHKIN, Major-General Dmitri

For six years, until 1982, he was the senior KGB man stationed in Washington. Although he appeared in diplomatic lists simply as one of the ten counsellors at the Soviet Embassy there, American intelligence considered him to be the most powerful officer in the service outside the Soviet Union.

YAMAMOTO, Admiral Isoroku

The Japanese admiral who planned the attack on Pearl Harbor. He became a victim of the success of American code-breakers in cracking the Japanese navy's operational signals.

American intelligence was able to keep Admiral Chester Nimitz fully informed of Japanese naval movements, which helped him to win a great victory in the battle of Midway in 1942. While Admiral Yamamoto was on a visit to bases in the South Pacific the Americans traced his movements accurately by signals interception. Finally they set a trap for him and shot down his aircraft. He died in the crash.

YARIV, Major-General Aharon

Another notable Israeli army officer who successfully moved into the intelligence business. He was born Aharon Rabinowitz in Moscow, before the family moved to Latvia and then Berlin. His father was murdered by the Nazis, and at the age of fourteen he arrived in Israel.

He joined the British Army during the Second World War, and was commissioned into the Jewish Brigade, set up by the British to fight the Germans in the Middle East. Spotted as a high-flyer when he joined Haganah, the Jewish underground army in Palestine, he was sent to the Ecole de Guerre in Paris, and after changing his name to Yariv was appointed military attaché to Washington in 1957.

From there he joined Aman, the Israeli Bureau of Military Intelligence. He became deputy to Meir Amit, and when Amit was transferred to take command of Mossad in 1963 Yariv moved up to take over Aman, a post in which he served for nine years, performing so successfully that for a time Aman overshadowed Mossad. 'I have never in my life,' he said 'had a more difficult but more engrossing assignment.' He was heavily involved in the espionage operations leading up to the Six

Day War in 1967, and in the series of raids the Israeli special forces carried out against Arab targets after the war.

Then, as his term of office was coming to an end, Black September terrorists carried out the Munich massacre at the 1972 Olympic games. Yariv — who was due to become an assistant to Moshe Dayan, the Defense Minister — was appointed 'Special Assistant for Terrorist Affairs' to the Prime Minister, Mrs Golda Meir. He worked with Major-General 'Zwicka' Zamir, who had taken over Mossad, and together they organized a series of assassinations of Palestinian terrorist leaders in Europe. Eventually a self-styled Israeli 'Wrath of God' squad killed an innocent man in Lillehammer, Norway, in mistake for the Black September chief, Ali Salameh.

This murder aroused such a storm of indignation in Israel, as well as in other countries, that it put an end to these operations in Europe.

Despite the Lillehammer scandal, Yariv was being considered for a post in the Cabinet, if the ruling Labour party won the forthcoming election. However, everything changed when the Egyptians and Syrians launched their surprise attack on Israel in October 1973. Military intelligence (which Yariv had made into such a formidable organization) was largely to blame for Israel being taken by surprise because its new commander, Major-General Eliahu Zeira, had refused to recognize signs of an impending attack.

Yariv, like so many other retired Israeli generals, simply put on his uniform again and went back to work, and nobody dared tell him to go away. It was then announced that with five other such fellow-officers he had been called up for 'special duties at the request of the Commander in Chief'.

It was after the war that Yariv performed probably his most important special duty for Israel. He conducted the initial military talks with Lieutenant-General Gamasy of the Egyptian army at Kilometre 101 which eventually led to the end of the war.

'Two valiant armies have fought for three weeks,' he told the Egyptians, 'now let's try to work out an honourable peace.'

YOSHIKAWA, Takeo

The Japanese Naval Intelligence Bureau agent installed in Honolulu in the summer of 1941 to report on movements of the US fleet as Tokyo put the finishing touches to the plan to attack Pearl Harbour. A 28-year-old junior naval officer who had studied English for four years, and followed that up while on the American desk of Japanese intelligence with a course in the colloquial language, he was appointed under a false name as Japanese vice-consul.

Carefully trained in naval intelligence work, his task was to report on all fleet movements. A versatile operator, Yoshikawa is credited with remarking that 'a spy without a love-life is a spy doomed', a maxim taken up enthusiastically by most fictional spies.

Aware that his telephone was tapped, he made endless calls to girl-friends, of whom he had many, to delude the listeners. On swimming expeditions with local Japanese girls he measured tide heights and beach gradients.

He knew that the Americans were reading his messages in Purple code, but he also knew there were long delays in transcription because of a shortage of Japanese translators. In fact he used his official position as vice-consul to take refuge in ostentation, often being seen around the bars and night spots. Less congenial was his activity in searching naval dustbins in the belief that they contained many useful clues about naval activity.

His most valuable piece of information was that Admiral Kimmel had rejected plans for anti-submarine nets in the harbour. He was still transmitting right up to the Japanese attack. Then he burned his code-books, was interned as a diplomat, and eventually returned to Japan under an exchange of diplomatic personnel.

YOUNG, George

An experienced British intelligence officer who specialized in Middle East affairs. He is a former deputy director of MI6.

When Sir Roger Hollis came under suspicion as a Soviet agent in MI5, the counter-espionage service George Young was firmly convinced that he was innocent. His theory was that Hollis came to be suspected because, he was in fact the wrong man in the wrong job, and he was by nature an indecisive man.

After his retirement George Young became a banker and a prominent member of the Monday Club of the Conservative party. He warned against the danger of Soviet 'agents of influence' at work in Britain, trying to affect opinion. He even suspected that such a person had penetrated either the government service or the Conservative party during the premiership of Edward Heath, which ended in 1974.

Z

ZABOTIN, Colonel Nikolai

Thinly disguised as the Soviet military attaché in Ottawa towards the end of the Second World War, he was in fact a senior GRU officer running one of the most important networks probing the Allied atomic-bomb programme. His star supplier of information was Dr Nunn May, the British spy.

He spent three years in Canada, and managed to recruit well-placed agents in the British High Commission, and the Canadian Ministries of Defence and External Affairs. Canadian communists like Fred Rose, who was a member of parliament, kept the network abreast of happenings in secret sessions. Other communists actively gave aid in the recruitment of spies.

Quantities of documentation from his own files were handed over to the Canadian authorities when his GRU cypher clerk, Igor Gouzenko, sought political asylum in Canada in September 1945. The Colonel's network was put out of action. Three months after the Gouzenko affair Colonel Zabotin, his GRU colleagues and the

Soviet Ambassador to Canada, were embarked on the Soviet ship *Alexandrov*, which sailed from New York without going through normal procedures. Zabotin was never seen or heard of again.

According to one account he jumped overboard and drowned at sea, rather than face the Kremlin inquisitors. But another version of the story claims that he died of a heart-attack within days of arriving in Moscow.

Stalin was furious when full details of the Zabotin operation were revealed in the report of the Royal Commission of Inquiry. GRU lost face to the KGB, stricter Soviet security measures at embassies were ordered, and case officers were instructed not to use national communists blatantly as espionage agents.

It was a cynical remark of Zabotin to GRU officers in Moscow in September 1945 which helped to encourage Gouzenko to defect. Speaking of the West, he said, 'Yesterday they were allies, today they are neighbours, tomorrow they will be our enemies.'

ZADNEPROVSKIY, V. F.

Yet another member of the staff of the Soviet Trade delegation in Highgate, North London, caught out indulging in strictly non-commercial activities, and asked to leave in February 1982. No announcement was made about the departure of this KGB agent until two months later.

All that is known about him is that he was up to the old Russian trick of trying to get classified information through a foreign national. Ever since the mass expulsion of Soviet diplomats and officials from Britain in 1971 it has been the London custom to insist that when a Soviet agent is expelled no replacement is accredited. The departure of Comrade Zadneprovskiy brought down the number from forty-seven to forty-six.

ZAMIR, Major-General Svi

A former military attaché in London, he succeeded Meir Amit as head of Mossad, the Israeli intelligence service, in 1969. An unobtrusive, Polish-born officer who had always kept out of the public eye, he was soon deeply involved in committing the Israeli intelligence services to a sustained campaign of counter-actions against the terrorist operations of extremist Palestinian organizations in league with European and Japanese international anarchists and leftists.

General Zamir brought under tighter control the semi-official Israeli hit-teams of army veterans which had been gunning for terrorist leaders in the late 60s and early 70s. He disciplined them, made their information more precise, and set up five special sections of highly trained men and women with one more in reserve.

He was a 'come on' leader, rather than a 'go on' one, who frequently went into the field to supervise operations. He himself had gone to Munich after the Olympic Games massacre of Israeli athletes in 1972, and planned the campaign for retaliation killing of Black September leaders who had organized it.

With the help of European Zionists to provide local support and information, a number of Arab terrorists were murdered and struck off the list. Then in 1973 a well-planned raid was carried out by one of his teams against the headquarters of Fatah, the Palestinian guerrilla organization in Beirut.

For two weeks agents infiltrated into the Lebanese capital with false passports, kept watch and set up the operation. They marked out a beach landing-site for special forces troops who came ashore in wet suits on 13 April with explosives and safe-breaking kit.

They raided the headquarters building, shipping out quantities of files and other documentation by helicopter, after killing the guards. Three prominent Black September leaders were killed in the operation before the spies withdrew with their special forces colleagues.

A brief and triumphant announcement in Tel Aviv spoke of a commando action, though it made no mention of the intelligence side, and reported that all had returned safely to Israel. It was put down as a triumph for General Zamir.

The Israelis were adept at such hit-and-run

operations in the Middle East, but when Zamir extended his operations to hunt down Arab activists in less familiar territory in Europe Mossad ran into difficulties, even though they enjoyed a certain measure of co-operation from Western services, in return for intelligence reports provided.

In particular, Ali Hassan Salameh, a trained Palestinian intelligence man in Black September, proved elusive. Mossad picked up his traces in Paris, but then Black September counter-intelligence led them astray with false information that he had gone to Scandinavia to plan a new campaign there. It is now suspected that a double agent was involved.

General Zamir, convinced that a courier from Switzerland was leading him to Salameh in Lillehammer, Norway, not far from the Swedish border, assembled a hit-team there. Knowing that it was a scratch team of ten because his resources were by now thin on the ground, he went in person to supervise the operation from Oslo.

Among the several women involved was Marianne Gladnikoff, a volunteer Swedish-born Jewess without previous experience. They also had on the spot Dar Aerbel, a Danish-born Israeli, but the rest of the team found it difficult to maintain cover in a small Norwegian town where everybody knew everybody.

In due course the courier arrived to make contact with the man they believed they had identified as Salameh. Tel Aviv gave the go-ahead, and on 21 July 1973 a man and a woman from the Israeli team leapt from a car and shot him dead at close range. His pregnant Norwegian wife was unhurt.

Panic and confusion set in when the Israelis discovered they had got the wrong man and killed a Moroccan waiter named Ahmed Bouchki. General Zamir left Oslo in a hurry, while his team, with the exception of the actual killers, were speedily rounded up by the Norwegian authorities.

In court Marianne Gladnikov spoke freely about the plot, was convicted of manslaughter, and served only half her thirty-month sentence before going back to Sweden. Dar Aerbel got five years, and two other team members, Sylvia Rafael

and Abraham Gehmer, five and a half years each. One man was acquitted, and their driver received a year's sentence.

It had been a disastrous experience. The same agent who directed Zamir's team to Lillehammer had also alerted the Norwegian authorities. Two of the arrested people had the telephone number of the Mossad 'legal' in the Oslo embassy, who was expelled. There was an international outcry against brutal Israeli methods.

From then on Mossad and its teams were far more circumspect about direct action in Europe. The commander on the spot survived to join the committee of inquiry into what had gone wrong, while the officer responsible for wrong identification of the victim was dismissed the service.

A further consequence of Mossad's obsession with hunting down terrorists was that political espionage had to be left to military intelligence, which failed to detect and report signs of the Egyptian and Syrian build-up for war. General Zamir belatedly delivered warnings, but by then it was too late. The government relied on the 'no war' predictions of military intelligence, and when the assault came in October 1973 Israel was taken by surprise and almost defeated by the Arab alliance.

After that war General Zamir retired, and became chairman of a construction company.

ZOTOV, Captain Anatoli Pavlovich

A rather jolly, sociable officer of the Red Fleet, and a specialist of undoubted skill in engineering and submarines, but by no means expert in carrying out his tasks as a GRU naval intelligence officer in London. He was the naval attaché at the Soviet Embassy in London who, having being caught out in rather clumsy efforts to set up a naval spy-ring, was given a week to leave Britain in December 1982 together with his blonde wife, Nina, who worked for Intourist.

The Soviets made a propaganda point by leaking information about his expulsion before the Foreign Office made an official announcement. This gave Captain Zotov — who had been a popular figure on the diplomatic circuit — a chance to say that it was all nonsense that he was a spy.

He was not untypical of the new generation of Russian intelligence officers, well brought up at service colleges and academies, good in English, and cosmopolitan. Captain Zotov had served in Washington. With a good voice, he used to tell people it had been difficult for him at one point to make up his mind whether to choose a naval career or to become an opera singer.

The Soviet Union replied to the Zotov expulsion by ordering the British naval attaché in Moscow, Captain Bruce Richardson RN, to leave.

'Z', Colonel

Well, half-colonel really, and 'Z' was the alias of a flamboyant Romanian claiming that rank. By figuring in an elaborate plot which involved President Mitterrand of France, the French counter-espionage service, and assorted Romanian exiles in France, he undoubtedly qualified for the title 'Ruritanian Spy of the Year 1981'.

His real name turned out to be Matei Haiducu. For eight years he had worked as a humdrum industrial espionage agent for Romanian 'Securitate', their equivalent of the KGB.

According to his version of events, he suddenly received orders direct from President Ceaucescu of Romania to kidnap Virgil Tanase, an equally flamboyant, long-haired novelist who had irritated the great man by describing him in print as 'His Majesty Ceaucescu the First, Communist King'.

Understandably put out by such outpourings from a fellow-countryman in exile, the Romanian President also instructed 'Z' to murder another novelist in Paris, Paul Goma, earlier expelled from Bucharest for setting up a dissident group.

Instead of carrying out these orders, 'Z' presented himself at the headquarters of the DST, French counter-espionage, and told all. It was at this point that the worldly chief of the French service hatched a Borgia-type plot to damage the opposition intelligence unit. With authorization from President Mitterrand himself, he arranged for his own men to kidnap Tanase and spirit him off to a pleasant hotel in Brittany. The trick worked so well that in no time there was an outcry in France about the missing Romanian, who was generally assumed to have been murdered.

The French President played along by issuing an official public protest. On the strength of it, he cancelled a visit to Romania planned for the following September.

The plot did not end there, for 'Z' had shown to the counter-espionage people the special fountain-pen filled with undetectable poison which had been issued to him by his masters in Bucharest. It is a piece of standard KGB equipment purpose-designed for assassination work.

With French co-operation, 'Z' posed as a literary buff, attended a dinner debate addressed by Paul Goma, and approached him to ask for an autograph. While Goma was signing, 'Z' with a deft gesture squirted the poison into his drink and swiftly moved away. With equal deftness, a DST man made sure that Goma did not drink it by accidentally smashing the glass.

Back at headquarters in Bucharest, Securitate and the President were happy when 'Z' reported the mission successful, though in fact Goma had joined his compatriot in the Brittany hotel. They rewarded their man Matei-'Z'-Haiducu with promotion, and a free holiday abroad with his family, from which he wisely failed to return.

Just to confirm the rather nostalgic nature of this spy story — which has a ring of the nineteenth century — Colonel 'Z' was known to his friends as 'Tufty'.

THE COUNTRIES

AUSTRALIA

ASIO The Australian Security and Intelligence Organization

The ASIO came into being in the early days of the cold war as an internal security organization with a counter-espionage mission similar to that of the American FBI and the British MI5. Before that, and during the Second World War, Colonel C.G. Roberts had served as director of Australian military intelligence with the Allied Intelligence Bureau established in Melbourne when General Douglas MacArthur began co-ordinating Allied operations against the advancing Japanese. The AIB was helped by an organization known as the Coast Watchers, a network of Australian spies on islands overrun by the Japanese.

It was from these historic origins that the ASIO developed with two branches; one intelligence-gathering; the other responsible for counter-espionage. The need for more professional intelligence was made plain after the defection of Vladimir Petrov, a KGB agent, from the Soviet Embassy in Camberra. He revealed details of extensive Russian operations in Australia. The KGB concentrated its attentions upon immigrants from Eastern Europe and infiltrated its agents among these 'new Australians'. It sought information about uranium-mining, and made attempts to subvert government servants.

In April 1983 ASIO successfully exposed as a spy Valery Ivanov, who worked under cover as Third Secretary at the Soviet Embassy. He was expelled, but his detection led to a political row when it was revealed that he had attempted to cultivate 'agents of influence' in the capital. He had been in touch with David Combe, a former Labour Party official, prominent lobbyist and friend of the Prime Minister, Bob Hawke. ASIO had tapped his telephone calls. Under opposition pressure the Prime Minister admitted that he had banned David Combe from any contact with his ministers.

A Royal Commission, known as the Hope Commission, was set up to look into the whole affair. As it proceeded a major political crisis developed. Mick Young, a special minister, was criticized by the commission for leaking cabinet details to a friend — namely that the Russian diplomat Ivanov was about to be expelled. He then resigned.

Six months later Mr Young returned to office as a Minister and member of the government security commission. Andrew Peacock, the opposition leader, promptly described his return as being like putting 'Dracula in charge of a blood bank'.

The end of 1983 brought another embarrassment for the Australian service, and a fresh opportunity for Australian phrase-makers, when a training exercise by intelligence officers in the Melbourne Sheraton Hotel ended in confusion. The officers were described by the *Sydney Morning Herald* as 'a bunch of stumblebums', and John Ryan, the sixty-year-old head of ASIS, the Secret Intelligence side of ASIO, was forced to resign. This distinguished former senior diplomat was rudely described by Senator Primmer as 'a crook, a bureaucratic bully, a professional liar, a bad drunk, and a social embarrassment' — words which would have been slanderous had they not been uttered under cover of parliamentary privilege.

The service had failed to inform either the hotel or the police that they were carrying out an exercise to simulate the rescue of a mock hostage held in a hotel room. Over-enthusiastic officers disguised in carnival masks and carrying sub-machine guns battered down a hotel door, sowed panic among guests and manhandled the manager who came to investigate these unseemly incidents.

To make matters worse, Melbourne police who arrested five of them outside the hotel complained that they were 'under the influence of alcohol'.

Dissatisfaction with ASIO was reflected in fresh curbs on the organization announced in February 1984. These new controls specify that the Prime Minister and the Attorney General must be briefed from the beginning about any case of espionage. ASIO must also make detailed reports to the federal Cabinet's security committee, and the Attorney General will have full access to the files concerning security matters.

CANADA

Security Intelligence Service

In 1981 a new organization was established by the Canadian Government with the title of Security Intelligence Service — borrowed, no doubt, from the similarly named service already functioning in Australia. Its task is to look after internal security and counter-espionage. For outside intelligence the Canadians rely largely on their close relationship inside NATO with the British and the Americans.

Earlier, counter-espionage operations were handled by the Royal Canadian Mounted Police. The force gained its first experience in 1945 when the Soviet defector Igor Gouzenko, who was a code clerk at the Soviet Embassy, took refuge in Canada. They then cleaned up the Soviet spy network in Canada.

But during the 1970s the RCMP overstepped the mark in its operations against terrorists of the Quebec Liberation Front, which was active at the time. Officers were accused of illegal wire-taps, breaking and entering, and acts of provocation.

As a result — and after a number of officers had been convicted of various offences — a committee was established to look into the whole question of internal security. It was as a result of its report that the government transferred responsibility for counter-espionage and anti-terrorist intelligence to the newly formed Security Intelligence Service.

CHINA

There is no precise equivalent in other parts of the world of the principal communist Chinese espionage organization, the Central External Liaison Department, for it works as much through the party as through the government, which is controlled by the party. There is also in existence a Central Control of Intelligence, but details of its functioning remain sparse.

The party itself is in charge of political security, responsible for counter-espionage and in general for keeping watch over citizens and their political activities. In addition, a State committee co-ordinates information-gathering through the Foreign Ministry and embassies abroad. A notable part in espionage is played by agents abroad working under cover of the New China News Agency.

Military intelligence too is important for a state which considers that it has powerful enemies, both communist and capitalist. Service attachés at Chinese embassies report to this organization, and they are expected to be equally alert for military developments in the Soviet Union, and in the United States and Europe.

CUBA

DGI Dirección General de Inteligencia

The Cuban secret service was formed on KGB lines; it is virtually a branch office of the KGB, with Russian officers holding high positions within the organization. At one stage General Viktor Simenov of the KGB was its operational boss.

It carries out missions for the Russians, and if its agents are caught it is Cuba which gets the blame, not Russia. One of its functions is to train Latin American agents and terrorists. Its prize alumnus was Carlos, the Venezuelan assassin, who was trained in a DGI camp before being sent to Lumumba University in Moscow.

It has close connections with the PLO, the Red Brigades, the IRA and the European urban terrorist groups.

Most of its activity is now concentrated on the West Indies and Central America. Grenada was a DGI base for subversion in the West Indies until the Americans invaded. DGI agents were heavily engaged in subversion and training of insurgents in Colombia, Costa Rica, El Salvador, Guatemala, and Honduras. Chile has also been said to be a target, and Nicaragua to have been turned into a forward base for the Soviet Union in the Americas, with the DGI acting as surrogates for the KGB.

EAST GERMANY
HVA Hauptverwaltung Aufklärung

Run since its establishment in 1956 by Lieutenant-General Markus Wolf, one of the most talented of Eastern Bloc spymasters, the 'Chief Administration, Intelligence', as it is called, is the thrustful external branch of East German intelligence. It developed from a cover organization set up after the war but before the establishment of the East German state. That organization bore the title Institute of Economic Research.

The HVA concentrates on espionage in the neighbouring Federal Republic of Germany, and has scored many successes. One of its men, Gunther Guillaume, managed to become confidential aide to Chancellor Willy Brandt.

The remarkable General Wolf broke with espionage tradition by deciding that women were better and more useful agents than men. The HVA's secret weapon was secretary-spies, of which it made prodigal use in West Germany. The theory was based on the fact that masses of papers cannot be watched, and that secretaries with uncontrolled access to secret documents can easily make an extra copy and take it home. Some women among the several hundred employed were specially trained. Others were hunted and wooed by specially schooled male seducers, and the targets were first-class typists and personal assistants, preferably over thirty. The organization succeeded in recruiting through the bedroom women working in key Ministries, political party headquarters and industrial concerns.

Werner Stiller, a highly placed defector from the HVA, revealed in 1979 how firmly committed it was to industrial espionage. The aim was to speed industrial development in the Eastern Bloc by saving time and money spent on research and development. The HVA also specializes in espionage on military, as well as industrial, high technology in the West.

There have been recent signs that East German intelligence is becoming more active in non-German countries, especially in Scandinavia. HVA also trains third-world security men, which helps them in their own state security operations, especially in Ethiopia and in South Yemen.

MfS Ministerium für Staats-Sicherheit

The Ministerium is East Germany's Ministry for State Security. Established in April 1950, it is modelled on the KGB, and acts as a surrogate for that organization. Operating out of East Berlin, it carries out the KGB functions of repression at home and espionage and subversion abroad. Its main target is West Germany, where it is estimated to have as many as 5,000 spies. In 1959 alone 2,802 MfS agents were caught in West Germany. These agents work for the élite foreign intelligence arm officially called the Chief Administration, Intelligence (HVA).

EGYPT
Mukhabarat el-Aam General Intelligence Agency

Egypt's espionage agency, set up in the 1950s with the help of former Nazis working for General Reinhard Gehlen. The GIA is responsible only to the President, and has almost unlimited powers. It carries out both espionage and counter-espionage, and in some cases police work.

While the GIA is all-pervasive in Egypt, relying on a network of informers and a comprehensive system of bugging and telephone-tapping, it is not particularly effective in espionage activities outside the Middle East. Working alongside it — and sometimes in competition with it — is another organization, Mahabes el-Aam, the Secret Police, which comes under the Ministry of the Interior and deals with internal security and political security.

The Mukhabarat gained a fearsome reputation for torture and cruelty under President Nasser, and when Anwar Sadat took over he promised to reform the organization and to destroy the bugging system. But it was not long before the Mukharabat was back to its old tricks.

It remains a potent force inside Egypt, if not in the world outside. It does not carry out strictly military espionage: that is reserved for the intelligence services of the armed forces.

FRANCE
DGSE Direction Général de Sécurité Extérieur

The French have been juggling with initials for forty years to describe their intelligence-gathering service, changing them whenever it was reorganized, which was frequently. The latest effort after President Mitterrand came to power in 1981 was DGSE, the General Direction of External Security.

Before that it had been called the SDECE, which at least had the advantage of being a nearly pronounceable acronym, for it was generally known as the 'S deck'. Its headquarters are in a disused barracks in Boulevard Mortier, Paris, near a municipal swimming-pool, so that the service is frequently referred to as the *piscine*, which has a slightly pejorative sense in French.

Name-changing reflects the confusion in French intelligence which arose out of the defeat of France by Hitler in 1940. The old Deuxième Bureau and sister services retired with Marshal Pétain and his collaborators to Vichy.

In London, General Charles de Gaulle and his Free French set up their own intelligence under the legendary agent and resistance fighter Colonel Passy, whose real name was Dewavrin. It was called BCRAM, Central Bureau for Information and Military Action. After the Allied landings in North Africa direction of the service — by now swollen with operatives who had come over to de Gaulle with their dossiers — was taken over by Jacques Soustelle, a young and enthusiastic Gaullist intellectual.

The history of the service is important, for it helps to explain why in the post-war years it became riddled with factions, pro or anti its British and American allies, and divided politically between left and right wing.

Then the Algerian War of independence forced the service to concentrate on North African spying at a time when other Western services were heavily engaged in the cold war. In the increasingly bitter struggles between Frenchmen over Algeria, before and after the return to power of General de Gaulle in 1958, the service became hopelessly entangled in domestic affairs. It was deeply involved with

Gaullist 'gorillas' in clandestine action against the Secret Army of settlers and disloyal French army officers.

It is not surprising, therefore, that the intelligence service was constantly being reorganized and its officers were often purged. The SDECE found itself embroiled in a number of scandals of a complexity which only France can produce. Among the best known are: 1) The Ben Barka affair in 1965. The mystery of the disappearance of this Moroccan exiled politician has never been satisfactorily solved. SDECE were deeply involved with Moroccan secret police in his kidnap. 2) The 'Topaz' business, so named because that was the title of a Leon Uris novel inspired by the experiences of Thyraud de Vosjoli, the SDECE liaison man with the CIA in Washington. It was claimed that a Soviet mole had been placed close to President de Gaulle. 3) The Markevitch affair, in which a small Gaullist faction tried to incriminate Georges Pompidou (who later became president) in a squalid gangster business involving the murder of the chauffeur of Alain Delon, the film actor. 4) In 1971 a fresh scandal brewed up after the arrest in New Jersey of Roger Delouette, an SDECE operator, for smuggling $12 million worth of drugs. He confessed, but said he was involved on the orders of his superiors, though he could not reveal the purpose of the exercise.

In the subsequent row General Pierre Billotte, a Gaullist deputy, who had the year before produced a government report on reorganization to prevent fresh scandals, roundly declared, 'I am convinced that the service should be dissolved'.

It did live to fight another day, but soon after his election in 1981 President Mitterrand — not one of its enthusiastic supporters — ordered a reshuffle, a change of name to DGSE, and brought in an outside management expert from Air France to head it.

That did not seem to work either, despite a purge in the ranks, for less than a year later the President appointed Vice-Admiral Pierre Lacoste to take over. Apparently he was not satisfied with the quality of foreign information presented to him and wanted to know more about international terrorism, the Mediterranean area and North Africa, especially Libya.

DST Direction de la Surveillance du Territoire

The DST, which for historical reasons has frequently, like its sister intelligence-gathering service, been involved in politics, is largely composed of ex-police officers. To its customary duty of detecting and arresting foreign spies in France, new tasks of counter-subversion and counter-terrorism were added in the 1970s as Paris became a centre of political violence.

President François Mitterrand appointed Yves Bonnet, a senior civil servant, as its head when he took over the Presidential office. The DST is controlled by the Interior Ministry, and the new Socialist Minister, Gaston Defferre, with his Resistance experience in the war, took a keen interest in the service.

One of his first acts was to call for papers on scandals which had embroiled the DST in the Gaullist era. In particular he wanted details about its eavesdropping on the offices of *Le Canard Enchaîné*, the Paris satirical weekly, which had so excited the Left at the time. DST runs a big phone-tapping operation from an HQ near Les Invalides in Paris.

The service keeps a tremendous number of dossiers, and now uses a computer to replace its amazing system of card indexes. It also employs the resources of the Renseignements Généraux, another police service which keeps track of foreigners, political and trade union militants.

The DST's record in tracking down foreign agents is good. It recruits clever young men, including many graduates, and has managed to attract far less moles and Soviet agents than for example MI5, the equivalent service in Britain.

IRAN

SAVAK Sazamane Etelaat va Amniate Kechvar

The intelligence service of the late Shah of Iran: the Iranian title of which SAVAK is an acronym means Security and Intelligence Organization. Created in 1956 with the help of the CIA and Mossad, it was controlled in its early years by the powerful feudal leader General Teymur Bakhtiar. After a number of assassination attempts the Shah came to rely on Savak more and more, and as its power grew so did its notorious reputation.

'Savak is everywhere', said one report. 'Every high official, every state secretary, even each minister has a Savak shadow who monitors everything he does and has the right to inspect his every move.' Savak reached out beyond Iran to intimidate and kill students and dissidents in exile.

Its agents even killed their former leader Bakhtiar after he had been dismissed for plotting against the Shah. Two Savak agents hijacked an Air Iran plane in 1970 and demanded to be flown to Iraq to join Bakhtiar in exile. He welcomed them with open arms, and invited them to go hunting with him. However, he was the quarry. Later, when the Shah was asked who had assassinated Bakhtiar, he replied, 'We did. The Savak did.'

The excesses of Savak agents who tortured everyone who fell into their hands was one of the major causes of the Iranian revolution. When that took place the hated Komiteh building, Savak's headquarters, was wrecked, its files thrown into the street and its instruments of torture burnt.

One of the main targets of the revolutionaries was General Nematollah Nassiri, the third and last head of Savak, who was described as 'not an appealing man.' His fat round pock-marked face, his cold yellowish eyes and lips as thin as knives made it obvious that he was exactly the right person to head a merciless outfit like Savak. It was perhaps appropriate that he was shot upon his own headquarters roof.

The irony is, of course, that the revolutionaries who suffered so much under Savak, and fought so desperately to destroy it, later set up their own equally cruel security organization which behaves in exactly the same way as Savak.

IRAQ

Al Mukharabat The Listening Post

Iraq's secret service, which is also known under the euphemism of the 'Public Relations Bureau'.

Established soon after the Ba'ath Party seized control of Iraq in July 1968, it controls all aspects of political, military and economic life, and carries out intelligence and violent operations abroad. It specializes in sending hit teams to murder opponents of President Saddam Hussein's regime. One such murder was done in London in July 1978 when General Abdul Razzak al-Naif, former Prime Minister of Iraq, was assassinated outside the Intercontinental Hotel. The assassination group is known as Al Hunain.

Commanded by Brigadier Khalil al-Wazir, the Public Relations Bureau has a fearsome reputation inside Iraq, but, unlike most Arab secret services, its role is not simply that of suppression of dissidents and plotters. It also carried out military and technical espionage on behalf of the Soviet Union. This came about because Iraq became so dependent on Soviet arms. In 1973, in the wake of the Yom Kippur war against Israel, a secret pact was concluded between Bagdad and Moscow. Under its terms Iraq's internal security set-up was reorganized on KGB lines, and Iraq security officers were sent for training at KGB and GRU schools in Russia. In addition the Russians supplied the Iraqis with modern espionage and interrogation equipment, while in return the Iraqis agreed to work on behalf of the KGB, undertaking missions for them where it was difficult for the Russians to operate, and providing assistance to KGB 'illegals' in countries where the Soviet Union had no diplomatic cover.

ISRAEL
MOSSAD The Central Institute for Intelligence and Special Assignments

This is Israel's much-vaunted intelligence service, often referred to briefly as The Institute. A number of freebooting intelligence organizations operated on behalf of various factions in Israel before that country achieved nationhood, but the Israeli Secret Service did not come into being officially until June 1948.

It was organized, on Prime Minister Ben Gurion's orders, into three divisions: 1. the Bureau of Military Intelligence, incorporating the Department of Counter-Espionage; 2. the Political Department of the Foreign Office, whose function was the collection of foreign intelligence; 3. the Department of Security (Sherut Habitachon), known to every Israeli by its Hebrew initials, Shin Bet.

The new organizations got off to a shaky start. It was found that the old slapdash methods could not be applied to the intelligence arm of a modern state, so in September 1951 the intelligence set-up was reorganized and Mossad came into being. It took over the espionage duties of the Political Department of the Foreign Office, and was also given responsibility for special operations. The director was to report directly to the Prime Minister. Its name gave it a psychological boost from its inception, for it was another organization known as Mossad which had smuggled many Jews into the Promised Land in the 1930s and 1940s.

Practically, the head of Mossad — the first director was Reuben Shiloach — was given precedence by being made chairman of the security committee whose other members were the heads of Shin Bet, military intelligence and the Special Branch of the police force. The new organization was considerably helped by the CIA with up-to-date training methods and with the latest equipment. (It is interesting to note that while Mossad turned to the Americans, military intelligence was run on British lines.)

In common with other modern secret services, Mossad makes great use of Elint and all the electronic paraphernalia of microchip espionage. It can call on some of the best mathematical brains in the world, and its cryptographers are especially talented.

It has a comprehensive disinformation department, and it works closely with Western security services. Sometimes the amount of information it feeds other services is embarrassing. At one stage the French complained that Mossad was giving them so much information about Arab terrorists heading for France that it would take all their men and all their time to process it.

Mossad can also call on a special army unit for

back-up in its operations. Called the Sayaret Matkal, the General Staff Reconnaissance Unit, it answers only to the Chief of Intelligence, and has the same sort of reputation as Britain's Special Air Service. It is some 200 strong, but is augmented with specialists for specific tasks. This unit is never mentioned by name in Israel, and its men are simply called 'The Guys'. It was they who carried out the assassination raid against Palestinian leaders in Beirut in 1973 and the rescue raid on Entebbe in 1976.

Both these operations were planned by Mossad and bolstered a reputation established by the coup of kidnapping from the Argentine Adolf Eichmann, the 'transport manager' of the 'Final Solution'. The often hilarious activities of Wolfgang Lotz, the 'Champagne Spy' in Egypt, the expert spycraft of Elie Cohen (who was eventually hanged in Damascus), the spiriting away of the gunboats from Cherbourg, the still untold story of the penetration of the PLO, are further items on the long list of Mossad successes.

Mossad does have two advantages denied to the majority of secret services: not only do most countries have a Jewish community into which an agent can be absorbed, but because Israel has been at war for virtually all its existence, Mossad's agents work in a wartime atmosphere rather than one in which they are bound by peacetime regulations and morals. Because it regards itself as being constantly involved in a struggle for survival, Mossad has never hesitated to use assassination as a tactic.

It was used against the former Nazi scientists who went to work for Nasser. It was used against the PLO in Europe following the Munich massacre. And it was used against the scientists building a nuclear reactor for Iraq which the Israelis feared would produce nuclear weapons for the Arabs.

One of Mossad's biggest blunders was the killing of a Moroccan waiter in Norway in July 1973 in mistake for Ali Hassan Salameh, the man responsible for the Munich massacre. Salameh was later killed by a bomb in Beirut.

This use of assassination without regard for the loss of innocent lives is the subject of much heart-searching within Mossad, especially among the younger members, many of whom regard it as the negation of the ideals of the Jewish state. The opposing argument is that Israel remains under attack, that terrorism is a form of warfare and that it can only be fought by counter-terrorism.

The cause of those opposed to assassination was strengthened when Israel was taken by surprise as the Egyptians and Syrians launched the Yom Kippur War in 1975. It became apparent that Mossad had been devoting so much attention to its private war against the Palestinian terrorists that its espionage role was taken over by military intelligence, which had in this instance failed to present all the evidence of the Arab military build-up to Israel's political leaders.

It was a mistake that Mossad would not normally have made, but its attention was directed elsewhere — to Vienna, where three elderly Jewish emigrants from Russia were being held hostage by Palestinian terrorists and Chancellor Bruno Kreisky had agreed to the terrorists' demands that he close the emigrant transient camp for Russian Jews at Schonau Castle.

The 'Institute' went through a troubled and introspective period after the Yom Kippur war. A certain lack of confidence became apparent and it took the dash and courage of the Entebbe hi-jack rescue to restore the confidence of the Israeli intelligence community. Since then Mossad has gone the way of most modern secret services. While retaining a certain individualistic flair, especially in penetrating Arab terrorist organizations, it now runs more on bureaucracy than on glory.

JAPAN

There are four intelligence agencies in Japan, all run on modest budgets. The most important is the Naicho, the Cabinet research office, which is the Prime Minister's own security service. With a staff of less than a hundred, it has built up a reputation for efficiency.

It makes full use of signals intelligence gathered at its Tokyo headquarters by the monitoring of military and diplomatic radio messages in neighbouring areas of the Soviet Union, China and North Korea. The efficiency of Japanese listening posts was demonstrated in September 1983, when they recorded radio talk between ground control and Soviet jet fighters which shot down a Korean Airlines Boeing near the Soviet island of Sakhalin to the north of Japan.

One interesting feature of Japanese intelligence-gathering is that up to two-thirds of the Naicho budget is spent on commissioning reports from private institutions and journalists. First steps towards the establishment of a central agency were taken in 1971 to work in co-operation with the United States in collecting and analysing information from the outside world about political as well as military developments.

Like the Japanese defence forces, the intelligence service had to be completely rebuilt after the War, in close co-operation with the United States. Under the Defence Agency a number of divisions, including research and operations, were set up.

The purpose of their activities was defined as the surveillance of maritime and air movements around the national territory. Naval intelligence is particularly vigilant in keeping track of Soviet naval developments, and in particular the expansion of the submarine fleet; for Japan never forgets the fact that it consists of islands. A security bureau is responsible for counter-espionage, against the spying actively conducted in Japan by both the Soviet Union and neighbouring China.

Japanese intelligence was very prompt in handling an incident in 1976 when a Soviet pilot, Lieutenant Viktor Belenko, flew to Japan with his latest-model MiG 25. They inspected the aircraft, and discovered explosive charges placed on those parts of the new aircraft which the Russians intended to remain secret.

Alarmed that an attempt might be made to destroy the MiG by Soviet air attack on the field at Hakodate where it landed, they quietly removed it to another air base. There they held it despite many Russian demands for its return, carefully examining every detail of design before crating up the aircraft and returning it by sea. They even asked for (but did not receive) payment for transportation.

SOUTH AFRICA
BOSS The Bureau of State Security

This much-feared South African intelligence organization represented everything that is ruthless about the Afrikaner's determination to keep South Africa white. Far more than an intelligence-gathering agency, it carried its war against opponents of apartheid wherever they could be found.

BOSS sent parcel bombs to black 'Freedom Fighters' in African bases, burgled the offices of anti-apartheid groups in London, including Amnesty International, and carried out a systematic campaign of disinformation. Much of its work involved infiltrating groups supporting workers in South Africa.

Led by the hardline General Hendrik van den Bergh, BOSS pursued its enemies so relentlessly, and caused such resentment in the countries in which it operated, that Prime Minister P.W. Botha restructured it in 1978. Van den Bergh was retired, and his empire disbanded.

BOSS was replaced by the National Intelligence Service, but it now appears that these changes were largely cosmetic. In March 1983 three South African journalists who reported that NIS had been involved in Colonel Michael Hoare's abortive attempt to overthrow the Seychelles government were tried in camera, found guilty and fined. The evidence could not be reported, but the South African government did admit that Martin Dolincheck, one of Hoare's men, was a member of the NIS. He was, said the government, on leave at the time.

SPAIN

CESID Centro Superior de Información de la Defensa

The Spanish intelligence service established in 1977, when Spain became a democracy after the death of Franco. It looks after both internal and external affairs, but may eventually have to split into two parts, in similar fashion to the American, British and French services; the advantage being that they can keep an eye on each other's activities.

Most of the Cesid staff came from the earlier military intelligence under General Franco, and most of its operatives are still ex-army officers. The new service showed its diligence, for example, by revealing that right-wing officers were planning a coup in 1982.

The old fascist state operated no less than eight secret services, and the police kept extensive political files. The first democratic Prime Minister, Adolfi Suarez, ordered the destruction of these files.

Felipe Gonzalez, the socialist who succeeded him, remains suspicious of secret services and keeps careful watch over their activities.

UK

GCHQ Government Communications Headquarters

This highly secret British signals intelligence organization based at Cheltenham can trace its origins back to Room 40 at the Admiralty, which provided valuable naval intelligence in the First World War. Commander Alastair Denniston, a founder-member of that Royal Navy group which boasted of deciphering 15,000 secret German messages, expanded a similar intelligence-gathering unit, the Code and Cypher School at Bletchley in the Second World War.

His most notable achievement was to assemble the team of cryptologists and scholars who broke the code of the German Enigma machine, in what was called the Ultra operation. In 1939 the British acquired Enigma by way of French and Polish co-operation, and a year later their primitive

electronic computer had broken down the German code. The first messages read by Commander Denniston were short Luftwaffe messages about personnel changes, but within a few years they were able to read the top-secret messages of Hitler's generals.

That was the beginning of electronic espionage of enormous complexity which is now carried out by GCHQ, and by America's much more ambitious National Security Agency. There is still close co-operation between the two which arose from the exchange of wartime information, when the British exchanged Enigma secrets in return for American secrets, after William Friedman had solved the riddle of the Japanese cryptographic machine known as Purple.

In 1947 the highly secret UKUSA Agreement was signed to establish signals intelligence co-operation, not only between those two countries, but also including Canada, Australia and New Zealand. The American operation is the most ambitious, covering vast areas. The other countries monitor regions best available to them. For example, GCHQ covers many Chinese communications from its station at Little Sai Wan in Hong Kong.

Under Commander Edward Travis — who had taken over from Alastair Denniston — GCHQ was moved in 1952 to Cheltenham from its wartime home at Bletchley. It was located in two large centres a few miles apart.

The task of the organization — which has feeding stations in different parts of the British Isles, two of them manned by Americans — is to intercept communications world-wide. Its principal interest is in hostile or potentially hostile diplomatic and military traffic, but commercial signals can also be intercepted, and searched for information about, for example, new weapons.

Sir Brian Tovey was director of this highly secret and important installation from 1978 until his retirement in 1983. After Oxford and the School of Oriental Studies, he entered naval then military intelligence, before spending the rest of his career at GCHQ. The fact that he retired early at the age of fifty-seven was undoubtedly connected with the discovery of Geoffrey Prime, the British spy who fed Cheltenham documents to the Russians, though this was officially denied.

He was replaced by Peter Marychurch, who had gone to GCHQ from the Royal Air Force thirty-one years earlier. As director he automatically became a member of the Joint Intelligence Committee, the Prime Minister's intelligence assessment group. As well as the British stations GCHQ operates others in Cyprus, Hong Kong and Berlin. More than 6,500 people are employed by it.

One branch of the service is responsible for producing codes and cypher machines used by the British government. Electronic eavesdropping on the grand scale amasses such a quantity of information that computers to store it and analysts to sift the vital information have become just as important as the gathering equipment.

JIO Joint Intelligence Organization

Based in the Cabinet Office, this body was virtually unknown outside intelligence circles until the Franks Committee reported on the Falklands conflict and commented sharply on the work of the JIO. Its main function is to make assessments for Ministers and officials of a wide range of external situations and developments. It draws for its assessment on all relevant information: diplomatic reports and telegrams, the views of government departments, and publicly available information, as well as secret intelligence reports.

It also has a co-ordinating role in the work of the security and intelligence agencies. Its assessments are prepared by Current Intelligence Groups which are serviced by the assessments staff, who are civil servants and serving officers seconded to the Cabinet Office from their own departments — usually the Foreign Office and the Ministry of Defence.

The CIGs are organized on a regional basis, and their membership is made up of those in the relevant departments with special knowledge of the area and the problem involved. Their assessments are normally considered by the Joint Intelligence Committee before they are circulated, and it is this Committee which is the very pinnacle of the intelligence set-up in Britain.

It is composed of the Chief of the Secret Intelligence Service (MI6); the Director-General of the Security Service (MI5); the Director of the Government Communications Headquarters; the Director-General of Intelligence at the Ministry of Defence; the Deputy Chief of Defence Staff (Intelligence); the Co-ordinator of Intelligence and Security; and a number of Foreign Service officials. The United States, Canada, Australia and New Zealand are also represented.

Before the Falkland crisis it was always chaired by a Deputy Under-Secretary of State at the Foreign Office, but because of the Franks Report's criticisms that appointment has been made a full-time post with a more critical and independent role. The man who holds it is a member of the Cabinet Office appointed directly by the Prime Minister.

The first man to be appointed to this new and extremely powerful post in 1983 was Sir Anthony Duff, an accomplished diplomat who was formerly Co-ordinator of Security and Intelligence in the Cabinet Office.

MI5 Military Intelligence, Department Five

This department of Military Intelligence, the British Security Service, emerged from the Haldane reforms of the War Office in 1905 which led to the creation of a General Staff and the recognition that military intelligence needed to be properly organized. As usual there was an inter-Service squabble over control of military intelligence. This was resolved in August 1909 by setting up MI5 along with MI6, the Secret Intelligence Service, which was to undertake secret espionage abroad. Both organizations, despite their military intelligence tags, were removed from the control of the War Office and handed over to the Foreign Office.

For the first thirty years of its experience MI5 was controlled by Captain Vernon Kell, who ended his career as Major-General Sir Vernon Kell, and might have progressed to even higher rank if he had not fallen out with Winston Churchill during the war. During his long term of office MI5 developed from dealing with purely military counter-espionage into something like the

FBI, except that it does not handle any criminal cases.

It deals with internal subversion, and tends to overlap with the Special Branch. Unlike the FBI, it has no powers of arrest and must call on the Special Branch not only to make arrests, but also to present MI5 evidence in court.

Operationally, MI5 is divided into six departments, the most important being 'A', dealing with intelligence resources and operations; 'C', responsible for protective security; 'F' for countering 'domestic subversion' from either the right or the left; 'D' for counter-espionage. These operational departments have the usual technical and administrative back-up. Like all modern security services, it makes full use of information stored in computerized data banks.

Throughout its existence MI5, despite its undoubted success — it rolled up the German spy networks in Britain in both world wars — has lived in the shadow of the more glamorous MI6, which tends to look down on 'the policeman'.

Inevitably, both services stray across the demarcation lines, but 'Six' always claims seniority and usually wins the struggle. It was only in the aftermath of the Burgess and Maclean fiasco that MI5 achieved superiority, but the case of Blunt, a wartime recruit to MI5, and a series of other spy scandals soon put the men from 'Five' back in their place. MI5 reached the nadir of its existence in 1970, when so much circumstantial evidence had been gathered suggesting that Sir Roger Hollis, former Director-General of the service, was a KGB agent that he was recalled for interrogation by his former colleagues. The case of Geoffrey Prime in 1982 can hardly have restored their self-confidence, for he was not caught by the counter-espionage service but betrayed by his taste for sexual perversion. And it was even further battered by the Bettaney case.

In these circumstances it is easy for politicians to make political capital out of MI5's difficulties and to demand that the security services be made accountable to Parliament. However, it must be remembered that 'Five' has an extremely difficult job. It must look after the nation's security on a limited budget, with limited manpower — and it takes a score of agents to mount a 24-hour watch.

Its failings are obvious to everybody when a spy or traitor is exposed and it is criticized even though it has been responsible for the capture. On the other hand, the failures of MI6 rarely become known to the public because 'Six' engages in positive espionage abroad, while 'Five' can only react to attempts at domestic subversion.

If things go wrong for 'Six' it withdraws in silence, but if they go wrong for 'Five' it is spread all over the front pages. It is not surprising, therefore, that MI5 has become a somewhat tetchy organization.

Since the reorganization of the Ministry of War, the Admiralty and the Air Ministry into the Ministry of Defence, MI5 and MI6 should properly be called DI5 and DI6, but few people use these designations, preferring the traditional and instantly recognizable versions.

MI6 Military Intelligence, Department Six

Otherwise known as the Secret Intelligence Service. A venerable and highly respected service whose origins may be traced back to the Elizabethan spymaster Sir Francis Walsingham. For hundreds of years British agents have gathered information and taken part in secret operations, at home, and in all parts of the world. Government accounts for 1982, the last figures available, show that the Secret Service spent £66 million. Despite that, a polite pretence is still maintained that officially the service does not exist.

In its modern form it has been with us since 1911, when it was established to conduct overseas espionage by Captain Sir Mansfield Cumming, RN, whose initial 'C' became the pseudonym for the head of the secret service. It is part of the MI6 legend that Sir Mansfield, an officer with a wooden leg, used to startle young members of his staff by plunging a knife into this artificial limb.

The service has had a chequered record, though it is not easy to judge the efficiency of such a secretive service, whose successes remain private and whose failures only become known through major scandals. In 1939 its networks in Europe were exposed by the Nazis, and the Special

Operations Executive took over many of its functions in wartime.

Both MI6 and the sister service MI5 suffered bitter blows when it became known that some of their brightest stars — Burgess and Maclean, Blake and Blunt — were traitors. What was even worse for MI6 was the defection to the Soviet Union of one of its senior agents, Kim Philby.

However, that setback did bring about a reorganization of the service. It was modernized, security and recruiting procedures were revised, and in the cold war (when its resources were concentrated against the Soviet Union) notable successes were achieved. In particular, MI6 handled the case of Colonel Penkovsky, its spy in Moscow, with great skill.

In the backlash of British security failures, and after the American scandals of the Central Intelligence Agency had been exposed, there were increasingly powerful demands in Britain that Parliament should have more information about, and tighter control over, the activities of military intelligence. Roy Hattersley, the prominent Labour politician, spoke for many when he said in December 1982, 'The failure of the security services' present organization stems largely from inbreeding, limited field of recruitment and its traditional attitudes, and the complacency that comes from the feeling that since its entire administration is cloaked in secrecy, its organizational failures can always be swept under the carpet.'

Critics of the over-secrecy of the British services, and their lack of democratic accountability, point to the success of watchdog committees in the United States, which at some cost in efficiency have curbed the over-enthusiastic activities of the CIA. Nevertheless, in May 1983 Mrs Thatcher, the Prime Minister, made clear her policy that the military intelligence services should remain accountable only to the Cabinet. She turned down requests for parliamentary select committees to supervise intelligence.

Traditionally the service recruited its officers either from the armed forces or from the ranks of the colonial police forces in the days of empire.

That has long since changed, and the new intake of secret-service men comes largely from young men spotted as likely candidates in the universities, with aptitude for languages. In fact they come from the same strata of society as their colleagues in the European and American equivalent services, and indeed as their opponents in the Soviet KGB.

The real tragedy of MI6 was that among the new entrants recruited from the universities at the beginning of the Second World War were a number so infected by the mood of the time that they were willing to betray their country to the Soviet Union. They may have been brighter intellectually than their predecessors from the Army, Navy and Air Force but they were certainly far less loyal and patriotic. Selection now is far less haphazard and more cautious. Positive vetting is an established procedure, and such devices as the polygraph are now coming into use.

Intelligence tasks and methods have changed a great deal. MI6 men and women are now likely to concentrate on espionage against the Soviet Union, having lost to a large extent their imperial role. They spend more time on collating, with the aid of computers, intelligence material in co-operation with the allied services of the NATO powers, than on cloak-and-dagger work.

The intelligence service also has to counter Soviet propaganda and disinformation, as well as to provide strictly military intelligence and forecasts. Electronic information derived from the Government Communications Headquarters at Cheltenham provides a significant part of the incoming material for assessment.

SPECIAL BRANCH

The special intelligence branch of the British police. It was formed in 1883 — suitably enough, on St Patrick's Day — to cope with an outbreak of Irish terrorism in London. Named the Irish Special Branch, it consisted of a mere dozen men.

In modern times its strength, spread among the various county forces, amounts to about 1,600. In its one hundred years existence it coped first with the Fenians, then with the anarchists, the German secret service in two world wars, and from 1917 onward the increasing problem of Russian espionage and communist subversion.

Throughout its history Irish terrorism has been a dominant theme, and in latter years the Branch has also had to deal with the complexities of international terrorism. Questioned in the House of Commons about the role of the Special Branch when he was Home Secretary, Mr Roy Jenkins replied, 'The Special Branch is only interested in subversion and possible subversion.' He added that the Branch is concerned with 'the activities of individuals who undermine the democratic party regime'.

Special Branch also acts as the executive arm of MI5, the Security Service. Because MI5 has no power of arrest, the Branch works closely with 'Five' and takes over its work when a case for an arrest is ready. It also collaborates with MI6, the Secret Intelligence Service, in infiltrating the Irish terrorist organizations, especially in Europe.

For some strange reason it also handles offences relating to the conduct of local and parliamentary elections. It is not to be confused with the 'Specials', the part-time policemen who deal with crowd-control and generally assist the uniformed police.

ULTRA

This was originally the prefix which the British attached to the word secret in order to designate intelligence material derived from intercepted code messages based on the war-time German Enigma code machine. Enigma was a complicated electro-mechanical device with a series of drums and wheels which first made its appearance on the commercial market in 1926.

The final model adopted by the German armed forces for battlefield use consisted of two electric typewriters connected jointly to the independently spinning wheels each bearing twenty-six crypto-graphic signs. It was modified by the introduction of obstacles intended to defeat code-breakers.

Polish, French and British cryptographers got to work on a stolen machine in 1939 on the eve of the outbreak of war. Gradually, and with the aid of captured codes, documents and Enigma wheels, they were able to read German radio signals from the highest military and naval commands downward.

The significance of this development was that Allied political heads and military commanders were frequently aware of the details of planned enemy operations before they began. This gave them an obvious advantage, though it has since emerged that commanders did not always take full advantage of it.

An establishment called the Government Code and Cypher School, housed in a Victorian mansion surrounded by huts in Bletchley Park, fifty miles north of London, was the source of all distributed Ultra information. Led by Dillwyn Knox, a devoted team of cryptographers worked on the incoming material with increasing success. Prominent among them was Alan Turing, creator of the 'Turing machine' capable of unscrambling Enigma messages, which eventually developed into an early computer.

The very success of the Bletchley operation brought difficulties, for Allied war leaders were sometimes reluctant to put their information from it to the best use in case the Germans might realize how they had acquired it and change their communications system. Elaborate subterfuges were devised to pass on the intelligence received, to say, the Russians, so that they would remain ignorant about the true source.

In the history of espionage the use of Enigma and the breaking of the machine at Bletchley, using the forerunner of the modern computer, marked the beginning of a secret technological war which has continued and become more sophisticated ever since.

Winston Churchill described the Bletchley people as 'geese that laid golden eggs and never cackled'.

UNITED STATES
CIA Central Intelligence Agency

There can be few secret services formed with more reluctance than the CIA, and the Americans have Pearl Harbour to thank for its creation. Until that

'Day of Infamy' the United States relied on a hotchpotch of military intelligence and the FBI to carry out its secret work, and there was no single central organization to analyse the collected information and pass it on to the people who had to make the decisions.

The need for such a central organization became evident when the Japanese launched their attack. Yet it was opposed by the established organizations, and by that streak of puritanism in the American public opinion which believes it is wrong to 'read other people's letters'.

In 1942, at President Roosevelt's behest, the United States did set up the Office of Strategic Services. It was led by William 'Wild Bill' Donovan, a former Attorney-General and a highly decorated First World War soldier. The OSS started its life under the tutelage of the British, and sometimes its early activities drove MI6 to despair. The British never did view it with sufficient confidence to provide total access to Ultra.

However, by the end of the war, with Allen Dulles operating into Germany, Austria and Italy from Switzerland, the OSS, backed by a large budget and bounding enthusiasm, was playing a significant role in the secret hostilities.

There were many in its ranks who felt that it had proved itself sufficiently to guarantee its peace-time survival. Then in 1945 President Truman wiped it out at the stroke of a pen, largely because he was fearful of establishing a 'Gestapo', and because the military intelligence services, and J. Edgar Hoover of the FBI, argued that it would merely duplicate their functions in peacetime. President Truman rapidly regretted his decision. He discovered that with the central role of OSS removed he was being fed unco-ordinated, unanalysed, raw and often conflicting intelligence.

He therefore set up a Central Intelligence Group under the command of Rear-Admiral Sidney Souers. Its task was to collate information and present assessments to the President. As such it did a useful but limited job.

Then in July 1947, under the pressure of the cold war which saw Eastern Europe falling to Russian control, America's defences were reorganized by the passage of the National Security Act, and the CIG was renamed the Central Intelligence Agency. The charter of the new agency specified that it should not only collect and evaluate intelligence but should also perform 'other functions and duties' as directed by the National Security Council.

At the very first meeting of the Council on 19 December 1947 Admiral Roscoe Hillenkoetter, the first director of the new CIA, was ordered to carry out covert activities to prevent the communists winning a general election in Italy which threatened to bring that country under Moscow's control. Backed by military, political and economic pressure, these activities were successful and brought prestige to the CIA. Much of the Agency's later eagerness to interfere in the affairs of other countries stemmed from that first success.

The CIA was largely staffed at this time by veterans of the OSS who simply picked up in Europe where they had left off in 1945 — only this time the enemy was the Soviet Union, not Nazi Germany.

As the cold war developed and spread across the world, so did the CIA. It became a major force in international affairs, especially after Allen Dulles became its Director in February 1953. Iran, Guatemala, Egypt, Congo, Indonesia — the CIA set out to influence them all, seeking to control or topple unfriendly governments of independent nations.

It used whatever tools it needed: bribery, disinformation, blackmail, guerrilla warfare, assassination, they were all judged legitimate in the world-wide struggle against the Soviet Union and its allies.

However, that was only part of its work. Pure espionage was also undertaken, and a number of coups were scored. Among them: obtaining the text of Khruschev's attack on Stalin, the U2 flights over the Soviet Union, the raising of part of a Soviet submarine sunk in the Pacific. It was a hectic period in which what was morally justifiable became confused with (and often subordinate to) what was expedient and realizable.

Naturally enough, there were operations which

went wrong. Nasser revealed the Agency's enormous bribery programme in Egypt. An attempted intervention in Indonesia failed; there was an embarrassing occasion when a CIA-backed Saudi force waged a small war for the Buraimi Oasis against Omanis supported by MI6. The CIA lost. It was not until Cuba and the Bay of Pigs fiasco in April 1961, though, that the CIA suffered the humiliating public disaster which is always a risk in the coup business. It was an operation based on bad intelligence mounted by the wrong people — émigrés — at the wrong place with insufficient strength.

The Bay of Pigs was such a disaster that Allen Dulles had to go. The story is told that President Kennedy said to Dulles, 'Under a parliamentary system it is I who would be leaving office. But under our system it is you who must go.'

President Kennedy allowed Dulles to stay on until the CIA had moved into his memorial, its custom-built headquarters covering 140 acres of countryside at Langley, Virginia. Anyone looking for it is guided by green and white signs to the building. It is only when the visitor arrives at the building — which looks rather like a university campus — that the security begins.

The staff is estimated at 18,000, and the cafeteria can seat a thousand people, while the car-parks can hold three thousand cars. Described as the Taj Mahal of bureaucratic architecture, it cost 46 million dollars. Behind its glass and concrete walls the most extraordinary collection of men and women practise their skills: cryptography, obscure languages, agronomy, chemistry, cybernetics, guerrilla warfare, demography; there are many mansions in the house of the CIA.

The Agency languished for a time after the failed Cuban adventure, and President Kennedy strengthened the hand of the State Department in dealing with foreign countries. But he needed the CIA to carry out the project which now obsessed him, Operation Mongoose, the overthrow of Fidel Castro of Cuba, and he hesitated to take too much power away from the Agency.

Under John McCone from November 1961 and the short unhappy rule of Vice-Admiral William Raborn from April 1965 until June 1966, it went about its business, more quietly. It looked with horror on the revelations of the traitors within MI5 and MI6. Nothing like that happened in the CIA.

Under the eagle eye and twitching nerve-ends of James Jesus Angleton, the Agency's chief of counter-espionage, the CIA remained clean of traitors. Its problems lay in other directions, and they were not revealed until the CIA was caught up in the aftermath of the Watergate scandal.

Like virtually every other institution in the United States, the CIA was damaged by the Vietnam war. When it began in earnest in 1965 CIA stations all round the world were stripped of trained men to man the so-called Office of Special Assistance in Saigon. At one stage it contained a thousand CIA agents, with another three thousand 'on contract'.

They ran operations in Vietnam, Laos and Cambodia. They had their own air force, under the guise of Air America. And, disastrously, the CIA became involved in spying on the anti-war protestors within the United States. Richard Helms, appointed director by President Johnson in June 1966, found it increasingly difficult to resist the demands of President Johnson, and later those of his successor, President Nixon, to become involved in domestic espionage, although he knew it was illegal under the CIA's charter. It was the FBI's job, but crafty old Hoover, smelling trouble, had refused to get involved, having stopped his own illegal domestic espionage programme in 1966. Helms got away with it until the Watergate investigations, and the Pentagon Papers, pointed towards CIA involvement in domestic affairs. Helms was sacked by President Nixon in February 1973 and given the post of ambassador to Iran, but he was recalled to give evidence before the Senate Select Committee to Study Government Operations with Respect to Intelligence Activities, the Church Committee, which prised open the Pandora's box of CIA evils.

The assassination attempts, the drug experiments, the spying on Vietnam protestors, the involvement in Chile — they all came hopping out. The American press campaigned against the Agency. All the old prejudices against a secret service emerged, and suddenly the CIA, once so powerful, became a whipping-boy. It became dishonourable to be a CIA agent.

Richard Helms was eventually fined two thousand dollars and given a suspended two-year gaol sentence for lying to the Senate Foreign Relations Committee in an attempt to conceal the CIA's secrets.

It was an exercise in public self-flagellation that must have had the KGB rolling in the aisles. It horrified the British secret service, and lent force to its determination never to be accountable to a Parliamentary committee.

The immediate result was the emasculation of the CIA. It reached the stage where every operation the Agency proposed to undertake had to be vetted by no less than seven committees. Obviously, no secret service could operate under these conditions, and the CIA turned to their friends in Israel, Britain and Germany for help, which was willingly given. Even here the Agency ran into trouble because the Freedom of Information Act, designed to uphold the principle of the public's 'right to know' about the background to major policy decisions, made other intelligence services reluctant to share information with their American counterparts for fear that their own secrets would be exposed.

It was President Carter who in 1979 began to lift the restrictions on the CIA, making it easier for the Agency to engage in small-scale covert actions by presenting legislation to allow the Director, then Admiral Stansfield Turner, to sanction some clandestine operations without the President's personal approval, and under special circumstances to spy on US citizens abroad.

The process of easing the shackles was speeded when President Reagan came to power, and by the beginning of 1983 the rehabilitation of the CIA under the directorship of William Casey, a self-made millionaire turned spymaster, was almost complete.

In an interview with the *New York Times* Casey revealed just how drastic the attack on the Agency had been. During the 1970s, he said, its 'workforce' was cut in half, and its budget was slashed by 40 per cent. The number of agents and staff

working on covert operations, involving paramilitary and political-action efforts to influence events abroad, had dropped from 2,000 to 200. But Casey made it plain that the bad times were past. He was, said the *New York Times*, 'overseeing the biggest peace-time build-up in the American intelligence community since the early 1950s . . . .'

With a 25 per cent budget increase for 1983 (compared with an 18 per cent increase for the Defense Department), the CIA was described by budget officials as 'the fastest-growing major agency in the Federal Government'. A career in the Agency has once again become acceptable to graduates who would have shunned it in the ten years before the Reagan administration. Radio stations carried advertisements for recruits: 'We are looking for very special people. You may be one of them.'

This return to confidence and power was reflected in the re-emergence of the CIA into the international field, not only in the acquisition and assessment of information but also in clandestine operations: support for the Afghan rebels, the arming of Iranian paramilitary groups opposed to the Ayatollah Khomeini's regime, and in particular the support of opponents to the left-wing government of Nicaragua. They all demonstrated that the CIA, with the encouragement of the President, had found ways to get round the controls introduced after 1974.

Admiral Stansfield Turner, who was Director from 1977 to 1981 and who welcomed the controls, is dismayed at the CIA's return to freedom. 'It was my observation,' he wrote in a *Guardian* article,

that quite a few "old hands" in the agency found it very difficult to accept these impediments. I forced several dozens of them into retirement because the controls were the law of the land, or the orders of the President, and I needed to feel comfortable that the people doing covert action would obey them. A large number of retired CIA have now apparently been called back into service to direct the Nicaraguan action.

So a new round starts in the forty-year-old battle over the CIA. Perhaps the Church Committee best summed up the problem in its final report:

> In some respects, the intelligence profession resembles monastic life with some of the disciplines and personal sacrifices reminiscent of mediaeval orders. Intelligence work is a life of service, but one in which the norms of American national life are sometimes distressingly distorted.

DIA Defense Intelligence Agency

Created by Robert McNamara in 1961 when he was President Kennedy's Defence Secretary, the DIA gathered into one organization all America's military intelligence services. This not only upset the individual services but created a serious rival for the CIA, because the combined strength of the military services exceeded that of the Agency. Rivalry developed between the CIA and DIA, particularly over programmes to acquire information about Russian rocket developments and in the control of spy-in-the-sky satellites. Some idea of the extent of DIA's ability to plug in electronically to what is going on in the Soviet Union was revealed in August 1983, when the Russians shot down a South Korean Boeing 747, killing 269 people, when the jumbo wandered into Russian airspace over the military bases on the fortress island of Sakhalin. It was the DIA which listened in to the flurry of radio traffic between the headquarters of the Far Eastern military region in China and Moscow, and subsequently recorded the orders being given to the Soviet fighter pilot to shoot down the airliner.

FBI The Federal Bureau of Investigation

Founded in 1908 by President Theodore Roosevelt as an investigative agency to help him in his fight against the land pirates in the West and the big-business pirates in the East. The FBI works out of Washington, and has offices in every state. Its men are hand-picked, mostly graduates. There are some 6,000 special agents, backed up by another 8,000 employees. The agents undergo a rigorous training, both in the classroom (where they learn investigative techniques, law and administration) and in the field (where they are taught self-defence and the use of firearms). Discipline is strict, and the agent is bound by a long list of rules such as 'He cannot fail to pay his taxes or to meet other financial obligations.'

The Bureau got off to an unhappy start, performing badly against gangs of German saboteurs in the First World War. It was not until J. Edgar Hoover was appointed Director in 1924 that proper standards and training were imposed. The FBI made its first real impact in the battle against the Prohibition mobsters, and it was during this time that its agents acquired the nickname of 'G-Men' (short for Government men), bestowed on them in the immortal plea 'Don't shoot, G-Men, don't shoot' by Machine Gun Kelly. In 1934 the Bureau achieved world-wide fame by arresting Bruno Hauptmann, the kidnapper of the murdered Lindbergh baby.

Then, when the Second World War broke out, President Franklin Roosevelt made the FBI responsible for guarding against espionage, sabotage and subversion. After a slow start, Hoover, mindful of the Bureau's failure in the previous war, cleaned up Nazi spy cells and picked up saboteurs as they were landed from U-Boats. However, as the war progressed Hoover became increasingly obsessed with the threat posed by the Soviet Union. He led his men into what was virtually a war against communism. Harry Gold, the Rosenbergs, Alger Hiss, Colonel Rudolf Abel, Morton Sobell — all fell victim to Hoover's investigators.

There is no doubt that the FBI performed extremely well in clearing up the Russian spy-rings in the United States, yet there was a great feeling of unease that all was not well with the Bureau. It lent itself only too willingly to Joe McCarthy. Hoover always protested that his duties were not to analyse or to make policy, and certainly not to pass judgment, only to acquire information. However, the sort of information that he set out to acquire was so tendentious that it was obvious that he intended not only to pass judgment but to impose it. Those were the days when to possess a book on the Russian Revolution meant that a scholar was immediately suspect.

In 1956 in a foreword to an officially approved book on the FBI by Don Whitehead, Hoover wrote:

> In recent years, a campaign of falsehood and vilification has been directed against the FBI by some ignorant and some subversive elements. In the world-wide struggle of free peoples, the truth is still one of our most potent weapons. And the record of the FBI speaks for itself. It is the best answer to the falsehoods, half-truths and rumours spread by Communists, their stooges and defenders.

When the truth about the FBI did emerge in the wake of Watergate it proved to be worse than anything the communists had said about it. Hoover had kept his Bureau clear of the Watergate scandal — he knew trouble when he saw it, and was happy to let the CIA fall into it. But the FBI was caught up, willy-nilly, in the rash of investigations that followed Watergate.

From these investigations emerged the fact that the FBI had been systematically breaking the law for a number of years. It had carried out 238 burglaries — 'black bag jobs' — against 14 'target organizations' from 1942 to 1968, and three other 'domestic subversive targets' were also the subject of numerous illegal entries from October 1952 to June 1966.

The New York City office of the Socialist Workers Party was broken into on no less than 92 occasions between 1960 and 1966, and ten thousand photographs of documents and correspondence were taken. These burglaries were carried out by specially trained teams of Federal agents who were paid bonuses because they were carrying out illegal acts and had no protection against being sent to prison if they were caught by local police. Finally, fearful that his illegal operations might be discovered, Hoover halted all 'black bag' jobs in 1966 except those involving foreign embassies whose code-books were needed by the National Security Agency to read diplomatic radio traffic.

Burglary was not the only 'dirty trick' indulged in by the FBI. There was also character assassination. The Church Committee reported that Dr Martin Luther King had been harassed for five years, even to the point where agents suggested anonymously that he should commit suicide, and tried to blackmail him into doing so. These attempts to 'neutralize and discredit' Dr King were said by the committee to be 'a sad episode in the dark history of covert activities directed against law-abiding citizens'.

Hoover never felt the weight of the nation's disapproval. The Committee made its report in 1976, and he had died in 1972. After his death L. Patrick Grey held the directorship for a brief and confused tenure before being succeeded by the highly professional Clarence Kelley, who began to put the Bureau together again. Kelley suffered, however, from being loyal to Hoover and being a Nixon employee. President Carter wanted him out. But it was no easy matter to find a suitable candidate. After a six-month search a liberal Alabaman, Federal Judge Frank Johnson, was chosen, but had to withdraw because of ill-health.

Kelley, who had announced his decision to retire, was asked to stay on, and the search went on until January 1978, when William H. Webster, Federal appellate judge in St Louis, was chosen, accepted and confirmed as Director. Described as 'a man of strength, intellect and integrity', he promised to carry out his duties 'within the framework of the constitution'.

The FBI is unique in that, unlike the security services of the other major nations, it handles criminal investigations, albeit only those involving the violation of Federal laws, alongside its security work. It must be said that while Hoover's paranoia with communism led the security investigators into excesses and illegalities, the criminal side of the Bureau's work has always been performed with great skill, rectitude and bravery.

By the autumn of 1983 it seemed that the Bureau was recovering from its troubles. Like the CIA, it was beginning to be released from the post-Watergate shackles, and after seven years of strict curbs it was given important new powers to investigate groups that might turn to terrorism.

NSA National Security Agency

The American organization responsible for all forms of signals and electronic espionage established by President Truman in 1952. Its main task is deciphering messages projected by all forms of sophisticated communications.

Its headquarters were described by James Bamford, author of a comprehensive book about NSA, *The Puzzle Palace*, as the 'largest single espionage factory' the free world could ever imagine. They are at Fort Meade, between Washington and Baltimore, in Maryland. Some 70,000 people work for the organization.

NSA has become the most important source of intelligence in the United States. Not only does it have a larger staff than the Central Intelligence Agency, but in power and influence with government it has often outclassed that Agency.

The operational part of NSA now has the capability to intercept every form of communication, and its staff regularly monitor the outpourings of neutrals, as well as of friend and foe. There are four code-breaking sections which take in messages from simple written or telephoned messages upward, and are also responsible for deciphering high-level coded military, diplomatic and commercial signals from around the world.

Special departments deal with even more complicated forms of electronic espionage. There is Elint, for electronics intelligence, and Radint for radar intelligence. Signals searchers track down the mysteries of spectrum spreading, where signals are hidden in noise, and frequency hopping to avoid detection.

Apart from the signals experts, the agency is well staffed with listeners, code-breakers, engineers, scientists and mathematicians. They have the back-up of extensive computer systems for storage and analysis.

The high secrecy and obvious importance of the Agency make it a target for Soviet penetration, so physical security is strong and an Office of Communications Security looks after counter-espionage within the organization.

In 1981 Lieutenant-General Lincoln D. Faurer, a 53-year-old air force officer, was appointed director of NSA in succession to Admiral Inman when that officer went to the CIA. General Faurer had great experience, and had earlier served as head of intelligence of the US European Command in Germany. He was also deputy chairman of the NATO military committee in Brussels.

The general rule seems to be that the director of NSA should have wide military and administrative experience. His deputy is traditionally a senior cryptologist in government service.

NSA works in close co-operation with the Government Communications Headquarters at Cheltenham, which is in control of similar though less extensive operations in Britain.

National Security Council

The most powerful group in the United States Government dealing with intelligence matters. It is a policy-making body under the direct control of the President, and is composed of senior members of the government, the armed forces and the intelligence community. It makes its decisions on intelligence briefings allied to government policy, and traditionally its meetings in the White House open with the Director of the CIA giving a briefing on the subject under discussion.

In some ways it is similar to the Joint Intelligence Committee of the British Cabinet. It was founded in December 1947 under the National Security Act, which was passed to reorganize America's intelligence services in the light of Russian aggression in Europe.

At its first meeting Admiral Roscoe Hillenkoetter, then Director of the CIA, was ordered to undertake a broad range of activities to prevent a communist victory in the Italian elections. It was one of the CIA's first and most successful operations, and gave the Agency the green light for undertaking covert action for which it had not previously had authority.

However, in 1955 the NSC formed a group known as the 5412 Committee which was given responsibility of approving all covert operations considered important or sensitive enough to warrant the President's approval. Its decisions were forwarded to the President, and he would initial one of two boxes marked 'Approve' or 'Disapprove'. This committee has undergone changes over the years, and has been variously called the Special Committee, the 303 Committee, and currently the Forty Committee. Its membership is based on representatives designated by the President, the State Department and the Defense Department, and it is serviced by the CIA. It has been described as the 'Directorate' of the NSC.

Office of Policy Co-ordination

A clandestine operations unit set up in June 1948 by the National Security Council to counter Russia's 'vicious covert activities'. It acquired a reputation for dilettantism, and was not highly regarded by the professionals of the Office of Special Operations, another covert group which had been placed under the control of the newly formed CIA. The OPC's operations were adventurous but not particularly successful. It tried to start a revolution in Albania, but all its agents were mopped up, through Philby's treachery. It was amalgamated with the OSO in 1952, and became the CIA's Directorate for Plans. Most of its remaining members were fired for their part in the Bay of Pigs débâcle in 1961.

United States Secret Service

This organization has nothing to do with espionage. It is a branch of the United States Treasury, and was formed after the Civil War to combat a wave of counterfeiting in currency and securities. It still has this role, but its most important function, given to it in 1901 following the assassination of President McKinley, is the protection of the President of the United States.

The men in dark glasses carrying Uzi submachine guns who surround the President in public do not belong to the CIA or the FBI but to the Secret Service. They check the food he eats at public functions, they search buildings for bombs and rooftops for snipers, they ride shotgun in Presidential motorcades.

Their orders are to protect the President's life at the cost of their own if need be. If shooting breaks out their technique is to form a human wall round the President, bundle him into a car and speed him out of danger, leaving a special weapons squad armed with automatic weapons behind to deal with the would-be assassin. They are highly trained, devoted men.

The fact that this 4,000-strong organization was unable to prevent the killing of President Kennedy and the wounding of President Reagan merely exemplifies the difficulty of protecting a well-known target who has to appear in public.

USSR
GRU Glavnoye Razvedyvatelnoye Upravleniye

GRU, the Chief Intelligence Directorate of the Soviet General Staff, is the military counterpart of the KGB. Working from 19 Znamensky Street, Moscow, a baroque palace which once belonged to a rich Tsarist merchant, the GRU's function is to acquire military intelligence.

This it does legally through the military attaché system — no military exhibition takes place without the Iron Curtain attachés filling their brief-cases with brochures — and illegally through espionage cells which are distinct and separate from the KGB.

Among the GRU's most successful illegals were Rudolf Abel and Konon Molody (Gordon Lonsdale). Klaus Fuchs and the Rosenbergs, the atom spies, were run by the GRU. This organization also trains foreign terrorists and keeps its own stable of assassins. It is estimated to number around five thousand operatives under its present director General Petr Ivanovich Ivashutin.

Divided into four main divisions — operations, information, training and auxiliary — the GRU is also subdivided into twenty-four geographical units. Despite its undoubted successes, the GRU remains subordinate to the KGB, with the latter having the power to investigate its members. Moreover, since the KGB was smartened up by Andropov the 'Chekists' tend to look down on the GRU as simple soldiers fit only for ordinary espionage while the KGB agents devote their time to the more sophisticated pursuits of international politics, running agents of influence and spreading disinformation.

One source of the rivalry and dislike between the KGB and the GRU is the fact that during Stalin's reign of terror the dictator played one off against the other while liquidating their leaders with equal ferocity. There is no doubt that the KGB, the state security organization, now has the upper hand — especially after the damaging 'defection in place' of Colonel Oleg Penkovsky, who was one of the best agents the West ever had — and he was GRU.

KGB Komitet Gosudarstvennoi Bezopastnosti

The KGB is the Soviet Union's Committee for State Security. This all-pervasive and increasingly sophisticated organization had its origins in the feared Tsarist secret police, and its main function remains the same: the repression of the Russian people.

When the Bolsheviks seized power in 1917 they replaced the Okhrana of the Tsars with their own Cheka, the Extraordinary Commission for Combating Counterrevolutions and Sabotage, but used the same files, the same prisons and, in a number of cases the same agents.

Its first head, the cruel Pole Felix Dzerzhinsky, who believed that means were justified by the ultimate end, quickly turned it from an arm of the workers' revolution into the punitive instrument of an unpopular State machine. KGB agents still proudly acknowledge the nickname of 'Chekist'.

In 1922 the Cheka became the GPU and then the OGPU, the State Political Administration. In 1934 it became part of the NKVD, The People's Committee of Internal Affairs, but in 1941 as a result of the huge wartime expansion of the NKVD's role the political police section was again detached and renamed NKGB, the People's Committee for State Security.

In 1946 in the post-war reorganization both organizations were upgraded to Ministries, becoming the MGB, the Ministry for State Security, and the MVD, the Ministry for Internal Affairs.

On Stalin's death Lavrenti Beria tried to merge the two organizations once again under his personal control. If he had succeeded he would have acquired enormous power: the secret police, both internal and foreign agents, the militia, an army of special troops amounting to 300,000 men equipped with their own tanks and aircraft, the labour camps, and a large part of Russia's industrial enterprises, including the nuclear and missile development programmes. He was thwarted then shot by Khruschev, Malenkov and Molotov, and the new leaders once again reorganized the secret police.

The KGB was given a threefold mission: the maintenance of communist rule at home, the guarding of the Soviet Union's borders and the conduct of foreign operations both legal and illegal in pursuit of the Soviet Union's aims.

It has been a long and bloodthirsty history. It was Dzerzhinsky who said, 'We stand for organized terror.... The Cheka is not a court. The Cheka is obliged to defend the Revolution and conquer the enemy even if its sword does by chance sometimes fall upon the heads of the innocent.'

That chance sword has fallen on the heads of millions of Russians killed by torture, the bullet in the back of the head, the Siberian labour camps, the forced migrations of whole peoples and the war of starvation against the peasants. The 'Chekists' reached beyond their frontiers to kill men like Trotsky, one of the founders of the Revolution, and still no Russian who defects is safe. The only element of satisfaction in this tale is that the KGB under its various names underwent the same sort of bloodletting in successive purges and its most brutal heads, Genrikh Yagoda and Nikolai Yezhov, were themselves both liquidated.

Today the KGB presents a very different aspect to the world. Part of its headquarters have moved to a modern office complex on Moscow's ring road to house its foreign department. and to accommodate the electronics so necessary to modern espionage. Dissidents are sent to 'psychiatric' hospitals rather than shot in the Lubyanka cellars.

The 'Chekists' prefer to concentrate on foreign

politics, running agents of influence, controlling 'Peace' movements and peddling disinformation. But that is only the outside skin. If need be the KGB will still undertake *Mokrie Dela* — wet affairs, or assassinations. It was the KGB which sanctioned the murder by poison pellet of Georgi Markov in London in 1979, while its repression of internal troubles beyond the eyes of the West is still swift and brutal.

It is difficult to estimate how many people work for the KGB, simply because it is so all-embracing. The village informant is just as much a member of the KGB as the expert in electronic decoding; but educated guesses put the strength of the *apparat* in the Soviet Union at around 1,750,000, while the agents in the field abroad, including diplomats, journalists, Aeroflot personnel, and co-opted members serving on international bodies, are estimated to amount to some 300,000, with another 100,000 to be added on to account for members of the satellite secret services. It is the biggest secret service the world has ever seen.

Managerially, the organization is controlled by a Chairman and two First Deputy Chairmen. It is split into four Chief Directorates: the First, which controls foreign operations; the Second, which runs internal security; the Fifth, whose role is to control political, religious and ethnic dissent; and the Border Guards.

Then there are eight Directorates: the Third, which makes sure the armed forces are loyal; the Seventh, which looks after surveillance; the Eighth, which attends to communications intelligence; the Ninth, which supplies bodyguards; the research directorate which develops the paraphernalia of espionage and assassination; and then the normal branches of technical support, administration, services and personnel.

The KGB can in fact be looked upon as an international conglomerate. It offers a splendid career to young men and women who are given special privileges, denied to those outside the protection of the organization. The work is well paid and offers opportunities to travel, and those employees who are not approved by the governments of the countries in which they work are simply reassigned.

Like all conglomerates, it has its malcontents and its bunglers, those who fake their expenses and copy their reports from Western magazines. And it has more defections from its ranks than any other secret service. Nevertheless, despite its problems — many of them caused by the arrogance of its agents operating abroad, who are made *persona non grata* in droves — the effort put into the KGB, the alternative state, is so huge that one way or another it affects the lives of nearly everybody in the world.

It must be emphasized that the KGB operates in a closed society with its own men guarding the doors. In America the CIA and the FBI now come under the closest scrutiny from Senate committees. In Britain security disasters are normally followed by an inquiry held at least partially in public, and whose members must submit a report to Parliament. But in Russia whatever inquiries are held into KGB disasters are held in secret, and as far as the Russian public is concerned the KGB never has disasters or defectors. All 'Chekists' are heroes, guardians of the Soviet Union. Their 'dirty tricks' are never exposed. When their agents are kicked out of a foreign country it is always a 'provocation'. And their defectors are never publicized, simply added to the death list. Only when something as serious as the Penkovsky affair surfaces, involving foreigners and a trial, are the Russians fed even a partial account. In these circumstances the KGB can, in contrast to the Western services, get away with murder.

SMERSH

Though it has been ruthlessly exploited by writers of spy fiction, SMERSH really did exist. It was the acronym for the Russian phrase *Smert Shpionam* — Death to Spies — and was said to have been coined by Stalin himself. It was set up in the late summer of 1942 on the basis of an organization called the Main Administration of Special Branches of the State Security Service in order to cope with the security problems in the front-line areas of the war.

Smersh was divided into five administrations. The first worked in every detachment of the army, and its job was to root out any suspicion of treachery or defeatism. The second was responsible for collecting information and dropping agents immediately behind the enemy lines. The third was the intelligence administration for collating and distributing information and orders. The fourth was the investigative branch whose members had the power of arrest. The fifth was composed of three-man tribunals which heard cases and passed sentence. Their sentences were final, and if they ordered an execution it was usually carried out on the spot.

Smersh only lasted until 1946, when it was absorbed into the MGB, the forerunner of the KGB, but in its short life it had killed thousands of men and women and left behind a legacy of terror unequalled in the bloody annals of the Chekists. Its modern equivalent is Department V of the First Chief Directorate of the KGB, the assassination department, and although it is no longer required to kill on the wartime scale of Smersh, it is no less ruthless.

Although Smersh's existence was well known in the West — it guarded Churchill and Roosevelt at the Teheran Conference — little was known about its structure until 1972, when a former member who had defected wrote a book about it: *Nights Are Longest There*. The author under the pen-name Romanov was Boris Hatton, formerly Bakhlanov. The book was translated for him by Gerald Brooke, who had spent four years in a forced labour camp. A London coroner returned an open verdict on Boris after he was found dead by drowning in a pond on Wimbledon Common in January 1984.

WEST GERMANY
BfV Bundesamt für Verfassungsschutz

The German name signifies Office for the Protection of the Constitution, and the BfV was established in September 1950 as West Germany's counter-espionage service. It is a purely domestic organization. It has no powers of arrest, and therefore can be compared with MI5, but instead of being a military organization, it is part of the Ministry of the Interior.

Its function is to provide a defence against espionage, sabotage and sedition, and its efforts are directed mainly against infiltration by communist agents, although in latter years it has been forced to shift its attentions to the urban terrorist gangs and their international allies. It does this by the classic counter-espionage techniques of infiltration and close surveillance, and also has the use of a highly efficient computer whose data banks are filled with information about communist agents and terrorists.

It has not had a smooth passage. BfV was born amid friction with General Gehlen's organization, and its first director, Otto John, defected — or, as he claims, was kidnapped — to the East Germans. John was produced at a press conference at which he attacked the West, but later he returned to West Germany. He was arrested and sentenced to four years' imprisonment, but was released after thirty-two months. He still protests his innocence, insisting that he was brainwashed.

Since then a number of double agents have been found lurking in the BfV offices. It is an occupational hazard which, given the geography and population interchange between East and West Germany, is extremely hard to overcome. A prime example of its problems is the case of Gunther Guillaume, the East German spy who became aide to Chancellor Willy Brandt, and whose exposure led to the latter's resignation.

The BfV finally nailed Guillaume, but not before he had done a great deal of damage, and it came under fierce attack for ever allowing Guillaume to worm his way into the administration. Given the number of agents infiltrated from East Germany, this must be the world's hardest-working security organization.

BND Bundesnachrichtendienst

The Federal Intelligence Service, the West German equivalent of the CIA or MI6, was established as a Federal Government Department in April 1956 by the transfer of the Gehlen Organization to government control. The Gehlen Organization had itself been assisted by the Americans after the Second World War, making use of the unique archives collected by Gehlen as Hitler's masterspy on the Eastern Front.

Gehlen became head of the BND, and he took all his operatives there with him. Many of them had Nazi pasts — and some of them were already communist 'doubles'. He remained head of the organization until April 1968, when he was succeeded by General Gerhard Wessel.

The function of the BND was laid down as 'to gather information on other countries which will be of importance in the shaping of foreign policy'. In practice the BND went further than that, and in its early days indulged in sabotage and subversion behind the Iron Curtain. Most of these operations proved disastrous, because the BND, like so many other West German intelligence groups, was riddled with communist agents and 'doubles'.

After Gehlen's retirement the BND's headquarters at Pullach were 'house-cleaned'. The old SS and Abwehr men were removed and the organization converted into a modern intelligence-gathering operation relying more on electronics and analysis than on 'cowboys'. It works closely with the CIA, MI6 and Mossad.

APPENDIX

THE BACKGROUND

Blackmail and Entrapment

The classical methods of forcing an unwilling target into treachery and espionage are gathered under the heading of MICE: Money, Ideology, Compromise, Ego. The money method can be quite crude — if the target is greedy an offer of money for information or services will do the trick, and once he has signed a receipt for the money he is in the bag. It can, however, be more subtle, where need rather than greed applies the pressure. Sympathetic help with hospital bills, school fees, gambling debts, a failing business — all these provide openings for the 'bagmen' to operate.

Ideology is perhaps the surest method. If a target can be convinced that what he is being asked to do is for the good of the cause and of mankind he will come willingly to treachery — although a little money helps as well. The only drawback with this method is that a person with strong ideological views is much more likely to reverse those views and confess than someone who cares little for ideology.

Compromise comes in various forms, the most usual and effective being sexual, with 'swallows' being provided for the men and 'ravens' for the women. Once hooked and shown the incriminating photographs, the victim knows that he or she is in trouble. Once the first piece of information has been handed over, the situation is irretrievable. There is a tale of a British diplomat who, when being shown a set of compromising pictures of himself with an attractive woman, held them up admiringly and ordered six sets. But that reaction is unusual, and it never happens when the honey trap is homosexual.

Ego is perhaps the most subtle of the methods, and the most difficult for counter-espionage agencies to pinpoint. This is dry fly fishing rather than coarse fishing. The victim has to be encouraged into impaling himself on the hook. He has to be made to think that he is either the saviour of the world or a super-spy. The victims of the ego method are usually fantasists, and in the end it is usually their own fantasies which betray them. Geoffrey Prime, the GCHQ traitor, was a classic example.

Counter-espionage

The art of spying on the spy. It is conducted in most countries by an organization enjoying a love-hate relationship with its sister services of espionage. In Britain these relations are between MI5 and MI6; in the US they are between FBI and CIA; in West Germany between BfV and BND. Each espionage organization also has a counter-espionage department within its own ranks. They would rather catch their own traitors than be humiliated by 'the policemen'.

The counter-espionage agencies have a much wider brief than the mere catching of traitors. They must also guard against the infiltration of agents and saboteurs from abroad, and the 'turning' of people involved in espionage into enemy agents. The armed forces also have their own counter-espionage departments.

The most renowned of counter-espionage agents was James Jesus Angleton of the CIA. It was he who first sniffed out the treachery of Philby and Maclean. Against this, he was accused of seeing a Red under every bed, and eventually William Colby, who restructured the CIA in the 1970s, forced him into bitter and suspicious retirement.

In all democratic countries the counter-espionage organizations must tread warily, taking care not to infringe the rights of individuals in their efforts to ensure the security of the nation. Angleton went over that line, and paid for it, though in the opinion of many counter-espionage agents his excess of zeal seemed well justified.

D Notice Committee

The Defence, Press and Broadcasting Committee which oversees the unique system of self-censorship on defence matters practised by the British press, radio and television. Dating from 1912, the committee is composed of media representatives and civil servants under the guidance of a Secretary, usually a retired senior naval officer.

Its function is to issue D Notices, which ask that certain matters should not be made public. There are in fact a surprisingly small number of permanent notices. Up to December 1981 there were only twelve. And then, because of some disquiet about the way the system was working, they were further reduced in that month to six. These deal with the security and intelligence services, military operations, details of nuclear-weapon capabilities, preparations for war and classified military equipment, plus intelligence, defence and diplomatic cyphers and communications.

Any journalist who has doubts about a story he has acquired is urged to consult the secretary of the committee. From personal experience, we know he is usually eager to find a way for the journalist to get his story printed.

There is no compulsion about this system, and some publications have consistently broken the notice requesting that the names of the directors of MI6 and MI5 should not be published. The security services are most sensitive on this matter, their argument being that although these men are usually well-known the publication of their names leaves them wide-open to terrorist attack. Obviously if the system breaks down some other method, probably with unpleasant teeth in it, will be introduced by the government.

Disinformation

The black art of spreading false stories about one's enemies. Developed by the British journalist Sefton Delmer in his German-language broadcasts to the German army over 'Soldiers' Radio Calais', which had a great effect on German morale, it is now one of the main weapons in the KGB's armoury.

The CIA estimates that the Russians spend some four billion dollars a year on these 'active measures'. The late Yuri Andropov set up the KGB's Department A which controls disinformation campaigns, and during his fifteen years at the head of the Soviet intelligence agency he promoted the use of forgery to embarrass the West.

Classic ploys include the use of forged letters written on stolen headed notepaper, forged inter-office memos and fake military instruction manuals. The KGB uses tame journalists to plant false stories which once printed in a Western newspaper are then syndicated throughout the world. Recent examples have been a forged State Department cable which purported to prove that the Polish Solidarity movement was connected with the CIA. Another, designed to embarrass the US in Latin America, was a forged Pentagon news release about US support for Britain during the Falklands crisis.

The latest technique is the forging of tapes of conversations and speeches. KGB technicians, once crude at the practice but now expert, splice together words and phrases from genuine speeches so that a completely false and derogatory effect is created.

Individually these examples would not seem to amount to much, but taken as part of a vast campaign, they snowball into effectiveness. The KGB's disinformation campaign was summed up for the Committee on Intelligence of the US House of Representatives by Mr John McMahon, Deputy Director of the CIA in July 1982: 'Active measures are in essence an offensive instrument of Soviet foreign policy. They contribute effectively to the strategic Soviet purpose, central to Soviet policy, of extending Moscow's influence and power throughout the world.

Elint

Electronic intelligence as distinct from Humint — that is, Human Intelligence, information gathered by agents in the old-fashioned way. Elint was born with the invention of radio, and no aspect of espionage has progressed so dramatically — at one time US satellites were listening to the car-radio conversations of the Russian leaders as they drove through Moscow.

The term encompasses not only listening in to telephone and radio messages but also radar frequencies and satellite signals. Satellites are increasingly taking over most Elint functions, but for a time ships and aircraft had to be used on nearly all 'Ferret' operations.

This gave rise to a number of incidents: the strafing of the USS *Liberty* by the Israelis during the Six Day War, the capture of the USS *Pueblo* by the North Koreans, the shooting down of Gary Powers' U2 over Sverdlovsk all stemmed from the need to acquire Elint. Moreover, it was Soviet sensitivity about American Elint probing along its coastline which led to them shooting down the Korean Air Lines Boeing 747 and killing 269 innocent people in August 1983.

Elint remains the most sophisticated and expensive form of acquiring intelligence and it still has its blind-spots — there was no satellite watching General Galtieri's invasion of the Falklands.

The Soviets play the game as well as the West. Their Bear ferret planes packed with electronic equipment make almost daily probes of Britain's northerly air defences, and their fleet of Elint ships disguised as fishing-trawlers patrol the US coastline and pop up whenever NATO conducts an exercise.

'Family Jewels'

A report prepared within the CIA when its world began to fall apart after Watergate. It was headed 'Potential Flap Activities', and listed every CIA activity which might embarrass the Agency if revealed. It included details of the CIA's drug-testing programmes; involvement in operations within the United States (Operation Chaos); plots to kill Fidel Castro (Operation Mongoose) and other foreign leaders; the bugging of journalists and the Agency's connection with the Watergate raiders. These activities were so delicate and potentially damaging that they were given the code-name of the Family Jewels.

Interrogation

The art of making someone reveal facts he is desperately trying to keep hidden. It can be done crudely: the mere threat of violence is often quite sufficient to make a prisoner 'sing', and actual violence will in the end make most people talk. The methods have been developed throughout history — the ancient Chinese had their water torture, the Inquisition had the rack, and most modern interrogators have learnt the value of electrodes fixed to genitals.

It is not our intention to go into detail — they can be seen most evenings on television. What is interesting is the way in which techniques have been perfected in which not a finger is laid on the victim.

The Russians, looking not only for information but for confession and recantation, concentrate on making their prisoners lose all hope. They are degraded; they have their clothes taken away from them; they are kept without sleep; they are summoned for questioning at all hours; they are given no idea of the time; they are questioned by a 'hard' man who threatens them and then by a 'soft' man who is kind; the hard man-soft man team is then replaced by a senior officer who speaks with authority, and gradually the prisoner comes to look on him as a father confessor — and tells all.

At the start of the current troubles in Ulster the British Army used a technique of disorientation which achieved quicker results than the Russian method. The prisoner was hooded, made to lean against a wall with only his finger-tips touching it, and then he was subjected to 'white noise', a continual high-pitched hum which went on for hour after hour until the prisoner became completely disorientated. This technique achieved remarkable results, and the man had no bruises or scars to show when he was released.

The use of this method was described in the British press. There was an international outcry, and it was dropped. There are, however, members of the security organizations in Ireland who argue that if they had not been forbidden to use this technique the emergency would have been swiftly ended, and many lives saved.

There are various modern aids to interrogation,

drugs and hypnosis among them. However, they are not always reliable, and prisoners sometimes die when being interrogated under drugs, which is not the object of the exercise.

Of all the techniques, the most skilful, most humane and in most cases the most successful (because the prisoner comes willingly to confession) is that of the professional interrogator, the man who assembles the evidence and then asks question after question, probing for a weakness, finding it, exploiting it and leaving the prisoner glad he has told all.

William Skardon of MI5 and James Angleton of the CIA were both masters of gentle interrogation. It was Skardon, always softly spoken, always polite, who broke Klaus Fuchs, and eventually induced Anthony Blunt to confess. Angleton relied on a perverse brilliance in argument and a meticulous matching of detail in which every scrap of information had to be checked. Skardon failed with Philby, although he was convinced of the traitor's guilt. When the information proving that conviction was acquired it fell to another man to confront Philby with proof of his guilt.

Operations

Chaos

The CIA's domestic intelligence programme which was formalized as a named operation in July 1968. It was aimed principally at the student organizations opposed to the Vietnam war.

As long as the CIA confined itself to investigating the foreign connections of the anti-war movements and carried out their operations outside the United States, Operation Chaos was legal. But as the war grew and the protests grew so the CIA became sucked into investigating and evaluating the protest movement within the United States. This was the province of the FBI, but Edgar Hoover, smelling trouble, refused to have anything to do with the operations except to act as a conduit for information.

So the CIA undertook work which was illegal under its charter, which forbids it to operate within the United States. Operation Chaos was

bitterly opposed within the CIA, where it was realized that the Agency was operating outside its charter. Director Richard Helms, under pressure from President Johnson and later President Nixon, nevertheless continued to spy on the anti-war groups. Operation Chaos was revealed in all its illegality in the aftermath of the Watergate and Pentagon Papers scandals.

Damocles

The Israeli campaign of intimidation and assassination mounted in 1962 against German scientists, some of them Nazis, working on weapons research for President Nasser. Like so many similar campaigns, it backfired. The weapons projects were crude and posed little threat to Israel, and the killings badly damaged the country's reputation.

The arrest of two Mossad agents on an intimidation mission against a German scientist's family in Switzerland led to a political row in Israel, and resulted in the resignation of Isser Harel, head of Mossad and the man who caught Eichmann. Damocles was ended, but was revived twenty years later in the undercover campaign to prevent the Iraqis building a nuclear reactor.

Gold

Code-name given to the tunnel dug under East Berlin in 1955 by the Special Intelligence Service and the Central Intelligence Agency to tap into the Russian military telephone system.

Mongoose

This code-name covers the continuing attempts by the Kennedy brothers to get rid of Castro following the Bay of Pigs disaster. Masterminded by guerrilla warfare expert General Edward Lansdale, it involved landing sabotage teams in Cuba to blow up copper-mines and set fire to sugar-cane fields.

Psychological warfare was also used. One plan was to convince the Cubans that Jesus Christ was about to make the Second Coming in Cuba — but only if they got rid of Castro first. Alongside this activity the CIA discussed and prepared a number of projects to assassinate Castro. These included giving him a box of poisoned cigars, planting an explosive seashell in an area where he was known to go scuba diving, presenting him with a wet suit impregnated with tuberculosis bacilli and the spores of a skin disease, stabbing him with a poisoned pen, even old-fashioned shooting.

The Mafia, which has its own reasons for hating Castro — he kicked them out of Cuba — was brought in, astonishingly at the same time that Robert Kennedy, then Attorney-General, was waging a bitter war against organized crime. There is no proof that the Kennedys knew of the assassination attempts, but it is difficult to believe that they were innocent. The weight of informed opinion is that they not only knew about the plots but actively encouraged them. Operation Mongoose ended after President Kennedy's own assassination in 1963.

No-Beef

Code-name for payments made by CIA to King Hussein of Jordan. These payments lasted for some twenty years, and totalled millions of dollars. They were stopped by Congress in February 1977 after the *Washington Post* had blown the gaff. The money was delivered personally to Hussein by the CIA station chief in Amman, and in return he allowed American intelligence agencies to operate freely in Jordan. Hussein admitted accepting the payments, but denied they were for his personal use. The money, he said, was used to help finance intelligence and security operations in Jordan. There were cries of outrage in Washington over the payments to Hussein and a number of other statesmen, but such payments are made in the normal course of events by intelligence services.

Noah's Ark

The Israeli operation mounted to smuggle five gunboats out of Cherbourg harbour on Christmas Day 1969. The boats, Israeli-designed, were built in Cherbourg shipyards but were prevented from leaving for Israel by General de Gaulle's ban on arms shipments to Israel following the raid on Beirut airport by Israeli commandos on 28 December 1968.

In the summer of 1969, with some of the boats still uncompleted, the Israelis pretended to give up hope that they would ever get possession, and demanded compensation. In November they set up a fake company called Starboat to negotiate the sale of the warships. All this time Israeli sailors were in Cherbourg, supposedly working on the boats on the pretext that they were of Israeli design. Towards the end of the year others slipped into Cherbourg.

The boats were fuelled for 'sea trials'. Supplies were taken on board over a period of weeks. By the end of December all was ready, and at 02.30 hours on Christmas Day all five boats opened up their engines and headed for the open sea, and Israel. Despite Israeli attempts at secrecy, it was immediately obvious that a number of people in Cherbourg knew precisely what was going on for they gathered to wave farewell to the boats they had helped build.

There is also reason to believe that the French government were not too displeased to see their embarrassing guests leave. The world — except the Arabs — enjoyed an adventurous coup and nobody got hurt, although President Pompidou was heard to complain that 'we have been made to look complete fools'.

Plumbat

An audacious Mossad coup in 1968 involving fake companies and a ship which was not what it appeared to be led to Israel acquiring 200 tons of uranium oxide for its nuclear reactor. The uranium was of the type which could be used for producing atomic weapons. A German-registered ship, the *Scheerbergs*, picked up 560 barrels of the oxide in Antwerp. It had been bought by the Asmara Chemie company of Hettenheim, West Germany, from the Belgian Société Générale des Minéraux. It was supposedly destined for an Italian company called SAICA for use in catalysts for the oil industry. It was actually shipped under the supervision of Euratom.

However, once the *Scheerbergs* was at sea both

it and the uranium disappeared. The uranium was never seen again, but the *Scheerbergs* reappeared under a different flag and with a different name and crew. The Israelis denied all knowledge of the affair, but confirmation of their involvement came later from Haakon Wiker, the former chief prosecutor of Norway, who in 1976 revealed that Dan Aerbel, a Mossad agent arrested in Norway, had told him that he had taken part in the operation.

Rice Bowl

This was the doomed dramatic attempt by the United States to rescue its fifty-three diplomats held hostage by the Iranians in the seized US Embassy and the Iranian Foreign Office in Teheran. It failed with the loss of eight dead because of equipment failure, the lack of a clear chain of command and over-ambitious planning. It was a great humiliation for the United States.

However, the intelligence work which had gone into the planning was impeccable. CIA and Defense Intelligence Agency men moved in and out of Teheran in a variety of guises, studying the target buildings, assessing the opposition, setting up bases, buying lorries and reactivating former Iranian agents who had gone to ground under Khomeini's revolution. They did all that was asked of them. When Rice Bowl had failed they were in great peril, and had great difficulty in making their way out of the country. It was a prime example of an intelligence success but an operational failure.

Suzanna

Code-name for the disastrous operation mounted by Israeli military intelligence in Egypt in 1954. A team of inexperienced young Egyptian Jews was ordered to mount incendiary bomb attacks against British and American property in Cairo and Alexandria for the purpose of breaking down what the Israelis saw as a rapprochement between President Nasser and the Western Powers.

The plot failed when an incendiary device exploded in the pocket of one of the saboteurs, and soon the whole gang had been rounded up,

including by mischance one of Israel's professional agents, Max Bennett. In the trial which followed two of the plotters were sentenced to death and six others were given long sentences. Max Bennett committed suicide in his cell. The Egyptians allowed one man, Paul Frank, to escape, and it is believed that he betrayed the plot.

Known as the Lavon Affair after Pinhas Lavon, the Defence Minister, who was accused of being responsible for Operation Suzanna, its repercussions in Israel were devastating, leading to a reorganization of Military Intelligence, the resignation of Lavon, and eventually the retirement of Ben Gurion from political life. The imprisoned plotters were rescued by the Israeli victory in the Six Day War of 1967. They were at the top of the list of Israelis whose freedom was demanded in exchange for the thousands of Egyptian prisoners captured by the Israeli army.

Positive Vetting

The system by which the Intelligence authorities try to exclude security risks from sensitive positions. In the late forties a system of 'Negative Vetting' prevailed in Britain. What it amounted to in those innocent days was that if nothing damaging was known about the candidate for a job no objections were raised. However, by 1947 Whitehall had begun to fear Soviet penetration, and a warning was made by the Chiefs of Staff to the Prime Minister, Clement Attlee, that a large number of communist scientists recruited into government research and development establishments during the war were still in position.

The Chiefs of Staff argued that when Hitler attacked Russia the British communist party had attracted people from the professional classes whose 'higher educational level' gave them access to important information. However, it was not until January 1952, after the Burgess and Maclean scandal, that Positive Vetting involving an active investigation of a man or woman's political and private life was introduced.

The investigation entails the candidate giving the names of two character witnesses and supposedly opening up his life to a vetting team of security officers, who are usually retired Service or police officers. What they look for are character faults which could lay a person open to blackmail and recruitment by a foreign espionage service.

According to the Ministry of Defence, 'there are certain character defects which could bar an individual from a positively vetted post: major indiscretion, drunkenness or drug taking, dishonesty, convictions for serious crimes, having substantial financial difficulties, being vulnerable as a result of irregular sexual behaviour and significant mental illness.

The basis of the vetting procedure is a long questionnaire about the subject's parents, grandparents, spouses, education, former employment, political affiliations and so on.

The answer to these questions provides the framework for the investigating officers who visit schools, universities, former employers, friends, relatives and neighbours and, finally the two character references.

The process does expose many people who might be liable to be blackmailed, but there have been a number of notable failures. The investigators failed to pick up the homosexual history of Commander Michael Testrail, the Queen's bodyguard, who, although absolutely loyal, would have been judged a security risk. It also failed to expose John Vassall, the naval traitor, who was an obvious homosexual. But the great weakness of the system is that it is simple for an enemy service to train a recruit to counter the vetting process. Geoffrey Prime, the GCHQ traitor, was positively vetted four times, and his sexual fantasies and espionage realities showed up in none of these.

It was the Americans who put pressure on the reluctant British to introduce Positive Vetting after the Klaus Fuchs and Burgess and Maclean scandals. After the Prime case they put the pressure on again, because Prime had been handling American as well as British material, and Britain has now agreed to introduce the American system of polygraph, lie-detector, tests into the vetting procedure.

However, is the lie-detector foolproof? It is believed that the KGB can teach its recruits how to block out the 'excitement factor' which registers on the polygraph, and if the investigating officers rely too heavily on the lie-detector for Positive Vetting it could have a 'negative effect'. The problem with introducing a really effective system of vetting is that which applies to all aspects of security. How much freedom and privacy, the fruits of democracy, can be given up to preserve democracy?

Project Jennifer

The CIA's attempt to salvage a sunken Russian submarine from three miles down in the Pacific in 1974. The Russian boat, a Golf-class diesel-powered craft with surface-fired atomic missiles mounted in the conning-tower, sank in 1968 after a series of explosions on board. After much debate the 40 Committee — headed at that time by Dr Henry Kissinger — gave William Colby, Director of the CIA, permission to go ahead with the salvage attempt.

Colby commissioned Howard Hughes's Summa Corporation to build a salvage vessel, the *Glomar Explorer*, ostensibly for deep-sea mining exploration. The *Glomar Explorer* was built with a 'moon pool' into which salvaged material could be lifted in secret by a 209-foot derrick capable of raising 800 tons. It was also equipped with refrigeration capacity for up to a hundred bodies; and copies of the American and Russian naval burial services were taken along.

The sunken submarine was found by the US Navy's underwater detection devices, and part of the hull was lifted. It is here that the story becomes opaque. One version says that the only part that was recovered was the forward section containing the bodies of seventy Russian seamen, which were then buried at sea with full military honours in both Russian and English. Another version says that it was the conning-tower which was brought up, and that one or more missiles were recovered, and that they were worth all the money and effort devoted to the project.

What is certain is that it was an extraordinary technical achievement, far beyond the capability of the Soviet Union. It is even suggested that the

CIA, through financing the *Glomar Explorer*, could claim to be responsible for the creation of a new industry — deep-sea mining for minerals.

Spy Aircraft

The extent of reconnaissance activity by extremely fast and high-flying aircraft over Soviet, Chinese, American and NATO territory is one of the most closely guarded secrets of the espionage war. What is known is that because of their technical superiority in aircraft development and in electronics, the Americans predominate in this field.

It is only when aircraft are shot down in time of peace — and there have been a number of such incidents — that public attention is drawn to aerial spy operations. The shooting down by Russian fighters of a Korean airliner flying off course over Soviet territory in the Far East in August 1983 was an outrageous example of the Kremlin's determination to protect its airspace, and its electronic secrets.

The Americans strongly denied Russian accusations that this civilian Boeing airliner was on a spying mission. Nevertheless, despite that, there can be little doubt but that American and Japanese monitoring stations were able to pick up a great deal of information about Russian air defences simply by recording the orders given to fighter pilots. They must also have registered intense radar activity as the Soviet command panicked at the approach of the civilian airliner.

It is certain that the Soviet Union has made use of Aeroflot flights on spy missions, though they provide far less rewarding intelligence than that provided by specially designed military aircraft. In November 1981 two aircraft from the Soviet airline strayed from their flight paths over the United States to pass over defence establishments in New England. They were not shot down, but explanations were demanded, and Aeroflot operations were suspended for seven days.

The Americans have been carrying out cold war reconnaissance flights by military aircraft since the 1950s. The record of one such spy flight shot down over the Caucasus in June 1958 by the Russians was only declassified and revealed in 1982.

In September 1958 President Eisenhower was forced to admit that a special version of a Hercules flying, as he claimed, along the Turkish-Soviet border had been shot down over Soviet Armenia. In an attempt to discover from Moscow what was the fate of the crew, he revealed for the first time that the US had tapes recording the conversation of Soviet pilots who shot it down.

By that time the US Air Force was operating a much more effective spy plane, the U-2, sometimes called the Black Lady. Twenty-two U-2 aircraft, specially designed for fast, high-flying reconnaissance, had been ordered at a cost of a million dollars apiece, and by 1955 the first was in service.

It was considered invulnerable over hostile territory until in 1960 the Russians managed to shoot down Gary Powers at the controls of a U-2' over Sverdlovsk. It was the uproar over this event which disclosed the use of specially designed spyplanes for the first time.

The U-2 still operates in a newer version produced by Lockheed and known as the TR-1A. It can carry nearly two tons of sensors and equipment for its all-weather surveillance role.

A spy aircraft with even more spectacular performance was then developed by the Americans. The Blackbird, the SR 71, is the world's fastest aircraft, capable of flying at three times the speed of sound, at a height of over 80,000 feet and with a range of 2,675 miles. It is used for photographic reconnaissance to pinpoint military activity even over hostile territory.

Viktor Belenko, a Soviet pilot who flew his MiG fighter to Japan, reported that SR 71s had been known to taunt Soviet chase planes by ostentatiously outflying them over Soviet territory, to prove their invulnerability.

Such aircraft are used for spot-checks on world danger-areas. They reported on the 1973 Yom Kippur war in the Middle East, and it is probable that they have overflown Afghanistan and China. The espionage work of this aircraft is given heavier backup from the RC-135, a special version of the Boeing civil airliner, the 707. Stuffed with advanced sensors and monitoring equipment, its task is to register the electronic order of battle of radar defenders and to spot holes for possible exploitation by bombers.

An RC-135 was flying off the Soviet islands at the time when the Russians shot down the Korean airliner in 1983. Such planes do not need to trespass over hostile airspace, for they are capable of monitoring radio signals from 135 miles' distance, and in favourable conditions that may extend to up to 1,000 miles. Their probing flights are manned by experts from the US National Defense Agency as well as by USAF crews.

America, Britain and other NATO countries also operate Awacs — Boeings in the case of America, and Nimrods of the RAF — to patrol national airspace, and by means of huge radar dishes they can peer into enemy territory to a depth of 200 miles.

For strategic reconnaissance reliance is placed upon unmanned satellites which hover at between 80 and 200 miles over the scene. The Russians too make extensive use of satellites.

Soviet airmen also operate high-flying, long-range reconnaissance aircraft for espionage missions. The most commonly sighted is the Bear, the TU-95, which regularly patrols the edge of British airspace, especially off the North of England. RAF Phantoms frequently scramble to intercept and photograph such planes.

The nearest Soviet equivalent of the American SR 71 is the supersonic bomber codenamed in NATO language the Backfire. It too makes its high-flying appearance over NATO territory, and photographs, for example, naval exercises.

Both super-Powers need to keep watch upon the other by satellite and spy aircraft flights. Each recognizes that this need-to-know is an essential part of maintaining the balance of nuclear power, and that each must strive to keep up to date with information.

If the United States places more emphasis on spying by aircraft and satellite than the Soviet Union, that is because military information is more difficult to obtain from on-the-ground sources in the closed societies of the communist world, both in the USSR and in China. The Soviets' task in penetrating the secrets of Western

defence by the more old-fashioned methods of spy networks is a great deal easier because of the nature of Western society.

Although the highest secrecy is normally maintained about flying espionage there is no doubt that its achievements over the last twenty years in particular have marked a revolution in the world of intelligence. Without such resources the Western alliance would have been blind to many areas of Soviet activity and expansion.

Spy Satellites

Parallel developments in rocketry and space-age technology in both the Soviet Union and the United States initiated entirely new techniques of espionage by satellite. In order to preserve the nuclear balance on which world peace delicately depends it is essential for each side to know with precision what the other is doing.

Without the kind of information provided from the man-made orbs in space, diplomatic treaties on arms-limitation and arrangements for nuclear containment are not worth the paper they are written upon. Both sides need to know the capability of the other.

For that reason the first war in space is already being fought, in the form of espionage satellite conflict high over the globe. Satellites are already spying upon each other, and it is only a question of time before killer satellites are readily available on each side to destroy spies in the sky.

The Americans are believed to have spare satellites 'hiding' in deep space, ready to be brought into action to replace others, if and when they are destroyed by Soviet hunter-killer satellites.

Equipment on board the satellites can survey photographically even small objects over huge areas; electronically they can record sounds and impulses, both written and spoken down to telephone-call level. Since it was first launched in 1961, the American Samos (Satellite and Missile Observer) programme has put into orbit with Atlas-Agena rockets hundreds of 18,000 m.p.h. satellites to criss-cross the skies. They detected nuclear-test explosions, rocket-launchings and troop-movements, and even recorded the orders given by foreign military headquarters.

Ten years later the higher-flying Rhyolite was placed into orbit, equipped with even more sensitive probing gear. It is supported by two new types of low-flying surveillance platforms known as Big Bird and Keyhole, crammed with new marvels. The one disadvantage of low-fliers is that Russian scientists can see them coming, and if need be postpone rocket-firing until they are out of range.

As spy satellites become bigger in order to accommodate more equipment they need more powerful rockets to propel them into orbit. The next generation of space spies will most likely go up in the space shuttle, which will give the Americans an advantage over the Russians who so far have not produced such a vehicle, and rely upon their successful rockets.

Both the Americans and the Russians will soon have operational permanently manned space stations which will undoubtedly be used for espionage and for warlike purposes.

The effect of satellite espionage on a battle situation may be gauged from the fact that in the 1973 Arab-Israeli war President Sadat was not aware how far the Israeli army had progressed in its counter-attack towards Ismailia, on the road to Cairo, until the Soviet ambassador showed him pictures taken from space to prove it.

Spy Ships

Although the Russians continue brazenly to operate some forty spy-ships, the Americans never had much luck with their signals intelligence fleet. Within less than a year in 1967–8, they lost two vessels in distressing circumstances.

The first was the USS *Liberty*, an old 10,000-tonner pressed into service as a floating platform for electronics. She was stationed in the summer of 1967 off the Sinai Peninsula, just in time for what was to be called the Six Day War between Israelis and Arabs.

Without warning Israeli Mirages and Mystères swooped down in a vicious machine-gun and cannon-fire attack which destroyed her electronic

equipment. Not content with that, the Israelis (who were determined to destroy this spy-ship, which was getting far too much information about their war) sent in three naval motor-vessels and torpedoed the *Liberty*. Finally, troop-carrying helicopters appeared to survey the damage.

The *Liberty* was packed with Arabic, and no doubt Hebrew, speakers, monitoring battle orders on both sides, from headquarters down to company level. Casualties were high. Israeli attacks killed thirty-four and wounded another seventy-five.

Cynically, the Israeli Government claimed to have mistaken the ship for an Egyptian vessel, despite the fact that (until it was shot away) she was flying a prominent Stars and Stripes. It was unthinkable in any case that Mossad, the Israeli intelligence service, which boasts of its efficiency, could have failed to know the whereabouts of the spy-ship.

There can be no doubt that Israel was determined to silence the electronic listeners. It was their aim to prevent their American allies from knowing the true extent of their victory in case Washington should seek to impose a cease-fire before they had achieved all their aims. It may also be suspected that they feared the Americans would learn too much about how they had contrived a war for which they wanted to place total blame upon President Nasser of Egypt.

Even though the US Sixth Fleet with the carrier USS *America* was only a few minutes' flying time away at the time, it failed to intervene effectively to protect the electronic scout ship. Although *Liberty* managed to get distress signals away, the only response was a Phantom sortie which came too late. Eventually the *Liberty* managed to limp away with her dead and wounded, and a half-hearted apology was wrung out of the Israelis.

It was a disconcerting experience for the Pentagon and NSA, demonstrating how vulnerable spy-ships can be to a determined enemy. The point was further made when the USS *Pueblo*, a similar espionage vessel operating off the coast of North Korea, was attacked by a Korean warship in January 1968. A boarding party captured the *Pueblo* and her crew, together with confidential papers and secret equipment which the captain had no time to destroy. The crisis which this action provoked continued for a year, and eventually in order to secure the release of the crew Washington was forced to confess to espionage and to apologize.

In the case of both the *Liberty* and the *Pueblo* naval officers had warned of the dangers facing them, but their signals had been ignored. Disillusioned by the two disasters, the Americans took their signals intelligence fleet out of commission and the ships were scrapped.

The Soviet Union, whose impudent trawlers loaded with spying electronics have never been victims of direct assault, continue to operate close in to spy upon all American and NATO naval manoeuvres.

United Nations

The organization which was set up by the victorious Allies at the end of the Second World War to unite the world in peace, but which has become the world's biggest — and most luxurious — base for Soviet espionage. In theory, employees of the UN are international civil servants. Article 100 of the UN Charter stipulates that they 'shall not seek or receive instructions from any government or from any external authority'. In practice, Russians in the UN are invariably seconded from government bodies in the Soviet Union. Few make any serious attempt to disguise the fact that they remain Soviet government officials.

There are approximately 700 Russian officials in New York, and of these nearly 200 are members of the KGB and GRU. Their particular targets include:

1. The use of UN records and personnel files to obtain information on potential agents.
2. The recruitment of officials from developing countries. Since the UN requires a high level of ability, these officials probably already hold senior positions in their home countries. Consequently, they will be of considerable importance to the Russian intelligence services.

3. The subversion of Western officials to influence UN policy and to act as espionage agents.
4. The use of the façade of neutrality afforded by the UN to maintain agents in the United States who are not subject to the travel and other restrictions imposed on members of Soviet embassies.
5. The recruitment of UN officials to collect scientific, technical and commercial intelligence made available to the UN by other countries.
6. The use of Russians working as genuine scientists and technicians within the UN to cultivate possible agents in the course of visits and conferences organized under UN auspices.
7. The use of UN buildings which are normally barred to local security authorities — the FBI is forbidden to enter the UN building in New York — to carry out clandestine activities.
8. The use of Russians working in the UN to feed disinformation.

The Soviet use of the UN for espionage purposes was highlighted in 1978 when Arkady Shevchenko became the highest-ranking Russian diplomat ever to defect to the West. Shevchenko held the powerful post of Under Secretary-General at the UN, and he was notorious throughout the organization for turning his department into virtually a sub-station of the Soviet mission.

He made every effort to staff it with communists, and his approach to his work was dedicated to ensuring that UN policy matters for which he was responsible were conducted along lines dictated from Moscow. When he defected Shevchenko admitted that the United Nations was 'the most important base of all Soviet intelligence operations in the world'.

It is the same story at the various UN agencies in Europe. UNESCO in Paris and the Atomic Energy Agency in Vienna are prime targets for Soviet espionage, and so is the International Labour Organisation in Geneva. The importance of these agencies to the Russians is the amount of technical knowledge that flows through their offices. This is so great that there is hardly a technical development in the West which is not copied by the Soviet Union — not by research and development, but by espionage within the United Nations agencies.

The host countries of these agencies are well aware of the Russians' activities, and every few months another batch is declared *persona non grata* and shipped back to Moscow. However, since the UN works on a nationality quota system they are simply replaced by other members of the KGB and GRU. If a genuine scientist is required to fill the post, then he is co-opted before he is allowed to leave the Soviet Union, which continues to use the United Nations and its agencies not for the good of the world but for the benefit of the Soviet Union.

SPYTALK

Agent
Abbreviation of secret agent acting as spy or saboteur.

Agent of influence
One who tries to affect opinion rather than to spy.

Agent provocateur
Person urging illegal acts by those under suspicion.

Asset
Agents or sympathizers positioned in target country.

Bagman
Agent who pays bribes.

Black-bag jobs
Bribery; paying for information, also burglaries.

Blown
Being discovered, either person or group.

Boxed
To be examined by polygraph lie-detector. Also known as being 'fluttered', because nerve-ends do.

Brainwashed
Object of psychological techniques to alter thought processes and loyalty.

Bugging
Use of electronic devices for eavesdropping.

Burnt
Compromised.

Case officer
Agent in charge of operation or network.

Cell
Basic unit of espionage network.

Chekist
Member of KGB (after Cheka, the first Soviet security service).

Cipher
Secret-message writing.

Cobbler
Forger.

Code
Use of symbols to represent letters and words in secret messages.

Codename
Substitute for actual name to ensure secrecy or to designate an operation.

Company, The
CIA.

Counter-espionage
Action against spies.

Counter-intelligence
System protecting secret information.

Counter-spy
A person in place to betray or forestall opposition spies.

Courier
Message or document carrier.

Cousins
SIS name for CIA.

Cover name
An alias.

Cover story
False biography to cover clandestine activity.

Covert
Concealed and deceptive activity, as in operation.

Cryptology
The craft of writing ciphered messages.

Cut out
Go between to protect identity of other network members.

Defector
Agent or dissident who changes sides in the cold war. Originally pejorative, but now multi-purpose for lack of a better word.

Desk man
Controller at headquarters.

Disinformation
False or misleading information to confuse or discredit the opposition.

Double agent
Person working for two organizations, loyal to one, betraying the other.

Drop
Place to leave message or item for clandestine collection. This is a 'dead drop', as opposed to a 'live drop', when people meet to pass material.

Dubok
Russian for dead drop.

Farm, The
Training-school for CIA in Virginia.

Field man
Agent in place and working.

Flaps and seals man
Expert at undetected opening and closing of the mails.

Friends
MI5 term for MI6.

Galoshes day
When galoshes are issued to KGB men for winter work.

Gebist
Russian slang for KGB member.

Hard target
Enemy country difficult for agent to penetrate. Thus also soft country.

Honey trap
Operation to compromise opponent sexually.

Illegals and legals
Soviet term to distinguish between agents abroad who are legal as diplomats and in international organizations, and those illegal, operating without immunity and on false papers.

Illness
Soviet slang for arrest.

In place
A working agent is said to be in place.

Invisible ink
The oldest trick in the spy book, but still useful.

Legend
Invented name and biography to hide identity of spies.

Line X
KGB field section for scientific and technological spying.

Microdot
Photograph of a message reduced for concealment to microscopic size.

Mole
Hostile spy burrowing into intelligence organization to report to enemy one.

Moscow Centre
No 2 Dzerzhinsky Sq, Moscow HQ of KGB.

Music box
Radio transmitter.

Musician
Radio operator.

Naked
Operating without back-up or cover.

Nash
One of ours, originally Russian.

Neighbour
Other branch of intelligence service.

Network
A spy ring working to one chief.

Onetime pad
Simple encoding method with five letter groups used only once.

Overt
Legally gathered information from published sources.

Paroles
Key words for mutual identification between agents.

Piscine
HQ French secret service (because of its proximity to municipal swimming pool).

Playback
Information which captured agents are forced to continue transmitting after discovery.

Plumbing
Infrastructure installed before big operation.

Polygraph
Lie-detector. A machine to indicate whether the suspect is lying, by measuring nervous reflexes.

Raven
Male seducer to lure woman into honey trap.

Resident director
Head of Soviet spy ring in foreign country.

Safe house
Place where agent is safe for meetings, or where a defector may be held.

Sanitize
Prepare or 'doctor' a document before release or publication. Edited to protect source or method.

Shoe
False passport.

Sleeper
A spy placed ready to be activated at a suitable moment.

Spook
American slang for a spy.

Spy
Defined by Hague Convention 1899: 'one who, acting clandestinely, or on false pretences, obtains, or seeks to obtain, information in the zone of operations of a belligerent, with the intention of communicating it to the hostile party.

Stringer
An occasional or freelance spy, non-staff.

Swallow
Female seducer to lure man into honey trap.

Swim
Travel (Sov.).

Take, the
Intelligence fruits of spying.

Tapping
Intercepting telephone calls.

Terminated with Extreme Prejudice
Murdered.

Turned
Persuaded or bribed to change sides.

Walk in
Anyone who walks in, volunteering services or information.

Watchers
Officers keeping persons under surveillance.

Wet job
Russian *Mokrie dela,* operation in which blood is shed.

BIBLIOGRAPHY

Adams, Sherman *First Hand Report,* Hutchinson, London 1962

Bamford, James *The Puzzle Palace,* Sidgwick & Jackson, London 1982

Barron, John *K.G.B.: The Secret Work of Soviet Secret Agents,* Hodder & Stoughton, London 1974

Barron, John *K.G.B. Today: The Hidden Hand,* Hodder and Stoughton, London 1984

Bar-Zohar, Michel *Spies In the Promised Land,* Davis-Poynter, London 1972

Beesly, Patrick *Very Special Intelligence,* Hamish Hamilton, London 1977

Bernikov, Louise *Abel,* Hodder & Stoughton, London 1970

Boyle, Andrew *The Climate of Treason,* Hutchinson, London 1979

Bulloch, John *Akin to Treason,* Arthur Barker, London, *MI5: The Origin and History of the British Counter-Espionage Service,* London 1961

Buranelli, Vincent & Nan *Spy Counter Spy, An Encyclopedia of Espionage,* MacGraw Hill, New York 1982

Cookridge, E. H. *Spy Trade,* Hodder & Stoughton, London 1971

Cookridge, E. H. *Gehlen, Spy of the Century,* Hodder & Stoughton, London 1971

Copeland, Miles *The Real Spy World,* Weidenfeld & Nicolson, London 1975

Dan, Ben *The Spy from Israel,* Valentine, Mitchell, London 1969

Dayan, Moshe *Story of my Life,* Weidenfeld & Nicolson, London 1976

Deacon, Richard *A History of the British Secret Service,* Muller, London 1969

Deacon, Richard *A History of the Russian Secret Service,* Muller, London 1972

Deacon, Richard *A History of the Israeli Secret Service,* Hamish Hamilton, London 1977

Deakin, F. W. & Storry, G. R. *The Case of Richard Sorge,* Chatto & Windus, London 1966

Driberg, Tom *Ruling Passions,* Jonathan Cape, London 1977

Dulles, Allen *The Craft of Intelligence,* Harper & Row New York 1963

Eisenburg, Denis, Dan, Uri, Landay, Eli *The Mossad, Israel's Secret Intelligence Service,* Paddington Press, London 1978

Fitzgibbon, Constantine *Secret Intelligence in the 20th Century,* Hart-Davis, MacGibbon, London 1976

Freemantle, Brian *KGB,* Michael Joseph, London 1982

Freemantle, Brian *CIA, The Honourable Company,* Michael Joseph/Rainbird, London 1983

Frolik, Joseph *The Frolik Defection,* Leo Cooper, London 1975

Gehlen, General Richard *The Gehlen Memoirs,* Collins, London 1972

Gott, Richard *Guerrilla Movements in Latin America,* Nelson, London 1970

Gramont, Sanche de *The Secret War,* André Deutsch, London 1962

Grey, Anthony *The Prime Minister Was a Spy,* Weidenfeld & Nicolson, London 1984

Hastings, Max *Yoni, Hero of Entebbe,* Weidenfeld & Nicolson, London 1979

Hinsley, F. H., Thomas, E. E., Ransom, C. F. G., Knight, R. C. *British Intelligence in the Second World War, Vols I and II,* H.M.S.O., London 1979 & 1981

Hoare, Geoffrey *The Missing Macleans,* Cassell, London 1955

Kirkpatrick, Lyman B., Jun, *Captains Without Eyes,* Hart Davis, London 1970

Levitsky, Boris *The Uses of Terror, The Soviet Secret Service 1917–70,* Sidgwick & Jackson, London 1971

Lewis, Flora *The Man who Disappeared,* Arthur Barker, London 1965

Lotz, Wolfgang *The Champagne Spy,* Valentine, Mitchell, London 1972

Maclean, Fitzroy *Take Nine Spies,* Weidenfeld & Nicolson, London 1978

Moorehead, Alan *The Traitors,* Hamish Hamilton, London

Montgomery Hyde, H. *The Atom Bomb Spies,* Hamish Hamilton, London

Mosley, Leonard *Dulles,* Hodder & Stoughton, London 1978

Myagkov, Aleksi *Inside the KGB,* The Foreign Affairs Publishing Co, London 1976

Page, Bruce, Leitch, David, Knightley, Phillip *Philby, the Spy Who Betrayed a Generation,* André Deutsch, London 1968

Penkovsky, Oleg *The Penkovsky Papers,* Collins, London 1965

Philby, Kim *My Silent War,* MacGibbon & Kee, London 1968

Phillips, David Atlee *The Night Watch: 25 Years Inside the CIA,* Robert Hale, London 1978

Pincher, Chapman *Their Trade is Treachery,* Sidgwick & Jackson, London 1981

Powers, Thomas *The Man Who Kept Secrets,* Weidenfeld & Nicolson, London 1980

Rositzke, Harry *The KGB, The Eyes of Russia,* Sidgwick & Jackson, London 1982

Seth, Ronald *The Encyclopedia of Espionage,* New English Lib., London 1972

Smith, R. Harris *OSS,* Univ. of California Press, Los Angeles 1972

Snepp, Frank *Decent Interval,* Random House, New York 1977

Steven, Stewart *The Spymasters of Israel,* Hodder & Stoughton, London 1980

Straight, Michael *After Long Silence,* Collins, London 1983

Tully, Andrew *Central Intelligence Agency,* The Inside Story, Arthur Barker, London 1962

Tully, Andrew *The Super Spies,* Arthur Barker, London 1970

Villemarest, Pierre de *L'espionage sovietique en France,* Nouvelles Editions Latines, Paris 1969

West, Nigel *MI5: British Security Ops 1909–45,* Bodley Head, London 1981

West, Nigel *A Matter of Trust: MI5 1945–72,* Weidenfeld, London 1982

West, Rebecca *The Meaning of Treason,* Macmillan, London 1952

Whitehead, Don *The FBI Story,* Random House, New York 1956

Whiteside, Thomas *An Agent in Place, the Wennerstrum Affair,* Heinemann, London

Winterbotham, F. W. *The Ultra Secret,* Weidenfeld & Nicolson, London 1974